Teacher Education and Black Communities

Implications for Access, Equity, and Achievement

A volume in
Contemporary Perspectives on Access, Equity, and Achievement
Chance W. Lewis, *Series Editor*

Teacher Education and Black Communities

Implications for Access, Equity, and Achievement

edited by

Yolanda Sealey-Ruiz
Teachers College, Columbia University

Chance W. Lewis
The University of North Carolina at Charlotte

Ivory Toldson
Howard University

INFORMATION AGE PUBLISHING, INC.
Charlotte, NC • www.infoagepub.com

Library of Congress Cataloging-in-Publication Data

A CIP record for this book is available from the Library of Congress
http://www.loc.gov

ISBN: 978-1-62396-697-3 (Paperback)
       978-1-62396-698-0 (Hardcover)
       978-1-62396-699-7 (ebook)

CONTENTS

PART I

PREPARING TEACHERS TO TEACH BLACK STUDENTS

PART II

PREPARING BLACK STUDENTS TO BECOME TEACHERS

PART III

IMPLICATIONS FOR ACCESS, EQUITY, AND ACHIEVEMENT

FOREWORD

TEACHER EDUCATION AND BLACK COMMUNITIES

Implications for Access, Equity, and Achievement

Gloria Ladson-Billings
University of Wisconsin-Madison

If you ask people in the general public what they know about teacher education you are likely to get a blank stare. Perhaps some might say something about it "not being very good" or "too hard (or easy) to get into" but for the most part teacher education is invisible to those outside of the field. Unlike medicine where shows like "Grey's Anatomy" provide the public with some window (albeit overly dramatic and sexualized) into the highly competitive and stressful task of becoming a doctor or law where films such as "The Paper Chase" or "Legally Blonde" do the same, there are no such analogues in teaching. Instead most films and television shows about teaching are not about *preparing* teachers. Instead they are about how awful teaching is as a profession and how good teachers almost always go it alone. They are mavericks who step away from their colleagues and peers (think

Teacher Education and Black Communities, pages ix–xiv
Copyright © 2014 by Information Age Publishing
All rights of reproduction in any form reserved.

"Dangerous Minds," "Stand and Deliver," or "Boston Public") and certainly never give credit to their teacher education programs for their skill and knowledge. Indeed, many of these depictions openly disparage teacher education either by choosing main characters that did not go through traditional preparation programs (e.g., "Music of the Heart") or have nothing good to say about these programs (e.g., "Freedom Writers"). The central message of these film depictions is that good teaching stems solely from the personal will and commitment of the individual teacher, not from careful or systematic study of a body of specialized knowledge.

Most people do realize that teachers are college graduates who probably have general humanities and science knowledge. If they are secondary teachers they have some specialized knowledge in a discipline. They may also know that their professional knowledge consists of some courses on child and/or adolescent development, how to teach specific subject areas, and some real-life practice experiences in the form of student teaching or internships. However, they also realize that on average teachers are drawn from the lower quartile of college students (according to standard scores like the SAT or ACT) and there is a cultural belief in the adage, "those who can't teach!"

The specific knowledge of the African American[1] community about teacher education may be even more limited. Historically, teaching along with preaching and nursing were stable professional careers for the African American community. In the 1950s and 60s many African American teachers were graduates of "teachers' colleges." Places like Historically Black Cheyney State University (in Pennsylvania) that was known as Cheyney State Teachers College (along with Bluefiled State in Virginia, Chicago State in Chicago and many others), were aspirational institutions for a rising working class and its chance to become solidly middle class.

Additionally, African American parents may have been less fixated on where their teachers were prepared and more concerned about their ability to teach effectively. It would be a rare instance where an African American parent would ask where her child's teacher was prepared or the nature of that preparation. Unlike physicians or lawyers who are likely to have their degrees prominently displayed in their offices, teachers rarely display the intellectual preparation that permits them to practice. Thus, teacher education remains invisible to parents.

Some groups of people who do have interests in the preparation of teachers are other teachers and administrators. Interesting, when I was a student teacher and a young professional I heard teachers in the schools I was assigned to specifically request student teachers from certain teacher education programs and reject those from others. For example, while student teaching in Baltimore, MD my cooperating teachers and her colleagues told me I was there because I was a student from Historically Black Morgan

State University (then College). "We like Morgan and Coppin (State) students. They are prepared to teach Black children. We don't have time to try to reteach those young girls from Towson (then a predominately White institution)." Similarly, when I was a new teacher and our principal solicited teachers to be cooperating teachers, my more experienced colleagues asked, "What school are they from?" When I asked why that question arose they told me, similar to my cooperating teacher and her colleagues, "We only want the teachers from Cheyney State or perhaps West Chester State. They're the ones who can teach our children. The ones from Penn (University of Pennsylvania) and Temple (University) just can't cut it. It's too much work to try to supervise them and our children."

Today, with the dwindling number of African American teachers, fewer experienced teachers concern themselves with the institutional pedigree of their student teachers. Thus, the second concern (after the invisibility of teacher education) I want to address is the invisibility of African American teachers from teacher education programs. Several phenomena are driving these lower numbers of Black teachers. First and foremost is the pipeline issue. With fewer Black students graduating from high school, the population of eligible African American teachers drops precipitously. Additionally, those African American students who do enter colleges and universities find themselves faced with many more career choices than previous generations. Instead of investing four-plus years pursuing a career that has fairly low financial remuneration and sinking prestige, today's Black collegian can become a physician, lawyer, businessman (or woman), engineer, or any other more lucrative profession. It may be that one of the "costs" of integration, affirmative action, and other civil rights victories (Ladson-Billings, 2004) is the loss of Black teachers. Additionally, those Black students who successfully matriculate at a college or university—especially those who are first generation—recognize the financial burden the cost of college imposes on them and their families. The expectation may be for them to go into a field where they can reciprocate and assist their families (or at least become self-sufficient).

In addition to the pipeline issues, Black college students who choose to attend one of the nation's 105 historically Black colleges or universities (HBCUs) may find that many are sharply reducing (or closing altogether) their teacher education programs. National accreditation mandates for specific pass rates on standardized exams (Praxis) inhibit the ability of these programs to remain open. Ironically, some HBCUs have failed their accreditation because they do not meet the "diversity" standard. As a HBCU that attracts primarily Black students and hires Black faculty, the programs are seen as "mono-cultural" rather than diverse of multicultural.

Another challenge that teacher education programs at HBCUs face is competing for scarce dollars. Few external grant dollars flow to teacher education and many colleges and universities hire adjunct and clinical faculty members to staff their programs. These faculty members do not participate in a reward structure that allows them to do grant-seeking. On the other hand, colleagues in STEM fields and business are able to access private and public funds to help with infrastructure (e.g., buildings, equipment), internships, and research projects. Schools like Xavier University, Florida A&M University, Tuskegee University, and Morgan State University are producing larger percentages of African American pharmacists, engineers, and computer scientists than their predominately White institutional (PWIs) peers. Teacher education is losing ground similar to the humanities (e.g., English, history, world languages, philosophy, etc.) but for different reasons. Humanities graduates are (erroneously) seen as less marketable while teachers are seen as less knowledgeable.

At the same moment that HBCU teacher education programs are shrinking, those programs at PWIs are increasing entrance requirements and time to degree. At my own university generally we accept students into our elementary teacher education program during their junior year. It is rare that we accept students with grade point averages of less than 3.0 and rarer still that we accept students who have not successfully passed the *Praxis I* exam. Because our program is a cohort one, it is almost impossible for students who have to work to pay for tuition, fees, books, and living expenses to participate in it. Our students must take their courses in a particular sequence during a specific semester. Currently our program takes 4½ to 5 years to complete. Students on our campus can complete engineering and business degrees in 4 years. They can earn a doctorate in pharmacy in 5½ to 6 years.

National critiques of teacher education argue that these programs fail to adequately prepare people to teach effectively in the nation's schools. Thus, colleges, schools, and departments of education along with state legislatures are demanding increased course requirements and evidence of deeper knowledge and skills. Raising program requirements may deter African American teacher candidates if such requirements include increasing the time to degree. Teacher education finds itself in the untenable position of attempting to recruit African Americans (and other candidates of color) into a field that is constantly raising its requirements, making it more difficult to enter, while simultaneously losing ground in terms of financial and prestige status.

More ironic than raising requirements for traditional teacher education programs while lamenting the loss of African American candidates is the current phenomenon of increasing alternative routes to certification. On one hand teacher education programs are asked to increase their requirements while we appear to sanction a "back-door" pathway to teaching that requires little in the way of requirements. The most notorious of these models is Teach for America (TFA) and while this discussion is not an indictment of TFA, it does point to the contradictory way we are dealing with the preparation of teachers. I will also point out that many of the alternative routes do provide greater access and outreach to African American teacher candidates. Many candidates who did not consider teaching while in college realize that the route to certification is long and arduous—sometimes requiring a second bachelor's degree. However, national, state, and local alternative programs provide a shorter pathway and are attractive to returning adults.

Unfortunately, some of the alternative route programs exhibit disdain for traditional teacher education. Some disparage the traditional preparation and make it appear that those who receive certification through traditional means are less intelligent and less qualified. Additionally, many of those who receive alternative certification are more likely to be teaching in schools and classrooms serving communities of color. The most dramatic case of this is what is happening in New Orleans. Orleans Parish Schools were among the nation's worst. They were failure factories where mismanagement and corruption abounded. When Hurricane Katrina hit and it was evident that the city would have to build a school system from the ground up I argued that this was indeed a great opportunity for a fresh start (Ladson-Billings, 2006). However, a series of neo-liberal policies made New Orleans Schools the largest quasi-public school system (or systems) in the nation. A variety of charter schools directed by management companies proliferated and their primary providers (i.e., teachers) came through alternative certification programs. The city and superintendent instituted a wholesale firing of the public school teachers who had taught in New Orleans prior to the storm. And, teacher education as we know it had little or no place in the revitalization of schooling in New Orleans.

It is important to note that teacher education in the United States *is* problematic. For some of the reasons listed above (pipeline issues, length of time to degree, etc.) along with the quality of some programs we need to take a hard look at the field. However, this does not mean we should "throw out the baby with the proverbial bath water." Teacher education is changing—not just in the United States, but also in most modern nations. This volume is an assemblage of important scholarship around three significant questions: (a) How do we prepare ALL teachers to teach Black students; (b) How do we encourage and prepare more Black students to become teachers; and (c) How do teachers' race and racial identities contribute to access, equity and achievement for Black students? The editors have pulled together a stellar group of scholars who are more than capable of providing the answers we need. The question is always about our political will.

NOTE

1. I use the terms African American and Black interchangeably throughout this foreword.

REFERENCES

Ladson-Billings, G. (2004). Landing on the wrong note: The price we paid for Brown. *Educational Researcher, 33*(7), 3–13.

Ladson-Billings, G. (2006). From the Achievement Gap to the Education Debt: Understanding Achievement in U.S. Schools. *Educational Researcher, 35*(7), 3–12.

ACKNOWLEDGEMENTS

This book evolved from Dr. Ivory A. Toldson's vision for a special issue of *The Journal of Negro Education* on preparing teachers to teach Black students, and preparing Black students to become teachers. That special issue, published in 2011, edited by Yolanda Sealey-Ruiz and Chance W. Lewis, received such an overwhelmingly positive response, we three decided to put out a call for papers for a book project. We are pleased to see this project realized and thank *The Journal of Negro Education* for being an initial conduit for these ideas, and for being a leading voice on issues concerning Blacks in education for nearly 80 years.

We are especially grateful to our contributing authors who responded to the call with interesting and innovative scholarship on the topic of teacher education and Black communities. Additionally, we are thankful for our critical friends who supported this project in various ways: Suzanne C. Choo, Juan C. Guerra, Violet J. Harris, S. J. Miller, Oliver Patterson, and Arlette Willis. Thank you for lending your time and energy to this book.

We are also grateful for the generosity and brilliance of other extraordinary teacher educators and scholars. We thank Gloria Ladson-Billings for writing the Foreword; Leslie Fenwick, Jacqueline Jordan Irvine, Suzanne C. Carothers, and Marvin Lynn for their section contributions; and H. Richard Milner, IV for writing the Epilogue. Through moments shared from their teaching and learning lives, each of these scholars boldly speak to many concerns regarding teacher preparation for Black communities, and they present us with hopeful possibilities for supporting the academic and social success of Black students.

Teacher Education and Black Communities, pages xv–xvi
Copyright © 2014 by Information Age Publishing
All rights of reproduction in any form reserved.

This book would not be possible without the teachers and young people featured in these chapters. We thank these individuals for allowing us to enter their teaching and learning spaces so that we may learn from them ways to improve the educational lives of Black students, and the practice of the educators who teach them. We thank our friends, family, and colleagues for their support, and the Ford Foundation for providing resources to complete this project.

Finally, we thank Information Age Publishing for supporting this project, and for its dedication to disseminating research that holds the potential for improving social and academic outcomes for all students, but particularly those students who continue to be made vulnerable by beliefs, policies, and practices that guide our schools and society.

INTRODUCTION

Yolanda Sealey-Ruiz, Chance W. Lewis,
and Ivory A. Toldson

For Black Americans, the most pressing issues in education are the persistent achievement disparities between Black students and their peers from other racial groups, along with the steady decline of Black teachers in our nation's classrooms. The authors included in this book acknowledge the teaching skills and contributions of thousands of dedicated professionals who currently serve in our nation's schools. Nevertheless, we strongly believe that an increase in the number of Blacks who enter the teaching profession and are firmly dedicated to creating a positive educational experience will assist in addressing the persistent underperformance of Black students.

In 2011, U.S. Secretary of Education, Arne Duncan and filmmaker/activist Spike Lee announced at Morehouse College (Atlanta, GA), that they were teaming up to create a task force that aims to recruit 80,000 Black males into the teaching profession by 2015. This is a good idea and a terrific start. Given the importance of this issue, we have assembled a cadre of education researchers and scholars that present evidence-based pedagogical practices for teaching Black students, and practical ways to enlist more Blacks to become teachers. It is our hope that this book will bring increased attention from the educational community to a topic that is of deep concern for the Black community and fortunately has appeared as a priority on America's education agenda. We, the editors of this book also hope that it will stimulate discussion and action among practitioners and policymakers to allow this population to take full advantage of educational opportunities that this great country has to offer.

In conceptualizing this important project, we understand that the "Black Community" as a whole is not monolithic; however, the need is the same—equity for all Black students in our nation's schools. It is our hope that as the educational community, parents, practitioners, and policymakers read the pages of this book, it helps to inform them about the imperative issues surrounding teaching Black students and developing Black teachers. We hope it inspires them to create or (re-imagine) ways they can contribute to improved educational outcomes for all students, particularly Black students. We believe the scholarship presented in these pages represents a diversity of thinking on a crucial topic. Seasoned and newer voices of scholars are brought together as a collective to address this issue. As we pass the torch to the educational community to continue this conversation, it is our hope that we (the education community) never lose our passion to improve the educational conditions in Black Communities. We must continue to produce the type of research and scholarly products that can aid in addressing policy issues that quietly impede the achievement levels of this population. We must remember that a child that we may never meet will count on us for their lives to be better.

PART I

PREPARING TEACHERS TO TEACH BLACK STUDENTS

PREPARING TEACHERS TO TEACH BLACK STUDENTS

A Story About a Journey to Teaching Excellence

Suzanne C. Carothers
New York University

BACKGROUND

The field of education has been and will continue to be essential to the survival and sustainability of the Black community. Unfortunately, over the past five decades, two major trends have become clearly evident in the Black community: (a) the decline of the academic achievement levels of Black students; and (b) the disappearance of Black teachers, particularly Black males. In 1940, the number one profession for Black men in the United States was teaching (Ruggles, Alexander, Genadek, et al., 2010). Approximately 36% of the working Black male population was standing in front of the classroom delivering instruction to young Black men and women. Today, only 8% are Black teachers, and approximately 2% of these teachers are Black males (NCES, 2010). Over the past few decades, the Black teaching force in the United States has dropped significantly (Lewis, 2006; Lewis, Bonner, Byrd, & James, 2008; Milner & Howard, 2004), and this educational crisis shows no signs of ending in the near future. As the population of

Teacher Education and Black Communities, pages 3–14

Black students in K–12 schools in the United States continue to rise—currently over 16% of students in America's schools are Black (NCES, 2010)—there is an urgent need to increase the presence of Black educators.

Historically, before integration, Black students performed well in school despite the "separate and unequal" conditions they often faced in their schools facilities and the challenges they had in getting to school. During that period, there was a robust number of Blacks teaching in America's schools (Foster, 1997; Perkins, 1989). Educational attainment and advancement were essential goals of the Black community. *Briggs vs. Elliot,* one of the five feeder cases to the 1954 *Brown vs. Board of Education of Topeka,* was the first case that challenged the constitutionality of "separate but equal." That case illustrates the determination of the Black community to procure quality education for their children. In 1947, Black parents in Clarendon County, South Carolina requested from the white Superintendent of Schools, a school bus, so that their children, like the white children, would not have to walk 16 or more miles daily to get back and forth to school.[1] The request was ignored. The Black community rallied under the leadership of Rev. Joseph Armstrong DeLaine, principal of Silver Elementary School, turning to the courts for remedy. What began as a simple request for a school bus and equal facilities which challenged the School Board's policies, ultimately attacked segregation as the *Briggs vs. Elliot* case.

Tillman (2004) noted that the 1954 *Brown vs. Board of Education of Topeka, Kansas* decision, led to a significant loss of Black teachers and Black school leaders. Education scholars point to the fact that since 1954, Black children have not experienced widespread educational success in our public schools (Edney, 2004; Foster, 1997; Irvine & Irvine 1983). As we have entered the second decade of the new millennium, familiar rhetoric continues to describe Black students. They are often depicted using the language of *achievement gaps, depravation* and that which is *lacking* or *problematic.* The contributors to this book believe it is important to shift this perspective and adopt the language of possibility grounded in those critical factors which allow Black students to thrive in school. For example, there is ample evidence that the unique bond that Black teachers and students share improves educational outcomes for Black students (Irvine & Irvine, 1983; Irvine, 1988; Foster, 1997; Perry, Steele, & Hilliard, 2003; Stewart, 2007; Watson & Woods, 2011); that Black students benefit in various ways from relationships they share with their Black teachers. It is also well-documented (Holmes, 1990; Irvine, 1988; King, 1993; Perkins, 1989) that the loss of Black teachers had a detrimental effect on the quality of education Black children received in schools.

In this current era of high stakes testing, common core standards, the proliferation of charter schools and demands for teacher accountability, all having strong implications for Black students' school success, we must turn our attention to instructive and productive ways to improve the educational outcomes for the millions of Black students in our nation's schools. Boosting the number of Black teachers is a major part of that effort as well as deepening our understanding of effective teaching practices that can work with Black students.

I believe that the story of one's journey to teaching excellence can speak to the preparation of teachers to teach Black children. Hear now that story.

The Journey Begins

It all began for me in that little segregated community of ours on the Westside of town where in 1955, folk in that new southern Black community in Charlotte, North Carolina became the proud owners of modest, single family homes with lawns scantly covered by infant trees and freshly sowed grass. It was a well-oiled, thriving community where the people got up and went to work each morning, the men and women. Where children went to school each day. Where children were safe and protected by all the adults in the community. Where each family looked out for and helped each other's family. It was a community that believed their children could succeed and that its adults could "make a way" for them to succeed.

University Park was the name of this new neighborhood. It was in a community, at that time, which was establishing its institutions that would nurture, strengthen, develop and guide its residents for decades to come. Already on the Westside of town was the Historic Black College, Johnson C. Smith University. As churches and doctors' offices also moved to the Westside, a new branch library was built and opened right up the street from our new house. From the perspective of the mothers and fathers of this community, what community would be complete without its educational institutions? West Charlotte High School, Northwest Junior High and Biddleville Elementary School were the three schools that served our community. As the elementary school was some distance away, a new elementary school was to build right in the neighborhood—a new elementary school for *Negro* children. As planning for the school began, our parents were invited to a meeting by the white Superintendent of Schools and asked for their input about the school as he elicited their thoughts concerning the school leadership role—asking who should be principal? In 1958, I began fourth grade at the new school—University Park Elementary School, a ten-minute walk from our house, where Mrs. Elizabeth Randoff was principal.

The context for understanding my perspective on "preparing teachers to teach Black students" starts in that community of my childhood where I was taught as a Black child, all by Black teachers who worked under the leadership of all Black principals. There for decades, teachers taught Black children successfully. What does it look like when a teacher has taught a Black child successfully? Stepping back into time can shed light on that question and offer insights for the challenges and opportunities we face today in preparing teachers to teach.

Teaching and Learning in an Era Past: Lessons From Home

Over the decades, I have had many teachers. As I think of my first 12 years of schooling, a name, face and classroom springs forth out of a sea of passing faces and classrooms bare. That would be Mrs. Evelyn Maxwell. Though I did not know it then, her classroom would be one that I would return to many, many times in years to come. No, I have not returned physically to the room but in the memories of my mind, she and her classroom are very intact, for reasons that I now understand as I have journeyed into teaching and preparing teachers to teach.

Mrs. Maxwell was of the generation of African American teachers who embodied teaching not simply as acts of pedagogical decisions but rather as a commitment, a duty and a privilege to develop the minds of young people who in-turn would contribute *positively to the Negro race* and beyond it. For she, and Black teachers of her day, believed that by improving our lot through education and advancing the race forward were the goals and they were dedicated to us achieving those goals—to reach our full potential. Black educators of that era understood that the generations of those who would come after them, would represent them and all of those who had come before them.

What did she do? Who was this woman whose way in a classroom is seared positively in my memory? Mrs. Maxwell was my teacher who helped me to see learning as the desire to know and she showed me how to make knowing happen for myself. For the two years she was my teacher, we actually learned by doing in that fifth and sixth grade class.

Mrs. Maxwell had such a way with words. Words sang out in her classroom. Language was full, rich, encouraged and enjoyed. She read to us, we to her. We wrote and produced plays. During the 1960 gubernatorial campaign, we gave campaign speeches right at University Elementary School standing in front of out make shift podium. We wrote poetry. She loved language in every form. We made books, bound them and on each page made a border using a potato on which we had cut a design. The books were quite pretty. They were very colorful. In retrospect, these must have been very simple words and ideas but, written in those books, they felt real important. I remember she called us *authors* of our books and put our books on the shelf with the real books.

I remember that Mrs. Maxwell would send three or four of us, at a time, to backboard to do arithmetic problems as she carefully observed what we did and talked with us about it. Working out long division problems at the blackboard using chalk and being able to erase your mistakes with the blackboard eraser, felt different from doing the same problems at your desk with paper and pencil. Even when the problems were hard, it was still more fun doing them on the board rather than at your desk. While she checked to see if you had the "right" answer; by the kinds of questions she peppered us with, she seemed so much more interested in having us explain to her how we figured out the answers thus seeking the "why" of our thinking.

In Mrs. Maxwell's class, after we had studied a unit in social studies, we were excited to take all we had learned and distill that knowledge in interesting formats to teach to others through the "Sharing Period." Those would be elaborate productions we would create through skits, TV like productions and game shows to show how much we had learned. Yes, in the 1950s Mrs. Maxwell did those things with us. Learning was lifted off the pages of text books in Mrs. Maxwell's class. In science, we did not just read about the weather, we built weather instruments—barometers and wind vanes—and went outside to look up in the sky to see cumulus or cirrus clouds.

Mrs. Maxwell believed that children can learn, that each child is special and has something special to give. But in the late 1950s when I was in elementary school, they called kids like me "late bloomers." This label explained why those like me did not do well on the California Achievement Test. I was never in the "Blue Jay" or "Cardinal" reading groups. Funny thing, in Mrs. Maxwell's class, I don't remember sitting in those dumb reading groups. Reading was all over the classroom and beyond its four walls. It was in the stories and plays we wrote. The campaign speeches we gave. The choral speaking we did. The newspaper articles we read. She taught reading but not like any teacher I had had before. Her idea of "learning to read" was connected to the world that I knew and the one that I began to discover. I, therefore, wanted to read to learn more about things that actually mattered to me. And, I did.

Mrs. Maxwell valued the knowledge we brought to school with us. She taught us that learning begins with desire—the desire to want to know more and the willingness to dig and find it. She seemed to understand that the process of digging to find out was not easy. The day that Chauncy threw the chair at her because he became angry when be could not do the long division problem; the whole class quaked with fear. What would happen next we thought? She calmly walked over to Chauncy and said, "Learning to do long division is hard but you can do it. Once you know how, you'll be able to do so many things with it. Now get the chair and put it back under the desk." Some of her exact words I may have lost over the years, but I will always remember the feeling of what she said and the way she said it. We all saw Chauncy go over and get the chair. He settled back to work and so did we.

I wonder had she ever read Dewey? Did she know about progressive education? How did she know what would work with us, her energetic, curious students in that all Black elementary school? Who was her teacher? How was she taught to teach?

I believe that Mrs. Maxwell understood the notion of holistic learning and that good learning happens when the left and right brain complement each other. For her, intellect was not a book to be read, an author to know or a thing in the abstract. Rather, it seems from the way that she taught, intellect was a matter of thinking, questioning and charting one's own course to knowing. She provided many tools. She awakened a deep curiosity in each of us and helped to release the confidence buried within us. As our teacher, Mrs. Maxwell figured out who each of us was, what each of us needed, held high expectations for us all and worked tirelessly to meet our needs as learners. Our parents were delighted that Mrs. Maxwell was our teacher for two years. While she created a classroom for her students, that classroom extended to welcoming our parents. Mrs. Maxwell got to know them, and they her. My mother once said about Mrs. Maxwell, "When she became my teacher, that's really when I started learning at school."

My mother created an annual tradition with my elementary school teachers. At the end of each school year, my mother, who loved to sew, would make and give my teacher a dress. It was her way of saying thank you to the teacher for teaching me. At the end of the school year when I was in her class, Mrs. Maxwell became part of my mother's tradition.

My journey as a teacher is initially anchored in the lessons I learned from Mrs. Maxwell and that Black community on the Westside of town. What does it mean to teach a Black child? How different is it from teaching children who are not Black? How does Mrs. Maxwell's teaching, model what children can learn when teachers teach in ways that engage them as learners?

Teaching and Learning in an Era Past: Lessons Beyond Home

No one needed to recruit me into teaching. Becoming a teacher was always my life's goal. Having taught summer school in my backyard for neighborhood children from 1959–1963 where I charged 25 cent tuition and 10 cent for each additional child in the same family, funds to offset the cost of materials I needed to purchase, I believed that I was already a teacher. While my family and neighbors supported my "teaching endeavors," upon graduation from West Charlotte High School in 1967, I was off to Bennett College to earn a degree by studying Nursery–Kindergarten Education.

It was there where I met Mrs. Mary Ann Scarlette who would become my advisor and major professor at Bennett. It was there where I would take the lessons learned from Mrs. Maxwell and my home community and draw upon them in my teacher education program. Mrs. Scarlette taught me about: (a) pedagogical excellence; (b) one's best is always the standard to be achieved; (c) intellectual challenge can be met creatively; as well as, (d) creating space and time for group gatherings builds community thus, become the first step in establishing meaningful relationships with others.

In that very first orientation for the nursery–kindergarten and elementary education majors, we freshmen sat in a circle as Mrs. Scarlette began to talk. She wove a story that included information about each of us in that circle. Just as she knew I had planned to start my own school called "Dreamland Nursery Kindergarten," she knew equally, the things that mattered to the other young women sitting in that circle—our hopes, fears and dreams. From the very beginning, she wanted us to know that our hopes and dreams were all possible. And, hard work would help us to achieve them as we overcome any fears we have. No doubt, Mrs. Scarlette really read those college essays. It was like, she already knew me but, we had never met. Even at 17 years of age, I knew what she did in that circle on that day was special. Three years later in 1970, I would be one of two African American students to be sent to an all-white elementary school as the first Black student teachers to do student teaching in the Public Schools of Greensboro, North Carolina. Mrs. Scarlette sent my friend Diane Earl and me to Claxton Elementary School the fall of our senior year because she knew us well and had prepared us well to enter those waters.

Graduating from Bennett, I was hired by the Charlotte Mecklenburg School System as a kindergarten teacher for the Educational Component of Model Cities, a federally funded program, for inner-city children. In this program, my students were all Black. My preparation to be a teacher served me well with the five-year old Black children I taught. The teacher preparation I received at Bennett positioned me well to further my education at Bank Street College of Education. It was at the Bank Street School for Children where I was hired as the teacher of the three-year-olds who were predominately white, for the next seven years.

Implications for Practice

As I reflect about my journey as a teacher—my work with children in pre-K to elementary school classrooms, the many student teachers whom I have supervised in those classrooms, the classroom teachers with whom

I have worked and the many students in the teacher education programs I have taught—there may be lessons learned from an era pass that can inform what we do on behalf of Black children's learning, what we do as teachers to teach them and what we do to prepare teachers to teach children like and unlike themselves. Since for me, my journey into teaching started in Mrs. Maxwell's classroom where I successfully learned as a Black child, what lessons can we learn from her teaching that speak to teacher education and preparing teachers to teach Black children?

Drawing from Mrs. Maxwell's classroom, Eight Guiding Principles emerge that can inform classroom practice which promotes teaching excellence that can lead to access, equity and achievement of Black students. They are:

- Know your students
- Care about your students
- Believe that your students *can* learn and that it is your job as their teacher to figure out the best ways to teach them
- Engage your students actively in learning that matters to them as the first step to learning about issues, ideas and concepts to which they will need to be exposed
- Have high expectations of your students
- Scaffold your students' learning process
- Involve the parents of your students in the life of the classroom learning community
- Enjoy teaching your students

For Black children to be taught successfully by their teachers, they must first, matter to their teachers. The relationship that teachers establish with their students becomes a critical piece of the teaching learning puzzle in promoting the academic success of Black children. According to Richard Bowman in "Relationship educates: An interactive strategy,"[2] "No one loves alone; no one heals alone; no one learns alone. Living is essentially a social process; 'learning is essentially a social process' (Combs, 1976, p. 67). In the ultimate sense, it is relationship which educates (Buber, 1967, p. 98)." The work that Mrs. Maxwell did in her classroom was anchored in the meaningful relationships that she established with her students and the parents in the community. From the vantage point of a 10 and 11 year old, it was clear to me that Mrs. Maxwell *loved* being a teacher. It gave her joy to work with us. As teachers create positive relationships with their students enabling their learning possibilities to soar, Mrs. Maxwell's Eight Guiding Principles can offer ways to demonstrate to children and their parents that they matter to their teachers.

The chapters that follow, in many ways, further explore the big ideas grounded in Mrs. Maxwell's Eight Guiding Principles. These chapters thoughtfully address issues of parental and community involvement with Black Parents, recruitment of Black teachers, generational education experiences of Black males and noticing how teachers' views of Black students has implications for the ways in which teachers engage with them as learners and how students, in turn, respond to their teachers.

The Six Chapters

In *Preparing Future Educators to Teach Black Students: Insights on Promoting Nonresident Black Father Involvement in Schools, Increasing Black Student Achievement, and Advancing Equity in Education*, Brianna P. Lemmons has contextualized the critical role of parental involvement in children's school success. She argues that one group which has been largely ignored and excluded from the debate on parental involvement is nonresident father families. This oversight disproportionately impacts Black children. Given the known positive effects of parental involvement on school performance, educators and school systems can play a key role in promoting educational equity by making greater efforts to engage the nonresident fathers of Black students. As many institutions have struggled to keep pace with changing family structures as well as federal and school efforts to promote parental involvement among diverse groups, many preservice teachers find themselves ill-prepared to partner effectively with the culturally varied families they serve.

In their chapter, *Making Space for Black Queer Teachers: Pedagogic Possibilities*, Lance McCready and Micia Mosley ask a series of hard-hitting questions: is it possible for Black women and men who identify as lesbian, gay, bisexual, transgender, queer or questioning to become teachers in K–12 urban schools? If they do, what must they give up? What could be gained by making urban teacher education queer? Their research seeks to make visible a group of individuals often rendered invisible from the conversation on Black teacher education.

As we plan schools, fix schools, close schools and change schools—how do people actually experience life in school?—is a question worth asking. Darrell C. Hucks in his chapter, *The New Visions of Collective Achievement: The Cross-Generational Schooling Experiences of African American Males*, presents research from a study with African American males across generations who share their perceptions of the factors that affected their schooling experiences and influenced their achievement in and beyond school. Hearing about their journeys in their own voices, brings a critical perspective that is often missing in our quest to plan, fix, close and change schools. Hucks argues that the schooling experiences of these participants call for establishing a model of collective achievement which captures and delineates the engagement and investment of the multiple stakeholders involved in their education. He contends that such a model will bring about a higher level of multiple stakeholder accountability that would likely improve students' schooling experiences and increase the academic and life outcomes.

The critical role of relationship in learning is brought to bear in Yolanda Sealey-Ruiz, Keisha Allen, and Erik Nolan's *Invisible Hands: Seeing and Noticing Black and Latino Male Youth*. Given the lenses that schools have historically chosen "to see" Black students, thwart with problems, Sealey-Ruiz, Allen, and Nolan examine the possibility of building genuine relationships with students that support their academic and socio-emotional development through their work with members of UMOJA, an all-male, mentoring group in an alternative high school. This chapter invites educators to explore ways to enhance their views of male students of color that further engage them in the classroom, and strengthen their practice as teachers.

Robert Simmons, Cheryl Moore-Thomas, and Audra Watson examine academic identity development among African American males in their chapter, *Young Scholars: African American Males and Academic Identity Development*. Using the lens of historical, institutional and sociocultural factors, their analysis draws a strong positive correlation between African American males' productive academic identity development and their academic achievement.

In the final chapter, *Not Strangers: How Social Distance Influences Black Male Teachers' Perceptions of Their Male Students of Color*, Travis J. Bristol examines survey data from a large public school district survey to gain insight on the ways in which Black male teachers make meaning of the schooling experiences of their male students of color. Applying the theory of Social Distance, Bristol investigates the tensions that arise when individuals from different social groups interact, and offer ideas on what an increase of Black male teachers may yield for the social and academic success of male students of color.

Summary

The six chapters that follow help us to understand:

- The role of parental involvement of nonresident fathers in the school success of Black children
- The possibility of recruiting those individuals not readily considered for the teaching profession
- The experiences of Black males in classrooms
- How young men Black want to be seen and noticed by their teachers

These six chapters build on the determination of the Black parents and Black community of Clarendon County, South Carolina who, in 1947, challenged policies and practices that were not in the best educational interest of Black children.

These six chapters illustrate how insights from a journey to teaching excellence can be instructive to educational dilemmas we face today.

These six chapters incorporate the lessons learned from an era past concerning what matters in the education of Black children.

These six chapters are in the spirit of the way Mrs. Maxwell taught, believed in and engaged the Black children in her classroom.

These six chapters become the latest voice in the continuing saga to promote access, equity and achievement of Black students.

Post Script

I never had the opportunity to tell Mrs. Maxwell about how my being in her fifth and sixth grade class became an experience for me that I would draw upon both personally and professionally, way beyond my time at University Park Elementary School. Mrs. Maxwell died long before I finished high school. So, I never had a chance to ask her about her journey to becoming a teacher and how she knew what to do with us energetic, active, seeking to be independent, at the beginning of puberty, 10, 11 and 12 year olds in her class. I did not know then that these would be things that one day, I would want to know. The chapters that follow further express issues about the education of Black children which I believe, Mrs. Maxwell would indorse.

NOTES

1. Ophelia DeLaine Gona, Dawn of Desegregation: J.A. D*eLaine and Briggs v. Elliott*, 2011. Richard Kluger, Simple Justice: The History of *Brown v. Board of Education* and Black America's Struggle for Equality, 1975, 2004.
2. pp. 101–103.

REFERENCES

Brown v. Board of Education (1954).

Buber, M. (1967). *A Believing Humanism*. New York: Simon and Schuster.

Combs, A. (1976). Fostering maximum development of the individual. In W. Van Til (Ed.), *Issues in secondary education*. Chicago: University of Chicago Press.

Edney, H. T. (2004). Black students still struggle in post-Brown era. *New York Amsterdam News, 95,* 37–38.

Foster, M. (1997). *Black teachers on teaching*. New York: The New Press.

Holmes, B. J. (1990). New strategies are needed to produce minority teachers. In A. Dorman (Ed.), *Recruiting and retaining minority teachers.* (Guest commentary, Policy Brief No. 8). Oak Brook, IL: North Central Regional Educational Laboratory.

Irvine, R. W., & Irvine, J. J. (1983). The impact of the desegregation process on the education of Black students: Key variables. *The Journal of Negro Education, 52,* 410–422.

Irvine, J. J. (1988). An analysis of the problem of disappearing Black educators. *The Elementary School Journal, 88,* 503–513. doi: 10.1086/461553

King, S. (1993). The limited presence of African American teachers. *Review of Educational Research, 63,* 115–149.

Lewis, C. (2006). African American male teachers in public schools: An examination of three urban school districts. *Teachers College Record, 108,* 224–245.

Lewis, C., Bonner, F., Byrd, D., & James, M. (2008). Recruiting African American males into urban teacher preparation programs from university athletic departments. *The National Journal of Urban Education and Practice, 1,* 224–238.

Milner, H. R., & Howard, T. C. (2004). Black teachers, Black students, Black communities, and Brown: Perspectives and insights from experts. *The Journal of Negro Education, 73,* 285–297.

National Center for Education Statistics (NCES). (2010). *Digest of Education Statistics* (NCES 2010-013). Retrieved from http://nces.ed.gov/programs/digest/d09/index.asp

Perkins, L. M. (1989). The history of Blacks in teaching: Growth and decline within the profession. In D. Warren (Ed.), *American teachers: Histories of a profession at work* (pp. 344–369). New York: American Educational Research Association.

Perry, T., Steele, C. M., & Hillard, A. G. III. (2003). *Young, gifted, and Black: Promoting high achievement among African-American students.* New York: Beacon.

Ruggles, S., Alexander, J. T., Genadek, K., Goeken, R., et al. (2010). *Integrated Public Use Microdata Series (IPUMS): Version 5.0* [Machine-readable database]. Minneapolis: University of Minnesota. Retrieved from usa.ipums.org

Stewart, E. B. (2007). Individual and school structural effects on African American high school students' academic achievement. *High School Journal, 91,* 16–34.

Tillman, L. (2004). Unintended consequences: The impact of *Brown v. Board of Education* decision on the employment status of Black educators. *Education and Urban Society, 36,* 280–303.

Watson, L., & Woods, S. (Eds.). (2011). *Go where you belong: Male teachers as cultural workers in the lives of children, families, and communities.* Netherlands: Sense.

CHAPTER 1

INSIGHTS FOR FUTURE EDUCATORS ON PROMOTING NONRESIDENT BLACK FATHER INVOLVEMENT IN SCHOOLS, INCREASING BLACK STUDENT ACHIEVEMENT, AND ADVANCING EQUITY IN EDUCATION

Brianna P. Lemmons
Howard University

Given the preponderance of research evidence underscoring the significant role of parents in the educational process, parental involvement has become a national priority. As outlined in the *No Child Left Behind Act of 2001*, schools across the county are now expected to ensure that parents play an integral role and are actively involved in their children's education. However, one group that has been largely ignored and excluded from the debate on parental involvement is nonresident father families. This is an oversight that

Teacher Education and Black Communities, pages 15–42
Copyright © 2014 by Information Age Publishing
All rights of reproduction in any form reserved.

disproportionately impacts Black children. Given the known positive effects of parental involvement on school performance, educators and school systems can play a key role in promoting educational equity by making greater efforts to engage the nonresident fathers of Black students. The ability of schools to successfully connect with parents is largely dependent on teachers who are expected to adequately possess the knowledge and abilities necessary for supporting all school-based parental involvement efforts. However, many institutions have struggled to keep pace with changing family structures and federal and school efforts to promote parental involvement among diverse groups, leaving many preservice teachers ill-prepared to partner effectively with the culturally varied families they serve. In order to uphold and promote the academic success and overall well-being of Black students, future educators must possess the requisite knowledge and skills for engaging their nonresident fathers. The information presented in this chapter is designed to provide future educators with insight on how to effectively promote Black nonresident father involvement in schools, thereby advancing Black student achievement and equity in education.

INTRODUCTION

Given the severe racial-ethnic and disciplinary gaps in achievement within America's education system, efforts to improve family engagement have accelerated over the past three decades. Many educators and policymakers have turned to parents to assist in the efforts toward closing these gaps (Trotman, 2001). These calls are grounded in the assumption that engaging parents in the educational process is key to resolving the deeply entrenched problems that exist within school systems (Jackson & Remillard, 2005; Smith, Wohlstetter, Kuzin, & De Pedro, 2011). For decades, educational researchers have contributed much to our understanding of the role of parental involvement in academic achievement by documenting the benefits for children, families, schools, and the larger society (Smith, Wohlstetter, Kuzin, & De Pedro, 2011). The significant role of families in promoting positive outcomes for children has been well established within the research literature (Abdul-Adil & Farmer, 2006). Parental involvement in education has been positively correlated with academic success and social competence (Hill & Taylor, 2004).

However, given the tendency of school systems and educators to operate from a nuclear family paradigm, one group that has been largely ignored and excluded from the debate on parental involvement is nontraditional, nonresident father families. Cabrera, Ryan, Mitchell, Shannon, and Tamis-LeMonda (2008) define the term nonresident as "the biological father not living in the home with his child at all" (p. 644). Hill (2007a) defines nonresidential parents as "fathers or mothers who *do not have legal custody* of their children and who *do not reside* with their children" (p. 130). While this particular form of family is a growing phenomenon within American culture generally, it is most prevalent among Blacks.

Today, more than half of all Black children live without their biological fathers (U.S. Census Bureau, 2012; as cited in The White House, 2012). Where many of their racial/ethnic and same race counterparts who reside in nuclear families enjoy the benefit of having both parents take part in their education, Black children who live in nonresident father families are not always afforded this same privilege. Although not all children in two-parent families have fathers who are actively engaged in their education, the potential for father involvement in these families is much greater than those wherein the father does not reside. Given the known positive effects of parental involvement on school performance, educators and school systems can play a key role in leveling the playing field and promoting educational equity by making greater efforts to engage not only the residential mothers of Black students, but also their nonresident fathers or father figures.

While many Black fathers may not be present within the homes of their children, their active participation within schools remains critical to the achievement outcomes of Black students. Research suggests that, despite their residential status, nonresident fathers' involvement in schools has a positive influence on children's school outcomes (Nord, Brimhall, & West, 1997; Nord, 1998; Powell, 2007). Thus, in order to uphold and promote the academic success and overall well-being of Black students, future educators must possess the requisite knowledge and skills for engaging their nonresident fathers as they may be key resources in increasing Black student achievement and eliminating inequities in education. The information presented in this chapter is designed to be utilized by teacher trainees in their efforts to gain awareness and insight on how to effectively partner with nonresident Black fathers in the educational process, thereby advancing the achievement of their children. In the same vein, this chapter may also be useful for in-service teachers looking to enhance their knowledge of how to involve nonresident Black fathers in schools.

First, this chapter will begin by discussing the various shifts that have occurred within the structure of Black families overtime, the variety of factors underlying these changes, and the consequent role of nonresident father for many Black men in families, particularly those that are of a lower socioeconomic status. Second, answering the question—"Who are nonresident fathers?"—a brief economic and demographic profile of this group will be provided, followed by an explanation of why their presence and involvement in schools is essential for increasing Black student achievement. Utilizing insights gleaned from the theoretical and empirical literature on fathering and families, one enduring misconception concerning the involvement of Black nonresident fathers with their children will be discussed and barriers to their involvement in schools will be identified. This chapter will conclude with recommendations and strategies for engaging Black nonresident fathers in schools, a brief dialogue on the role of social fathers or father figures in the lives of Black children, and conclusions and implications for Black student achievement and equity in education.

BLACK FATHERS AND THE BLACK COMMUNITY: PAST AND PRESENT

Although decades of research provide evidence for the powerful influence of the home environment on the academic achievement and cognitive development of children, overtime, the home environments and living arrangements of Black children have changed drastically. Between the years of 1865 and 1866, Gutman (1976) notes that the majority of Black households were comprised of either a husband and wife or two parents and children. Furthermore, most families had a male head of household and relatively few Blacks lived as single parents (Gutman, 1976). Billingsley and Morrison-Rodriguez (2007) and Ruggles (1994) note that just 15 years post the abolition of slavery (around 1880), 90% of Black families were comprised of two parent households. Furthermore, in 1925, six of seven households had either a husband or father present (Franklin, 1997). Even in 1950, 91% of Black families were comprised of two parent households (Conner, 2011). During this time, Black family life in America was described as "solid" (Conner, 2011, p. 9). In other words, the Black family structure was considered stable and intact according to traditional and generationally distinct conceptions of family.

Franklin (1997) notes that from early to late 1960s, "a remarkable 75% of Black families included both husband and wife" (p. 8). By the late 1970s, the percentage of Black families that remained nuclear in structure had dropped to 67.7% (Glick, 1997; Hogan-Garcia, 1997). Major shifts within the Black family structure occurred between the years of 1970 and 1990 (Kreider & Fields, 2005). As noted by Glick (1997), in 1980, the number of two parent homes had further decreased to 54.2%. In addition, as documented by Hogan-Garcia (1997), by 1990, only 50% of Black families had two parents, an 18% decline from 1970. Furthermore, independent analysis of data from the United States Census Bureau's Current Population Survey (2011) revealed that in 1990, the number of Black children living in mother only homes ($N = 5,132$) exceeded the number of Black children living in two parent homes ($N = 3,781$) (see Figure 1.1), demonstrating the trend toward female headed households that began to accelerate rapidly in the latter part of the twentieth century.

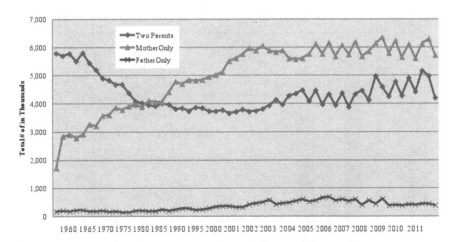

Figure 1.1 Living arrangements of Black children under 18; 1960–present.

Today, more than half of all Black children live without their biological fathers (U.S. Census Bureau, 2012; as cited in The White House, 2012) and nearly 80% of all Black children can now expect to spend at least a significant part of their childhood living apart from their fathers (Morehouse Research Institute for American Values, 1999; Perry, 2009). An independent analysis of data from the United States Department of Education's National Household Education Survey (NHES), Parent and Family Involvement Survey revealed that in 2007, 41% of Black children lived in mother only homes, in comparison to 23.9% of Hispanic children and 11.5% of White children. Thus, in contrast to their racial/ethnic counterparts, Black children were the least likely to live in two parent homes and the most likely to live in mother only and nonparent guardian homes (see Figure 1.2).

Furthermore, independent analysis of data from the United States Census Bureau's Current Population Survey (2011) suggests that among Black children, the number of mother only homes continues to exceed the number of two parent homes (mother only homes = 6,296; two parent homes = 4,982). In fact, this trend has been remained fairly stable and unchanged from the latter part of the twentieth century through the twenty-first century (see Figure 1.2).Taken together, in comparison to other racial/ethnic groups, statistically speaking, mother only homes are indeed more prevalent within the Black community (Lamb, 1997; Morehouse Research Institute for American Values, 1999; Hill, 2007a; Billingsley & Morrison-Rodriguez, 2007). A recent report by Livingston and Parker (2011) reveals that although today's fathers are more active in the lives of their children, they are also more absent than in any other period in American history. While fathers have increased their level of involvement in caregiving roles,

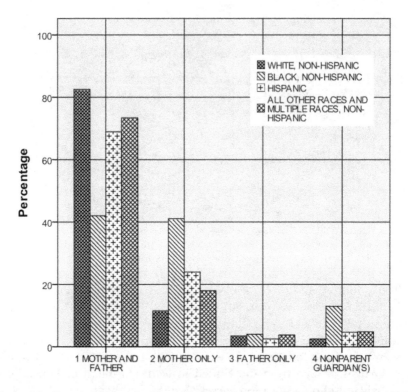

Figure 1.2 Race/ethnicity of subject child and subject child's household composition.

the number of fathers that live apart from their children continues to in-crease rapidly (Amato, Meyers, & Emery, 2009; Livingston & Parker, 2011).

Highlighting these statistical trends is important for understanding the various changes that have taken place within the Black family structure throughout history. However, similar types of data have been utilized in the past as a means of characterizing Black families as pathological, disor-ganized, matrifocal (a family structure where the mother heads the family and the father plays a less important role), and unstable (Moynihan, 1965). Thus, in order to prevent the formation of negative and deficit-oriented perspectives, it is important to place these data within their proper context and to make especially clear that the current structure and functioning of twenty-first century Black families is indeed the product of a complex web of factors that together reflect a response to their social environment, lived experiences, and unique history in this country (Franklin, 1997; Lowe & Hopps, 2007; Coles & Green, 2009; Delpit, 2012). As noted by Franklin (1997), these experiences have been created as "the cultural expectations of African American families interacting with societal institutions, and it is the combination of these factors that has generated changes in family structure over time" (p. 19).

Family structure, and in turn, fathering roles, are largely shaped by social and historical factors (Pleck & Pleck, 1997). In order to truly understand the challenges confronting contemporary Blacks families, long-standing inequities related to unemployment and labor market disparities, mass incarceration, urbanization, poverty, educational achievement and attainment, institutional racism, and criminal justice and social welfare policies *must* be a part of the discourse as each of these factors have unquestionably shaped the foundation of family life (Lowe & Hopps, 2007; Lu et al., 2010; Toldson & Morton, 2012). Along with drastic changes in family structure naturally came major shifts in the role and place of Black fathers within the family unit (Rasheed & Stewart, 2007; Livingston & Parker, 2011). Consequently, many Black fathers now serve in nonresident father roles.

WHO ARE NONRESIDENT BLACK FATHERS AND WHY DO THEY MATTER?

In 1997, an estimated 10.2 million men identified as nonresident fathers in the National Survey of America's Families (Nelson, 2004). In 2001, nearly 11 million fathers in the United States reported living apart from their children (Sorenson & Zibman, 2001) and these figures continue to increase overtime. Overall, minority men are much more likely to be nonresident fathers, in comparison to their White counterparts (Stykes, 2012; as cited in The White House, 2012). In fact, Livingston and Parker (2011) note that "Black fathers are more than twice as likely as White fathers to live apart from their children (44% vs. 21%), while Hispanic fathers fall in the middle (35%)" (p. 2). Despite the limited data available on nonresident fathers, a small group of scholars have attempted to construct profiles of this population that reveal their demographic and economic characteristics.

For example, Mizell (2002) found that divorced or "ever-married" nonresident fathers tend to be White, older (i.e., over the age of 25), fairly educated (i.e., high school education or higher), have stable patterns of employment, and thus higher child support payments. By contrast, single or "never-married" nonresident fathers tend to be nonwhite, younger (i.e., under the age of 25), fairly uneducated (i.e., high school education or less), have unstable patterns of employment, and thus lower child support payments. More recent data suggests that among fathers who never completed high school, "40% live apart from their children; this compares with 7% of fathers who graduated from college" (Livingston & Parker, 2011, p. 2).

As a whole, nonresident fathers tend to be younger, less educated, earn less, have fewer assets, and less healthy than resident fathers (Garfinkel,

McLanahan, & Hanson, 1998; Nelson, 2004). Responding to the question "who are nonresident fathers?" is complex as their characteristics vary greatly. The men that comprise this group are best understood when taking into consideration the interplay between the following key demographic and economic characteristics, which all function as strong correlates of nonresident fatherhood: (a) racial/ethnic background, (b) socioeconomic status (as measured by educational attainment and/or real income), (c) marital status, (d) age at the time of the child's birth, (e) criminal history,and (f) family history.

Although the characteristics of nonresident fathers may be ostensibly off-putting, the literature clearly suggests that they matter and are important for academic success and overall child well-being. For example, the work of Nord, Brimhall, and West (1997) suggests that the effects of nonresident father involvement seem to vary by grade level or the age of the child. Among children in grades 1–5 and 6–12, nonresident father involvement is positively associated with involvement in extracurricular activities. However, among older children (grades 6–12), having an involved nonresident father increases the likelihood of school attachment and academic success (i.e., receiving mostly A's in school).

Not much is known about the influence of nonresident Black fathers on the school outcomes of their children. However, a recent study provides some insight. Powell (2007) examined the influence of nonresident African American fathers' involvement in school-based activities on the educational outcomes of their middle school children. Although they were not found to influence the academic achievement outcomes (i.e., school grades) of their children, they did have a significant impact on their behavior and conduct. Specifically, children with involved nonresident fathers had fewer in-school and out-of-school suspensions, in comparison to those with uninvolved nonresident fathers. Taken together, regardless of their racial/ethnic background, nonresident fathers may be salient resources in eliminating the discipline and achievement gaps that exist within the American educational system.

Despite insight offered through the literature on the positive influence that nonresident fathers can have on the educational outcomes of their children, there remains a disconnect between research and practice. Educators continue to grapple with how to effectively engage two-parent families in schools and nonresident fathers are often left out of the debate on parental involvement entirely. Given their physical absence from the home, they are often an invisible and untapped resource within school systems, perhaps due to ambiguity regarding their place within families and attitudes toward the paternal role. One common misconception that exists about nonresident Black fathers is that they are unwilling to accept their parental responsibilities and have no desire to be involved in their children's lives. This presumption can stand in the way of educators making concerted and genuine efforts to support nonresident fathers in taking part in the education of their children. Henceforth, the goal of this chapter is: (a) to assist teacher trainees in addressing and eliminating potential biases by dispelling the common misconception of the "uncaring" and "uninvolved" Black nonresident father, (b) to discuss some of the realities and barriers to the involvement of nonresident Black fathers in schools, and (c) to provide insight on how future educators can effectively engage nonresident Black fathers as partners in the educational process.

OUT OF HOME, OUT OF HEART: THE PERENNIAL MISCONCEPTION REGARDING THE INVOLVEMENT OF NONRESIDENT BLACK FATHERS IN THE LIVES OF THEIR CHILDREN

Nonresident Black fathers that do not reside in the home with their children are often assumed to be uninvolved, uncaring, and totally disengaged from their parenting responsibilities (Miller, 1994; Nelson, 2004; Conner & White, 2006; Hill, 2007a; Perry, 2009; Mills, 2010). As noted by Johnson (1998), "the principal attribution regarding absent fatherhood is that African American fathers are peripheral in the lives of their children" (p. 216). Mills (2010) notes that although father absence is a major issue within the Black community, it is only "one slice of the fatherhood pie" (p. 3). Given the overwhelming focus on absence, the numerous ways in which nonresident Black fathers impact the lives of their children *positively* are often concealed and the various efforts made by these men to engage in proactive parenting are frequently hidden and overlooked (Perry, 2009).

The literature on fathering suggests that physical absence from the home does not necessarily preclude father–child contact (Danziger & Radin, 1990; Coley & Chase-Lansdale, 1999; Hill, 2007a; Perry, 2009) and that residential status is not necessarily an indicator of the extent to which nonresident fathers involve themselves with their children (Nelson, 2004; Conner & White, 2006; Mills, 2010). In fact, several research studies have found evidence that challenges the assumption that nonresident Black fathers are negligent in their parenting responsibilities (Mott, 1990; King, 1994; Salem, Zimmerman, & Notaro, 1998; Hill, 2007a; Cabrera, Ryan, Mitchell, Shannon, & Tamis-LeMonda, 2008).

King (1994) found that Black nonresident fathers were over three times more likely (10.5%) to visit their children every day, in comparison to their White (3.2%) and Hispanic (3%) counterparts. Compared with White or Hispanic children, Black children were found to be the least likely to have a nonresident father who never visits and the most likely to be in contact with their fathers almost daily. Several other recent studies have also found evidence of higher levels of involvement among nonresident minority fathers, in comparison to their White counterparts (King, Harris, & Heard, 2004; Cabrera, Ryan, Mitchell, Shannon, & Tamis-LeMonda, 2008). Cabrera, Ryan, Mitchell, Shannon, and Tamis-LeMonda (2008) found that even after controlling for parents' education, age, and child gender, White nonresident fathers had lower levels of involvement than their minority counterparts.

All in all, these studies have shown that Black nonresident fathers are more involved than originally thought (Mott, 1990; Hill, 2007a; Mills, 2010) and in ways that often go unrecognized by policymakers, educators, and the general public (Miller, 1994; Nelson, 2004; Hill, 2007a). Yet, there remains a great deal of variability in the relationships that Black students have with their nonresident fathers. While some students may see their fathers daily, others may have only minimal contact. The literature suggests that the intensity and nature of involvement among urban Black nonresident fathers has the tendency to change overtime as children age (Coley & Chase-Lansdale, 1999). In comparison to resident fathers, nonresident fathers often face formidable challenges that defy their sustained presence in the lives of their children (Seltzer, 1991; Nelson, 2004; Julion, Gross, Barclay-McLaughlin, & Fogg, 2007). Notwithstanding these impediments, consistent involvement from both parents, regardless of their residential status, is essential for advancing Black student achievement. Nevertheless, effectively promoting and gaining the involvement of nonresident Black fathers in their child's learning can be difficult for a variety of reasons. To successfully overcome these obstacles, there is a need to understand the various factors that may create barriers to their involvement in schools.

BARRIERS TO NONRESIDENT BLACK FATHER INVOLVEMENT IN SCHOOLS

Much of the scholarship on contemporary men and fathers highlights their inadequacies (Hawkins & Dollahite, 1997a) such as low levels of involvement in schools (Nord, Brimhall, & West, 1997; Nord, 1998) and declines in their contribution to caregiving responsibilities for children overtime (Coley & Chase-Lansdale, 1999). However, given the limitations of quantitative data, researchers are seldom able to provide evidence of the underlying factors that may help to explain and accurately interpret these outcomes. In other words, simply knowing that they are not involved is only part of the story. Consideration of barriers to involvement would provide a more comprehensive understanding. The involvement of Black nonresident fathers in the lives of their children must be understood within the context of ongoing challenges and complex dynamics that create situations where far too many fall short of fulfilling the responsibilities of fatherhood (Doherty, Kouneski, & Erickson, 1998; The White House, 2012). Underlying inconsistencies in involvement are often complicated circumstances that influence fathering behaviors.

Although many nonresident fathers would like to have a strong and sustained presence in the lives of their children, there are several mutually influencing factors that make maintaining this kind of relationship difficult (Halle, Moore, Greene, & LeMenestrel, 1998). Research suggests that the role of fathering, in comparison to mothering, is not highly prescribed (Cabrera, Fitzgerald, Bradley, & Roggman, 2007). It is extremely sensitive to and strongly influenced by a variety of forces that exist on intrapersonal, interpersonal, neighborhood, community, cultural, and societal levels (Belsky, 1984; Doherty, Kouneski, & Erickson, 1998; Coley & Chase-Lansdale, 1999; Parke, 2000; Wood & Repetti, 2004; Cabrera, Fitzgerald, Bradley, & Roggman, 2007; Hill, 2007a; Lu et al., 2010). Such forces combine to either facilitate or hinder the extent to which nonresident fathers are involved in advancing the education and overall well-being of their children (Doherty, Kouneski, & Erickson, 1998; Marsiglio, Amato, Day, & Lamb, 2000; Parke, 2000; Lu et al., 2010). Although there are many, two major factors will be discussed: family conflict and school policies and practices.

Family Conflict

Within nonresident father families, the mother–father relationship context is critical to understanding a father's involvement with his children (Sobolewski & King, 2005). In these families, fathering is often treated as a "package deal," wherein a man's ability to fulfill his parenting obligations is highly intertwined with and contingent upon the nature of his relationship with the child's mother. Research suggests that men who attempt to father outside of a relationship with the child's mother experience major barriers to successfully fulfilling their parental responsibilities (Doherty, Kouneski, & Erickson, 1998; Ryan, Kalil, & Ziol-Guest, 2008). Studies have shown that closeness and harmony in the mother–father relationship protects against paternal disengagement, encouraging active fathering and high levels of paternal involvement among urban, African American resident and nonresident fathers (Coley & Chase-Lansdale, 1999). However, high levels of mother–father conflict often result in low levels of paternal involvement among both adolescent and adult nonresident fathers (Coley & Chase-Lansdale, 1999; Gavin et al., 2002; Sobolewski & King, 2005; Castillo & Fenzl-Crossman, 2010).

Furthermore, intimacy between parents has been found to be instrumental in the reduction of conflict and facilitative of high levels of father involvement (Gavin, et al., 2002; Cabrera, et al., 2004; Bradford & Hawkins, 2006; Varga & Gee, 2010). On the other hand, studies of unwed nonresident fathers have shown that high levels of conflict and the likelihood of negative parental alliances tend to be especially high when parents are not engaged in a romantic relationship (Tach, Mincy, & Edin, 2010). Under these circumstances, fathers may be less likely to have consistent contact with their children as the biological mother may engage in "gatekeeping" practices that bar fathers' regular access to their children or she may have a new significant other (i.e., boyfriend, cohabiting partner, or husband) who serves as a father figure in place of the child's natural father.

As noted by Bzostek (2008), given the pervasive practice of family formation within the United States, which now places parenthood ahead of marriage, many children will witness the separation of their biological parents and their formation of new intimate relationships apart from each other. Such practices have consequences for father involvement, and in turn, the relationships of children with their biological fathers. For example, it has been found that post nonmarital separation, father involvement is likely to gradually decline as children age (Seltzer, 1991; Leite & McKenry, 2006; Laughlin, Farrie, & Fagan, 2009; Cheadle, Amato, & King, 2010). All in all, it is important for educators to understand the status of the relationship between parents and levels of family conflict at any given time in the lives of Black students as it is one of the most significant predictors of nonresident father involvement.

School Policies and Practices

Despite the increased interest in fatherhood within research and policy arenas and mounting evidence suggesting that fathers are becoming more involved in caregiving (Badalament, 2008; Livingston & Parker, 2011), men are often left out of the decision making process when it comes to the schooling of their children. Although school systems frequently speak of their efforts to engage parents, in reality, fathers are seldom included in these attempts (Badalament, 2008). As noted by Eardley and Griffiths (2009) female dominated systems that serve children (i.e., school and child welfare systems) often operate from a deficit-oriented perspective that assumes that men are either uninterested, disengaged, or are somehow a threat to the lives of their children.

In comparison to resident fathers, nonresident fathers, experience even greater struggles and frustrations in their interactions with various systems that serve their children. As noted by Hawthorne (2002), despite the various social and economic trends that have led to precipitously high rates of nonresident father families in the United States over time, school policies and practices continue to reflect the underlying assumption that all students reside within intact families. Catering to the nuclear family structure, schools often overlook and fail to recognize the parental presence and value of fathers that do not reside in the home with their children. Previously, it was made clear that nonresident Black fathers do desire to be involved in the lives of their children. However, existing school practices and policies consistently communicate the unspoken view that they are substandard and shoddy in their parenting responsibilities, contributing to their alienation and low levels of involvement in schools.

In fact, Austin (1994) examined the impact of school policies on noncustodial (or nonresident) parents in 79 school districts in the Midwestern region of the country, finding that nearly 50% of the school districts surveyed excluded noncustodial parents from the educational process. What's more, such practices were often executed largely on the basis of unwritten policy guidelines. School systems cannot lawfully deny biological nonresident fathers the right to student records, progress reports, school visits, parent–teacher conferences, or other school-based activities, unless a court order restricts such rights. However, they can indirectly discourage and undermine their involvement through exclusionary practices (Austin, 1992). In comparison to resident parents, nonresident fathers are virtually ignored in school initiated parental engagement efforts.

For example, traditionally, school systems have been expected to reach out to and routinely advise parents of parent–teacher conferences and other educational activities concerning their child. However, in many school districts (i.e., Lincoln, Nebraska's Public School System; The School District of Philadelphia; Fairfax County, Virginia's Public School System), noncustodial parents—most likely to be fathers—are *not* automatically notified as they are held responsible for making a formal request for any information concerning their child's school performance. In other words, although schools systems are required to provide access to student information, they are *not* required to initiate the engagement of noncustodial parents in the educational process. Such practices stand in stark contrast to the requirements outlined in the *No Child Left Behind Act of 2001* which hold schools responsible for initiating regular communication with parents and ensuring that they play an integral role in their child's learning.

In addition, such practices are also particularly problematic for Black nonresident fathers who often feel victimized in their interactions with societal institutions such as school, healthcare, child welfare, and judicial systems (Hawthorne, 2002). Overall, fathers have historically had an adversarial relationship with social systems (Robinson, 2012). Perceived victimization has, in turn, negatively impacted the help-seeking behaviors of these men, causing them to feel reluctant to reach out to agents within various systems for information, guidance, and assistance (Gary, 1981; Hawthorne, 2002). Some have speculated that current school practices are due to society's ambiguity about the role of nonresident fathers in the lives of children (Hawthorne, 2002; Baldalament, 2008). It has also been argued that such practices are due to the negative perception that systems and the larger society have of nonresident fathers (Eardley & Griffiths, 2009). These images are often shaped by statistical data that are intended to highlight demographic trends in the United States. However, these data have inadvertently contributed to obscuring our understanding of Black nonresident fathers.

These figures, when misused, fuel deficit perspectives as they can be manipulated in a manner that emphasizes father absence, concealing the various ways in which nonresident fathers are present and involved with their children, despite their physical absence from the home. Pessimistic views can thwart the ability of educators and schools systems to effectively engage nonresident Black fathers in their child's learning. Thus, a nondeficit perspective is critical for meaningfully involving these men in the educational process. Though engaging the nonresident father presents a novel and unique challenge to school systems, educators must contend with the contemporary realities of changing family structure by making genuine efforts to reach out to them as doing so could make a considerable difference in the achievement outcomes and overall well-being of Black students (National Center on Fathering, 2000b). However, in order to successfully reach this group, a variety of innovative strategies are needed. Prior to providing recommendations and strategies for engaging nonresident Black fathers in schools, a brief overview of Hawkins & Dollahite's (1997a; 1997b) *Generative Fathering Perspective* will be provided. This strengths-based perspective can be drawn upon by preservice teachers, teacher education programs, teacher educators, and school systems as a framework for understanding, encouraging, and promoting the involvement of nonresident Black fathers in schools.

THE GENERATIVE FATHERING PERSPECTIVE

The work of Hawkins and Dollahite (1997a; 1997b) asserts that much of what we know about fathers to date is based a deficit-oriented perspective that emphasizes the inadequacies of men. Similarly, the work of Rasheed & Steward (2007), which examines the social science literature on Black fatherhood, suggests that much of the early literature on Black fathers was also based on a model of deficiency that condemned culturally-specific styles of fathering and imposed Eurocentric forms of paternal involvement as the norm or ideal. By and large, today, we know more about what fathers are *not* doing, than we know about what they *are* doing. As underscored by Hawkins and Dollahite (1997a; 1997b) and Rasheed and Steward (2007), the literature on fathers and families is laden with perceptions of men as ineffectual, distant, peripheral, emotionally inept, failed contributors to household labor, incapable of willingly taking on the paternal role and investing in their children. While these assertions may be true of some, all men do not fit this description. Preoccupation with the deficiencies of a few, in effect, masks the experiences and efforts made by others who are motivated to be responsible, caring, and involved fathers. Hawkins and Dollahite (1997a; 1997b) highlight the counterproductive nature of approaching work with men and fathers from a place of lack and instead offer a strengths-based framework, referred to as the *Generative Fathering Perspective.*

In short, the Generative Fathering Perspective draws on Erik Erikson's Psychosocial Stages of Development, specifically the stage of *Generativity vs. Stagnation.* It is in this stage that individuals are expected to complete a variety of developmental tasks related solidifying their legacy in the world such as the establishment of careers, families, and giving back to society through the raising of children (Longres, 2000). Based on this theory, generative fathers are committed not to simply fulfilling social expectations for the paternal role, but to the important work of caring for and ensuring a better life for the next generation (Askeland, 2006). The principles of the Generative Fathering perspective are illustrated in Table 1.1. Applying Hawkins and Dollahite's (1997) notion of *Generative Fathering*, the following section offers four strategies that can be employed as best practices for successfully engaging nonresident Black fathers in schools.

TABLE 1.1 Principles of the Generative Fathering Perspective

---

1. Assume that most fathers accept the obligation to meet the needs of the next generation
2. Assume that good fathering is consistent with mens' healthy development
3. Assume that most fathers want to provide resources and opportunities for their children
4. Assume that most fathers love and care for their children deeply
5. Assume that most men have the capabilities to care for children in meaningful ways
6. Appreciate the varied capabilities that men bring to their fathering
7. Recognize that manifestations of generative fathering vary across time and context
8. Realize that fathering occurs in a context of constraints on fathers, mothers, and children
9. Engage in respectful, accurate, and constructive discourse about fathers and fathering
10. Identify the factors that lead to good fathering across culture and circumstance
11. Work to improve cultural and institutional supports for good fathering
12. Call forth and facilitate generative fathering from fathers
13. Care for the next generation in your personal lives.

Source: Dollahite and Hawkins (n.d.)

RECOMMENDATIONS AND STRATEGIES FOR ENGAGING NONRESIDENT BLACK FATHERS IN SCHOOLS

Seek Out Specialized Coursework and Training in the Engagement of Nonresident Fathers

As outlined in the *No Child Left Behind Act of 2001*, schools across the county are now expected to ensure that parents play an integral role and are actively involved in their children's education. However, the ability of schools to successfully connect with diverse groups is largely dependent on teachers who are expected to adequately possess the knowledge and abilities necessary for supporting all school-based parental involvement efforts. Given the growing diversity within the United States, teacher educators should prepare preservice teachers to engage a wide range of students and families.

However, research suggests that, in practice, many institutions have struggled to keep pace with changing family structures and federal and school efforts to promote parental involvement among diverse groups (Shartrand, Weiss, Kreider, & Lopez, 1997; Flanigan, 2005). Specifically, many institutions that do offer curriculum content in parental involvement seldom focus on multicultural or special populations, opting instead to provide generalized parental involvement courses. Such shortcomings have left many preservice teachers ill-prepared to effectively partner with the culturally varied families they serve (Shartrand, Weiss, Kreider, & Lopez, 1997; Flanigan, 2005). In fact, studies have shown that while preservice teachers feel the most prepared to work with students, they often feel inept in the area of parental and community engagement (Flanigan, 2005; Pedro, Miller, & Bray, 2012).

While the research literature suggests that family engagement is necessary for achieving optimal results for children, few teachers have had formal training experiences, and as a result, have a minimal understanding of how to successfully connect with diverse groups of parents (Pedro, Miller, & Bray, 2012). Flanigan (2005) found that among faculty within 20 colleges of education in the Midwestern region of the country, 89% believed that it was important to prepare preservice teachers to partner with parents and communities. However, only 30% believed that preservice teachers were well prepared to do so. In addition, Pedro, Miller, and Bray (2012) found that although 54% of the preservice teachers they studied understood the value of parental involvement, only 15% felt very well prepared to determine parent knowledge of educational needs and only16% felt very well prepared to hold parent–teacher conferences. Given the complexity and diversity that characterizes the unique experiences of nonresident fathers and contemporary, nontraditional families, it is imperative that teacher trainees possess the knowledge and specialized skills that are necessary for successfully meeting the challenges that come along with being a twenty-first century educator (Pedro, Miller, & Bray, 2012). Courses or training programs that provide a specific focus on multicultural/special populations, preferably ones that include content on working with men and fathers, can significantly strengthen the efforts of educators to engage nonresident fathers.

Develop a Positive Disposition and Believe That Nonresident Fathers are Valuable Resources for Increasing Student Achievement

The notion of nonresident fathers as valuable resources for enhancing the educational well-being of students is well supported within the empirical literature (Nord, Brimhall, & West, 1997; Nord, 1998; Powell, 2007). However, translating this knowledge into one's own personal beliefs about these men can be difficult given negative perceptions manufactured by the media, popular and academic literature, and life experiences. Accomplishing any task, particularly ones that are difficult, starts with examining systems of belief and attitudes toward others, particularly those you serve such as students and parents. One major barrier to believing and seeing nonresident fathers as valuable resources is judgmental and negative attitudes. Such attitudes often stem from cultural disparities between teachers and parents. Cultural mismatches and misunderstandings pervade today's education system, particularly within urban school districts, due in part to the lack of diversity within America's teaching force.

Numerous books (Delpit, 2006; Landsman & Lewis, 2011; Delpit, 2012) have pointed to the reluctance of school systems and educators to effectively draw on the real life experiences and culture of students and families of color in order to promote positive student outcomes and educational equity. Many teachers may misinterpret the circumstances of the families they serve because they fail to engage in the perspective taking that is necessary for bringing a since of cultural competency and compassion to their work. Forming a genuine belief in nonresident fathers as valuable resources requires serious introspection and examination of any biases, perceptions, and attitudes that may prevent effectively working with this group. Seeking out opportunities for exposure and hands-on, authentic, real-life experiences with nonresident fathers will also assist in combating any unhelpful or counterproductive belief systems. This may include field experiences, internships, and volunteer work. Upon riddance of any negative attitudes, the emergence of a positive disposition will allow educators to draw upon the strengths of nonresident fathers and begin to engage them as an integral and necessary resource for advancing the education of their children.

Create a Father-Friendly Environment

Despite the growing body of literature which suggests the important role of fathers in the lives of their children (Lamb, 1997), within many school systems and other nonschool contexts, *parenting* is often synonymous with *mothering*. Even within two-parent families, it is often an unspoken assumption that mothers are the "go to" parent for all matters concerning the education of children. However, there is over 30 years of evidence to suggest that students and schools experience higher levels of academic success when *both* parents are involved (National Center on Fathering, 2000a). As a preservice teacher in the field and even as an in-service teacher, the creation of a father-friendly environment is critical to the successful engagement of nonresident fathers in schools (National Center on Fathering, 2000b).

Furthermore, intentionally creating an environment that is welcoming and supportive can potentially prevent their discouragement from the educational process. It has been recommended within the literature that a good starting point for creating a father friendly environment is evaluating your classroom and school environments' current practices and readiness for father involvement (National Center on Fathering, 2000a; National Center on Fathering, 2000b; White, Brotherson, Galovan, Holmes, & Kampmann, 2011). Several agencies, organizations, and research scholars offer instruments that are designed to assess and build father friendly approaches within organizational settings. These tools are listed in Table 1.2.

Reach Out, Offer Invitations and Opportunities for Meaningful Involvement

Making efforts to foster a friendly and inclusive environment empowers nonresident fathers and helps them realize that they matter and make a difference in their child's education (National Center on Fathering, 2000b). One way of instituting a manner of friendless within educational settings is by reaching out and offering open invitations and opportunities for meaningful involvement (National Center on Fathering, 2000b). The work of Hoover-Dempsey and Sandler (1995) suggests that teacher-specific or personal invitations to involvement are highly important for creating a warm environment and a primary motivator of parental participation in schools. Thus, it is probable that when nonresident fathers feel that schools are in support of their participation, they are more apt to increase their levels of involvement, barring any of the barriers that were previously mentioned, such as family conflict. Given their unique circumstances, it is important to note that locating nonresident fathers in order to extend invitations to

TABLE 1.2 Tools for Father-Friendly Environmental Assessment

Name of Tool	Website/Reference
Dakota Father Friendliness Assessment	(White, Brotherson, Galovan, Holmes, and Kampmann, 2011) http://mensstudies.metapress.com/content/ m1049673557m6215/
The Father Friendly Check-Up	National Quality Improvement Center on NonResident Fathers and the Child Welfare System http://fatherhood.ohio.gov/LinkClick. aspx?fileticket = EZ3EmgH2_dM%3D&tabid = 285
The Father Friendliness Organizational Self-Assessment and Planning Tool	The National Partnership for Community Leadership (NPCL) http://calswec.berkeley.edu/files/uploads/pdf/CalSWEC/ Fatherhood_AssessTool.pdf
Fatherhood QIC Toolkit	American Human Society http://www.americanhumane.org/children/programs/ fatherhood-initiative/qic-fatherhood-toolkit/qic-9-steps.html
40+ Top Fatherhood Resources	Annie E. Casey Foundation http://www.aecf.org/~/media/Pubs/Topics/Special%20 Interest%20Areas/Responsible%20Fatherhood%20and%20Marri age/40TopResources/40TopResourcesFINAL5%2011%2011.pdf

involvement may present a challenge, due in part to their physical absence from the home.

Custodial mothers often facilitate fathers' involvement with children following a separation or divorce (Hawthorne, 2002). Thus, custodial mothers are key players in getting nonresident fathers involved in schools and should be consulted in the strategy development and implementation process. Although custodial mothers may be looked to for assistance, depending on the status of her relationship with the nonresident father, this may not be an option and other avenues would need to be pursued. Outside of the dynamics of the mother–father relationship, educators and school systems must also be cognizant of legal issues concerning custody and visitation arrangements when attempting to reach out to nonresident fathers.

Under the most optimal conditions, educators can work cooperatively with custodial mothers and other family members to assist nonresident fathers in taking part in the educational achievements of their children (National Center on Fathering, 2000b).

As mentioned previously, given the unique patterns of help-seeking among Black men (Gary, 1981), and the experiences of nonresident fathers with societal institutions (Hawthorne, 2002), teacher-initiated communication is critical to their participation in schools—at least until a rapport is established. By and large, intervention and encouragement from educators is particularly important as they play a vital role in keeping nonresident fathers engaged and involved, not only in education, but in the lives of their children more generally. Once efforts have been made to create a father friendly environment, and to provide opportunities for meaningful engagement, it is important to begin to expect high levels of involvement from nonresident fathers. In an effort to obtain their participation as equal partners in the educational process, future educators must start from the assumption that they want to be involved, and in turn, expect active participation. (Hawkins & Dollahite, 1997a; Hawkins & Dollahite, 1997b; National Center on Fathering, 2000b). Among educators, the importance of having high expectations for realizing student academic success cannot be understated. And, the same is true of nonresident fathers—you get what you expect.

STANDING IN THE GAP: THE ROLE OF SOCIAL FATHERS IN THE LIVES OF BLACK CHILDREN

While all attempts should be made to engage students' biological nonresident fathers, in circumstances where this cannot be achieved, it is important to consider what may be the next best option: their social fathers. If is often assumed that Black students who live in nonresident father families are fatherless (Jayakody & Kalil, 2002.; King, 2010). Such assumptions obscure the involvement of other men, such as social fathers, in the lives of Black children. Given the rigidity and overwhelming focus on biological ties within America's definition of family (Guzzo, 2011), the notion of "social fathers" is often overlooked and understudied. Jayakody and Kalil (2002) define a social father as "a male relative or family associate who demonstrates parental behaviors and is 'like a father' to the child" (p. 3).

Overtime, the definition of family and fatherhood within America has expanded, moving further away from the necessity of genetic ties and toward more expanded definitions that are inclusive of nongenetic relationships (National Center on Fathering, 2000b). However, within the Black community, the boundaries for what constitute family and fathering roles have *always* been highly permeable and elastic (Hill, 2007b). Historically, Black biological family systems have been augmented to include nonbiological adults who share in the responsibilities of caring for children (Hill, 2007b; Schiele, 2007). In many ways, such flexibility and openness has been a source of strength, resilience, survival, comfort, and a protective buffer against the ills of a very hostile and oppressive social environment (Hill, 2007b; Schiele, 2007).

In the absence of biological fathers, many low-income African American families look to grandfathers and stepfathers as primary role models and teachers (Hunter, Pearson, Ialongo, & Kellam, 1998; Butler, 2000). Social fathers or fathers figures can also be uncles, family friends (King, 2010), and romantic partners with whom mothers may or may not cohabit

(Jayakody & Kalil, 2002; Bzostek, Carlson, & McLanahan, 2006). The circumstances by which children come to be reared by a social father vary largely by race and socioeconomic status. Today, "7,113,594 (nearly 70%) Black children do not have both a mother and father in the home primarily because their parents never married" (Toldson & Morton, 2012, p. 96). Sharp declines in marriage, and the resultant high rates of children born to unwed parents within the Black community, have had the most significant impact on Black children's exposure to social fathers, particularly those of a lower socioeconomic status. However, given the higher rates of marriage among their parents, divorce is the factor that is most likely responsible for the involvement of social fathers in the lives of children from other racial/ethnic and socioeconomic groups.

Demonstrating the commonness of social fathers within the Black community, in their study of low-income African American families, Jayakody and Kalil (2002) found that 51% of children in their study had social fathers. Understanding the role of social fathers in the lives of Black children is particularly important for future educators who plan to teach in low-income urban communities. The literature suggests that, by the age of three, a sizeable portion of children born to unmarried ("never-married") parents will be exposed to social fathers (Bzostek, Carlson, & McLanahan, 2006). In addition, increasingly, children of divorced ("ever-married") parents are also being reared by father figures. These numbers are expected to continue to rise overtime (Bzostek, Carlson, & McLanahan, 2006). Thus, it is imperative that educators and school systems make deliberate efforts to expand and modify their current practices to include social fathers. While these men may not take the biological or emotional place of natural fathers in the hearts and minds of their children and families, they often stand in the gap and should be recognized as potentially vital and powerful resources for increasing Black student achievement (Jayakody & Kalil, 2002; National Center on Fathering, 2000b).

CONCLUSIONS AND IMPLICATIONS FOR BLACK STUDENT ACHIEVEMENT AND EQUITY IN EDUCATION

As evidenced in the literature, family does provide an important context for the growth and development of children (Bronfenbrenner 1979; 1994) and when *both* parents are involved, children achieve at higher levels. Yet, we know that the circumstances and experiences of nonresident fathers are complex and distinctive, in comparison to men in other family configurations. This underlying tension suggests that in order to increase achievement among Black students who live in nonresident father families, it is important for future educators to possess knowledge of how to appropriately interact with and engage their biological fathers. Though some nonresident Black fathers deeply love their children and demonstrate high levels of motivation and desire to take part in their lives, family processes and parental relationship status continue to play a large role in determining their actual levels of involvement. An awareness of how factors such as family conflict influence the participation of nonresident Black fathers in schools can provide valuable background knowledge that can be drawn upon when attempting to engage them in the educational process.

Although educators may have little influence on family dynamics, school-related factors may be an area in which they can exercise their skills as advocates by seeking changes to policies and practices that undermine the participation of nonresident fathers in schools. Given their overrepresentation among students who have nonresident fathers, minority children are the most disadvantaged by school policies and practices that cater to nuclear families, while ignoring the unique experiences and needs of nonnuclear families. Bearing in mind the present realities of the rapidly changing demographics of American society, future educators have a responsibility to do what is necessary to address any courses of action taken (or not taken) at the school level that may create barriers to meeting and supporting the needs of students and families that are nontraditional in form.

However, more is also required of teacher education programs in terms of curriculum design and development than what has taken place in the past. Courses that provide a generalized knowledge of parental involvement are simply not sufficient, nor are they consistent with the diversity and complexities that now characterize the families served by American school systems. Though numerous attempts have been made, the education system has consistently failed in eradicating persistent racial/ethnic academic achievement and disciplinary gaps within the United States. Given the absence of substantive increases in Black student achievement, particularly in urban areas, it is abundantly clear that previous efforts have been ineffectual. In light of the evidence that points to parental involvement as a potential solution for eliminating disparities, future educators can utilize the information offered in this chapter to assist in leveling the playing field by positioning themselves to effectively engage nonresident Black fathers, thereby increasing Black student achievement and advancing equity in education.

REFERENCES

Abdul-Adil, J. K., & Farmer, A. D. (2006). Inner city African American parental involvement in elementary school: Getting beyond urban legends of apathy. *School Psychology Quarterly, 21,* 1–12.

Amato, P. R., Meyers, C. E., & Emery, R. E. (2009). Changes in nonresident father-child contact from 1976–2002. *Family Relations, 58,* 41–53.

Askeland, K. (2006). *Infosheet 10: What is a good father?* Retrieved from http://www.mnfathers.org/Resources/Documents/InfoSheetGenerativeFathering.pdf

Austin, J. F. (1992). Involving noncustodial parents in their student's education. *NASSP Bulletin, 76,* 49–54.

Austin, J. F. (1994). The impact of school policies on noncustodial parents. *Journal of Divorce and Remarriage, 20,* 153–170.

Badalament, J. (2008). Engaging modern dads in schools. *Independent School, 67,* 122–131.

Belsky, J. (1984). The determinants of parenting: A process model. *Child Development, 55,* 83–96.

Billingsley, A., & Morrison-Rodriguez, B. (2007). The black family in the twenty-first century and the church as an action system: A macro perspective. In L. A. See (Ed.), *Human behavior in the social environment from an African American perspective* (2nd ed., pp. 57–74). New York: The Haworth Press, Inc.

Bradford, K., & Hawkins, A. J. (2006). Learning competent fathering: A longitudinal analysis of marital intimacy and fathering. *Fatheirng, 4,* 215–234.

Bronfenbrenner, U. (1979). *The ecology of human development: Experiments by nature and design.* Cambridge, MA: Harvard University Press.

Bronfenbrenner, U. (1994). Ecological models of human development. In T. Husén & T. N. Postlethwaite (Eds.), *International encyclopedia of education* (2nd ed., Vol. 3, pp. 1643–1647). Oxford: Elsevier.

Butler, J. (2000). *Being there: Exploring fatherhood experiences and beliefs of low-income urban African American males.* Paper presented at the meeting of National Association of African American Studies & National Association of Hispanic and Latino Studies, Houston, TX.

Bzostek, S. (2008). Social fathers and child well-being. *Journal of Marriage and Family, 70,* 950–961.

Bzostek, S., Carlson, M., & McLanahan, S. (2006). *The second time around: Social fathers in fragile families.* Retrieved from http://paa2006.princeton.edu/papers/61324

Cabrera, N. J., Brooks-Gunn, J., Moore, K., Bronte-Tinkew, J., Halle, T., Reichman, N., Teitler, J,.. Boller, K. (2004). The DADS initiative: Measuring father involvement in large-scale surveys. In R. D. Day & M. E. Lamb (Eds.), *Conceptualizing and measuring father involvement* (pp. 417–452). Malwah, NJ: Lawrence Earlbaum, Publishers.

Cabrera, N. J., Fitzgerald, H. E., Bradley, R. H., & Roggman, L. (2007). Modeling the dynamics of paternal influences on children over the life course. *Applied Developmental Science, 11,* 185–189.

Cabrera, N. J., Ryan, R. M., Mitchell, S. J., Shannon, J. D., & Tamis-LeMonda, C. S. (2008). Low-income nonresident father involvement with their toddlers: Variation by fathers' race and ethnicity. *Journal of Family Psychology, 22,* 643–647. doi: 10.1037/0893-3200.22.3.643

Castillo, J. T., & Fenzl-Crossman, A. F. (2010). The relationship between nonmarital fathers' social networks and social capitol and father involvement. *Child & Family Social Work, 15,* 66–76. doi: 10.111/j.1365-2206.2009.00644.x

Cheadle, J. E., Amato, P. R., & King, V. (2010). Patterns of nonresident father contact. *Demography, 47,* 205–225.

Coles, R. L., & Green, C. (2009). Introduction. In R. L. Coles & C. Green (Eds.), *The myth of the missing black father.* New York: Columbia University Press.

Coley, R. L., & Chase-Lansdale, P. L. (1999). Stability and change in paternal involvement among urban African American fathers. *Journal of Family Psychology, 13,* 416–435.

Conner, M.E. (2011). African descended fathers: Historical considerations. In M. E. Conner & J. L. White (Eds.), *Black fathers: An invisible presence in America* (2nd ed., pp. 3–19). New York: Routledge Taylor and Francis Group.

Conner, M. E., & White, J. L. (2006). Fatherhood in contemporary Black America: Invisible but present. In M. E. Conner & J. L. White (Eds.), *Black fathers: An invisible presence in America* (pp. 3–16). Malwah, NJ: Lawrence Earlbaum, Publishers.

Danziger, S. K., & Radin, N. (1990). Absent does not equal uninvolved: Predictors of fathering in teen mother families. *Journal of Marriage and Family, 52,* 636–642.

Delpit, L. (2006). *Other people's children: Cultural conflict in the classroom.* The New Press: New York.

Delpit, L. (2012). *Multiplication is for White people: Raising expectations for other people's children.* The New Press: New York.

Doherty, W. J., Kouneski, E. F., & Erickson, M. F. (1998). Responsible fathering: An overview and conceptual framework. *Journal of Marriage and Family, 60,* 277–292.

Dollahite, D. C., & Hawkins, A. J. (n.d.). *Father work: Generative fathering defined.* Retrieved from http://fatherwork.byu.edu/generativeDefined.htm

Eardley, T., & Griffiths, M. (2009). *Nonresident parents and service use.* Retrieved from http://www.sprc.unsw.edu.au/media/File/Report12_09_Non_Resident_Parents.pdf

Flanigan, C. B. (2005). *Partnering with parents and communities: Are preservice teachers adequately prepared?* Retrieved from http://www.hfrp.org/publications-resources/browse-our-publications/partnering-with-parents-and-communities-are-preservice-teachers-adequately-prepared

Franklin, J. H. (1997). African American families: A historical note. In H. Pipes McAdoo (Ed.), *Black families* (3rd ed., pp. 5–8). Thousand Oaks, CA: Sage Publications.

Garfinkel, I., McLanahan, S. S., & Hanson, T. L. (1998). A patchwork portrait of nonresident fathers. In I. Garkinkel, S. S. McLanahan, D. R. Meyer, & J. A. Seltzer (Eds.), *Fathers under fire: The revolution in child support enforcement* (pp. 31–60). New York: Russell Sage Foundation.

Gary, L. E. (1981). *Black men.* Beverly Hills, CA: Sage Publications, Inc.

Gavin, L. E., Black, M. M., Minor, S., Abel, Y., Papas, M. A., & Bentley, M. E. (2002). Young disadvantaged fathers' involvement with their infants: An ecological perspective. *Journal of Adolescent Health, 31,* 266–276.

Glick, P. C. (1997). *Demographic pictures of African American families.* In H. Pipes McAdoo (Ed.), *Black families* (3rd ed., pp. 118–138). Thousand Oaks, CA: Sage Publications.

Gutman, H. G. (1976). *The black family in slavery and freedom, 1750–1925.* New York: Pantheon Books.

Guzzo, K. B. (2011). New fathers' experiences with their own fathers and attitudes toward fathering. *Fathering, 9,* 268–290. doi: 10.3149/fth.0903.268

Halle, T., Moore, K., Greene, A., & LeMenestrel, S. M. (1998). What policymakers need to know about fathers. *Policy and Practice of Public Human Services, 56,* 21–35.

Hawkins, A. J., & Dollahite, D. C. (1997a). *Generative fathering: Beyond deficit perspectives.* Thousand Oaks, CA: Sage.

Hawkins, A. J., & Dollahite, D. C. (1997b). Beyond the role-inadequacy perspective of fathering. In A. J. Hawkins & D. C. Dollahite (Eds.), *Generative fathering: Beyond deficit perspectives* (pp. 3–16). Thousand Oaks, CA: Sage.

Hawthorne, B. (2002). *Nonresident fathers' struggle with the system.* Retrieved from http://mhaweb.squarespace.com/storage/files/NONRES%20FATHERS.pdf

Hill, R. B. (2007a). Family roles of noncustodial African American fathers. In L. A. See (Ed.), *Human behavior in the social environment from an African American perspective* (2nd ed., pp. 117–131). New York: The Haworth Press, Inc.

Hill, R. B. (2007b). Enhancing the resilience of African American families. In L.A. See (Ed.), *Human behavior in the social environment from an African American perspective* (2nd ed., pp. 75–90). New York: The Haworth Press, Inc.

Hill, N. E., & Taylor, L. C. (2004). Parental school involvement and children's academic achievement: Pragmatics and issues. *Current Directions in Psychological Sciences, 13,* 161–164.

Hill, N. E., & Tyson, D. F. (2009). Parental involvement in middle school: A meta-analytic assessment of strategies that promote achievement. *Developmental Psychology, 45,* 740–863. doi: 10.1037/a0015362

Hogan-Garcia, M. (1997). African Americans as a cultural group. In L. L. Naylor (Ed.), *Cultural diversity in the United States* (pp.145–157). Westport, CT: Greenwood Publishing Group, Inc.

Hoover-Dempsey, K. V., & Sandler, H. M. (1995). Parental involvement in children's education: Why does it make a difference? *Teachers College Record, 97,* 311–331.

Hunter, A. G., Pearson, J. L., Ialongo, N. S., & Kellam, S. G. (1998). Parenting alone to multiple caregivers: Child care and parenting arrangements in black and white urban families. *Family Relations, 47,* 343–353.

Jackson, K., & Remillard, J. (2005). Rethinking parental involvement: African American mothers construct their roles in the mathematics education of their children. *School Community Journal, 15,* 51–73.

Jayakody, R., & Kalil, A. (2002). Social fathering in low-income African American families with preschoolers. *Journal of Marriage and Family, 64,* 504–516.

Johnson, W. E. (1998). Paternal involvement in fragile, African American families: Implications for clinical social work practice. *Smith College Studies in Social Work, 68,* 215–232.

Julion, W., Gross, D., Barclay-McLaughlin, G., & Fogg, L. (2007). It's not just about mommas: African American nonresident fathers' views of paternal involvement. *Research in Nursing & Health, 30,* 595–610.

King, M. B. M. A. (2010). Fathering in low-income black communities: Studying father figure flows. In R. L. Coles & C. Green (Eds.), *The myth of the missing black father* (pp. 147–169). New York: Columbia University Press.

King, V. (1994). Variation in the consequences of nonresident father involvement for children's well-being. *Journal of Marriage and Family, 56,* 963–972.

King, V., Harris, K. M., & Heard, H. E. (2004). Racial and ethnic diversity in nonresident father involvement. *Journal of Marriage and Family, 66,* 1–21.

Kreider, R. M., & Fields, J. (2005). *Living arrangements of children: 2001.* Retrieved from http://www.census.gov/prod/2005pubs/p70-104.pdf

Lamb, M. E. (1997). Fathers and child development: An introductory overview and guide. In M. E. Lamb (Ed.), *The role of the father in child development* (3rd ed., pp. 1–18). New York: John Wiley & Sons, Inc.

Landsman, J. & Lewis, C. W. (Eds.). (2011). *White teachers/diverse classrooms: Creating inclusive schools, building on students' diversity, and providing true educational equity* (2nd ed.). Sterling, VA: Stylus Publishing, LLC.

Laughlin, L., Farrie, D., & Fagan, J. (2009). Father involvement with children following marital and non-marital separations. *Fathering, 7,* 226–248.

Leite, R., & McKenry, P. (2006). A role theory perspective on patterns of separated and divorced African American nonresidential father involvement with children. *Fathering, 4,* 1–21.

Livingston, G., & Parker, K. (2011). *A tale of two fathers: More active, but more absent.* Retrieved from http://www.pewsocialtrends.org/files/2011/06/fathers-FINAL-report.pdf

Longres, J. F. (2000). *Human behavior in the social environment* (3rd ed.). Wadsworth/Thomson Learning: Belmont, CA.

Lowe, T. B., & Hopps, J. G. (2007). African Americans' response to their social environment: A macro perspective. In L. A. See (Ed.), *Human behavior in the social environment from an African American perspective* (2nd ed., pp. 27–53). New York: The Haworth Press, Inc.

Lu, M. C., Jones, L., Bond, M. J., Wright, K., Pumpuang, M., Maidenberg, M., Jones, D., Garfield, C., & Rowley, D. L. (2010). Where is the f in mch? Father involvement in African American families. *Ethnicity & Disease, 20,* S2-49-S261.

Marsiglio, W., Amato, P., Day, R. D., & Lamb, M. E. (2000). Scholarship on fatherhood in the 1990s and beyond. *Journal of Marriage and Family, 62,* 1173–1191.

Miller, D. B. (1994). Influences on paternal involvement of African American fathers. *Child and Adolescent Social Work Journal, 11,* 363–378.

Mills, C. E. (2010). Fostering fatherhood: Understanding the effects of child-support policy on low-income, noncustodial African American fathers. In R. L. Coles & C. Green (Eds.), *The myth of the missing black father* (pp. 327–350). New York: Columbia University Press.

Mizell, L. (2002). *Nonresident father involvement: Do mothers and fathers see eye to eye? An investigation of the impact of reporting discrepancies on parameter estimates.* (Doctoral dissertation, RAND Graduate School). Retrieved from http://www.rand.org/pubs/rgs_dissertations/2005/RGSD164.pdf

Morehouse Research Institute for American Values (1999). *A statement from the Morehouse Conference on African American Fathers: Turning the corner on father absence in Black America.* Retrieved from http://www.americanvalues.org/turning_the_corner.pdf

Mott, F. L. (1990). When is a father really gone? Paternal–child contact in father-absent homes. *Demography, 27,* 499–517.

Moynihan, D. P. (1965). *The Negro family: The case for national action.* Retrieved from http://www.dol.gov/oasam/programs/history/webid-meynihan.htm

National Center on Fathering (2000a). *A call to commitment: Fathers' involvement in children's learning.* Retrieved from http://www2.ed.gov/pubs/parents/calltocommit/fathers.pdf

National Center on Fathering (2000b). *Involving nonresident fathers in children's learning.* Retrieved from http://fatherhood.hhs.gov/involv-nonres00/chapter2.htm

Nelson, T. J. (2004). Low-income fathers. *Annual Review of Sociology, 30,* 427–451.

Nord, C. W. (1998). *Nonresident fathers can make a difference in children's school performance.* Retrieved from http://nces.ed.gov/pubs98/98117.pdf

Nord, C. W., Brimhall, D., & West, J. (1997). *Fathers' involvement in their children's schools.* Retrieved from http://nces.ed.gov/pubs98/98091.pdf

Parke, R. D. (2000). Father involvement: A developmental psychological perspective. *Marriage and Family Review, 29,* 43–58.

Pedro, J. Y., Miller, R., & Bray, P. (2012). *Teacher knowledge and dispositions towards parents and families: Rethinking influences and education of early childhood pre-service teachers.* Retrieved from http://www.hartford.edu/enhp/files/pdf/research/article04.pdf

Perry, A. R. (2009). The influence of the extended family on the involvement of nonresident African American fathers. *Journal of Family Social Work, 12,* 211–226.

Powell, P. (2007). *Relationship of nonresident African American father involvement in school-related activities to middle school student outcomes.* (Doctoral dissertation, Walden University). Retrieved from http://search.proquest.com.cassell.founders.howard.edu/docview/304762659/fulltextPDF?accountid = 11490

Pleck, E. H., & Pleck, J. H. (1997). Fatherhood ideals in the United States: Historical dimensions. In M.E. Lamb (Ed.), *The role of the father in child development* (3rd ed., pp. 33–48). New York: John Wiley & Sons, Inc.

Rasheed, J. M., & Stewart, R. (2007). The impact of racism, poverty, educational attainment, and masculine identity on the efficacy of African American fatherhood. In L. A. See (Ed.), *Human behavior in the social environment from an African American perspective* (2nd ed., pp. 117–131). New York: The Haworth Press, Inc.

Robinson, M. (2012). *The importance of engaging fathers in social work practice.* Retrieved from http://www.nacsw.org/Publications/Proceedings2012/RobinsonMTheImportanceFINAL.pdf

Ryan, R. M., Kalil, A., & Ziol-Guest, K. M. (2008). Longitudinal patterns of nonresident fathers' involvement: The role of resources and relations. *Journal of Marriage and Family, 70,* 962–977.

Ruggles, S. (1994). The origins of African American family structure. *American Sociological Review, 59,* 136–151.

Salem, D. A., Zimmerman, M. A., Notaro, P. C. (1998). Effects of family structure, family process, and father involvement on the psychosocial outcomes among African American adolescents. *Family Relations, 47,* 331–341.

Shartrand, A. M., Weiss, H. B., Kreider, H. M., & Lopez, M. E. (1997). *New skills for new schools: Preparing teachers in family involvement.* Retrieved from www.hfrp.org/content/download/1145/48650/file/skills.pdf

Schiele, J. (2007). Strength behaviors for African American socialization and survival. In L.A. See (Ed.), *Human behavior in the social environment from an African American perspective* (2nd ed., pp. 91–116). New York: The Haworth Press, Inc.

Seltzer, J. A. (1991). Relationships between fathers and child who live apart: The father's role after separation. *Journal of Marriage and Family, 53*, 79–101.

Smith, J., Wohlstetter, P., Kuzin, C. A., & De Pedro, K. (2011). Parental involvement in urban charter schools: New strategies for increasing participation. *The School Community Journal, 21*, 71–94.

Sobolewski, J. M., & King, V. (2005). The importance of the co-parental relationship for nonresident fathers' ties to their children. *Journal of Marriage and Family, 67*, 1196–1212.

Tach, L., Mincy, R. D., & Edin, K. (2010). Parenting as a "package deal": Relationships, fertility, and nonresident father involvement among unmarried parent. *Demography, 47*, 181–204.

The White House (2012). *Promoting responsible fatherhood.* Retrieved from http://www.whitehouse.gov/sites/default/files/docs/fatherhood_report_6.13.12_final.pdf

Toldson, I. A., & Morton, J. (2012). *Black people don't read: The definitive guide to dismantling stereotypes and negative statistical claims about Black Americans.* Washington, DC: iYAGO Entertainment Group.

Trotman, M. F. (2001). Involving the African American parent: Recommendations to increase the level of parent involvement within African American families. *The Journal of Negro Education, 70*, 275–285.

United States Census Bureau. (2011). *Current population survey: Annual social and economic supplements, March 2011 and earlier* [Data file]. Retrieved from http://www.census.gov/population/www/socdemo/hh-fam.html

United States Department of Education, National Center for Education Statistics. (2007). *National household education surveys: Parent and family involvement survey* [Data file]. Washington, DC: Institute of Education Sciences.

Varga, C. M., & Gee, C. B. (2010). Racial identity, father involvement, and co-parenting in adolescent African American mothers and fathers. *The New School Psychology Bulletin, 8*, 29–37.

White, J. M., Brotherson, S. E., Galovan, A. M., Holmes, E. K., & Kampmann, J. A. (2011). The Dakota father friendly assessment: Measuring father friendliness in head start and similar settings. *Fathering, 9*, 22–43.

Wood, J. J., Repetti, R. L. (2004). What gets dads involved? A longitudinal study of change in paternal child caregiving involvement. *Journal of Family Psychology, 18*, 237–249. doi: 10.1037/0893-3200.18.1.237

CHAPTER 2

MAKING SPACE FOR BLACK QUEER TEACHERS

Pedagogic Possibilities

Lance T. McCready
University of Toronto

Micia Mosely
Independent Researcher

They used their teaching to prepare children for a world that did not yet exist.
—Siddle Walker, 2008, p. 121

INTRODUCTION

Black queer teachers, or Black teachers of African descent who identify as sexual minorities, gender nonconforming, or deviant in the context of heteronormative power structures (Brockenbrough, 2012) may be troubling for teacher educators because they disrupt dominant discourses and ideas about Black teachers that circulate in the scholarly literature and professional communities related to urban education, Black Education, and teacher education. In this

Teacher Education and Black Communities, pages 43–58
Copyright © 2014 by Information Age Publishing
All rights of reproduction in any form reserved.

paper the authors Lance McCready and Micia Mosely argue these disruptions contain "pedagogic possibilities" meaning they have the potential to confront the normalizing practices and discourses that marginalize queer people of color in educational studies, and expand, more generally, the possibilities for antioppressive equity and social justice work in teacher education. The question that guides the authors' exploration of these topics is, *"What pedagogic possibilities lie in 'making space' for Black queer teachers in teacher education?"*

The authors begin by describing their conceptual framework and how their "outsider within" standpoints as Black queer teachers working in and across multiple professional contexts such as academia, university-based preservice teacher education and in-service professional development facilitates "making space." They then review the academic literature on Black teachers, critiquing the way this literature depicts the roles and responsibilities of Black teachers through a heteronormative lens. In the second part of the chapter the authors discuss what needs to be done to "make space" for Black queer teachers in preservice and in-service education for Black teachers. In this section McCready discusses the pedagogic possibilities of Black queer teachers disrupting the formal or "official" curriculum. Mosely discusses making space through self-reflection processes that facilitate alternative ways of thinking about and exploring Black teacher identity and power dynamics. In conclusion the authors discuss the significance of mobilizing a queer politic in the education of Black teachers, in particular how a queer politic can make schooling a more inclusive experience for administrators, teachers and students alike through disrupting commonsensical understanding of what it means to be a Black teacher.

PART I: THEORIZING MAKING SPACE
AS OUTSIDERS WITHIN

Conceptual Framework: Making Space

In *Punks, Bulldaggers, and Welfare Queens*, Cathy Cohen (1997) argues that the radical potential of queer politics lies not in simply incorporating queer people of color into existing canons and social movements, but rather "if there is truly any radical potential to be found in the idea of queerness and the practice of queer politics, it would seem to be located in its ability to create a space in opposition to dominant norms, a space where transformational political work can begin." (p. 438) Here Cohen is arguing that what is truly radical about queer theory is the possibility of enacting a politic built on creating spaces that oppose all forms of dominance and oppression. *What would it mean to mobilize such a politic in the education of Black teachers? What does it mean to make space for Black queer teachers in teacher education?*

In *"Making Space for Ourselves: Gay/Gender-Nonconforming and Lower-Track African American Student Responses to Their Marginalization"* the authors explain that the notion of "making space" is derived from the work of critical theorists who use the concept of "spatiality" to show how struggles over geographic control create social boundaries that have material effects on individual and collective identities, and people's access to space (Venzant-Chambers & McCready, 2011; Foucault, 1986; Lefebvre, 1991; Soja, 1996). More recently, scholars of social geography endeavor to show how young people figure in these struggles to constitute public space in urban communities and schools (Ruddick, 1996; Skelton & Valentine, 1998).

Urban social geography is the study of the patterns related to how social groups use urban space (Knox, 2006). It also involves consideration of the social patterns and processes arising from the distribution of and access to scarce resources for urban residents (Knox, 2006). In the context of public schools, I treat urban social geography as the study of the ways social groups of students and/or teachers use school space, and of patterns of student participation in academic and extracurricular programs. How teachers and students use school space and participate in academic and extracurricular programs is a function of normalizing social and cultural forces in and beyond the walls of the school that seek to marginalize and consequently regulate teacher and student subjectivities. Susan Ruddick uses social geography through an investigation of the importance of "safe space" or "third space" where the marginality of homeless youth in Los Angeles could be affirmed or even celebrated by "suturing" (p. 196) spaces for themselves within the public eye (Ruddick, 1996).

John Ogbu and Signithia Fordham have a long record of publication on the normalizing social and cultural dynamics of African American peer groups, in particular how they create social boundaries. Some African American students' decision to adopt a "raceless" persona can put them at odds with their peers who practice "fictive kinship" with other African American students through speaking Black English and de-emphasizing academic achievement (Ogbu, 2003; Fordham, 1996). Similarly, in *Race in the Schoolyard,* sociologist Amanda Lewis (2001) provides several examples of how racial boundary norms between students of color and White students are constructed in "everyday interactions" where young people ascribe specific racial identities to particular bodies. Lewis is careful to note that the notion of "doing race" in daily interaction applies to a range of social identities including race, gender, social class, and sexual orientation.

Developmental psychologist Beverly Tatum (1997) draws on the concept of spatiality to explain why "all the Black kids [are] sitting together in the cafeteria." From Tatum's perspective, "When one is faced with what Chester Pierce calls the 'mundane extreme environmental stress' of racism, in adolescence or in adulthood, the ability to see oneself as part of a larger group from which one can draw support is an important coping strategy"

(p. 70). Overall, the notion of "making space" is meant to capture the social, cultural, geographical, and psychological strategies used by marginalized groups to respond to and/or cope with the normalizing forces that undergird their marginalization. In the next section McCready and Mosely discuss their own strategies for making space based on their standpoints as "outsiders within" teacher education.

Outsider Within Standpoints

In *Learning From the Outsider Within: The Sociological Significance of Black Feminist Thought,* Patricia Hill Collins (1986) defines a person's standpoint as the societal knowledge located within an individual's specific geographic location. From this perspective, knowledge becomes distinctly unique and subjective—it varies depending upon the social conditions under which it was produced. Collins refers to the concept of the "outsider within" as a special standpoint encompassing the self, family and society (Collins, 1986, pg. S14). This relates to the specific experiences to which people are subjected as they move from a common cultural world (i.e., family) to that of the modern society. Therefore, even though people of color and sexual minority educators, in particular Black queer teachers, may become influential in a particular profession such as formal education, they may feel as though they never quite belong. Essentially, their personalities, behaviors, and cultural beings overshadow their true values as individuals; thus, they become the outsider within (Collins, 1986, p. S14). Both of the authors, McCready and Mosely, view themselves as outsiders within Black teacher education, albeit for different reasons. The authors explain their standpoints below. These standpoints inform their praxis for making Black teacher education more inclusive of Black queer teachers.

Micia Mosely
Mosely began her formal teacher education in a credentialing program in the mid-1990s. The program offered 1 two-hour workshop on "Multicultural Education." The highlights included "cutting edge" research that Black students were kinesthetic learners. She was the only person of color in her program and there was no space for her or any of the students to discuss who they were in the context of teaching. Once she began teaching the trend continued where most of her professional development centered on good pedagogy and connecting those practices to science (a major emphasis in the mid-90s .com era of Bay Area education).

In her second year of teaching Mosely decided to officially come out to her students. She also spent a lot of time bonding with her Black colleagues (who were all straight) and her queer colleagues (who were all White). Mosely had a small hand in advising the Black Student Union (which got push back for being exclusive and eventually because the Multicultural Student Union). She watched her colleagues support the creation of a Gay Straight Alliance. Within a month she was asked to be more active and come to meetings because in a school where less than 10% of the students were White, they comprised 80% of the GSA (there were also several Asian students). From her colleagues' perspective she needed to be the face of Black queerness. Her students were overwhelmingly supportive. She had a few who said they "still" thought she was cool, but "disagreed with her lifestyle" for religious reasons. There was no formal space for Mosely to learn how to navigate how these shifts in relationships with her students would impact her teaching. Mosely ended up "making space" for identity as a Black queer teacher by engaging her colleagues in conversations about what it meant for her to be in the middle of two separate social worlds, Black and LGBTQ, in the school. It was this constant self-reflection and inquiry that led Mosely to think about the pedagogic possibilities of self-reflection designed to "make space" for bringing together multiple social worlds. Mosely eventually left the classroom to work as a school coach with San Francisco Coalition of Essential Small Schools. Working for this organization, which is led by a White gay man who is explicitly antiracist, continued to facilitate Mosely learning more formalized structures for "making space" through self-reflection.

Lance McCready

McCready teaches social foundations courses in university-based preservice teacher education programs. McCready's research program does not focus on teachers, rather on urban youth studies, specifically Black males and sexual minorities. McCready engages teacher candidates in reading critical theories of race, gender relations and sexuality, and gaining a better understanding of the everyday lives of youth in disadvantaged urban environments. From 1997 to 2002, McCready gained invaluable experience working on a collaborative action research project that investigated the origins of achievement gaps and racial separation at a multiracial high school located in Northern California. The focus of McCready's individual research on this project was to understand the interplay between the structural dimensions of race and gender segregation in extracurricular activities and identity formation processes of gay and gender nonconforming Black male students. McCready conducted ethnographic fieldwork with queer students of color and in doing so learned about their everyday lives in the segregated school environment. He gained insight into the "troubles" they experienced and how they were both similar to and different from "troubles" of heterosexual Black male students in the school (see Noguera, 2009 for a discussion of structural vs. cultural explanations of the "troubles" of Black male students.

McCready's research experiences with Black queer youth as an openly gay Black man position him as an "outsider within" Black teacher education. On the one hand McCready can be seen as a part of Black teachers educators as a group of professionals because they share a commitment to preparing and building the capacity of Black teachers who work with Black students in elementary and secondary education systems. On the other hand, putting Black queer youth at the center of professional development work in teacher education may position him as an outsider since these students disrupt the normalizing discourses of who Black students are and therefore how Black teachers should support them and facilitate their learning. Including theories and concepts such as intersectionality and queer or color analysis is crucial for this work since these concepts take into account multiple, intersecting social identities and forms of oppression and discrimination. With a few exceptions, critical theories such as these are virtually absent in the scholarly literature on Black teachers.

Literature Review: Who are Black Teachers?

The literature on Black teachers can be understood relative to three major themes: historical accounts of Black teachers' experiences relative to segregation, Black teacher identity & cultural competence relative to Black students. Much of the work on Black teachers draws on narratives and teachers' self-reflection about who they are and their practice. These narratives and reflections contain normalizing discourses that construct Black teachers as predominantly heterosexual, rather than possessing a range of sexual and gender identifications.

For example, Michelle Foster, in her seminal work *Black Teachers On Teaching*, shares the voices of 20 teachers in different stages of theirs careers. While the reader gains a generational perspective on Black teaching, the voices of queer Black teachers and the challenges they face are absent. Foster focuses on Black teachers' commitment to educating Black students, a theme that runs through almost all of the literature about Black teachers.

Vanessa Siddle Walker's work (1996) looks at the historical underpinnings of community connections in the segregated south. In *Their Highest Potential* Siddle Walker focuses on the context of these connections and relates them to larger educational issues such as the goal of local communities to 'take care of their own.' Adam Fairclough (2000, 2009) also unpacks the experiences of Black teachers in the segregated south highlighting the larger context of Black schools being seen as inherently inferior. In *A Class of Their Own: Black Teachers in the Segregated South* Fairclough examines the role of Black teachers as connectors between Black communities and the White educators who acted as gatekeepers to resources. Black queer teachers are absent in both accounts of Black teachers struggling to make sense of who they are as agents of change in multiple communities. In later work Siddle Walker does complicate how Black teachers were seen in the segregated south "as either victims of oppressive circumstances or as caring role models." (Siddle Walker, 2001). In particular Siddle Walker highlights the relationship between identity and context and that these teachers in fact saw themselves as trained professional who had a responsibility to their Black community.

Research about Black teachers in desegregated schools has focused on Black teachers' relationship to Black students. Specifically, how Black teachers' assumed racial bonds and deep understandings of Black culture enable them to enact culturally relevant pedagogies that effectively engage Black students. For example, Michelle Foster asserts that effective Black teachers across generations have a cultural solidarity with Black students. This solidarity allows them to connect the curriculum to the everyday lives of their Black students (Foster, 1998). Jacqueline Jordan Irvine attributes this connection and its resulting success to "cultural synchronization—the values, communicative patterns, and worldviews that are shared by Black teachers and Black students (Irvine, 2002). Cultural synchronization can be seen as an extension of Black teachers' belief in Black students' potential, a connection to spirituality, and an ethic of caring (Brockenbrough, 2012).

The literature on Black teachers makes connections between the personal and political roles of Black teachers; however, it does not explore how these roles are complicated by nonnormative gender and sexual identifications or sexual minority status. Historically speaking, did sexual minority teachers exist in the segregated south? If so, how might our notions of southern Blackness be expended by the inclusion of their voices and experiences? In contemporary debates, how might sexuality and sexual minority status trouble dominant discourses of culturally relevant and responsive pedagogy? As researchers continue to highlight the challenges Black males face in schools (Noguera, 2009), Black male teachers (Brown, 2009; Lynn, 2006) are expected to be disciplinarians and serve as role models for navigating an unjust system. Likewise, Black female teachers are also expected to model a particular politic of respectability and perform a race-specific feminine expression care (Beauboeuf-Lafontant, 2002; Dixson, 2003; Foster, 1993; Irvine, 2002).

What happens when the Black male teachers transgress gender norms and act like "queens"? What does an ethic of care look like between an effeminate Black male teacher and his students? Similarly, Can a Black lesbian teacher who "looks like a man" shows a teenage girl how to be a strong Black woman? Can "butch" Black women teachers serve as "othermothers" to their students? (Beauboeuf-Lafontant, 2002) How do gender nonconforming and/or sexual minority Black teachers relate to Black students with whom they share racial identification and but not gender or sexual identification?

A few notable studies on the experiences of Black queer teachers show these teachers have the potential to interrupt the heteronormative discourses of care and culturally responsive teaching that run through the scholarly literature on Black teachers. For example, Bryant Keith Alexander states (in Holland & Cohen, 2005), "How can I not respond both as a teacher and as a black gay man when some of my "straight" black female students write papers in my class about the scarcity of "good black men," or about the "breakdown of the black family," or when they proceed to demonize black gay men for not "acting right," for not "being black," for not taking "responsibility" as black men—thereby equating sexuality, character and racial identity? How can I not respond to those papers in detail?" (p. 251). Alexander goes on to highlight the work it takes for Black queer teachers to bring their multiple identities into the classroom: "I embrace myself as a black/man/gay and celebrate the problematic and glorious intersection of that positionality—and dear student—while I have teased these individual strains from my complex identity, and enumerated them, please note that it has been for your benefit-for they are intricately interwoven into the tapestry of my being" (p. 252).

Ed Bockenbrough's research on the experiences of Black male teachers who are not openly gay is similarly instructive (Brockenbrough, 2011). Brockenbrough explores how five Black queer male educators negotiated pressures to keep their queerness "in the closet." For these Black queer teachers remaining in the closet left them vulnerable to homophobic surveillance, which set the stage for a range of power struggles between teachers and students. Students, through a variety of speech acts ranging from homophobic innuendos to direct inquiries into teachers' sexual identities, produced a heightened visibility of Black queer male teachers' suspected queerness. The Black queer male teachers, in response, employed a range of strategies to either address of deflect these accusations. These strategies often interrupted the norms of cultural responsiveness and caring attributed to Black teachers. Brockenbrough recounts the experience of one teacher, Maxwell, who had particularly contentious interactions with students on account of being gender nonconforming:

> Maxwell recalled dramatically contentious interactions with students over the visibility of his queerness: There are a whole bunch of kids who just call me faggot that I don't even teach. And one of them, he called me a faggot, and I was like, "You're gonna be fat, dumb, and f--- ugly for the rest of your life." And I blew the s--- out of him, like just railed him a new one in the hallway in front of everybody. And then he ended up sending me [an email] message saying, "A-yo, you f------ faggot, you gay as s---." I went to the administration, I did what I had to do [i.e., reporting the student's actions]. (Brockenbrough, 2011, p. 13)

The above scenario illustrates the difficulties of maintaining traditional roles of Black teachers as disciplinarians, role models, culturally responsive and caring in the context of a school where there are gender and sexuality boundaries of Blackness. Black queer teachers, in these settings, may feel anything but caring when students and colleagues who demand they uphold heteronormative roles of Black teachers persecute them. Black queer teachers in these settings are understandably less effective at enacting culturally relevant and responsive pedagogies that foster engagement and academic learning.

PART II: PEDAGOGIC POSSIBILITIES OF MAKING SPACE

How can Black queer teachers be effective teachers of Black students? Black teacher educators need to "make space" for Black queer teachers by moving away from the dominant discourses in scholarly literature that essentializes the identities and roles of Black teachers in static, heteronormative ways. Instead, teacher educators might look toward literature and professional development experiences that illustrate the pedagogic possibilities that can result from "making space" through challenging the normalizing gender and sexuality discourses. Below, we provide two examples of what this might look like in the context of teacher education. Regarding teacher education for Black male teachers Mc-Cready suggests drawing on Patricia Hill Collins' notion of "progressive" Black masculinities to interrupt the dominant discourses of what it means to be caring, which would "make space" for the experiences of Black queer teachers. A more progressive ethic of care for Black male teachers might focus on caring for those whose social identifications in relation to race, class, gender, and sexuality categories make them "queer" or nonnormative in society; in the words of Cathy Cohen (1997), "punks, bulldaggers and welfare queens." Mosely draws on her experience facilitating professional development for teachers to consider how transformative self-reflection exercises could "make space" for Black queer teachers through more critical reflection on race, gender and sexuality power relations. Together, these discussions of pedagogic possibilities, one more theoretical, the other more practical, make the case for confronting the normalizing practices and discourses that marginalize queer people of color in teacher education. "Making space" for Black queer teachers is worthwhile because it holds the potential to make Black teacher education more inclusive and socially just.

Pedagogic Possibilities of More Progressive Notions of Black Masculinity

Black teacher educators can "make space" for Black queer male teachers, in particular, by taking a more progressive stance towards Black masculinity. In *Black Sexual Politics: African Americans, Gender, and the New Racism* Patricia Hill

Collins (2006) makes an important distinction between masculinity as dominance versus masculinity as strength that holds important pedagogical possibilities in Black teacher education. Making this distinction is crucial for making space for Black queer teachers. Below, I summarize her argument towards posing a different set of questions related to what it means for Black teacher educators to care for Black queer teachers and in doing so model an ethic of care for Black students.

In the book chapter "A Telling Difference: Dominance, Strength, and Black Masculinities," Patricia Hill Collins presents a compelling case for Black men being able to tell the difference between dominance and strength. She begins by asserting that definitions of Black masculinity in the United States "reflect a narrow cluster of controlling images situated within a broader framework that grants varying value to racially distinctive forms of masculinity" (p. 75). All of the representations, she argues, hinge on questions of weakness, "whether it is a weakness associated with an inability to control violent impulses, sexual urges, or their black female, heterosexual partners or a weakness attributed to men whose lack of education, employment patterns, and criminal records relegate them to inferior social spaces" (p. 75).

The possibility of masculinity being a form of weakness is based on hegemonic White masculinity which is fundamentally a relational construct where gender boundaries are defined through a series of oppositional relationships whereby normal masculinity becomes defined in opposition to women, gay men, poor and working-class men, boys, and Black men. Each of these groups serves as an important social group for constructing the ideas of hegemonic White masculinity as well as actual social practices of dominance that maintain power relations that privilege elite White men. As social groups, women, gay men, poor, and working-class men, boys and Black men are socially stigmatized with a particular form of weakness that is juxtaposed to the seeming strengths of hegemonic White masculinity. Hegemonic masculinity reflects a cognitive framework of binary thinking (real men are not like women, real men are not gay, real men are not poor, real men are not boys, real men are not Black) that defines masculinity in terms of its difference from and dominance over multiple others. The dominance is the strength of hegemonic White masculinity.

Collins believes strongly that Black men are harmed and constrained by popular images that hinge on questions of weakness, and to the extent that they internalize this thesis, "their own strategies to combat their oppression will be misguided" (p. 75). Collins asserts that progressive Black masculinities require rejecting the images currently associated with Black masculinity, as well as the structural power relations that cause them. This includes rejecting images of heteronormative physical dominance and aggressiveness celebrated by hip-hop artists and professional athletes.

These entertainers' reputations are built on physically dominating others through living the "thug life" and playing sports. Developing progressive Black masculinities also requires rejecting sexual dominance and the popular images associated with it such as "the playa" who has multiple sexual partners and the "baby daddy" who fathers children by more than one mother.

In addition to rejecting physical and sexual dominance, the development of progressive Black masculinities requires the rejection of political and economic dominance as well. The fact that many African American men work in the informal labor market, mainly the global drug industry, and have prison records which precludes them from invoking their voting rights as citizens to change labor laws, creates a situation where African American men are less able to contribute financial support to their families and communities. In the context of globalization where job flight, mechanization and downsizing, and punitive domestic social welfare policies leave Black boys in poor schools with bad housing and poor opportunities, economic dominance modeled by elite White men seems a distant dream.

Collins acknowledges that the process of moving beyond the notion of masculinity as dominance is challenging work because it requires Black men to exhibit strength in two areas: relinquishing privilege and personal accountability. Progressive Black masculinities recognize and subsequently relinquish real and imagined privileges gained through domination, "in particular the benefits and costs attached to sexism and heterosexism. Relinquishing benefits of dominance is difficult because it inevitably fosters marginalization and alienation from those very groups that long served as places of belonging" (p. 92). In the context of Black teacher education, this means rejecting some of the institutions that have served as a refuge from systemic racism if those institutions uphold sexist, homophobic politics that reject sexual diversity and nonnormative gender expression.

The second area Black men must learn to exhibit strength in is "incorporating an ethic of personal accountability in relation to women, children, parents, siblings, and one another" (p. 92). Gay men, lesbians, bisexuals, transgender, queer, and questioning people could be added to this list. Collins points out that "historical patterns of black sexual politics provide the overarching context for black men's behavior," but asserts that, "each individual African American man is responsible for his actions and the choices he makes in everyday life" (p. 93). Personal accountability to self and others means rejecting the negative outcomes of the weakness thesis and redefining Black male strength in terms of relationships with others. From this perspective, Black male teachers must work to become allies with those for whom middle class, White, Heterosexual male logic considers weak such as men who identify as gay, or men who are incarcerated.

What would it mean for Black teacher educators to hold themselves personally accountable in relation to caring for Black teachers and students who are "punks, bulldaggers, and welfare queens?" What would it take for teacher educators to facilitate the kinds of critical inquiry that rejects middle class, White, Heterosexual male in favor of logics that defines this relinquishing of privilege and subsequent accountability as strength? From Mosely's perspective, one way of "making space" for these kinds of logics is through transformative self-reflection.

Pedagogic Possibilities of Transformative Self-Reflection

In order to understand the nested contexts of racialized expectations relative to Black queer teachers we must take a critical inquiry stance towards transformative education. That is, teacher education must support Black queer teachers (and everyone else) in investigating and understanding the power and difference in the multiple contexts in with they teach as well as in key relationships that inform their work. This inquiry stance allows Black queer teachers to position their local experiences relative to the larger work of transformation in schools (Cochran-Smith & Lytle, 2009). Transformation is rooted in interrupting policies and practices that are currently enacted in educational settings (SFCESS, 2013). This inquiry stance manifests in transformative teacher education primarily through self-reflection that actively considers power relations, multiple identities and hierarchies of privilege (Darling-Hammond, 2012).

One structure that supports self-reflective teacher education is the affinity group. This is a space where a group of teachers with shared identity deliberately meet to address issues in their practice through the lens of that common identification. Black queer teachers may find themselves with the opportunity to be a part of several affinity groups on account of their multiple marginalized affiliations as nonWhite, sexual minorities, gender nonconforming, etc. Part of what becomes available by being in a group of all Black teachers, however, is an explicit interrogation and interruption of heteronormativity in Black communities.

Who are you relative to what you do and who you interact with? By examining their relationships with their students, content and other adults, Black queer teachers can make informed strategic choices based in their reality. This shifts the power dynamic of who has the knowledge of what it takes to be a successful teacher from the professor or professional development provider to a shared control. Like all good teaching it positions professors & providers to hold space and guide the exploration of learning for Black queers teachers, with strategic inputs when needed.

For example, Keith Clark (in Holland & Cohen, 2005) describes a Black gay male teacher who states that he is going to teach *Go Tell It On The Mountain* and "go there" with his 11th graders regarding the gay themes that the text address. This would be a powerful opportunity for his professors and/or professional support providers to support him in examining what that can look like and what it means for him and his students given the context of the school community he is in. Having that conversation in a Black affinity group or a queer affinity group created the possibility for interrupting heteronormativity and White racial centering, respectively. His curricular decision can impact not only his students, but his colleagues as well.

The foundation of a queer politic is rooted in opposing all forms of dominance and oppression. Preparing and supporting Black queer teachers involves engaging in an educational system that is designed to reproduce dominance and oppression. In the late twentieth century an emergence of a critical analysis of teacher education has led to more open discussions of power and identity. Specifically, organizations like The National Equity Project (formerly the Bay Area Coalition of Equitable Schools) have named systemic racism as the cause for the disproportionate underachievement of Black students. Their curriculum supports current classroom teachers & administrators to reflect on their practice using and "inquiry stance" that often names race, gender and class.

For example, protocols offer the temporary space to ease out labels and to share thoughts, opinions and feelings in ways that help us avoid centering particularly identities. When used properly they can give voice to previously marginalized communities whether they are in the room or not. Fictional scenarios can involve descriptors that highlight particular issues. In the case of SFCESS (San Francisco Coalition of Essential Small Schools), the facilitators always describe people's race, class and gender. More and more they are including sexuality whether or not it seems related to the issue being discussed. Including that information can explicitly make space for Black Queer teachers and center their complicated identities instead of simply marginalizing an essentialized notion of it.

This kind of exploration does not privilege race over sexuality, but allows us to use race as the primary lens to examine relationships, expectations and outcomes. This is also a familiar framework for most educators because of the focus on race-class achievement gaps in school reform. Complicating the heteronormative assumptions about Blackness can support teachers in staying in an inquiry stance. In the absence of assumptions about who the Black teachers are in classrooms, we must actually build relationships and get to know and understand each other. This is a space where Black queer teachers can be heard and understood for all that they are. This is not just good for Black queer teachers, but it's also good teaching practice in that it interrupts a binary of race and gender that we see in traditional professional development discussions that focus on "who we are."

CONCLUSION: TOWARDS A MORE INCLUSIVE BLACK TEACHER EDUCATION

As we consider what it takes to make Black teacher education more inclusive we must look to the expectations we have of those teachers. As role models for Black students in the twenty-first century we can no longer reproduce notions that Black adults are all heterosexual people who conform to traditional ways of expressing who they are. The research on Black teachers must continue to expand to include the experiences of Black queer teachers so that we can understand their impact on urban education, curriculum, pedagogy and professional development in particular. "Making space" for Black queer teachers not only makes for a more nuanced understanding of the role of Black bodies in education, but it also pushes on multiple points of reproductive marginalization and allows us to call into question our implicit expectations and assumptions about those roles. In making space for that inquiry Black queer teachers force us to look at power dynamics from multiple perspectives and that process is where we see the real opportunity for transformative education.

REFERENCES

Beauboeuf-Lafontant, T. (2002). A womanist experience of caring: Understanding the pedagogy of exemplary Black women teachers. *The Urban Review, 34*(1), 71–86.

Brockenbrough, E. (2012). Agency and abjection in the closet: The voices (and silences) of black queer male teachers. *International Journal of Qualitative Studies in Education, 25*(6), 741–765.

Brown, A. L. (2009). "Brothers Gonna Work It Out:" Understanding the pedagogic performance of African American male teachers working with African American male students. *The Urban Review, 41*(5), 416–435.

Cochran-Smith, M., & Lytle, S. L. (2009, April). *Inquiry as stance: Practitioner research for the next generation.* Practitioners Inquiry Teachers College Press.

Cohen, C. J. (1997). Punks, bulldaggers, and welfare queens: The radical potential of queer politics? *Glq, 3*(4), 437–465.

Collins, P. H. (2006). A telling difference: Dominance, strength and Black masculinities. In A. D. Mutua (Ed.), *Progressive Black masculinities* (pp. 73–97). New York: Routledge.

Collins, P. H. (1986). Learning From the outsider within: The sociological significance of Black feminist thought. *Social Problems, 33*(6). S14–S32.

Holland, S. P., & Cohen, C. J. (2005). *Black queer studies: A critical anthology*. In E. P. Johnson & M. G. Henderson (Eds.). Duke University Press.

Darling-Hammond, L. (2012, June). *Powerful teacher education: Lessons from exemplary programs, Edition 1*. John Wiley & Sons.

Delpit, L. (2006). *Other people's children: Cultural conflict in the classroom*. The New Press.

Dixson, A. D. (2003). "Let's Do This!" Black women teachers' politics and pedagogy. *Urban Education, 38*(2), 217–235.

Fairclough, A. (2000). "Being in the field of education and also being a Negro...Seems...tragic": Black teachers in the Jim Crow south. *The Journal of American History, 87*(1), 65–91.

Fairclough, A. (2009). *A class of their own: Black teachers in the segregated South*. Harvard University Press.

Fordham, S. (1996). *Blacked out: Dilemmas of race, identity, and success at Capital high school*. Chicago: University of Chicago Press.

Foster, M. (1998). *Black teachers on teaching*. The New Press.

Foucault. M. (1986). Of other spaces. *Diacritics, 16*, 22–27.

Irvine, J. J. (2002). *In search of wholeness: African American teachers and their culturally specific classroom practices*. New York: Palgrave.

Knox, P. L., & Pinch, S. (2006). *Urban social geography: An introduction* (5th ed.). Harlow, Essex ; New York: Pearson/Prentice Hall.

Lefebvre, H. (1991). *The production of space*. Oxford: WileyBlackwell.

Lewis, A. E. (2001). There is no "race" in the schoolyard: Color-blind ideology in an (almost) all-white school. *American Educational Research Journal, 38*(4), 781–811.

Lynn, M. (2006). Education for the community: Exploring the culturally relevant practices of Black male teachers. *The Teachers College Record, 108*(12), 2497–2522.

McCready, L. T. (2010). *Making space for diverse masculinities: Identity, intersectionality, and engagement in an urban high school* (pp. i–140). New York: Peter Lang.

Monroe, C. R. (2009). Teachers closing the discipline gap in an urban middle school. *Urban Education, 44*(3), 322–347.

Noguera, P. A. (2009). *The trouble with black boys: And other reflections on race, equity, and the future of public education*. Wiley. com.

Ogbu, J. (2003). *Black students in an affluent suburb: A study of academic disengagement*. Mahwah, NJ: Lawrence Earlbaum Associates.

Ruddick, S. (1996). *Young and homeless in Hollywood: Mapping social identities*. London and New York: Routledge.

SFCESS (2013) San Francisco Coalition of Essential Small Schools ongoing professional development for K–12 schools.

Siddle Walker, V. S. (1996). *Their highest potential: An African American school community in the segregated South*. University of North Carolina Press.

Siddle Walker, V. S. (2001). African American teaching in the south: 1940–1960. *American Educational Research Journal, 38*(4), 751–779.

Siddle Walker, V. (2008). A thought from another world: The professional education of Black teachers in Georgia, 1930–1965. In M. Cochran-Smith, S. Feiman-Nemser, D. J. McIntyre, & K. E. Demers (Eds.), *Handbook of research on teacher education: Enduring questions in changing contexts* (3rd ed., pp. 117–121). New York: Routledge/Taylor & Francis and the Association of Teacher Educators.

Skelton, T., Valentine, G. (Eds.) (1998). *Cool places: Geographies of youth cultures.* New York: Routledge.

Soja, E. W. (1996). *Thirdspace: Journeys to Los Angeles and other real-and-imagined places.* Cambridge, Mass.: Blackwell.

Tatum, B. D. (1997). *"Why are all the black kids sitting together in the cafeteria?" and other conversations about race* (1st ed.). New York: BasicBooks.

Venzant Chambers, T., & McCready, L. (2011). "Making space" for ourselves: African american student responses to their marginalization. *Urban Education, 46*(6), 1352–1378.

CHAPTER 3

NEW VISIONS OF COLLECTIVE ACHIEVEMENT

The Cross-Generational Schooling Experiences of African American Males

Darrell Cleveland Hucks
Keene State College

The purpose of this study was to allow African American males across generations to share their perceptions of the factors that affected their schooling experiences and influenced their achievement in and beyond school. Individual interviews were conducted with men and boys within the context of their home environment; outside of the schools the boys attended. The participants' schooling experiences call for establishing a model of collective achievement that captures and delineates the engagement and investment of the multiple stakeholders involved in their education. Such a model will bring about a higher level of multiple stakeholder accountability that would likely improve students' schooling experiences and increase the academic and life outcomes for African American males.

Teacher Education and Black Communities, pages 59–86
Copyright © 2014 by Information Age Publishing
All rights of reproduction in any form reserved.

INTRODUCTION

In today's educational context of the "Achievement Gap" and "Disproportionality in Special Education," as well as the so-called "Crisis With Black Males" (Jackson & Moore, 2006; Pluviose, 2008; Watson, 2006), there are longstanding debates regarding the engagement and investment of African American boys in school (Mincy, 2006; National Urban League, 2008; Noguera, 1996; Noguera, 2003; Schott Foundation for Public Education, 2008; Watson, 2006). A significant body of research has supported quantitative measures, which reveal low test scores, high dropout rates, and crime and incarceration statistics that suggest that African American males are unsuccessful in school and within society (Duncan & Magnuson, 2005; Fryer & Levitt, 2006; Hoffman, Llagas, & Synder, 2003; Schott Foundation, 2008; Toldson, 2008). In decades of school reform, from *Brown v. Board of Education* (1954) to the current era of the federal *No Child Left Behind Act* (2001), and the recursive educational reforms these have ushered into our schools, African American males continue to occupy the bottom tiers in terms of achievement at all levels of school (Donnor & Shockley, 2010; Hughes & Bonner, 2006; Mincy, 2006; National Center for Education Statistics, 2007; Noguera, 2003; Swanson, Cunningham, & Spencer, 2003). This concern raises the question, why, for generation after generation, have African American males not been successful academically?

Historically, African American males bear the weight of timeless atrocities, experiencing a painful history of discrimination that continues to influence their marginalization in society. African American males are the least employed, the most imprisoned, and oftentimes, the most oppressed people in America (Davis, 2003; Majors & Billson, 1992; Noguera, 2003; Ogbu, 1974; Polite, 1999). According to data from the United States Census Bureau (2003), 35% of African American males between grades seven and twelve were suspended in 2000, while the National Center for Education Statistics (2007) reports that in that same year, 15% of African Americans males between grades 10 and 12 dropped out of high school. The U.S. Department of Justice (2000) has also documented that 50% of the American prison population consists of African American men. Statistics such as these clearly indicate a cause for better solutions to the challenges African American males face in schools and society.

In this article, the author focuses on the contextual factors that have influenced the cross-generational schooling experiences and achievement of African American males, revealing both the continuities and discontinuities that have been underexplored in past research, by using the voices of African American males to suggest directions for educational reform and future research.

School

On many levels the promise of educational advancement rendered in the 1954 landmark case *Brown* has not been fully actualized. Years after *Brown* for some students, education did improve; for instance, some received far better access to resources and materials than their fathers have received. For most, however, advancement never occurred. Despite recent reform efforts, such as smaller schools, vouchers, charter schools, and the federal legislation of the *No Child Left Behind Act* (2001), a large number of African American males are still trailing behind other students in schools and in society. Today's standardized test achievement data demonstrate that African American males across all grade levels continue to lag significantly behind their counterparts. Legislators, administrators, and teachers still fail to offer constructive and engaging ways of addressing and countering these problems. In this way, African American boys are caught between a school system that holds low expectations and negative perceptions of their academic abilities and a society that often mirrors and distorts these images (Davis, 2003; Howard, 2008; Lewis & Moore, 2008; Noguera, 2003; Osborne, 1999; Steele, 1990, 1998). This poses significant challenges for African American boys and their families. Many African American families continue to struggle for equal educational opportunities for their children. This is especially true for poor and working-class families living in inner cities and rural areas.

Society

The American public image of the African American family is one that is broken, weak, and unstable (Frazier, 1966; Hill, 2003; Lewis, 1966; Moynihan, 1965). Furthermore, the rise in number of African American single-parent, female-headed households have had a tremendous impact on how African American fathers are viewed. These fathers are believed to be disengaged from their families, or worse, seen as deserters of their children. This negative public perception of absent African American fathers has raised much debate regarding the presence of positive male role models for African American boys (Hutchinson, 1997). In understanding and confronting these perceptions, people must examine the causes of this phenomenon, whether perceived or actual, so that one can explore the structural changes in society and the impact they have had on our children. This exploration requires qualitative information that census data has not captured. Qualitative research allows the lived experiences and perceptions of research participants to be captured in ways that quantitative research does not (Denzin & Lincoln, 2000; Glaser & Strauss, 1967; Lawler, 2002; Lincoln & Guba,

1985; Rubin & Rubin, 1995; Weiss, 1995). The increasing number of single-parent African American male- or female-headed households has been studied only recently (Hill, 2003). Findings from this study suggest that the changes in the structure of African American families belies the complexity of making generalizations about the influences that fathers have on their young children. The complexities of these relationships should be examined in ways that go beyond only knowing *how many* family members reside at the same address and start to address *why* this is occurring.

Family

Family plays a significant role in the lives of children and a powerful influence on children's orientation to education and school. Many researchers have noted the crucial role the family has in shaping children's beliefs, perceptions, and values about their schooling (Kohn, 1999; Meier, 2002; Perry, Steele, & Hilliard, 2003; Sampson, 2002; Scanzoni, 1971; Thompson, 2003). Research suggests that parents' beliefs regarding past experiences of their own education are often passed on, directly or indirectly, to their children (Daniel & Effinger, 1996; Hale, 1994; Neblett, Chavous, Nguyên, & Sellers, 2009; Osborne, 1999; Sampson, 2002). Until recently, research focusing on the intergenerational-schooling experiences of African American males within the context of their families has been underexplored (Hucks, 2008). In 2009, Rowley and Bowman suggested that successful academic outcomes for African American males in higher education are impeded by "cross-generational family and student role strains"—specifically citing the absence of African American fathers and male role models as negatively influencing student motivation and peer-risk behaviors both in and out of school. Furthermore, a limited number of studies report how African American role models actually do influence the children in their lives and their education (Hale, 1994; Hill, 2003; Perry, Steele, & Hilliard, 2003). Some of these studies have focused more on the relationships between African American mothers and their sons (Ferguson, 2001; Hale, 1982; Thompson, 2004), while others have focused on the role of fathers in their daughters' education (Draughn & Waggenstock, 1986). Additionally, others have been intergenerational studies of the educational experiences of grandmothers, mothers, and daughters (Carothers, 1990; Daniel & Effinger, 1996; Sealey-Ruiz, 2007; Willie & Reddick, 2003). It is only recently that studies have begun to examine the impact of African American fathers on their sons' education (Harris, 1999; Polite & Davis, 1999; Scott, 1997).

While intergenerational studies of fathers, sons, and other male role models in the immediate and extended family may have offered males an opportunity to speak about education, these studies have not used a multi-theoretical framework as the current study.

Achievement

Existing research shows that African American males are oftentimes, most likely, to be overrepresented in categories associated with school failure (Mincy, 2006, Moore, 2006; Noguera, 2008). The challenge for addressing this overrepresentation in underachievement is great and will require a level of engagement, investment, accountability, and achievement for all who play a role and have a stake in bringing change for African American males.

The collective voices of African American males regarding their school and life experiences, and the issues and challenges they face are missing from the literature. In examining the schooling experiences and achievement of African American males, educators and researchers have often not viewed them as being knowledgeable informants of their own experiences (Dance, 2002; Laubasher, 2005; Mincy, 2006; Sampson, 2002; Sewell, 2000; Swanson, Cunningham, & Spencer 2003; Thompson 2004). Contrary to that approach, the researcher asked African American boys and men to share their schooling experiences with him and they did.

Collective Achievement

A model of collective achievement provides a new way of examining and understanding student achievement and provides important applications for the investment, engagement, accountability, and achievement of all stakeholders (Hucks, 2008). All of the themes from the current study shed light on the overarching metatheme of collective achievement that runs across the generations and ties these participants' schooling experiences together. Collective achievement has important implications for enacting change, not only with the educational outcomes for African American males, but also for the schools and communities that are serving them.

Collective achievement is not a new term or phrase. In a study conducted in the 1960s, of students in historically Black colleges, Gurin and Epps (1975) used the term "collective achievement" to discuss issues of Black consciousness, identity, and achievement in the lives of their participants. The researchers focused on achievement as a collective phenomenon, stating:

> It focuses on the collective commitments and action of the students through which they tried to exact legal, economic, and social changes that would benefit Black people. The activists were striving to achieve, but they were work-

ing for group products and accomplishments rather than for individual goals. Their motivation carried all the usual connotations of achievement motivation: it prompted hard and persistent effort as well as setting group goals that were both difficult and realistic. When successful in creating change, they evinced the kind of pleasure usually related to achievement. They were elated with a job well done; they were proud of the process of working together. (p. 189)

The current study expands on this term by extending its application to the work of multiple stakeholders around the issue of student achievement.

Where educational policy and research have primarily focused their lens on the achievement and academic outcomes of African American boys at all levels of school, it is often aimed at what is problematic about them (Donnor & Shockley, 2010; Gibbs, 1988; Noguera, 2003, 2008). There is a void in capturing the accountability and achievement of all the stakeholders involved with children's academic success and life outcomes (Davis, 2003; Ferguson, 2001; Howard, 2002; Majors & Billson, 1992; Moore, 2006; Noguera, 2003; Ogbu, 1997; Osborne, 1997, 1999; Steele, 1992). The lens of collective achievement forces people to go deeper than the *what* of engagement and investment to the *whowho* as it relates to accountability and achievement, and not just for the students, but for everyone involved in the educational process. The current study, in combination with past research, suggests that school leaders may need to identify and put into operation, a collective achievement model, which capitalizes on the investments and honors the engagement of all stakeholders.

The demographics of the majority who are teaching in public school classrooms today are White, middle-class females, in contrast to those they teach, who are students of color (Delpit, 1995; Gay, 2000; Kozol, 2005; Ladson-Billings, 1995; Sleeter, 2001; Tate, 1994). What assumptions do teachers make because of differences regarding race, ethnicity, gender, and class? How do teachers view and respond to the educational legacies that are walking into schools and classrooms each day? These are critical questions that schools and teachers must ask themselves.

THEORETICAL FRAMEWORK

The current study contributes to the research on African American males by closely examining the intergenerational educational experiences of boys and men in a select number of families. This research explored the connections that have gone unexamined by past researchers about the education and achievement of African American males. The goal of the study was to explore how African American males characterize their schooling experiences across generations, which is crucial in understanding the intergenerational conflicts, continuities, and interwoven experiences involved in their educational stories and how they currently impact students' academic performance in schools.

Due to the researcher's shared ethnicity with the participants in the study, years of past experience teaching African American boys, and after engaging with the literature on African American males, it was quickly realized that not one isolated theory, model, or perspective could, nor should, be applied to the complex lives of African American males. This approach to the research design was also informed by preliminary conversations with African American males prior to the current study, the researcher discovered that one theory or concept on its own could not capture the range of factors that informed the schooling experiences of African American males on an intergenerational scale. But enacting them as a collective allowed for a more open-ended research design that captured the intergenerational continuities and discontinuities that exist among the participants, and also gave rise to this new theory of collective achievement. The idea of seeing them collectively, not separately, made more sense and told a richer story. The following researchers provided this collective framework:

- Osborne's (1997, 1999) perspective on disidentification with academics suggests that the educational achievement of African American males is directly related to whether or not they identify with academics.
- Steele's (1992, 1997) stereotype-threat model suggests that if you belong to a minority group in which there are negative stereotypes about that group's academic ability, then that group's academic performance in school will be adversely affected.
- Majors and Billson's (1992) "cool pose" theory suggests that African American males adopt a pose of acting "cool" in school as a coping mechanism for the challenges they face.
- Noguera (2003) and the environmental and cultural perspective suggests that the interaction of harmful environmental and cultural factors have an impact on young African American boys both in and out of school.
- Ogbu's (1997) cultural-ecological model suggests that the home culture and community with which a student identifies will impact their school performance. He also argues that students, coming from a culture that has viewed itself as being oppressed, may view school as a continuation of that oppression.

The current study intended to address the deficit of African American male voices in the literature by engaging with African American males from within the same family unit across generations through qualitative interviews and observations in their homes and communities. This study focused on understanding schooling experiences across generations from the perspectives of African American males. In exploring their schooling experiences across generations, this study investigated how these experiences shed light on the ways African American males were and continue to be served by the U.S. public educational system. In a quest to delve deeper, the researcher used the following questions as a guide to framing the study and to generate interview questions:

- What are the educational stories of African American males?
- How do the educational experiences of previous generations of African American males inform those of the next generations?
- What "human capital" (parents, siblings, extended family, friends, and role models) do African American males use to navigate the public school systems?
- How do African American males evaluate their public school education?
- How do African American males see the value of their education and that of their families who send them to school?
- In what ways do African American males see the connections between their schooling experiences and life outcomes?

METHODOLOGY

This current study documented over a six-month period, through a series (two to three per individual) of in-person interviews conducted in participants' home environments, the educational histories of a group of urban African American boys, between the ages of eight and twelve, and those of the older males in their immediate and extended families. The age group of eight to twelve was specifically chosen for two reasons: First, it is a group that has not been intensively studied around issues of schooling. Second, it is also the age group where standardized testing becomes the method for evaluating students' academic achievement in public schools—evaluations that resonate throughout the rest of these students' academic lives.

Data Collection

Qualitative research is as much about the researcher as it is about those studied (Carothers, 1990). The journey in recruiting the participants allowed me to track my own reflections of discovering and rediscovering connections and involvement within the African American community. Flyers were posted in African American neighborhoods, churches, barbershops, community organizations, and any places where African American families might visit. However, the families that participated in the study were found through informal referrals from community members who initiated contact with the researcher. Three families participated in this study: the Andersons, the Wallaces, and the Freemans. All of the families, and the individual members in each, have been given pseudonyms to protect their identities. A total of 11 participants ranging in age from 9 to 73 were interviewed. Of the 11 males, three of them were boys between ages 9 and 12. Two participants were biological fathers and one participant was a stepfather. One participant was an older sibling to one of the boys and three participants were cousins within each separate family. There was one participant who was a great-grandfather (See Table 3.1).

Individual interviews of the 11 participants were all conducted outside of the school environment. The researcher arranged to conduct the interviews at the participants' homes. One of the fathers participating in the study invited the researcher to his place of employment and an interview was conducted in the conference room, and another interview was conducted using public transportation after this same father asked the researcher to accompany him on a business call. Before interviewing individual members of each family, the researcher visited the families' homes to explain the purpose of the study and secure their permission and consent.

The researcher used methods of active interviewing as developed by Holstein and Gubrium (1995) who explained that this kind of conversation allows

TABLE 3.1 Demographic Profile of the Participants (N = 11)

Family	Relationship	Age	Education	Occupation
The Andersons				
Charles	Father	45	Master's degree	Art teacher
Shaun	Son	14	10th grade	Student
Jeremy	Son	10	4th grade	Student
James	Charles' cousin	19	College freshman	Student
The Wallaces				
Martin	Father	48	1 year of college	Project manager
Tyreek	Son	11	5th grade	Student
Malik	Tyreek's cousin	14	8th grade	Student
The Freemans				
Joshua	Step-father	23	High school graduate	Store clerk
Tyrone	Step-son	10	4th grade	Student
Jacob	Tyrone's great-grandfather	73	High school graduate	Retired
Larry	Joshua's cousin	22	College graduate	Office assistant

both interviewer and informant to use the "dynamic interplay between the two, to reveal both the substance and process of meaning-making in relation to research objectives" (p. 76). Using these methods, over a two-year period, interviews were conducted with the three families, spending six to eight months with each family before going to the next. While the data from the interviews were used to answer the primary research questions of the study, the interviews also expanded the researcher's understanding of African American males and their schooling experiences in a more holistic way. As is often the case in qualitative research, participant observation and in-depth interviewing were combined to conduct more naturalistic research (Bogdan & Biklen, 2003; Wolcott, 2001). Therefore, there is never an in-person interview without an observation. Detailed written descriptions were collected to capture contextual and relational factors that may influence the lives of the participants.

Data Analysis

In creating a road map to analyze the data generated in this study, themes and metathemes were instrumental in interpretations. Analysis revealed four important intergenerational-thematic categories that emerged from the data. Into those categories, recurring themes across individuals and families that fit into the collective framework (cited earlier in methods) were placed. The significant metatheme of collective achievement was an overarching construct that came from the experiences and insights shared in the narrative accounts of the participants. With the recursive analysis of these narratives, simply put, good schooling is invested in collective achievement and bad schooling is not invested in collective achievement. Most of the males in the study have experienced more of the latter.

Limitations of Study

This study was designed to explore African American males' perceptions of the factors that impact and influence their schooling experiences. The study does not include the perceptions of teachers and administrators; therefore, it is limited to the participants' viewpoints. The number of participants in the study was also limited by the availability of African American families with multiple generations of males, with boys currently attending elementary school, and their willingness to participate. The participants were recruited from a single city within the northeastern section of the United States. The findings may hold significance for multiple stakeholders who seek ways to improve the achievement outcomes for African American males across multiple grade levels.

FINDINGS

The following provides an overview of four major thematic categories that emerged from the data. Through detailed, written descriptions of the observations made after interview sessions with the participants, the researcher gained a greater understanding of the contextual and relational factors at work (Ely et al., 1997; Lofland & Lofland, 1995).

The three families' stories of their educational journeys, spanning over 63 years, share a common path through four major thematic categories: (a) Resiliency, (b) Role Models and Role of Community, (c) Resources, and (d) School Experiences. The thematic categories have been identified in order to offer a road map for understanding African American males' educational experiences in American society (see Table 3.2). The themes under each category were derived from identifying patterns in the data that repeated across the participants' experiences. Many of the theme titles were lifted directly from the participants' language used in their narrative accounts.

Resiliency (Understanding Issues of Safety and Masculinity)

Prior research suggests that a study about African American males schooling experiences would typically focus on problematic behaviors on their part (Ferguson, 2001; Gibbs, 1988; Noguera, 2003). However, the participants' stories reveal that their behaviors are grounded in defensive and

---

TABLE 3.2 Thematic Categories and Themes (Within and Across Generations and Families)

Resiliency (Safety & Masculinity)
Negative Incidents with Teachers
Threat of Racism
Role Models and Role of Community
"Ballers and Rappers"
Same Ole Black History Month
Is School an Option?
Resources
Lack of Resources to Engage Students
We Like Science, too
Outdated Curriculum
School Experiences
Supportive Teachers
Supporting Culturally Responsive Teachers
Status Quo Teachers
Power of Teachers and Teaching

---

offensive stances they employ in response to feeling unsafe in the various contexts they must negotiate in their lives. The theme of resiliency, specifically looking to issues of safety and masculinity, was a common thread that ran across the generations. Understandings of and responses to resiliency were clearly grounded in the participants' experiences as African American males and those of other African American males in their families and communities.

Negative Incidents With Teachers

Most of the participants in the study talked about the impact of negative incidents with teachers that have left indelible impressions on their minds. These encounters left many of them angry and confused about their teachers' perceptions of them. Oftentimes, these negative incidents happened in the classroom and range from the following: teachers not being fair to them; accusing them of cheating; not keeping private information confidential as promised; making fun of their mistakes in front of classmates; openly accusing them of trying to do more than what's expected; encouraging them to lower their own expectations for themselves as learners; not following through on promises, lying to their parents; being physically inappropriate (i.e., pushing or grabbing them); making racist and culturally offensive comments to them; and expressing disdain for students' interests. Participants suggested that at an early age, boys have a systematic way in which they identify and connect to the adults who support them and have a clear sense of those who do not through "reading" their behaviors.

Threat of Racism

For many, if not all of the participants, the threat of racism manifesting itself was a daily reality both inside and outside of school. On a generational scale, racism and discrimination continues to be a part of their lives as African American males in our society. Starting with a comment from the oldest participant, Jacob Freeman, who talked about the possibility of prison or even death in the antebellum South:

> Listen, racism was no joke, we had to be very careful around White folks because they hated us and they weren't afraid to hurt us. You didn't give them a reason by being in the wrong place at the wrong time. You could come up dead. The rules were clear it was their world and they didn't want us in it— laws or not.

Moving a few generations forward, after desegregation, one finds that schools and classrooms may be integrated, but with integration, racism is now both in and outside of the classroom.

This was exhibited with Charles Anderson and Martin Wallace who both went to school during the early years of desegregation, which both attested, did not change people's perceptions of African American males. Charles remembers White students alongside their parents who picketed outside of his school when Black students were bused into their neighborhood. Martin commented on racism at his school at the time:

> The racial tension was thick. Mobs of White kids would come after the Black kids after school. It was hell getting to school in the morning and another hell at the end of the day. It was ridiculous! In class you be sitting next to somebody that wanted to get you once you left the building. Nothing ever happened in the classroom but it affected people. How do you concentrate on learning anything when you thinking about that?

These older males' stories, across the generations, reveal their struggles within a racist society.

For the three youngest participants, racism still exists. Unlike their elders, it is more subtle, more insidious, and closer than ever before. It exists in their classrooms. Ten-year old Jeremy Anderson, discussed how comments made by some of his former teachers have racist undertones, explaining, "There are certain things you just don't say, like I'm going to 'hang you' to a student—especially a Black one." Additionally, 11-year old Tyreek Wallace discussed how racism lives in the low expectations of some of his former teachers: "You can just tell that White teachers treat you differently if you're Black and not in a good way." Tyrone Freeman, age 11, best illustrates these boys' perspectives:

> Sometimes I just watch teachers and I can tell which ones don't like Black people. They act real funny and mean. I can tell by what they don't tell us, and what they don't let us do. They racist, but they be trying to hide it. We ain't stupid, we know, we just can't do nothing about it.

Across the generations, racism has existed in and out of school and it is the responsibility of the child to make sense of it along with understanding the power dynamics at work.

Role Models and Role of Community

Across the generations, the participants in this study stated that finding role models in the context of schools was a major challenge. They shared their insights concerning a dearth of positive African American male role models. Despite this difficulty in the schools, the boys and men said they believed positive role models existed in their homes and communities, and questioned why schools and teachers did not tap into them as resources.

"Ballers and Rappers"

Four participants made comments about the problematic nature of the two major career options associated with successful African American males: basketball and the rap-music industry. Based on the researcher's work in urban schools, these are often the two choices most frequently shared by young African American males in response to the question: "What do you want to be when you grow up?" The following comments demonstrate the problematic nature of this widely spread phenomenon in urban settings.

First to address this issue is Tyrone, age 11, who believes his only possibility for future success is tied to receiving a scholarship to play college basketball. Then there is Joshua, his step-father, who sees basketball as a viable way for many urban low-income youth to get out of the environment in which they live. Joshua shared; however, that basketball should not be the only option for poor urban youth and that schools need to help them have more options. According to 21-year old James Anderson:

> Teachers and schools automatically just assume that all African American males are only interested in basketball and rap music and never bother to challenge these perceptions for themselves and for the benefit of their students. Not every Black boy wants this deep down—it's almost like we're being brainwashed to think we should want to be a rapper or a basketball star. That's about making money for somebody else; that ain't about us. Besides most of these kids are not gonna make it and it's not their fault. If we're not showing them something else to aspire to why should they believe they could do anything else and be successful?

Tyreek Wallace along with James Anderson, both believe that the media and the recording industry are responsible for perpetuating these images into the minds of society to the point that African American males buy into the image of what African American males must do in order to be financially successful. Despite the fact that many of these images run counter to who these boys are, this creates unrealistic expectations and unfulfilled dreams for young African American males. Joshua made the point that, "There are many rappers with degrees but they don't ever talk about getting an education because it doesn't fit the image that sells." Larry Freeman also explains, "Schools are supposed to help children see more options through education; unfortunately many kids don't experience that." According to these African American males, schools are clearly not providing viable career options for them to pursue in their lives.

Same Ole Black History Month

Three participants addressed the lack of culturally responsive curriculum and teaching in their schooling. They claimed that the contributions of African Americans is lacking across subject areas and that African Americans are visibly absent in the books that they are required to read in their classes. They believe that this causes African American students to disengage from learning. James Anderson explained, "The only time we read about Black people was when the textbook had a page or two on slavery and even then it was like it happened a long time ago and now everything is fine." Twenty-three year old Joshua Freeman continues this argument, stating:

> It's like Black people never did anything except be slaves, play sports, and make music. Which is not true, we made a whole lot of contributions to this country, to the world. It's like they don't want us to know who we really are. It's like this is our history: slavery, Martin Luther King, Malcolm X, Michael Jordan, Jay-Z, Oprah, and Tiger Woods. And that's not history those are people who made history. There's a whole lot more than that but White people are really scared of us. The teachers don't know Black history and most them wouldn't know what to do with it. They ain't scared of the people I just said—two of them ain't alive no more and they love Oprah. Oprah needs to do a show on Blacks in history. Maybe we'll all learn something. Make teachers learn history, real history, not just Black history. We are a part of history, period. It's not separate.

Even 11-year old Tyreek, commented on when and how the contributions of African Americans are regularly found in schools, he explained:

> February is Black History Month and that's when we hear about the same four or five people, year after year. It's a waste of time to keep hearing the same speeches, the same books, the same stuff. There's got to be more and why only in February, we're Black all year long. It's just the same ole Black History month every time.

From the 11-year old to the 23-year old, these African American males make astute observations of the ways in which schools are not culturally responsive to them and the possibly negative impact this can have on the learning for "all" students. Schools have the power to impact students' embracing of diversity, but instead schools often perpetuate stereotypes and promote prejudice when they are not culturally responsive.

Is School an Option?

Seeing school as an option was a theme that flowed consistently through all of the participants' stories. The question of whether schools, as they are currently structured, are a viable option for African American males was frequently addressed. Many participants believe that African

American males have fallen victim to teachers and schools because they have not been truly invested in their achievement. As James Anderson suggested, "Schools are invested in maintaining the status quo and the status quo has African American males as low achievers. And low achievers don't have any power to change anything." For Martin Wallace, the public school system is simply, "not working for us." He goes further to say, "We as a people can believe in education all we want, but until the people who are running the schools believe in *our* education, then it's just an uphill battle for us." Schools can have a tremendous impact on how students experience the learning environment and student achievement by investing in countering negative media images, enacting culturally responsive and culturally relevant pedagogy, and providing students with positive options for the future.

Resources

The participants in this study turned a critical eye to what was, and is, missing for them in their schools. The boys who are currently in school offered a very clear understanding of the impact a lack of resources has on their trust and engagement in the learning process. They also made astute observations about how this lack of resources affects the curriculum and the way that they are taught in school. Many believe that for African American males, the system has been designed to exclude their interests from the start. Several participants also suggested that teachers' negative perceptions of African American males perpetuate the negative cycle occurring in schools, which ultimately affects their academic achievement.

Lack of Resources to Engage Students

Student engagement is an important topic in today's urban classrooms. Oftentimes, urban schools are the most under-resourced settings. For all three boys participating in this study, the lack of resources at their schools was cited as a reason for their disengagement. Jeremy talked about the need for better books at his school and more computers. Tyreek called attention to the lack of science materials and curriculum in his former classroom; he also commented on the need for more up-to-date books. Lastly, Tyrone had the most to say about the lack of resources at his school. He was adamant about the need for "better books," more "hands-on" materials, "instruments for music class" and "more computers." Several older males in the study also reflected on the lack of access to resources at their schools when they were younger. They noted how these materials would have helped them connect to their work in positive and constructive ways.

We Like Science, Too

Several participants discussed their interest in science; however, most have not had experiences in school that have consistently nurtured their interest in the subject. While describing a science project Tyreek did at home, which ultimately won a school award, he complained that his own teacher offered no support or acknowledgment of his work. Tyrone also talked about why he liked "doing science" but how his experiences with science are noticeably tapering off as he moves along through school. According to Tyrone, "They be acting like we only like art and gym. You know we like science, too. They should ask us." Some of the older participants, like James and Joshua, also expressed a love of science despite the lack of encouragement in their schools. Larry; however, had a science teacher in middle school who helped students appreciate science as much as she did because of her enthusiasm for the subject. The participants in this study suggest that their schools' lack of support for their science education does not match the interest and the desire that they genuinely have for learning science.

Outdated Curriculum

For many of the participants, the curriculum they experienced as African American males was lacking in substance, especially in how it reflected the African American experience. Several of the participants, as suggested by "Same Ole Black History Month" discussed frequent encounters with texts that only mentioned slavery and a few key historic figures. According to James, "Teachers need to learn African American history beyond what is presented in textbooks to inspire and motivate their students." He strongly suggested that White students should also be taught African American history. For Joshua and Jacob, their experiences with outdated curricula gives African American students a skewed view of their community and has little connection to their lives, which negatively impacted their self-esteem.

School Experiences

For the participants in this study, teachers are major players in their lives. Many of them cited negative encounters with teachers that seemed to open old wounds. All the males had experienced, however, at least one good teacher. Needless to say, one good teacher, against a cadre of bad teachers, lowers the odds of outstanding academic achievement for African American boys in today's schools.

Supportive Teachers

The boys in this study have a systematic way in which they identify and connect to the adults who support them and have a clear sense of those who do not. The three young boys in this study all shared stories of incidents with teachers that let them know whether this teacher truly supported them or not. In their stories, it appears that unsupportive teachers do not have an understanding of the impact of their actions or never addressed how the boys may have interpreted their actions. According to all the participants, supportive teachers are culturally responsive, caring, smart, engaging, humorous, and loving.

Supporting Culturally Responsive Teachers

Two participants remembered specific teachers who were invested in understanding and embracing the cultural backgrounds of their students. As a result, these teachers were popular teachers among students and their families. Unfortunately, these teachers were often not well-received and supported by their colleagues at school. Joshua talked about one teacher he had in high school who left the school because according to him, "The other teachers did not like this teacher 'cause the teacher looked out for us." Tensions among the faculty about how some teachers "work well" with students of color make invested teachers targets by their colleagues. Joshua suggested that the school system needs to be more embracing of teachers "who look out for us" and use them as models for other teachers to emulate.

Status Quo Teachers

In describing some of their teachers, both past and present, the participants revealed that some of these individuals have an investment in maintaining the status quo—keeping African American males from succeeding in school. The participants shared many stories of teachers who upheld and maintained this status. For James, he shared how one teacher's low expectations for him colored her interactions with him and his schoolwork. For Jacob, these low expectations were a constant reality with which African Americans from the South had to contend, especially with White teachers who taught their children in the North. Joshua also talked about teachers who just did not seem to want to see their students do any better in school and there was no investment in making things different. Status-quo teachers have wreaked havoc on the educational achievement of African American males. Educational policies need to be directed at identifying and removing these problematic teachers from schools serving African American males.

Power of Teachers and Teaching

All the participants discussed the power that teachers have in changing the negative images of African American males through their work in classrooms. Three participants in particular commented on the responsibility of teachers in countering existing negative images. Martin commented on how teachers are image-makers along with parents for African American males. James discussed how teachers must understand that a few supportive actions and words can have a tremendous impact on a child's future. Jacob discussed how male teachers can and should embrace the responsibility of being a positive father figure for their students. His stance is that, "Classrooms need to be more like family, if we are going to change things for the better." Ironically, the youngest participant, Tyrone, claimed that he does not want to consider teaching as a career because he does not want to be like the negative teachers whom he has experienced. However, James definitely wants to teach in the future. Whether or not they want to pursue a career in teaching, all of the participants hold strong ideas around educational reform to bring change for African American males and all students—despite the negative experiences that have overshadowed their own experiences in schools.

DISCUSSION

This study argues that school-reform strategies must take into account the lived experiences of African American males across generations. The field of education is in desperate need of a lens that reveals the achievement of not just students, but their families, their teachers, school administration, school staff, and the community. A collective achievement model can provide this necessary lens.

The African American males who participated in this study are a diverse group of individuals with similar and differing educational experiences. Unlike quantitative studies that cover breadth involving many people in large samples, allowing for in-depth focus on a small number of participants is a recognized strength of qualitative research (Carothers, 1990). This sample of three families, with 11 participants, may not necessarily be applicable to the schooling experiences of all African American males across generations. What these narratives do, however, is demonstrate the complexity involved in how African American males view and discuss their schooling experiences and how these stories are connected across generations.

Osborne's (1997) perspective on African American male academic success being directly attributed to whether students identify with academics is deepened by the current findings. The participants in this study revealed that they do indeed identify with academics; yet, they question whether the academic environment of schools and teachers identifies with them. This perspective shifts the sole ownership of academic success and achievement from the students, suggesting a multiple stakeholder gap in the achievement of African American male students.

Regarding Steele's (1992) stereotype threat model, which suggests that negative stereotypes hinder the academic performance of African American males, findings from the current study support his work. At the same time, the current findings complicate Steele's work in a major way. Steele's research was limited to students experiencing stereotype threat under testing conditions. The participants in the current study have indicated that the threat of negative stereotypes impact their school performance on a daily basis beyond the parameters of testing. While Steele used a larger sample for his research, the group was narrowly defined due to their identification as gifted students of color. The current work uses a smaller sample but a more diverse group on a generational scale, which raises questions regarding the influence of stereotype threat on the nontest taking schooling experiences of Steele's group of students. By focusing solely on students' performance on standardized tests, Steele has overlooked the significant contextual factors that the current study has identified as being at work, both beyond schools and in schools—even when testing is not taking place. These contextual factors can negatively impact their performance on both formal and informal assessments as well as diminish students' learning experiences. In light of the findings suggested in this study, curiosity is piqued about the classroom learning experiences of Steele's "gifted and talented" students of color. Does stereotype threat exist in other areas of their academic lives? Eleven year old, Tyreek and 10-year old, Tyrone, would answer, "Yes, it does."

Ogbu's (1997) cultural ecological perspective, which suggests that the home culture and community with which students identify will impact their school performance, scratches the surface of the dynamics in urban communities. The current study has looked more in-depth at those dynamics across generations. Ogbu's theory on voluntary (by choice such as Caribbean Americans and their descendants) and involuntary (not by choice such as U.S. slaves and their descendants) immigrants identifies African Americans as historically not having an investment in education and attributes low educational engagement and achievement to membership within this group. The current study, however, challenges Ogbu's theory on multiple levels. This work found that the participants did come from home cultures that placed value on education. The home value was not enough; however, to overcome the obstacles they met and still meet in school. Challenges students and their families face while operationalizing this belief in school is not usually taken into account by researchers in their attempts to explain the achievement gap. The responses of the participants in this study are in keeping with Ogbu's perspective that schools are a continuation of societal oppression. Seventy-three year old Jacob Freeman expressed this sentiment well:

> For African American males, schools try to get you ready for society. But society don't want you there. So the bad schools are getting you ready for a bad place, a bad position in society. That's how they see you. So many schools are just not trying to educate our kids for a better future. It's just more of the same thing.

His comment is based on years of life experience and watching how the generations after his generation are faring in schools and society.

These findings also support Majors and Billson's (1992) cool-pose theory, which purports that African American males adopt a "cool" stance in school as a coping mechanism. Findings further suggest that this stance is also connected to mirroring media images that African American males encounter and is peer-motivated and connected to peer dynamics that adults do not fully understand. The current findings complicate the source of the motivating factors behind this cool-pose and the expectations for its existence based on the influence of peers in school and media's influence on both students and teachers regarding the interpretation and acceptance of this stance.

Findings from the current study also support Noguera's (2003) environmental and cultural perspective, which suggests that the interaction of harmful environmental and cultural factors have an impact on young African American males in and outside of school. The current study expands on this by suggesting that these harmful factors should not be viewed as being isolated to the African American community. On the contrary, many of these harmful factors are originating in schools themselves and are not helping African American males positively negotiate these different contexts.

In addition, notions of the nuclear family simply do not convey the wondrous array of family groupings that have always existed in the African American community (Stack, 1997). This is directly related to the existence of unrecognized role models in the African American community.

As a collective, these various theories surrounding the education of African American males address particular factors that must be considered in their academic achievement. By adding the intergenerational voices of African American males themselves, the strengths and weaknesses of the individual theories are exposed. The current study reveals that school reform initiatives and interventions must enact models of collective achievement to have a sustainable positive impact on the educational achievement of African American males.

The participants taught us how they negotiate their identity as African American males and navigate the terrain of availability and access to opportunity regarding their education. These are voices of experience that can inform the work of educators, administrators, researchers, parents, community organizations, and policymakers. Collective achievement is a model of reciprocity. As teachers and students, our fates are linked. It raises shared responsibility, shared accountability, and shared achievement. Collective achievement encapsulates all of the suggestions and possibilities that the schooling experiences of African American males participating in this study discussed.

The narratives of the African American males across the generations revealed a common thread about education. It is multifaceted and it involves the work of many including students, parents, community members, teachers and school administrators. Upon recursive analysis of these narratives, simply put, good schooling is invested in collective achievement and bad schooling is not invested in collective achievement. Most of the males in the study have experienced more of the latter. Regardless of age, the participants in the study articulated and extrapolated what teaching invested in collective achievement should look like. It is caring, filled with high expectations, resourceful, culturally responsive, dynamic connected to and built on other stakeholder contributions, no matter who that stakeholder is— male, female, Black or White. Most importantly, according to the youngest participants in this study, it should be fun. Ladson-Billing's (1994) work on culturally responsive curriculum and pedagogy provided a framework for reforming teacher education and impacting student achievement for marginalized students. Collective achievement builds on her culturally responsive theory by offering another framework that will reach not only students and teachers, but also all stakeholders in and outside the classroom.

Implications

This study has implications for the design and implementation of present and future school-reform efforts, educational policy and research, and teacher education. Where educational policy and research have primarily focused their lens solely on the achievement and outcomes of African American boys at various levels of school, there seems to be a void in earlier educational reform models that have not used the voices or lived experiences of students as a means to engage and measure the achievement of all the stakeholders involved in children's academic success and life outcomes.

African American families value education. Their engagement and investment in the schooling process of their children has often been interpreted in ways that point out their limitations instead of the limitations of the public school system in this society. Existing research has relied heavily on quantitative measures to tell the educational experiences of African American males. This approach leaves many aspects of African American males schooling experiences unexamined and it leaves many avenues for reform unidentified and unexplored. While quantitative data has given us statistics on how African American males are performing in and beyond school, qualitative data will help give deeper meaning to existing data and help us understand why schools are not working for African American males. The implications for practice are overwhelmingly clear; the adoption and implementation of collective achievement strategies are of the utmost importance in changing educational outcomes for African American males.

Recommendations for Research

- Findings from this study call for research that further explores the schooling experiences of African American boys to better understand how they experience the captive environments of classrooms and schools.
- There is also a need for research that captures and examines the experiences of multiple stakeholders in young African American boys schooling.
- Research that captures and delineates successful models of schools that are enacting collective achievement theory frameworks is needed.

Recommendations for Practice

- The findings suggest that culturally responsive professional development must be mandated for teachers and administrators.
- Teacher education programs must provide prospective teachers with culturally responsive pedagogy and teach them history through multiple perspectives.
- Findings from this study suggest that outdated and culturally exclusionary curriculum must become a thing of the past to truly engage and positively impact teacher investment and student achievement.
- Schools need to build stronger relationships within the communities they serve and find the various human resources that exist. In collaboration, schools and communities can redefine collective achievement.
- Local, state, and federally funded academic-intervention programs must be grounded in a model of collective achievement to constructively impact student achievement and for sustainability and accountability.

CONCLUSION

Understanding the cross-generational schooling experiences of African American males from their perspective has much to contribute to the field of education. The collective voices of African American males are missing from the research literature in two significant areas: (a) on an intergenerational level and (b) at the elementary school level.

There is also a need for research that captures and examines the experiences of multiple stakeholders in young African American boys schooling. Such research could help schools identify and understand the continuities and discontinuities occurring in the education of African American males across age levels. As the narratives in this study suggest, research focused on schools who adopt a model of collective achievement can have significant impact on how we understand the relationship of African American male students' schooling experiences and their achievement.

NOTE

All comments and queries regarding this article should be addressed to dhucks@keene.edu

REFERENCES

Bogdan, R. C., & Biklen, S. K. (2003). *Qualitative research for education: An introduction to theory and methods* (4th ed.). New York: Pearson Education.

Carothers, S. (1990). Catching sense: Learning to be Black and female from our mothers. In *Uncertain terms: Negotiating gender in American culture* (pp. 232–247). In F. Ginsberg & A. Lowenhaupt-Tsing (Eds.), Boston, MA: Beacon Press.

Dance, J. (2002). *Tough fronts: The impact of street culture on schooling.* New York: Routledge Falmer.

Daniel, J. L., & Effinger, M. J. (1996). Bosom biscuits: A study of African American intergenerational communication. *Journal of Black Studies, 27,* 183–200.

Davis, J. E. (2003). Early schooling and academic achievement of African American males. *Urban Education, 38,* 515–537.

Delpit, L. (1995). *Other people's children: Cultural conflict in the classroom.* New York: The New Press.

Denzin, N. K., & Lincoln, Y. S. (Eds.). (2000). *Handbook of qualitative research.* Thousand Oaks, CA: Sage.

Donnor, J. K., &,Shockley, K. G. (2010). Leaving us behind: A political economic interpretation of NCLB and the miseducation of African American males. *Educational Foundations, 24,* ,43–54.

Draughn, P. S., & Waggenstock, M. L. (1986). Fathers' supportiveness: Perceptions of fathers and college daughters. In R. A. Lewis & R. E. Salt (Eds.), *Men in families* (pp. 197–209). Beverly Hills, CA: Sage.

Duncan, G. J., & Magnuson, K. (2005). Can family socio-economic resources account for racial and ethnic test score gaps? *Future of Children, 15,* 35–54.

Ely, M., Vinz, R., Downing, M., & Anzul, M. (1997). *On writing qualitative research: Living by words.* Washington, DC: The Falmer Press.

Ferguson, A. A. (2001). *Bad boys: Public schools in the making of Black masculinity.* Ann Arbor, MI: University of Michigan Press.

Frazier, E. F. (1966). *The Negro family in the United States.* Chicago: University of Chicago Press.

Fryer, R. G., & Levitt, S. D. (2006). The Black-White test score gap through third grade. *American Law and Economics Review, 8,* 249–281.

Gay, G. (2000). *Culturally responsive teaching: Theory, research, and practice* (2nd ed.) New York: Teachers College Press.

Gibbs, J. T. (1988). *Young, Black, and male in America.* New York: Auburn House.

Glaser, B. G., & Strauss, A. L. (1967). *The discovery of grounded theory.* Chicago: Aldine.

Gurin, P., & Epps, E. (1975). *Black consciousness, identity, and achievement: A study of students in historically Black colleges.* New York: John Wiley.

Hale, J. E. (1982). *Black children: Their roots, culture, and learning styles.* Baltimore, MD: Johns Hopkins University Press.

Hale, J. E. (1994). *Unbank the fire: Visions for the education of African American children.* Baltimore, MD: Johns Hopkins University Press.

Harris, W. G. (1999). Conceptions of the male familial role by African American youth revisted. In W. G. Harris & G. M. Duhon (Eds.), *The African American male perspective of barriers to success* (pp. 89–108). New York: Edwin Mellen Press.

Hill, R. B. (2003). *The strengths of Black families.* Lanham, MD: University Park Press.

Hoffman, K., Llagas, C., & Synder, T. D. (2003). *Status and trends in the education of Blacks.* Washington, DC: U.S. Department of Education, National Center for Educational Statistics.

Holstein, J. A., & Gubrium, J. F. (1995). *The active interview.* Thousand Oaks, CA: Sage.

Howard, T. C. (2002). Hearing footsteps in the dark: African American students' descriptions of effective teachers. *Journal of Education for Students Placed At Risk, 7,* 425–444.

Howard, T. C. (2008). Who really cares? The Disenfranchisement of African American Males in PreK–12 schools: A critical race theory perspective. *Teachers College Record, 110,* 954–985.

Hucks, D. C. (2008). *New visions of collective achievement: The cross-generational schooling experiences of African American males* (Doctoral dissertation). Available from ProQuest Dissertations and Theses database (UMI No. 3332512)

Hughes, R., & Bonner, II, F. A. (2006). Leaving Black males behind: Debunking the myths of meritocratic education. *Journal of Race and Policy, 2,* 76–87.

Hutchinson, J. F. (1997). *Cultural portrayals of African Americans: Creating and ethnic/racial identity.* Westport, CT: Bergin & Garvey.

Jackson, J. F. L., & Moore, J. L. III. (2006). African American males in education: Endangered or ignored? *Teachers College Record, 108,* 201–205.

Kohn, A. (1999). *The schools our children deserve: Moving beyond traditional classrooms and "tougher standards."* New York: Houghton Mifflin.

Kozol, J. (2005). *The shame of the nation: The restoration of apartheid schooling in America.* New York: Crown.

Ladson-Billings, G. (1994). *The dreamkeepers: Successful teaching of African American children.* San Francisco: Jossey Bass.

Ladson-Billings, G. (1995). Toward a theory of culturally relevant pedagogy. *American Educational Research Journal, 32,* 465–491.

Laubasher, L. (2005). Toward a (de)constructive psychology of African American men. *Journal of Black Psychology. 31,* 111–129.

Lawler, S. (2002). Narrative in social research. In T. May (Ed.). Qualitative research in education (pp. 242–258). Thousand Oaks, CA: Sage.

Lewis, A. (1966). *The second American revolution: A first-hand account of the struggle for civil rights.* London: Faber.

Lewis, C. W., & Moore, J. L. III. (2008). African American Students in K–12 Urban Educational Settings. *Urban Education, 43*(2), 123–126. doi: 10.1177/00420859083141147

Lincoln, Y., & Guba, E. (1985). *Naturalistic inquiry.* Newbury Park, CA: Sage.

Lofland, J., & Lofland, L. H. (1995). *Analyzing social setting: A guide to qualitative observation and analysis* (3rd ed.) New York: Wadsworth.

Majors, R., & Billson, J. (1992). *Cool pose: The dilemma of Black Manhood in America.* New York: Lexington Books.

Meier, D. (2002). *In schools we trust: Creating communities of learning in an era of testing and standardization.* Boston: Beacon.

Mincy, R. (2006). *Black males left behind.* Washington, DC: Urban Institute.

Moore, J. L. III. (2006). A qualitative investigation of African American males' career trajectory in engineering: Implications for teachers, school counselors, and parents. *Teachers College Record. 108,* 246–266.

Moynihan, D. P. (1965). Employment, income and the ordeal of the Negro family. *Daedalus, 94,* 745–769.

National Center for Education Statistics. (2007). *National assessment of educational progress: The nation's report card 2007.* Retrieved from http://www.nces.ed.gov/nationsreportcard

National Urban League .(2008). *The state of Black America 2007: Portrait of the Black male.* New York: Author.

Neblett, E. W., Chavous, T. M., Nguyên, H. X., & Sellers, R. M. (2009). "Say It Loud-I'm Black and I'm Proud": Parents' messages about race, racial discrimination, and academic achievement in African American boys. *The Journal of Negro Education 78,* 246–262.

No Child Left Behind Act of 2001, 20 U.S.C. § 6319 (2008).

Noguera, P. A. (1996). Responding to the crisis confronting California's Black male youth: Providing support without furthering marginalization. *The Journal of Negro Education, 65,* 219–236.

Noguera, P. A. (2003). The trouble with Black boys: The role and influence of environmental and cultural factors on the academic performance of African American males. *Urban Education, 38,* 431–459.

Noguera, P. A. (2008). *The trouble with Black boys . . . and other reflections on race, equity and the future of public education.* San Francisco: Jossey Bass.

Ogbu, J. U. (1974). *The next generation.* New York: Academic Press.

Ogbu, J. U. (1997). Understanding the school performance of urban African Americans: Some essential background knowledge. In H. Walberg, O. Reyes, & R. Weissberg (Eds.), *Children and youth: Interdisciplinary perspectives.* (pp. 190–222). London: Sage.

Osborne, J. W. (1997). Race and academic disidentification. *Journal of Educational Psychology, 89,* 728–735.

Osborne, J. W. (1999). Unraveling underachievement among African American boys from an identification with academics perspective. *The Journal of Negro Education, 68,* 555–565.

Perry, T., Steele, C., & Hilliard, A. III. (2003). *Young, gifted, and Black: Promoting high achievement among African American students.* Boston, MA: Beacon Press.

Pluviose, D. (2008). Remedying the Black male "crisis." *Diverse Issues in Higher Education, 25*, 5.

Polite, V. C. (1999). A cup runneth over: Personal reflections on the Black male experience. In *African American males in school and society*. New York: Teachers College.

Polite, V. C., & Davis, J. (1999). *African American males in school and society: Practices and policies for effective education*. New York: Teachers College Press.

Rowley, L. L., & Bowman, P. J. (2009). Risk, protection, and achievement disparities among African American males: Cross-generation theory, research, and comprehensive intervention. *The Journal of Negro Education, 78*, 305–320.

Rubin, H., & Rubin, I. (1995). *Qualitative interviewing: The art of hearing data*. Thousand Oaks, CA: Sage.

Sampson, W. A. (2002). *Black student achievement: How much do family and school really matter?* Lanham, MD: Scarecrow.

Scanzoni, J. H. (1971). *The Black family in modern society*. Boston, MA: Allyn & Bacon, Inc.

Schott Foundation for Public Education (2008). Given half a chance: The Schott 50-state report on public education and Black males. Retrieved from www. blackboysreport.org

Scott, J. W. (1997). Making a way out of no way. In C. Johnson & J. McCluskey, Jr. (Eds.), *Black men speaking* (pp. 1–28). Bloomington, IN: Indiana University Press.

Sealey-Ruiz, Y. (2007). Rising above reality: The voices of reentry Black mothers and their daughters. *The Journal of Negro Education, 76*, 141–152.

Sewell, T. (2000). *Black masculinities and schooling: How Black boys survive modern schooling*. London: Trentham Books.

Stack, C. B. (1997). *All our kin: Strategies for survival in a Black Community*. New York: Basic Books.

Sleeter, C. (2001). *Culture, difference and power*. New York: Teachers College Press.

Steele, C. (1992). Race and schooling of African Americans. *Atlantic Monthly, 4*, 68–78.

Steele, C. (1997). A threat in the air: How stereotypes shape intellectual identity and performance. *American Psychologist, 52*, 613–629.

Steele, S. (1990). *The content of our character: A new vision of race in America*. New York: Harper Collins.

Steele, S. (1998). *A dream deferred: The second betrayal of Black freedom in America*. New York: Harper Collins.

Swanson, D. P., Cunningham, M., & Spencer, M. B. (2003). Black males' structural conditions, achievement patterns, normative needs, and opportunities. *Urban Education, 38*, 608–633.

Tate, W. (1994). From inner to ivory tower: Does my voice matter in the academy? *Urban Education, 29*, 245–269.

Thompson, G. (2003). *What African American parents want educators to know*. Westport, CT: Praeger.

Thompson, G. (2004). *Through ebony eyes: What teachers need to know but are afraid to ask about African American students*. San Francisco, CA: Jossey-Bass.

Toldson, I. A. (2008). *Breaking barriers: Plotting the path to academic success for school-aged African American males*. Washington, DC: Congressional Black Caucus Foundation, Inc.

United States Bureau of Justice Statistics (2000). Correctional Populations in the United States, 2001. U.S. Department of Justice. Washington, D.C. Retrieved from www.ojp.usdoj.gov/bjs/

United States Census Bureau (2003). School Enrollment Data, Census 2000. U.S. Department of Commerce, Economics, and Statistical Administration. Washington, D.C. Retrieved from www.census.gov/

Watson, J. (2006 August). Scholars and activists debate the 'crisis of young Black males.' *Diverse Issues in Higher Education. 23,* 8–9.

Weiss, R. (1995). *Learning from strangers: The art and method of qualitative interview studies.* New York: Free Press.

Willie, C. V., & Reddick, R. J. (2003). *A new look at Black families* (5th ed.).Walnut Creek, CA: Altamira Press.

Wolcott, H. F. (2001). *Writing up qualitative research* (2nd ed.). Thousand Oaks, CA: Sage.

CHAPTER 4

YOUNG SCHOLARS

African American Males
and Academic Identity Development

Robert W. Simmons, III and Cheryl Moore-Thomas
Loyola University

Audra Watson
City University of New York

Academic identity, which is socially and culturally constructed through interactions within and across activities, spaces, and time, contributes to the way
students think of themselves as learners and behave in educational settings
(Kane, 2011; Murrell 2007). Academic identity contributes to students' general academic success and professional goals (Murrell, 2007). In light of this
important connection, this chapter examines African American males' academic identity development. Using the lens of historical, institutional and sociocultural factors, consideration is given to the discourses and practices that
affect the academic identity development of African American male students.
Both school-based and community-based factors that facilitate healthy development are discussed and examined as they are operationalized in current
programs and educational practices. In conclusion, this chapter discusses the

Teacher Education and Black Communities, pages 87–98
Copyright © 2014 by Information Age Publishing

unique and substantive contribution facilitation of healthy academic identity could have for the achievement of African American males and their presence in today's schools as teachers, educational leaders, and agents of social change. Examples of educational enterprises that have effectively created a space for the healthy academic identity development of African American males are discussed.

> *There is nothing wrong with our young men.*
> *They just need the right kind of supports and people believing in them,*
> *and they can go and manifest their greatness like everybody else.*
>
> —David Banks

And the booming voice from the room said—you are somebody. And the students responded—I am somebody. This call and response lasted for 15 minutes between this African American male teacher and his all African American male class in an eighth grade social studies classroom in a large, urban city in the Midwest. As I observed this interaction it became clear that Smitherman's (1977) assertion that the call and response interactions commonly found in African American culture are providing these students an opportunity to be encouraged by someone who looks like them and sounds like them. With class ending I noticed how this young twenty-something teacher with long dreadlocks gave an index card to each of his students as they left. On each card was the following quote by Dr. Benjamin Mays— "The tragedy of life doesn't lie in not reaching your goal. The tragedy lies in having no goal to reach." The goals he had in mind for them were not things measured on a standardized test but goals deeply rooted in his belief about education but also getting more African American male teachers— "I can't see more of me in teaching unless they see themselves as learners, scholars, and intellectuals."

The commitment of the previously discussed teacher isn't anything new when one considers Walker and Tompkins' (2004) assertion that the legacy of African American teachers, dating back to legally segregated schooling practices, was grounded in efforts to provide African American children with encouragement and wise counsel. Furthermore, specific to African American males teachers, they have demonstrated a commitment to social change (Lynn, 2006) while also affirming the socio-emotional needs of African American youth (Lynn & Jennings, 2009) and contributing to humanity (Lewis, 2006). Despite their passion and willingness to serve African American males comprise less than 2% of the teaching force (Lewis, 2006). In an effort to increase their numbers numerous collaborations between colleges and universities, schools districts, and state departments of education have materialized. While these efforts have produced some results through programs like *Call Me MISTER* (Clemson University); MenTeach (Minnesota); African American Males into Teaching Program (Howard University); Men

Equipped to Nurture (Bowie State University); Griot Program (Detroit, Marygrove College) (Brown & Butty, 1999; Lewis, 2006; Zeichner, 2003), we have continued to struggle to increase the number of African American males who become teachers.

The larger issue associated with increasing the number of African American male teachers lies in their K–12 educational experiences as students. As significant segments of the American public have expressed a view of African American males with fear and indifference (Spencer, 2001), the quality of life for many has existed at the bottom of many measures of success—overrepresentation in the prison system and consistent racial profiling by law enforcement officials (Parks & Hughey, 2010); high rates of illiteracy (Zamani-Gallaher & Polite, 2010) and graduation rates as low as 27% in the Detroit Public Schools (Schott Foundation for Public Education, 2010). As a result, far too many African American males are being rendered obsolete by our educational system. As such, the authors of this paper would like to contribute to this discussion by suggesting that efforts to increase the number of African American teachers are meaningless unless we ensure their academic identities are sufficiently nurtured.

It is our intention to ground our discussion in a psychological theoretical framework grounded in extant literature that focuses on the academic identity development of African American males during their K–12 experiences. As the first step toward becoming a teacher requires the successful completion of an accredited secondary education program, we believe that it's imperative to ensure these young men have their academic identities nurtured and supported. As the observations from the teacher in the all male classroom demonstrated, supporting the academic identity development of African American males in schools is linked to such things as discourses and practices in schools as well as their views about the future possibilities for their own lives (Zirkel, 2002).

It is our intention to articulate a view of academic identity development using the lens of historical, institutional and sociocultural factors. Additionally, consideration is given to the discourses and practices that affect the academic identity development of African American male students. Both school-based and community-based factors that facilitate healthy development are discussed and examined as they are operationalized in current programs and educational practices. In conclusion, this chapter discusses the unique and substantive contribution facilitation of healthy academic identity could have for the achievement of African American males and their presence in today's schools as teachers, educational leaders, and agents of social change. By focusing on specific practices embedded in school and nonschool based enterprises we offer insights into current practices being animated in the lives of African American males.

GROUNDING THE ACADEMIC IDENTITY DEVELOPMENT
OF AFRICAN AMERICAN MALES

Academic identity, which is socially and culturally constructed through interactions within and across activities, spaces and time, contributes to the ways students think of themselves as learners and the ways they behave in educational settings (Kane, 2011; Murrell, 2007). Academic identity contributes to students' general academic success and professional goals (Murrell, 2007), and begins to explain how they make sense of themselves and is made sense of by others (Kane, 2011). There is general agreement among educators and researchers that academic identity influences the strategies students practice and their resultant academic achievement (Irving & Hudley, 2008; Was & Issacson, 2008; Whiting, 2006).

While there are a variety of theories of academic identity construction, most have emerged from the foundational study of identity construction by Erikson (1963) and Marcia (1993). The work of these theorists suggests that during periods of personal examination, typically thought to occur in adolescence and early adulthood, individuals develop by making choices about their values and beliefs, experiencing crises or deeply significant personal experiences related to those choices, and exploring options. The process of identity development immediately and over the long term informs interactions, decisions, strategies and life choices. As a specific outgrowth of this work, Marcia (1993) identified four identity statuses that individuals navigate during development. The first, *identity foreclosure,* is marked by the adoption of the values and beliefs of significant others. *Identity diffusion,* the second status, occurs when individuals have no intentional direction because they have not yet experienced a developmental crisis that spurs commitment to a particular set of values or beliefs. The third status, *identity moratorium,* involves an experienced, personalized crisis, which leads to a gradual exploration of values, beliefs and choices. *Identity achievement,* the fourth identity status identified by Marcia, occurs when an individual's developmental crisis leads to a personal commitment to values, beliefs and choices with the intent to pursue particular, self-selected outcomes.

Moving from this broad-spectrum work on the construction of identity, Berzonsky (1997) made a significant contribution to the academic identity literature by suggesting that students' identity processing styles affect their academic achievement. Specifically, Berzonsky (1985) found that students with foreclosed identity which is marked by the taking on of values and beliefs of significant others were likely to be underachievers in college while those students who had reached achieved identities by college age were more successful choosing, pursuing and attaining academic goals. This important research finding linked cognitive and school-related practices to academic identity development theory and models.

Was and Issacson (2008), in pursuit of more clearly understanding and measuring academic identity, developed the Academic Identity Measure (AIM). The AIM distinguishes four statues of academic identity: *foreclosed academic identity status* (the student takes on the academic values of important people in his/her life); *diffuse academic identity status* (the student fails to explore and make decisions about academic goals and values); *moratorium academic identity status* (the student navigates academic uncertainty and tries to reach conclusions about academic goals and values); and *achieved academic identity status* (the student personally commits to a set of academic values formed after a period of exploration). Importantly, Was and Issacson's research conceptualized academic identity as a construct separate and distinct from global identity investigated by Erikson (1963) and Marcia (1993).

While this conceptualization of academic identity and its development is significant, other models of academic identity also exist. Noteworthy are the models that conceptualize academic identity development as a nonlinear, recursive process through which people gain a sense of their academic selves by responding in the moment and in light of given historical, institutional and sociocultural forces. It is through these dynamic interactions that individuals practice and perform in ways that shape their ever-changing stories or narrative of self. Moreover, members of particular communities, such as African American males, use the resources and contexts of their day-to-day lives to construct and reconstruct culturally relevant and embedded narratives of identity and ways of being (Kane, 2011). These ways of being, narratives and practices are not to be understood or explained in comparison with those of other communities or by applying deficit approaches, but through strength-based, identity affirming lenses that recognize and value authentic, community specific contexts and practices.

The Situated-Mediated Identity theory posited by Murrell (2007) suggests that identity is a work in progress that in not achieved in adolescences, but continually enacted as we move from one setting to another. It is rooted in who we are, what we do, and how we choose to invest in what we are doing. It draws together basic principles of social identity, critical theory and communication. Murrell suggests that academic identity is explored in a person-in-context framework in a variety of broad sweeping contexts including schools, homes and communities. Academic identity, therefore, is simply not something that is developed by students in schools, but something that students develop in homes, on the streets, and in relationships. Furthering Murrell's understanding of Situated-Mediated Identity Theory, Stinson (2006) uses mathematics to animate Murrell's view that students' academic identities are constructed through a multiplicity of interactions— homes, streets, community, etc. Stinson's study of African American males academic identities in mathematics reinforces Murrell's assertion in that, in this case, a mathematics academic identity isn't something that remains static but best understood in context, and negotiated and developed over time. Furthermore, Stinson indicates that when given space to engage in a discourse that opposes the alleged inferiority of African American males in mathematics African American males effectively "articulated a view that could succeed in spite of the structural deficiencies or inequities" (p. 21).

This model may have particular relevance for African American males because it accounts for the acquisition of cultural practices and notes the importance and roles of self-efficacy, intellectual agency, and emotional resilience. The complex nature of models of academic identity that account for contributions of context can be found in Graham and Anderson's (2008) study of African American male students in an urban high school. Their study discussed the interplay of students' emerging academic identity with the context of their cultural heritage; Black identity; local orientation including geography and time; and the beliefs, values and teachings of their significant others (i.e., parents, guardians, teachers, administrators and counselors). Corroborating the use of a context rich model for understanding the academic identity construction of African American males, Howard, Flennaugh and Terry (2012) suggest that educators and researchers consider the influence and intersections of the collective, social narrative of media and the public; gender (see Wright, 2011); and class. Moreover, while recognizing the contributions of cultural community and context to academic identity construction, Howard, Flennaugh and Terry remind us that African American males are not a monolithic community. Those of us committed to understanding the academic identity development of African American males must continually work to hear and affirm the individual voices of African American males as they unfold and navigate the unique and critical narratives of their academic identity trajectories (Wright, 2011).

SCHOOL AND COMMUNITY BASED FACTORS IMPACTING ACADEMIC IDENTITY DEVELOPMENT

As we aim to unpack some of the factors that impact the academic identity development of African American males, the previous discussion of Murrell's (2007) Situated Mediated Identity Theory offers a pathway. Along this pathway that we believe Murrell's work has provided, the role of agency amongst African American males is critical. At the core of our understanding of agency, based on our own experiences as educators and researchers, as well as the work of Murrell, caring is essential. As such, we believe that the caring that's missing in the schooling experiences of far too many African American males, which limits their ability to develop a sense of agency, is located in their individual interactions with teachers as well as a system that doesn't provide them with access to quality programs.

Lee & Ransom (2011) issued a report for the College Board that substantiated numerous claims related to the systemic failure of African American males. While the report discussed all males of color throughout the paper, they gave significant attention to the ways that schools systemically destroy the dreams of a disproportionate number of African American boys by placing them into special education or under enrolling them in gifted or honors courses. Furthering a discussion of the systemic role in limiting the academic identity development, Darling-Hammond & Bransford (2007) posit that the deep inequities in the allocation of resources to schools serving low income and students of color contributes to their marginalization. These systemic issues, structural and cultural, have a direct impact on the sense of agency that these students need in order to build a solid academic identity (Noguera, 2003) as well as their understanding of who matters in schools (Darling-Hammond & Bransford, 2007). Aside from the systemic explanation for what's contributing the academic identity development, Murrell (2008) ask us to also consider popularly held notions of the decline of racism. This "new racism," that is at play in our public schools is, in our estimation, a cultural racism that is a fundamental part of American cultural, social, and political life. As noted by Murrell (2008), "cultural racism inheres in those practices and policies that outwardly intend to deal with issues of equity and difference, but end up maintaining or increasing the disadvantage of the subordinate group" (p. 7).

SOURCES OF HOPE AND INSPIRATION: A PROGRAMATIC EFFORT TIED TO ACADEMIC IDENTITY DEVELOPMENT

Fortunately, there are individuals and organizations who are giving voice to these issues through their scholarship, work in classrooms, and development of more all-encompassing supports for our African American males. Ginwright (2010) who has worked toward the "radical healing" of black youth includes care as a critical component of radical healing. He contends that care "moves beyond coping and surviving and encourages black youth to thrive and flourish as they transform community conditions" (Ginwright, 2010, p. 57). Through *Leadership Excellence*, his community-based organization, Ginwright has worked with more than 40,000 African American young people in California. Built on a foundation of caring relationships, community, developing critical consciousness about their world, and connecting students to their culture, Ginwright's program is supporting youngsters, many of whom are African American males, to thrive academically and to positively impact their communities.

Duncan-Andrade and Morrell (2008) have sought to create contexts in which African American males and other urban youth succeed in classrooms through their use of critical pedagogy beyond classroom. Through their careful creation and enactment of a literacy curriculum that enables youngsters to "understand, interpret, and produce in the Language of Wider Communication" (p. 50), they use canonical texts, popular films, and music to integrate Freire's "problem-posing pedagogy." Accordingly, they have managed to foster the richer exchange of ideas and simultaneously enable students to sift through school knowledge using their lived experiences as the primary lens.

One Example of What Works—Eagle Academy

Building on the previous examples, Eagle Academy secondary schools serve as both a counterpoint and a targeted approach to improving the experiences faced by many African American males in the nation's schools. This unique network of public schools is deeply embedded within the communities they serve and is having significant success in preparing future generations of African American males as scholars and leaders within their communities. Founded in 2004 by One Hundred Black Men, Inc. and The Eagle Academy Foundation, the first Eagle Academy for Young Men School opened in the south Bronx under the leadership of Principal David Banks. The Eagle Academy School for Law, Government, and Justice, now both a middle and high school, was supported by city advocates concerned about the poor graduation rates and other academic statistics of African American males in New York City public schools. Schools have now opened in Brooklyn, Queens and Newark, with a mission to facilitate academic excellence, leadership, and character development. A fifth school opened in Harlem in September 2013.

Eagle's promise is the result of carefully selected, highly skilled teachers who serve in the role of coaches simultaneously maintaining high expectations, attending to the pulse of the school's social environment, and adeptly utilizing culturally and gender-relevant pedagogies to engage Eagle scholars during and beyond the school day. Professional development is particularly focused on promoting the academic and social success of young men through strategic approaches to engagement and motivation.

At the core of Eagle's success is the widely held belief of school administrators, faculty, and support staff that more extensive engagement with African American males is needed to foster success. As such, three programs serve to complement the traditional school day. The first is a daily Extended Learning Forum. Between the end of the regularly scheduled school day and 5:30 p.m. each evening, students participate in mandatory academic groups in which they complete homework or receive tutoring as necessary. The second takes place two Saturdays a month during which individualized academic support is provided to the young men. Finally, a Summer Bridge program is mandatory for all entering freshmen to acclimate them to the increased cognitive demands of high school. Parents of new students must attend two family workshops that address learning skills and parenting styles, respectively. Other programmatic elements that serve to facilitate student success include: integral roles for family and community in the lives of the young men; a mission shared across multiple stakeholders; engaging curricula; and clearly defined behavioral standards.

Also integral to the success of young men at Eagle is a deliberately planned and executed mentoring program that is provided through graduation. The mentoring curriculum provides Eagle scholars with multiple models of African American male success that are frequently absent in media and, at times, in their own lives. Mentoring takes varied forms including one-on-one mentoring, small group sessions, and Saturday morning convocations. Moreover, at the high school level mentoring takes on added significance and is accompanied by a peer-mentoring framework in which seniors mentor sophomores, while juniors mentor their freshmen peers.

Eagle Academies now have had approximately 4,000 students in New York City alone which attests to its potential to reach significant numbers of young African American men. More importantly, however, the schools have nearly doubled graduation rates for young men of color in the New York City public school system. Currently, the average graduation rate for the four schools is 84%, with 90% of the 2010 graduating class heading to four-year colleges and/or universities. Founder David Banks, while pleased with the model's success, is not prepared to replicate the model through developing additional schools. Instead, he provides an annual Professional Development Institute in an effort to share strategies and insights for implementing the components of the Eagle model in other locales.

CONCLUSION

Despite continual efforts at school reform and change over the past three decades, we have yet to positively alter the outcomes for large numbers of African American males. If we don't take on Noguera's (2003) assessment that "changing the culture and structure of schools such that African American male students come to regard them as sources of support" (p. 455), their academic identity will never be developed. While the mainstream media and certain segments of the African American community propagate a mythology that something is wrong with "those African American boys" we stand against such assertions. It is our contention that the academic identity of African American males must be nurtured through systemic and individual efforts. The lack of attentiveness to consequences of racial inequities in schools as well as the failure to fundamentally restructure our educational institutions or school-based supplementary has resulted in merely symbolic attempts to adequately support their needs. We believe that we can offer three concrete next steps. First, we must lift up and exemplify those individuals and programs, like those illustrated in this chapter, that are succeeding with our young men. In this way, we will accurately identify the true nature of the problem and provide a markedly different representation of African American males. Second, we must seek to establish and financially support additional models such as these that have proven to be successful. To do this we must insist that our schools are staffed with personnel who know how to love, care for, and provide high academic standards for our sons rather than those whose practices are tied to notions of Black inferiority or color-blindness (Murrell, 2008). Simultaneously our schools must create structures within and beyond the school day that nurture these students through mentoring, community service, and cultural activities. Such opportunities should not be available only to a mere precious few. Finally, we must articulate for those who suggest that we need more African American males in classrooms as teachers that this effort doesn't sit as an isolated enterprise from efforts to nurture the academic identity of African American males.

REFERENCES

Berzonsky. M. D. (1985). Diffusion within Marcia's identity status paradigm: Does it foreshadow academic problems? *Journal of Youth and Adolescence, 14,* 527–538.

Berzonsky. M. D. (1997). Identity development, control theory and self regulation: An individual differences perspective. *Journal of Adolescent Research, 12,* 347–353.

Brown, J. W., & Butty, J. M. (1999). Factors that influence African American male teachers' educational and career aspirations: Implications for school districts recruitment and retention efforts. *Journal of Negro Education, 68,* 280–292.

Darling-Hammond, L., & Bransford, J. (Eds.). (2007). *Preparing teachers for a changing world: What teachers should learn and be able to do.* San Francisco: John Wiley & Sons, Inc.

Duncan-Andrade, J., & Morrell, E. (2008). *Possibilities for moving from theory to practice in urban schools.* New York, NY: Peter Lang Publishing.

Erikson, E. (1963). *Childhood and Society* (2nd ed.). New York: Norton.

Ginwright, S. (2010). *Black youth rising: Activism & radical healing in urban America.* New York, NY: Teachers College Press.

Graham, A., & Anderson, K. (2008). "I have to be three steps ahead": Academically gifted African American male students in an urban high school on the tension between ethnic and academic identity. *Urban Review, 40,* 472–499.

Howard, T. C., Flennaugh, T. K., & Terry, C. L. (2012). Black males, social imagery, and the disruption of identities. *Educational Foundations, 26,* 85–102.

Irving, M. A., & Hudley, C. (2008). Cultural identification and academic achievement among African American males. *Journal of Advanced Academics, 19,* 676–698.

Kane, J. (2011). Young African American children constructing academic and disciplinary identities in an urban science classroom. *Science Education, 96,* 457–487.

Lee, J., & Ransom, T. (2011). The educational experience of young men of color: A review of research, pathways and progress. Retrieved from http://advocacy. collegeboard.org/sites/default/files/EEYMC-ResearchReport_0.pdf

Lewis, C. (2006). African American male teachers in public schools: An examination of three urban school districts. *Teachers College Record, 108,* 224–245.

Lynn, M. (2006). Dancing between two worlds: A portrait of the life of a black male teacher in South Central LA. *International Journal of Qualitative Studies in Education, 19,* 221–242.

Lynn, M., & Jennings, M. (2009). Power, politics, and critical race pedagogy: A critical race analysis of Black male teachers' pedagogy. *Race, Ethnicity & Education, 12*(2), 173–196.

Marcia, J. E. (1993). The status of statuses: Research review. In J. E. Marcia, A. S. Waterman, D. R. Matteson, S. L. Archer, & J. L. Orlofsky (Eds.), *Ego identity: A handbook for psychology research* (pp. 22–41). New York: Springer-Verlag.

Murrell, P. (2007). *African centered pedagogy: Developing schools of achievement for African American children.* Albany, NY: State University of New York Press.

Murrell, P. C. Jr. (2008). *Race, culture, and schooling: Identities of achievement in multicultural urban schools.* New York, NY: Routledge.

Noguera, P. A. (2003). The trouble with Black boys: The role and influence of environmental and cultural factors on the academic performance of African American males. *Urban Education, 38*(4), 431–459.

Parks, G., & Hughey, M. (Eds.). (2010). *12 angry men: True stories of being a Black man in America today.* New York: The New Press.

Schott Foundation for Public Education. (2010). *Yes we can: The Schott 50 state report on public education and Black males.* Retrieved from http://blackboysreport.org/

Smitherman, G. (1977). *Talkin and Testifyin: The Language of Black America.* Wayne State University Press.

Spencer, M. B. (2001). Identity, achievement, orientation, and race: Lessons learned about the normative developmental experiences of African American males. In W. Watkins, J. Lewis, & V. Chou (Eds.), *Race and education: The roles of history and society in educating African American students* (pp. 100–127). Boston: Allyn and Bacon.

Stinson, D. W. (2006). African American male adolescents, schooling (and mathematics): Deficiency, rejection, and achievement. *Review of Educational Research, 76*(4), 477–506.

Walker, V., & Tompkins, R. (2004). Caring in the past: The case of a southern segregated African American school. In V. Walker & J. Snarey (Eds.), *Race-ing moral formation: African American perspectives on care and justice* (pp. 77–92). New York: Teachers College Press.

Was, C. A., & Isaacson, R. M. (2008). The development of a measure of academic identity status. *Journal of Research in Education, 18,* 94–105.

Whiting, G. W. (2006). Enhancing culturally diverse males' scholar identity: Suggestions for Educators of gifted students. *Gifted Child Today, 29*, 46–50.

Wright, B. L. (2011). I know who I am, do you? Identity achievement of successful African American male adolescents in an urban pilot high school in the United States. *Urban Education, 46*, 611–638.

Zamani-Gallaher, E., & Polite, V. (2010). Preface. In E. Zamani-Gallaher & V. Polite (Eds.), *The state of the African American male* (pp. xix–xxvi). East Lansing, MI: Michigan State University Press.

Zeichner, K. (2003). The adequacies and inadequacies of three current strategies to recruit, prepare, and retain the best teachers for all students. *Teachers College Record, 105*(3), 490–519.

Zirkel, S. (2002). Is there a place for me? Role models and achievement among White students and students of color. *Teachers' College Record, 104*, 357–376.

CHAPTER 5

INVISIBLE HANDS

Seeing and Noticing Black and Latino Male Youth

Yolanda Sealey-Ruiz
Teacher's College, Columbia University

Keisha Allen
Teacher's College, Columbia

Erik Nolan
UMOJA Network for Young Men

Invisible Hands
Black and Brown boys raise their hands.
We believe the world is ours. Or can be.
We dream that raised hands mean a brighter future,
We believe that raised hands mean raised voices.
We want to tell our stories, too.

But what happens when the system
that taught us to raise our hands

Teacher Education and Black Communities, pages 99–115
Copyright © 2014 by Information Age Publishing
All rights of reproduction in any form reserved.

renders them invisible?
What happens when our hands,
inflicted with wounds from a racist society,
are seen as dangerous weapons?

We want to wonder aloud.
We want to ask questions.
We want to know if you were there
when it was decided that our beliefs
and dreams were a threat to ourselves
and others.
—Erik Nolan, UMOJA founder and mentor

INTRODUCTION

Males of color often talk about how they are made to feel invisible in school settings and society (Fergus, Hurtado, & Noguera, 2012). In his poem "Invisible Hands," Erik Nolan reflects on his experience of feeling ignored as a student. He imagines that he and other Black and Latino males are overlooked in schools because adults are not willing to accept that they are part of a system that does not support Black and Latino boys. Ralph Ellison evoked a similar image in 1952, with the publication of his epic novel, *Invisible Man*, in which he cemented into the public's imagination the trope of being Black, male, and invisible. In the novel's opening lines Ellison's protagonist tells us:

> I am an invisible man. No, I am not a spook like those who haunted Edgar Allan Poe; nor am I one of your Hollywood-movie ectoplasms. I am a man of substance, of flesh and bone, fiber and liquids—and I might even be said to possess a mind. I am invisible, understand, simply because people refuse to see me. (Prologue, 1)

Ironically, Ellison's character spends years trying to make himself visible to others, and once he is seen he must go into hiding to save his life.

This tension between the binary of invisibility and hypervisibility (Collins, 2005) is one many Black and Latino males negotiate daily in their school contexts (Sealey-Ruiz & Greene, 2011; Sealey-Ruiz, Noguera, & Handville, 2008). Today's educational climate presents a host of challenges for young Black and Latino males (Watson, Sealey-Ruiz, Jackson, in press; Knaus, 2007; Lynn, 2006; Watson, Sealey-Ruiz, & Jackson, in press; West-Olatunji, Baker, & Brooks, 2006). Black and Latino boys face a litany of stereotypes held by peers, administrators, and classrooms teachers (Haddix, 2008; Haddix & Sealey-Ruiz, 2012; Noguera, 2008; Steele & Aronson, 1995), which makes it difficult for them to be viewed as individuals who are smart, talented, complex, and have the potential to be academically successful (Ferguson, 2000; Toldson & Lewis, 2012).

The purpose of this chapter is to share insights from our experiences with an all-male mentoring program focused on the social, emotional, and academic success of its male participants. As Erik explains in his narrative, one of the main reasons he created UMOJA Network for Young Men (UMOJA) at the Sunset Hills Academy East (SHAE)[1] alternative high school in New York City, was to help disrupt the "invisibility" felt by some of the Black and Latino males who had a significant presence in the school (93% of the school's students are Black and Latino, 47% of them are male). During the years we worked with the young men of UMOJA (2009–2012) we observed how they shared similar experiences with many Black and Latino males in schools across the country who lament about being viewed through stereotypical lenses of what it means to be a young man of color in America (e.g., Caton, 2012; Harrison, Sailes, Rotich, & Bimper, 2011). These stereotypes prevent them from being viewed in positive and authentic ways, or noticed for their unique style and abilities.

In this chapter, we briefly discuss a selective body of literature associated with the misrecognition of male youth of color, and literature on seeing and noticing. In our discussion, we argue for a more nuanced way of viewing and relating to Black and Latino male students. We make a distinction between seeing, which is a passive activity, and noticing which requires deliberate attention to what one sees in order to guide future action. Next, we offer a brief vignette of Ricky, a participant in the UMOJA program. We believe that Ricky's experiences in his previous school and at SHAE, provide some insight on how young men of color, similar to Ricky, value interpersonal relationships and respect (Saez, Casado, & Wade, 2009).

Finally, we share our personal narratives about how we came to work with Black and Latino males and why we continue to engage in work in schools that seek to affirm the experiences of these youth and make them visible in positive ways. Through sharing our own stories, we hope to encourage other educators to invest time and energy in becoming an advocate for the Black and Latino young men they teach.

THE MISRECOGNITION OF BLACK AND LATINO MALE YOUTH AND EDUCATIONAL OUTCOMES

Taylor's (1994) conceptualization of recognition highlights how educational experiences of Black and Latino males may be oppressive and at times violent. For example, the way in which teachers and staff misrecognize and position Black and Latino males as social deviants, often leads to the overrepresentation of these youth in special education for behavior disorders (Gregory, Skiba, & Noguera, 2010). Taylor's conceptulization also offers an explanation for how this misrecognition by school personnel may contribute to lower educational outcomes for them. Taylor further argues that misrecognition can cause individuals to develop self-deprecating identities. In his seminal book, *The Mise-ducation of the Negro*, Woodson (1933) provides one example of the damaging outcomes of a racist system that intentionally misrecognizes Blacks. He argues:

> If you make a man feel that he is inferior, you do not have to compel him to accept an inferior status, for he will seek it himself. If you make a man think that he is justly an outcast, you do not have to order him to the back door. He will go without being told; and if there is no back door, his very nature will demand one. (p. 55)

The miseducation of young Black and Latino males in schools and in the media influences how they are perceived and positioned not only in and by society, but by themselves. The systematic miseducation and undereduca-tion of Black and Latino males have caused irreparable damage to many of them because they come to doubt their intellectual abilities and live on the margins of society. Taylor (1994) asserts that the development of our authentic self lies within our dialogical relationships with others. As we are recognized and affirmed by others, our identities are also affirmed.

Ikäheimo (2002) distinguishes among three possible meanings of rec-ognition: (a) identification, (b) acknowledgment, and (c) recognition that entails respect and esteem. We see promise in Ikäheimo's analyses of these three possible meanings of recognition, and find that they are applicable to the social, emotional, and academic development of the Black and Latino males we have worked with over time, as well as Black and Latino males featured in the literature about their schooling experiences.

In her ethnography of an ethnically and economically diverse elemen-tary school in a Midwestern U.S. city, Ferguson (2000) examines both the ways in which schools maintain social order through norms and procedures, and how images and racial myths influence the way individuals perceive Black males and Black males perceive themselves. One of her findings was that school personnel viewed Black males as either "endangered species" or "criminals," and these identifications influenced teachers' decision-making practices. These categories are not unique to this school or even schools in general; rather, they are a reflection of how males of color, and in this example, how Black males are positioned within schools.

Murrell's (2008) theory of situated-mediated identity also speaks to the ways in which identities and positionalities are constantly evolving and forming in concert with our interactions with others. He argues through his framework that Black students' academic achievement is produced through the "dynamic interplay of racial identity development and academ-ic identity development" (p. 90). Additionally, Murrell's theory complicates recognition and misrecognition by acknowledging the agency that students possess to oppose how others position them.

Unfortunately, Black and Latino males' acts of resistance to their imposed positionality seem to perpetuate how they are perceived within school and society. There is an abundance of research that examines how Black and Latino males respond to school curricula and practices that are harmful to their identity formation (Gregory, Skiba, & Noguera, 2010; Halx & Ortiz, 2011; Milner, 2013; Noguera, 2008). Regarding Black males in particular, the adoption of coping mechanisms such as Majors and Billson's (1991) cool pose is one way researchers argue that Black males protect themselves against the "annihilation" and "dehumanization" they face in school and society (Stevenson, 2004). In fact, it is a fear of nonexistence that Stevenson (2004) argues is at the heart of the enactment of anger and social conflict by Black adolescent males.

SEEING AND NOTICING
BLACK AND LATINO YOUTH IN SCHOOLS

In his article, "Seeing and noticing: An optical perspective on competitive intelligence" Michael L. Neugarten (2003) writes, "It's all about noticing. The first step of any intelligence process is not to scan, but to notice" (p. 1). Seeing is an immediate response to sense impressions. Through seeing, we match images with established schematas. Noticing, however, involves experiencing and exploiting moments with complete and full attention. It requires a set of practices for living in and hence learning from experiences that can inform future practice. To disrupt the old adage "seeing is believing," Neugarten argues it is more accurate that what we *believe* impacts what we see. For example, we suggest that when some teachers look at their Black and Latino male students, many only see stereotypes or partial representations of their identity, yet they often rely on these beliefs and this reductionist way of thinking when they engage with them (e.g., Lynn, Bacon, Totten, Bridges, & Jennings, 2010). Noticing, on the other hand, implies that a person is *paying attention.* We rarely notice unless we are being deliberate. For instance, one teacher may see a young Black or Latino male with sagging pants; this same student is known for his forceful and confident personality. The other teacher may be intimidated by this student, and read his clothing as part of a gang culture or make other judgments about his choice of clothes. Whereas, another teacher committed to noticing his or her students beyond stereotypes and performances may notice a connection between the passion in his way of being, and the role he plays in bettering his community as a youth leader in an anti-violence coalition. This same teacher may also notice that his student is an active participant in urban youth culture (Sealey-Ruiz & Greene, 2011), hence his choice of clothing. Both teachers may notice this student; however, one teacher may frame his personality and way of being as a threat, while the other recognizes it as a strength.

In his book, *Researching your own practice: The discipline of noticing*, Mason (2002) reminds us that life in the classroom passes quickly. As teachers and mentors, we are so often 'in the moment' and it becomes a challenge to be fully present and notice important details about our students at all times. As Mason notes,

> In many ways it is a relief that classroom life goes by quickly, but in many ways it is a tragedy. For the more you probe what happens, for example, by listening to audio-tapes of yourself or watching video-tapes, the more you realise the complexity of 'being taught.' The more you probe children's thinking, the more you realize how sophisticated and powerful children's thinking can be. Experience of life in general, and of classrooms in particular can become much more full and satisfying when there are occasional moments of complete and full attention, producing moments which can be re-entered. (p. 26)

If teachers and school personnel begin to take notice of their male students of color, this may facilitate connections between the performance of Black and Latino males and the structural elements in schools that pose a threat to them. These structures impose particular ways of knowing, being, and acting that are oftentimes in conflict with the ways in which these young men experience relationships and expectations in their home and school communities (Sealey-Ruiz & Lewis, 2012). As these young men realize their potential and experiment with identity and notions of masculinity, their actions and bodies are often misread. As a result, many are disproportionately placed in special education and lower-track classrooms, and are often expelled from school because of the ways in which they are seen and viewed. The focus and intent for our work with the young men of UMOJA was to present opportunities for them to know more about themselves and be known differently (Vasudevan, 2006) in their school context.

The UMOJA Network for Young Men

The UMOJA Network for Young Men (UNFYM) began in the fall of 2004 at SHAE. Erik Nolan started the group with 11 young men. The school's site director, Christine, had first conceived this initiative because she and her staff recognized the urgent need to support some young men in the school community. Erik stepped to the fore to give shape and breathe life into the group. The young men, who were predominantly Black (African American, Caribbean, and African descent) and Latino (Mexican, Puerto Rican, and Dominican), had experienced challenges in their academic and home lives. Some had brushes with the law that caused them to be on probation.

In other cases, some were being bombarded with court dates that caused disruptions in their educational progress.

UMOJA is an organization that focuses on the holistic development of young men in the SHAE community. Erik, the founder of the group, believes that young people should be academically prepared, socially smart, and emotionally strong. The young men who join the UMOJA brotherhood are transfer students from traditional high schools. Since its inception, over 100 young men have experienced UMOJA. With 93 of the young men graduating from the program, and only seven dropping out or leaving to attend another school, the group has been credited with making their experiences more tolerable and fruitful in school, and providing many of them with internship and part-time work opportunities. During our work with UMOJA the brothers met for "family group" (similar to homeroom in traditional schools) two days a week. Family group was an opportunity for them to check-in about issues related to their high school credits, progress on their PBAs (Portfolio Based Assessments), discuss the progress the young men of UMOJA were making in their personal and school lives, among other issues. It was also time the young men discussed how to grow UMOJA's membership, and what issues they needed to take to the administration on behalf of Black and Latino males in the school. UMOJA's mission was foregrounded at every meeting, and often the young men were asked to recite the mission to, "Live with Purpose, Learn with Morals, and Lead with Integrity" as a reminder for the ways in which they should behave as young men. The mission statement, created by Erik, was conceived to inspire the men to have respect for self and others; take pride in their home and school communities, and build the moral strength to make choices guided by integrity and honesty throughout their lives. Each of us supported the young men in various ways. For example, Erik conducted "family group" for two sessions during the week, and Yolanda designed and cotaught with Erik the UMOJA Readers and Writers (URW) course which the young men attended one day per week. Keisha brought her expertise on culturally responsive pedagogy to the course design process, and as Yolanda's graduate assistant, helped to identify articles and develop ideas for the URW class. The URW curriculum, guided by theory and principals of culturally responsive pedagogy, invited the young men to discuss issues that impacted or influenced their lives beyond their school experiences at SHAE.

NOTICING AS PEDAGOGY:
THE CREATION OF UMOJA READERS AND WRITERS

As we designed URW, we kept in mind that many adolescent males of color are reluctant readers and writers in high school (Kirkland, 2013). Their love for reading and writing is often not developed to its full potential. In part because most of what they read and are asked to write about in their classrooms is irrelevant to their everyday lives and/or cultural backgrounds. Quite often, there appears to be a mismatch between how these young men express themselves and the school's expectations for their communication skills (reading, writing and speaking). Many are labeled as underperforming and this often leads to feelings of failure and disconnection from school. For some, this disengagement leads to their dropping out of school. The major goal of the UMOJA Readers & Writers (URW) course was to encourage a love of reading and writing among its participants. Another goal was to empower young men as they learn how to navigate the terrain of life as well as to develop skills and confidence in speaking and expressing themselves competently in any environment.

As the participants engaged with relevant reading and writing prompts, their curiosity was piqued for reading and, as a result, they confronted multiple issues relating to school and home. The young men were vocal about how the readings offered in URW were "easier to access" and "easier to relate to" (researcher journal, 10/8/2010, 11/7/2011, 11/18/2011) when compared to the texts assigned in their regular English class. We also observed how the young men used the readings as a point of departure to examine a concept or share an experience from their own lives, furthering their connection to the literature. We observed how the curriculum welcomed the opportunity to build their overall confidence in reading, writing, thinking, and self-expression. The URW course included six elements: (a) brotherhood building activities, (b) freewriting, (c) shared reading, (d) open discussion, (e) article distribution, and (f) performance. Twice a week during a lunch period, URW sessions took place. The major projects in URW included a digital storytelling project based on their "Where I'm From" poems, and writing assignments which populated a portfolio with six themed sections: (a) self, (b) family, (c) gender/relationships, (d) community, (e) school/education, and (f) next steps/future. Some of the texts the young men read and interacted with in URW included the spoken word poem *Nigger Recan Blues* by Willie Perdomo, the novel *The House on Mango Street* by Sandra Cisneros, and the films *Coach Carter* and *Roots*.

Noticing Ricky

Ricky, one of the members of UMOJA, helped us to understand how he experienced feelings of invisibility as a male who is both Black *and* Latino. Ricky hated the school he attended before coming to SHAE. He often talked about how there were 40–45 students in each of his classes, which made it impossible for teachers to know their students. Although SHAE was a much smaller school than where Ricky came from, he believed that he would be ignored at SHAE just as he had been in his previous school. Before joining UMOJA

Ricky would cut school for weeks at a time, and when he was in school, he would often get into altercations with his teachers. When asked if he thought anyone noticed his absence at SHAE, he replied "yes, but only because they have to be recorded on the attendance sheet" (researcher journal, 10/2010).

Ricky often talked about how being a part of UMOJA made him feel seen for who he was instead of "who people think I should be" (researcher journal, 10/2010). Even though he lived with his mom and two younger brothers, at 19, Ricky considered himself emancipated.[2] He worked after school and contributed money to his household. In family group and URW, he often talked about being a father figure to his two brothers. Because of his family and work responsibility, Ricky saw himself as an adult and refused to tolerate what he experienced as "teachers talking down to me all of the time" (researcher journal (10/2010). The role Ricky played outside of SHAE made it difficult for him to allow himself to be treated as a kid while in school. He explained,

> Are you kidding me? You know how I have to hold it down at home? If you think I'm gonna let some lady talk to me like I don't have no sense and don't know what I'm doing, you've got to be out of your damn mind. I respect you. You respect me too. It goes both ways.

Ricky's relationships with many of his teachers led to him experiencing some dissonance with school. When he became frustrated he often chose to cut class or to go to work instead of school.

Ricky's story helped us to think about the many Black and Latino male youth who are often only "seen" through the lenses of absence, expulsion, suspension, truancy or underachievement. In general, the ways we see and talk about Black and Latino males in schools, social science research, and the media tend to be negative (Brown, 2011). For example, it's only a recent phenomenon for educational research to be focused on the success of Black and Latino males (Harper & Associates, 2013; Howard & Flennaugh, 2011; Toldson & Lewis, 2012), and not just their underachievement in school. We found that Ricky's two-year involvement with UMOJA helped him develop more positive experiences in school, particularly with teachers he determined were "difficult to vibe with" (researcher journal, 11/2010). Ricky has attributed his success in graduating high school to some of his teachers, but mostly to the brotherhood of UMOJA and the support he received from his mentors.

OUR JOURNEYS: WORKING WITH AND ON BEHALF OF BLACK AND LATINO MALES

In this next section we discuss why we work with and on behalf of Black and Latino males. We think it is important to speak about our intentions and commitments for doing this work. How one reads educational issues and identifies solutions is often framed by their own personal experiences, and/or the experience of young people they care about. Taken together, our individual journeys are a testimony to the ways in which educational inequities have long-term effects on those students who are marginalized and on the adults who care for them.

Yolanda's Journey

The root of my commitment to the social and academic success of Black and Latino male students dates back to the time when a primary focus of my life was playing stickball, skelzies, and hopscotch with the other kids on the streets of my South Bronx neighborhood. The experiences of my youth—the schools I attended, my teachers, the kids in the South Bronx who played with me—continue to shape and guide my research and teaching today. My memory is clear: Our classrooms were filled with mostly Black and Latino children, but nearly all of our teachers were White. I remember the girls were taken care of—recommended to skip a grade or placed in "enrichment" programs on Saturday afternoons or during the summer. However, I also remember some of my smartest and most energetic playmates falling behind; especially vivid are the boys who could keep scores in their heads, outwit adults at card games, and grocery shop for their mothers. These were the kids—Black and Latino boys—who headed to the special education classes once we entered the school building. I recall many of them fading in my rear-view mirror as I moved on to high school and college. I knew something was deeply wrong with this picture in my schools, and this knowledge remained with me and motivated me to choose education as my focus in graduate school.

My first teaching position was at Manhattan Comprehensive Night and Day High School, an alternative high school in New York City serving mostly Black and Latino males who were overage and undercredited and had been kicked out of their previous schools: schools with 40 students or more in one classroom—schools that ultimately failed them. My experiences with these young men, who were academically wounded and emotionally discouraged, were completely positive. They responded to my instruction, progressed, and stayed out of trouble; many graduated high school. My colleagues and I gave students the support structures and programs that served their needs. We also had an understanding of who our students were and from where they came. We saw them as whole beings neglected by their previous schools, and as teenagers who were going through a rough patch filled with obstacles, which we wanted to mitigate as much as possible. Our goal was to find ways to reach our students and ensure they had the tools to take care of themselves and become productive citizens.

Many years later when I began to volunteer at Sunset Hills Academy East (SHAE) with the young men of UMOJA, I carried with me the belief that schools have the ability (and the responsibility) to make positive change for overage and undercredited male students of color. From 2009–2011, I spent time with Black and Latino males who are a part of UMOJA. During my work with the young them, I have learned that *noticing* them is harder than I thought. Even on my best days, the education literature that I spend so much time reading overwhelms me with statistics and visual imprints of who these young men are supposed to be. As I work alongside them while they labor against stereotypical images of their identities at home and in their communities, I realize that how I see them is influenced by these statistics and images. I am working to develop a discipline *noticing* these young men, and as I do so, I am learning so much about myself as an educator.

My hope for Black and Latino males is that they have equitable opportunities to receive an education that prepares them for full citizenship. I also hope—and this is a necessary complementary component—that America transforms its attitude toward children of color in our public schools, especially our male students of color. The work I do in schools, and particularly the work I have done with the young men of UMOJA, is helping to create a world for them, as much as it is for myself, and my own daughters. The ways in which most urban schools are currently treating Black and Latino males negatively impacts their future life chances, and also diminishes society by creating the absence of whole and visible Black and Latino men.

Keisha's Journey

My commitment to studying and improving the educational experiences and outcomes of Black and Latino males has been inspired by my own desire to understand the qualitative differences and outcomes of my two younger brothers' educational experiences, as well as my own. While I excelled academically and was always embraced by my teachers during my K–12 schooling, my brothers often either managed to eke by or struggled to simply pass their courses.

This pattern was also repeated with other young Black men in our high school as well as with my own Black male students once I became a teacher.

My work done on behalf and with Black and Latino male youth is creating a space in which they can become their best selves. It is a space that fosters and informs them of the history and legacy of their ancestors' struggles and successes, so that they can fill their store of cultural memory and knowledge and draw their resiliency from it. It is a space in which they can freely express joy, fear, wonder, future hopes, and pain without judgments. My part in creating this space is twofold. By conducting research that examines the academic and social outcomes of culturally sustaining (Paris, 2012) pedagogy and curriculum, I hope to make these practices systemic within K–12 policy. Second, my research and work with teachers and Black and Latino males informs my work with preservice and in-service teachers. I concur with bell hooks (2004) who argues that "Black women cannot speak for black men. We can speak with them. And by so doing embody the practice of solidarity wherein dialogue is the foundation of true love" (p. xvii). As a Black woman, I cannot speak to the challenges and lived experiences of Black and Latino young men. I can, however, make sure that my research and teaching helps to disrupt the policies and practices that disproportionately marginalize them.

A number of economic, democratic, and spiritual implications are connected to the success of Black males. On a practical level, the vitality of the United States is connected to the success, health, and civic engagement of its citizens, including Black males. The undereducation and mass incarceration of Black males stifles intellectual and economic contributions that go unrealized through neglected potential. The genius displayed by young Black men who become ensnared in the legal system, for instance, could otherwise be used for innovation and problem solving, had they the opportunity. Because their gendered and raced ways of knowing and being are not mainstream, they are not recognized as producers of knowledge and are thus considered a drain on national resources.

I ascribe to the South African concept of *ubuntu*, a philosophy that "I am what I am because of what we all are." I recognize that my humanity and quality of life on this earth are intertwined with the humanity and quality of life of others. Though others may not acknowledge this principle, it still holds true and we must do a better job of caring for one another as a reflection of our humanity. It is my hope that as we (re)think noticing the potential and brilliance of Black and Latino males that they will be able to enact academic identities that are compatible with their cultural ones.

Erik's Journey

My own personal journey into this work has been one of overcoming my own struggles with invisibility in academic settings and, more importantly, identifying who I am as a man. This work now lives in my heart and spirit. I do this work within a system that sees Black and Latino males as worthless. Often these young men find few people or no one at all to help them work toward positive outcomes for themselves. As a recent father of a Black male, my work has intensified and shifted: I now recognize that the work of UMOJA needs to begin as an early intervention. Self-identity starts from early childhood.

For as long as I can remember, I've always wanted to help improve educational experiences for Black and Latino students. As a young adult, I was active in my church and community. The work I have done in my community prepared me for my work as a parent coordinator and mentor. I was ready to help start something when, ten years ago, I was approached by Christine, the site director Sunset Hills Academy East about starting a group for the males of color on or campus. As Director, she recognized the dire need to support the males in our learning community. As someone who graduated from Sunset Hills two decades before, and as a person who worked closely with the Black and Latino males in the school, she knew I has some ideas about what that support should look like.

My connection to the young men of Sunset Hills, and my passion to serve and develop them is what guided me as I formed UMOJA. Despite the early challenges I faced from colleagues who doubted my ability to do this work, I was able to motivate and assist these youth in seeing their personal value and worth as young Black and Latino men. UMOJA has a strong curriculum that focuses on true self-identity. Through mentorship and peer support, the members of UMOJA are able to share their knowledge with the rest of the school community through the various forums we create in the school. These forums are an opportunity for the young men to show their leadership skills, and be in the spotlight in positive and productive ways.

I do this work because I believe I am called to do it. It comes from my heart as well as my own experience which is strongly connected to theirs. The work I do with them creates spaces for them to learn, share, and think about ways that they can impact the world in a positive way. Over the years UMOJA has been a solid foundation for nearly 100 Black and Latino male youth, and in 2014 will celebrate its tenth year anniversary.

My hope for the young men of UMOJA, and for other young Black and Latino males is for them to understand who they are and not what they have been brainwashed to believe they are. These young men come from a strong heritage and have a strong constitution, and these are valuable tools they need to let them guide them along their journey toward positive change.

RESISTING PARTIAL REPRESENTATIONS
OF BLACK AND LATINO MALES

Returning to Ikäheimo's (2002) definitions of recognition, another way we may misrecognize Black and Latino males is in how we identify them in school. Many scholars have studied and drawn attention to Black and Latino male overrepresentation in special education and underrepresentation in gifted and talented programs (Bonner, 2003; Noguera, 2003). One of the ideas that several young men of UMOJA communicated to us was that they wanted to be recognized and/or seen in school in the ways they were seen in their home communities.

What would it mean for us to see all Black and Latino males as college-going or going somewhere in life that is meaningful? In what ways might we revise our practices so that we notice their strengths and talents? How do we avoid exceptionality narratives which in another way renders them invisible?

So how do we do notice Black and Latino male youth? Our teacher education programs do not always teach this explicitly, even when a critical pedagogy is applied. Often, once we hit the ground in our classrooms, our experience suggests that we should value thinking on our feet and responding quickly. This contrasts with noticing because, at first, noticing is inherently slow. It happens over time and is the way we orient our minds and hearts. Noticing requires practice, patience, and discipline to become deliberate. Increasingly, education scholars are joining metaphysicians, philosophers, and optical researchers in carefully examining the differences between seeing and noticing. We reflect on the scholarship of Lalitha Vasudevan (2006, 2011) who writes about the enactment of multimodal selves and invites us to see differently, pause, and take notice in our work with young people.

While noticing is an inquiry that cannot be proscribed, we can consider specific ways to notice for our classroom practice. Mason (2002) talks about intentional noticing and professional noticing. *Intentional noticing* is exactly what it sounds like: taking mental pauses and time to notice, and allowing that noticing to alter our actions and deepen our sensitivities to notice our practice. With *professional noticing,* one may take note of how a person teaches a lesson, conducts a workshop, speaks to a group, and one can identify ways to incorporate this into one's own work. It is a form of modeling for the one who is noticing. In this way, noticing is a pragmatic approach to improving practice.

Based on our work with the young men of UMOJA, we argue that teachers need to recognize the limitations of their seeing and do more noticing in their classroom. That is, teachers must learn to be more deliberate in their noticing and think about ways to increase incidents of noticing in order to look beyond the partial representations of students in the classroom. How *do* we notice? And, then, how do we make noticing our pedagogy? For those of us who feel we already notice our students, we ask: how will you sustain noticing in a hyper-standardized test environment; with the continual negative media onslaught of who Black and Latino students are categorized, and in light of the incredible injustices that communities of color live with? One way is to be explicit with our students about our intent to notice them, and then set about noticing *and* affirming their brilliance, potential, and the characteristics that make them unique and worthy beings. We noticed that approaching Ricky and the other young men of UMOJA in this way resulted in positive outcomes for them. We believe that if educators look beyond the partial representations of Black and Latino males in their classroom they will begin to notice them as complex and unique beings, persons with cultural capital (Yosso, 2005), and cofacilitators whose life experiences can make what happens in the classroom more meaningful for both the student and teacher.

NOTE

1. All names are pseudonyms.
2. New York State has no formal process for emancipation. Youth must be over the age of 16; not live with or receive assistance from parents, guardians, or court ordered supervision; and must their own job as their source of income.

REFERENCES

Bonner II., F. A. (2003). To be young, gifted, African American, and male. *Gifted Child Today, 26*(2), 26–34.

Brown, A. L. (2011). Same old stories: The Black male in social science and educational literature, 1930s to the present. *Teachers College Record, 113*(9), 2047–2079.

Caton, M. T. (2012). Black male perspectives on their educational experiences in high school. *Urban Education, 47*(6), 1055–1085.

Collins, P. H. (2005). Booty call: Sex, violence, and images of Black masculinity *Black sexual politics: African Americans, gender, and the new racism* (pp. 149–180). New York: Routledge.

Ellison, R. (1952). *Invisible Man.* New York: Random House.

Ferguson, A. A. (2000). *Bad boys: Public schools in the making of black masculinity.* Ann Arbor, MI: The University of Michigan Press.

Gregory, A., Skiba, R., & Noguera, P. A. (2010). The achievement gap and the discipline gap: Two sides of the same coin? *Educational Researcher, 39*(10), 59–68.

Haddix, M. (2009). Black boys can write: Challenging dominant framings of African American adolescent males in literacy research. *Journal of Adolescent & Adult Literacy, 53*(4), 341–343.

Haddix, M., & Sealey-Ruiz, Y. (2012). Cultivating digital and popular literacies as empowering and emancipatory acts among urban youth. *Journal of Adolescent & Adult Literacy, 56*(3), 189–192.

Halx, M. D., & Ortiz, M. (2011). Voices of Latino male high school students on their disconnect with education: Perspectives of "drop-outs" and those on the brink. *Latino Studies, 9*(4), 416–438.

Harper, S. R., & Associates. (2013). *Succeeding in the city: A report from the black and Latino male high school achievement study.* Philadelphia, PA: University of Pennsylvania, Center for the Study of Race and Equity in Education.

Harrison, L., Sailes, G., Rotich, W. K., & Bimper, A. Y. (2011). Living the dream or awakening from the nightmare: Race and athletic identity. *Race Ethnicity and Education, 14*(1), 91–103.

hooks, b. (2004). *We real cool: Black men and masculinity.* New York, NY: Routledge.

Howard, T. C., & Flennaugh, T. (2011). Research concerns, cautions, and considerations on black males in a 'post-racial' society. *Race Ethnicity and Education, 14*(1), 105–120. doi: 10.1080/13613324.2011.531983

Ikäheimo, H. (2002). Taylor or something called recognition. In A. Laitinen & N. H. Smith (Eds.), *Perspectives on the philosophy of Charles Taylor* (Vol. 71). Helsinki, Finland: Acta Philosophica Fennica. HAVE AN ACCENT ON "A" of this name. Please add or delete in text as necessary.

Jackson, I. J, Sealey-Ruiz,Y., & Watson, W. (in press). Daring to care: The role of culturally relevant care in mentoring Black and Latino male high school students. *Race, Ethnicity, and Education.*

Kirkland, D. (2013). *A search past silence.* New York: Teachers College Press.

Knaus, C. B. (2007). Still segregated, sill unequal: Analyzing the impact of No Child Left Behind on African-American students. In *The state of Black America, 2007.* Washington, DC: National Urban League.

Lynn, M., Bacon, J. N., Totten, T. L., Bridges, T., & Jenning, M. (2010). Examining teachers' beliefs about african american male students in a low-performing high school in an african american school district. *Teachers College Record, 112*(1), 289–330.

Lynn, M. (2006). Education for the community: Exploring the culturally relevant practices of black male teachers. *Teachers College Record, 108*(12), 2497–2522.

Majors, R., & Billson, J. M. (1991). *Cool pose: The dilemmas of black manhood in America.* New York, NY: Lexington Books.

Mason, J. (2002). *Researching your own practice: The discipline of noticing.* New York, NY: Routledge.

Milner, H. R., IV. (2010). *Start where you are, but don't stay there: Understanding diversity, opportunity gaps, and teaching in today's classrooms.* Cambridge: Harvard Education Press.

Murrell, P. C. (2008). Identity, agency, and culture: Black achievement and educational attainment. In L. Tillman (Ed.), *Sage handbook of african american education* (pp. 89–105). Thousand Oaks: Sage.

Neugarten, M. L. (2003). Seeing and noticing: An optical perspective on competitive intelligence. *Journal of Competitive Intelligence and Management 1*(1). 93–104.

Noguera, P. A. (2012). Saving Black and Latino boys. *Phi Delta Kappan, 30*(20), http://www.edweek.org/ew/articles/2012/02/03/kappan_noguera.html.

Noguera, P. A. (2003). The trouble with Black boys: The role and influence of environmental and cultural factors on the academic performance of African American males. *Urban Education, 38*(4), 431–459.

Noguera, P. A. (2008). *The trouble with Black boys: And other reflections on race, equity, and the future of public education.* San Francisco: Jossey-Bass.

Noguera, P. A., Hurtado A., & Fergus, E. (Eds.) (2011) *Understanding and responding to the disenfranchisement of Latino males: Invisible no more.* New York: Routledge.

Paris, D. (2012). Culturally sustaining pedagogy: A needed change in stance, terminology, and practice. [Essay]. *Educational Researcher, 41*(3), 93–97.

Saez, P. A., Casado, A., & Wade, J. C. (2009). Factors influencing masculinity ideology among Latino men. *The Journal of Men's Studies, 17*(2), 116–128.

Sealey-Ruiz, Y., & Greene, P. (2011). Embracing urban youth culture in the context of education. *The Urban Review, 43,* pp. 339–357

Sealey-Ruiz, Y., Noguera, P. A., & Handville, N. (2008). In pursuit of the possible: Lessons learned from district efforts to reduce racial disparities in achievement. *The Sophist's Bane: Society of Professors of Education, 4*(1/2), 31–41.

Steele, C. M., & Aronson, J. (1995). Stereotype threat and the intellectual test-performance of African-Americans. *Journal of personality and Social Psychology, 69*(5), 797–811.

Stevenson, H. C. (2004). Boys in men's clothing: Racial socialization and neighborhood safety as buffers to hypervulnerability in African American adolescent males. In N. Way & J. Y. Chu (Eds.), *Adolescent boys: Exploring diverse cultures of boyhood* (pp. 59–77). New York, NY: New York University Press.

Taylor, C. (1994). The politics of recognition. In A. Gutmann (Ed.), *Multiculturalism: Examining the politics of recognition* (pp. 25 –73). New Jersey: Princeton University Press.

Toldson, I. A., & Lewis, C. W. (2012). *Challenge the status quo: Academic success among school-age African American males.* Washington, DC: Congressional Black Caucus Foundation.

Vasudevan, L. (2006). Making known differently: Engaging visual modalities as spaces to author new selves. *E-Learning, 3*(2), 207–216.

Vasudevan, L. (2011). An invitation to unknowing. *Teachers College Record, 113*(10), 1154–1174.

Watson, W., Sealey-Ruiz, Y. & Jackson, I. (in press). Daring to care: The role of culturally relevant care in mentoring Black and Latino male high school students. *Race, Ethnicity and Education.*

West-Olatunji, C. A., Baker, J. C., & Brooks, M. (2006). African American adolescent males: Giving voice to their educational experiences. *Multicultural Perspectives, 8*(4), 3–9.

Woodson, C. G. (1933). *The mis-education of the Negro.* Washington: Associated Publishers.

Yosso, T. J. (2005). Whose culture has capital? A critical race theory discussion of community cultural wealth. *Race, Ethnicity and Education, 8*(1), 69–91.

CHAPTER 6

NOT STRANGERS

How Social Distance Influences Black Male Teachers' Perceptions of Their Male Students of Color

Travis J. Bristol
Columbia University

Social distance, or the perceived dissimilarities between groups based on race, class, or gender, appears to be one of the prevailing assumptions that underlie a policy initiative to increase the number of Black male teachers to improve Black boys' academic outcomes. Using survey data from the Boston Public Schools 2012 Black Male Teacher Environment Survey (BMTES), findings shed light on how Black male teachers perceive the schooling experiences of male students of color. According to respondents in this sample, using the number of Black male teachers on staff as a proxy to measure the social distance between male students of color to the school, boys of color experience less social distance when there are many Black male faculty members.

Teacher Education and Black Communities, pages 117–128
Copyright © 2014 by Information Age Publishing
All rights of reproduction in any form reserved.

INTRODUCTION

On January 31, 2011, Secretary of Education Arne Duncan, along with filmmaker Spike Lee and civil rights leader John Lewis, visited Morehouse College to, as the department's website proclaims, "Call Black Men to the Blackboard." The Department of Education's targeted recruitment strategy is part of a larger effort to diversify the teacher workforce. One aim of this recruitment campaign is to increase the percentage of Black male teachers; 2% of the nation's teachers in public schools are Black men (Lewis & Toldson, 2013). The focus by national policy makers to increase the number of Black male teachers might be an attempt to bridge the social distance Black students, specifically males, experience in schools.

As one U.S. Department of Education official at Morehouse suggests: "faced with the startling fact that Black males represent 6% of the U.S. population yet 35% of the prison population and less than 2% of teachers, I can't help but think how far we have to go" (Graham, 2011). As such, implicit in this policy response to increase the number of Black male teachers could well be the belief that Black men, in the classroom, have the ability to ameliorate the educational and social outcomes for this marginalized group, Black boys. Moreover, for the 75% of Black boys living in female-headed households (Snyder, McLaughlin, & Finders, 2006), having a Black man serve in a father-figure role, it is assumed, might improve academic achievement (Kunjufu, 2005). As a result of their racial matching and similar perceived shared encounters with institutionalized racism, Black male teachers, researchers argue, are well positioned to increase Black boys' educational and social outcomes (Lynn & Hassan, 1999; Lynn, 2006). To address this tension, an investigation of the relationship between the presence of Black male teachers and the experiences of male students of color in one U.S. urban school district is warranted.

Below, I first provide a theoretical framework, social distance, which lays out the tensions that arise when individuals of different social groups come in contact with each other. Next, I present the research strategy and data used to explore how social distance influences Black male teachers' perceptions of their male students of color. After analyzing that data, I discuss the results, and address threats to validity. I conclude with the study's significance.

THEORETICAL FRAMEWORK

Black Male Teachers and Social Distance

Social distance (Parks, 1924; Simmel, 1950), or the perceived dissimilarity between groups based on race, class, or gender, appears to be one of the prevailing assumptions that underlie a policy initiative to increase the number of Black male teachers. In "The Stranger," Georg Simmel (1950) discusses the precarious role of the "stranger" who, while dwelling among the individuals of a particular locale, is, in the end, distant from the experiences of those people. About the stranger, Simmel writes, "his position in this group is determined, essentially, by the fact that he has not belonged to it from the beginning, that he imports qualities into it, which do not and cannot stem from the group" (pg. 1). In Simmel, we observe the nascent thinking around how one's identity shapes the ways in which people interact in a particular space. In many urban school environments, on average, White teachers are strangers to the daily experiences of their Black students (Brown, 2009).

Applying Social Distance to Urban Schools

From Simmel's (1950) early theorizing about how the assumed similarities between persons can affect their relationship to each other, we begin to observe manifestations of social distance in urban spaces across the United States, specifically as it relates to race. Parks (1924) describes how the population shift away from towns to the metropolis brought varying ethnic groups within close proximity to each other. These groups, even when living and working together, believed that they were, indelibly, different from each other. Such recognitions of difference evolved into prejudicial attitudes by the majority Whites and the ways they interacted with the "other." More recent applications of social distance focus on the race of teachers and students. Specifically, sociologists investigate the perceptions of White teachers with regards to working-class Black students (Diamond, Randolph, & Spillane, 2004; Hyland, 2009). These investigations attempted to understand the relationship between teacher characteristics and students' academic outcomes. Researchers found that many White teachers in urban areas have low expectations of Black students, who are, on average, from economically disadvantaged communities. Specifically, White teachers are more inclined to see student failure as a result of students' racial background rather than their socialized worldviews, or the quality of instruction received (Hale, 2001; Milner, 2006). Thus, social distance often exists between White teachers and Black students, due to differences in lived experience.

It is critical, then, to explore how teachers of the same race as their students describe students' experiences. More precisely, how might the numerical composition of Black men in schools influence the perceived experiences for Black boys, or boys of color more generally? Such an exploration becomes even more important given continued efforts to increase the number of Black male teachers in U.S. public schools. I use the number of Black male teachers in a school as a proxy to measure the social distance between male students of color to the organization. My theory is based on the premise that having more Black male teachers in schools can decrease the social distance between the organization and Black male students. Black male teachers, based on their personal experiences and training, might create socioemotional environments in schools that can shelter Black boys from societal and institutionalized racism.

This study was guided by two research questions.

1. Is there a relationship between the numerical composition of Black male teachers in schools and how these teachers perceive the academic and social in school experiences for male students of color?
2. How do Black male teachers view their colleagues' interactions with Black male students?

Below, I describe the research method used to answer the two aforementioned research questions.

RESEARCH METHODOLOGY AND STUDY DESIGN

In June 2012, I designed the Black Male Teacher Environment Survey (BMTES) [Appendix A], the first of its kind for any U.S. public school district. BMTES was administered under the auspices of the Office of the Achievement Gap in Boston Public Schools (BPS).[1] Superintendent Carol Johnson sent an email with a link to the survey to each Black male teacher of record in BPS. Thirty-two percent responded;[2] or 86 of the 266 Black male teachers in the district. Approximately 67 completed all survey items.

I use descriptive statistics (Winkler & Dyckman, 2010) to analyze data from BMTES. Descriptive statistics serves as a useful methodological tool to describe patterns in a dataset with the aim of drawing attention to particular social phenomena. The initial analysis of BMTES provided insight into how a nonrepresentative sample of Black male teachers in one northeast urban school district, Boston, viewed the academic and social experiences of the male students of color in their schools.

Research Strategy

I use the number of Black male teachers in the school as a proxy to measure the social distance between male students of color and the organization. As a way to explore further how, if at all, the presence, or lack thereof, of other Black men on a school's faculty might influence how Black male teachers describe the experiences of male students of color, the unit of analysis focuses on the responses of two groups of teachers: Loners, or those respondents who are the only Black men on their faculty, and Groupers, respondents in schools with four or more Black male teachers. I provide responses to specific questions from the BMTES when there was greater than a 10% difference between Loner and Grouper responses. I also present the sample mean as a way of demonstrating the degree to which Loners and Groupers differ from their combined average.

In this chapter, I analyze a sub-set of BMTES. Using a Likert Scale, I focus on how respondents rated their perceptions of the experiences of male students of color. For categories on the Likert Scale, respondents were asked to "1 = Strongly Disagree, 2 = Disagree, 3 = Neither Agree nor Disagree, 4 = Agree, 5 = Strongly Agree" to items. In an attempt to highlight if respondents had positive, negative, or neutral feelings about each measure, I collapsed strongly disagree and disagree into one measure; similarly, I collapsed strongly agree and agree into one measure. I aggregate the responses from Loners and Groupers in order to create average values for each question for Loners and Groupers.

It is important to note that the absolute size of Loner (n = 8) and Grouper (n = 33) teachers for whom the analysis is conducted only provides an impression of potential patterns in the district. An increase in response rate could change some findings. All the Loners answered each question but a number of Groupers did not. No questions were excluded from the analysis; I analyzed questions with incomplete responses.

FINDINGS

Teacher Characteristics

More than three-quarters (77%) of all respondents taught in their current schools during the 2010–2011, the year before the survey's administration. The majority of Loners (72%) and Groupers (70%) taught in their current school during the 2010–2011 school year. Thus, the responses to survey items were based on, at minimum, two years of experience in that organizational setting. Seventy five percent of all respondents had six or more years of teaching experience: five percent of the sample was comprised of first year teachers. All Loners (100%) taught a minimum of five years and, 81% of the Groupers had five or more years of experience. The length of teaching seems significant because it is quite different from existing patterns in the district. After five years, approximately 51% of district teachers leave. Further, both the time respondents have spent in their schools and their years of teaching underscore the unique insight they have into exploring the conditions of male students of color as their view is based on multiple years of teaching as opposed to simply an anomalous year.

Relationships With Students

On average, Black male teachers said that males of color experienced school differently than their peers (see Table 6.1). Almost two-thirds (63%) of respondents noted that male students of color struggled academically more than other students. While Loners and Groupers both agreed that male students of color struggled, they did so at a different rate; 87.5% and 60%, respectively. Thus many more Loners felt that male students of color faced academic challenges.

Approximately 45% of Groupers believed their colleagues cared as much as they did about helping males of color academically: 26% of Loners believed this to be true. This finding seems particularly interesting because it suggests that, according to respondents, schools with more Black male teachers are more caring organizations for male students of color.

More than half of respondents (57%) suggested that boys of color got into trouble more so than other groups. Loners and Groupers disagreed starkly on the degree to which male students of color got into trouble. Eighty seven point five percent of Loners agreed that boys of color got into more trouble than their peers, and 45% of Groupers believed that male students of color were more likely to get into trouble than other students. About one-quarter (26%) of Loners and one-tenth (9%) of Groupers believed that girls were treated more fairly than boys.

A little more than two-thirds, or 67%, of respondents noted that colleagues were as concerned as they were for the academic performance of male students of color. However, Loners and Groupers had very different responses to this question (see Table 6.2). Fifty percent of Loners noted that their colleagues were as concerned as they were for the academic performance of males of color, compared to 73% of Groupers.

About half (52%) of the respondents believed that their colleagues shared as much concern for male students of color's problematic behavior as they did. Almost two-thirds, or 63% of Loners, however, noted that their colleagues expressed more concern than they did for males of color problematic behavior. Slightly more than one-quarter (30%) of Groupers believed that their colleagues expressed more concern than they did for the problematic behavior of males of color. However, 57% of respondents suggested that their colleagues were less likely, when compared to them, to take responsibility for talking with male students of color to solve personal problems. The rate at which Loners and Groupers described their colleagues' responses to talking with males to help them solve their problems was particularly stark. Twice as many Loners (88%) as Groupers (45%) noted that their colleagues were less likely, when compared to them, to help males of color solve their problems.

TABLE 6.1 Perceptions of the Experiences of Male Students of Color by Loners and Groupers (*n* = 41)

Male students of color at my school tend to struggle academically more than other students

	Only Black Male Teacher (*n* = 8)	Four or More Black Male Teachers (*n* = 33)
Disagree	0.0%	21%
Neither agree nor disagree	12.5%	19%
Agree	87.5%	60%

My colleagues care just as much as I do in efforts to help males of color academically

	Only Black Male Teacher (*n* = 8)	Four or More Black Male Teachers (*n* = 32)
Disagree	25%	21%
Neither agree nor disagree	50%	34%
Agree	25%	45%

Male students of color tend to be in trouble for their behavior at this school more than other groups

	Only Black Male Teacher (*n* = 8)	Four or More Black Male Teachers (*n* = 33)
Disagree	12.5%	39%
Neither agree nor disagree	0%	16%
Agree	87.5%	45%

Female students at this school are treated more fairly than the boys are

	Only Black Male Teacher (*n* = 8)	Four or More Black Male Teachers (*n* = 31)
Disagree	25%	52%
Neither agree nor disagree	50%	39%
Agree	25%	9%

Discussion

According to respondents in this sample, boys of color experienced less social distance when there were multiple Black male faculty members. Specifically, survey respondents in schools with more Black male teachers described the organization as more caring and attuned to the academic challenges faced by boys of color in schools—as observed on the measure—My colleagues care just as much as I do in efforts to help males of color academically. Loners believed that female students in their schools were treated more fairly than males, as opposed to Groupers who did not believe females were treated any differently

TABLE 6.2 Perceptions of Colleagues' Interactions With Males Students of Color by Loners and Groupers (*n* = 41)

In general, how much do other teachers at your school take responsibility for helping male students of color to improve academically?

	Only Black Male Teacher (*n* = 8)	Four or More Black Male Teachers (*n* = 33)
Less than I do	50%	33%
The same as I do	50%	63%
More than I do	0%	3%

In general, how much do other teachers at your school take responsibility for redirecting male students of color who have misbehaved?

	Only Black Male Teacher (*n* = 8)	Four or More Black Male Teachers (*n* = 33)
Less than I do	50%	46%
The same as I do	37%	51%
More than I do	13%	3%

In general, how much do other teachers at your school express concern about the academic performance of male students of color?

	Only Black Male Teacher (*n* = 8)	Four or More Black Male Teachers (*n* = 33)
Less than I do	50%	24%
The same as I do	50%	73%
More than I do	0%	3%

In general, how much do other teachers at your school express concern about the problematic behavior by male students of color?

	Only Black Male Teacher (*n* = 8)	Four or More Black Male Teachers (*n* = 33)
Less than I do	13%	9%
The same as I do	24%	61%
More than I do	63%	30%

In general, how much do other teachers at your school take responsibility for talking with male students of color to help them solve personal problems?

	Only Black Male Teacher (*n* = 8)	Four or More Black Male Teachers (*n* = 33)
Less than I do	88%	45%
The same as I do	12%	48%
More than I do	0%	6%

In general, how familiar are other teachers at your school with the life circumstances that male students of color experience?

	Only Black Male Teacher (n = 8)	Four or More Black Male Teachers (n = 33)
Less than I am	88%	78%
The same as I do	12%	18%
More than I am	0%	0%

than males. Groupers were more likely to suggest that their colleagues cared as much as they did to help males students of color improve academically. In contrast, Loners felt that their colleagues did not care as much as they did. Moreover, respondents in schools with many more Black male teachers reported that other teachers spoke with males to help them solve personal problems.

It stands to reasons, from an analysis of BMTES, that the perceived experiences of male students of color differed based on the number of Black male teachers on the faculty. When compared to Groupers, a higher percentage of Loners described their male students of color as struggling more with academics and behavior. Schools in my sample with more Black male teachers place greater emphasis on redressing the academic, rather than the behavioral, needs of boys of color. There may be several reasons for this occurrence. It may indeed be the case that the types of male students of color in schools with one Black male teacher on the faculty differ in distinct ways to those in schools with many more Black male teachers.

While I do not address the types of schools that male students of color attend in this book chapter, findings from the larger dataset suggest that the school characteristics with one Black male teacher differ from the school characteristics with many more Black male teachers (Bristol, 2013). Specifically, schools with one Black male teacher tend to screen students, have smaller student enrollment, and a larger percentages of White students: simply put, schools with one Black male teacher are, on average, higher performing in this urban district, when compared to schools with many more Black male teachers.

Although the schools with one Black male teacher have a higher academic performing student population, Loners reported that their male students of color struggled at a higher rate, when compared to schools with many more Black male teachers. It is particularly troubling, then, that Loners suggested their colleagues were more preoccupied with the behavioral, rather than the academic, challenges faced by boys of color. According to Loners, the disproportionate rate at which other teachers focus on males of color behavior, choose not to help these students solve personal problems, and treat female students more fairly, may well heighten the social distance in these schools compared to spaces with many more Black male teachers.

Regardless of how many Black male teachers there were on the faculty, respondents universally agreed that part of their work was to mentor or act as a father figure to male students of color. Herein, we observe that Black men saw one of their many roles on the faculty as supporting their male students of color's socioemotional development by helping them address social concerns. Loners did not feel that their colleagues attended to boys of color nonacademic challenges. It might be the case that Black male teachers are more apt to relate to some of the personal problems faced by their male students of color by having experienced similar challenges as an elementary or secondary student, or in everyday life. Other teachers (e.g., White and female teachers) who are more socially distant may feel uncomfortable, or lack the tools, to address some of the out-of-school challenges faced by boys of color.

In the end, by using the number of Black male teachers on staff as a proxy to measure the social distance between male students of color to the school, I observe from my sample that boys of color experience greater social distance in schools with one Black male teacher. In contrast, schools with many more Black male teachers operate as organizations that are more attuned to male students of color's socioemotional and academic needs.

Validity Threats

One threat to the validity of my overall findings is that I attempt to make claims about how male students of color experience the organization without, directly, soliciting their input. However, given the average years of teaching, both in the profession and in the particular school, I feel confident in respondents' perceptions of the schooling experiences of male students of color. Also, given the pattern that began to emerge (e.g., differences in Loner and Grouper responses) this survey should, at the minimum, give practitioners and policy makers pause around the relationship between the number of Black men on the faculty and male students of color social and academic experiences in schools.

Significance

The findings here are significant in that, for the first time, there exists large-scale survey data to link the organizational conditions of particular schools to the experiences of male students of color. Confirming Simmel's early theorizing about the social distance, I observe that boys of color experience less social distance when there are many more Black male faculty members. Consequently, as policy makers look to increase the number of Black male teachers in hopes of increasing learning for Black boys, it might be useful to consider the findings from this study: an increase in the number of Black male teachers, in this sample, might be associated with more supportive academic and socioemotional environments, for male students of color. As such, policy makers might find it more useful to place a concentrated number of Black male teachers in particular schools rather than scattering such new recruits across schools.

NOTES

1. The Office of the Achievement Gap has a copy of the data.
2. The email was sent on Tuesday, June 26th—three days before the end of the school year.

REFERENCES

Bridges, T. L. (2011). Towards a pedagogy of hip hop in urban teacher education. *Journal of Negro Education, 80,* 325–338.

Bristol, T. J. (2013). Organizational purgatory: An exploration into how the within school experiences of Black male teachers differ across one urban school district. Paper presented at the 2013 American Educational Research Association Annual Meeting, San Francisco, CA.

Brown, A. L. (2009). Brothers gonna work it out: Understanding the pedagogic performance of African American male teachers working with African American male students. *Urban Rev, 41,* 416–435.

Creswell, J. W. (2007). *Research design: Qualitative, quantitative, and mixed methods approaches.* (2nd ed.), Los Angeles: Sage Publications, Inc.

Diamond, J. B., Randolph, A., Spillane, J. (2004). Teachers' expectations and sense of responsibility for student learning: The Importance of race, class, and organizational habitus. *Anthropology & Education Quarterly, 35*(1), 75–98.

Duncan, A. (2011). Leading a life of consequence. Speech presented at Fayetteville State University, Fayetteville, NC.

Graham, J. (2011). Secretary calls Black men to the Blackboard. Retrieved October 1, 2012, from http://www.ed.gov/blog/2011/02/secretary-calls-Black-men-to-the-Blackboard/

Hale, J. E. (2001). *Learning while Black: Creating educational excellence for African American children* . Baltimore, MD: The Johns Hopkins University Press.

Hyland, N. (2009). Opening and closing communicative space with teachers investigating race and racism in their own practice. *Action Research, 7*(3), 335–354.

Kunjufu, J. (2005). *Countering the conspiracy to destroy Black boys.* Chicago: African American Images.

Lewis, C. W., & Toldson, I. A. (2013), Black male teachers: Diversifying the United States' teacher workforce. In C. W. Lewis & I. A. Toldson (Eds.), *Black male teachers advances in race and ethnicity in education, 1.* Emerald Group Publishing.

Lynn, M. (2006). Dancing between two worlds: A portrait of the life of a Black male teacher in South Central L.A. *International Journal of Qualitative Studies in Education, 19*(2), 221–242.

Lynn, M., Johnson, C., & Hassan, K. (1999). Raising the critical consciousness of African American students in baldwin hills: A portrait of an exemplary African American male teacher. *Journal of Negro Education, 68*(1), 42–51.

Milner, H. R. (2006). But good intentions are not enough: Theoretical and philosophical relevance in teaching students of color. In J. Landsman & C. W. Lewis (Eds.), *White teachers/diverse classrooms: A guide to building inclusive schools, promoting high expectations and eliminating racism* (pp. 79–90). Sterling, VA: Stylus Publishers.

Parks, R. E. (1924). The concept of social distance as applied to the study of racial attitudes and racial relations. *Journal of Applied Sociology, 8,* 339–344

Simmel, G. (1950). *The sociology of Georg Simmel.* Compiled and translated by Kurt Wolff, Glencoe, IL: Free Press.

Snyder, A. R., McLaughlin, D. K., & Findeis, J. 2006. Household composition and poverty among female-headed households with children: Differences by race and residence. *Rural Sociology, 71*(4), 597–624.

Winkler, O. W., & Dyckman, T. R. (2010). Interpreting economic and social data: A foundation of descriptive statistics. *The Accounting Review, 85*(5), 1820–1822.

PART II

PREPARING BLACK STUDENTS TO BECOME TEACHERS

TEACHERS AND TEACHING FOR THE NEW MILLENNIUM

Jacqueline Jordan Irvine
Emory University

Leslie T. Fenwick
Howard University

Although progress has been made, the lack of teacher diversity continues to be a problem in the field. Currently, 43% of students in our nation's schools come from ethnically diverse backgrounds and at least half of the students are African American and Latino in our largest school districts (Orfield & Lee, 2007). However, in the 2003–04 academic year, African American teachers represented only 7.6% of the teaching force. The absence of a critical mass of teachers of color is an important matter. All students benefit from exposure to effective teachers of color who serve as role models and authority figures in the schools. As the Carnegie Forum on Education and the Economy asserted decades ago, "We cannot tolerate a future in which both white and minority children are confronted with almost exclusively white authority figures in their schools" (1986, p. 32).

There is clear evidence that a larger pool of effective teachers of color makes a difference in the lives of students of color as well as White students (Foster, 1997; King, 1993). Teachers of color do more than just teach content. They dispel myths of racial inferiority and incompetence and serve as

Teacher Education and Black Communities, pages 131–141
Copyright © 2014 by Information Age Publishing
All rights of reproduction in any form reserved.

surrogate parents, guides, and mentors to their students (Dilworth, 1992; Dilworth & Brown, 2007). They also serve as accessible models of intellectual authority. Moreover, diversity among teachers increases teachers' and students' knowledge and understanding of different cultural groups, thereby enhancing the abilities of all involved to interact with each other. It is clear that diversifying the nation's teaching force is essential to the racial and ethnic integration of American society, a goal that the majority of Americans supports.

Education is one of the top-10 most popular fields of study pursued by African American college students. Nine percent of African American college students earn a bachelor's degree in education which is slightly more than the percentage (7%) of other students earning a bachelor's degree in education (NCES, 2004). Increasing the number of African American teachers is a pipeline issue.

STAFFING HIGH-NEED SCHOOLS

In this age of increased educational accountability, providing high-quality teachers for all students is critical because the single most important school factor affecting student achievement is teacher quality (Darling-Hammond, 2000). Indeed, the difference between an effective and ineffective teacher can be a full grade level of achievement in the course of a single school year (Hanushek, 1986; Vandevoort, Amerein-Beardsley, & Berliner, 2004). Exposure to a series of ineffective teachers has obvious detrimental consequences for students (National Association of State Boards of Education, 2000).

One of the nation's major educational concerns is the search for qualified and caring teachers for low-income students of color and for immigrant students, who will soon become the majority population in public schools (Gordon, 2000). Using a quantitative measure to define "opportunity to learn," The Schott Foundation (2009) stated in a report that Native American, Black, and Latino students, taken together, have just over half of the opportunity to learn as White, non-Latino students in the nation's best-supported, best-performing schools. A low-income student, of any race or ethnicity, also has just over half of the opportunity to learn as the average White, non-Latino student. The Foundation concluded that "half a chance is substantively no chance at all" (p. 6). Therefore, the availability of qualified, effective, and caring teachers for schools that enroll these types of students is especially acute. When disaggregated by the racial and economic composition of the school, the data disclose alarming trends.

Ingersoll's (2004) analyses revealed that 33% of new teachers leave teaching within the first three years, and by five years after being hired, nearly half (46%) of all teachers have left the profession. The annual turnover rates in urban high-poverty schools are nearly 70% higher than are the turn-over rates in low-poverty schools.

The severity of this attrition problem is noted by the continuing Black-White test score gap. A 2009 Educational Testing Service (ETS) report updated and expanded its 2003 quantitative analyses of the correlates of achievement and concluded that although the gap narrowed in some areas and widened in others—"overall there is little change" (Barton & Coley, 2009, p. 3). ETS reported that among 8th graders in 2007, 52% of African American students had a teacher who left before the school year ended compared to 28% of White students. Equally disturbing is the finding that 11% of African American students, as compared to 8% of White students, attended a school where 6% or more of the teachers were absent on an average day. Research suggests that the absence rate of teachers is important to track because it is associated with low student achievement (Clotfelter, Ladd, & Vigdor, 2007; Miller, Murnane, & Willett, 2007).

Teacher attrition and absences are not the only concerns in predominantly African American high-poverty schools; students in these schools are also twice as likely as students in other schools to be taught by the most inexperienced teachers. Studies of inexperienced teachers consistently find that they have difficulty with curriculum development, classroom management, student motivation, and teaching strategies (Darling-Hammond & Baratz-Snowden, 2005). A recent *Washington Post* study of 12 metropolitan Washington, DC, school systems reveals that in schools where fewer than 10% of the students received free or reduced lunch, first- or second-year teachers make up only 12% of the staff (de Vise & Chandler, 2009). In high-poverty schools in these districts (75% or more subsidized meals), the percentage of novice teachers rises to 22%. Researchers note that experience alone does not make for an effective teacher and most novice teachers improve their practice over time (Rockoff, 2004). Unfortunately, many students of color in high-need schools are taught by a revolving door of mostly inexperienced teachers, and the financial costs associated with this turnover are tremendous. The cost of teacher turnover in this country is $2.6 billion annually (Alliance for Excellent Education, 2004).

The literature suggests that teachers of color, particularly African American teachers, could reduce the acute shortage and high turnover of teachers in urban schools that enroll mostly low-income African American students. Using data from the Status Survey administered every five years by the National Education Association, Villegas (2006) found that a significantly larger percentage of teachers of color than White teachers taught in urban communities between 1981 and 2001. Specifically, at least half of all teachers of color reported teaching in urban settings, compared to only about one-fifth of all White teachers. The concentration of teachers of color in urban schools has also been reported by Choy (1993); Clewell and Villegas (2001); Clotfelter,

Ladd, and Vigdor (2005); Gay, Dingus, and Jackson (2003); Kirby, Berends, and Naftel (1999); and Villegas and Geist (2008).

Scafidia, Sjoquistb, and Stinebrickner (2007), using quantitative economic risk models, revealed a more complex finding about the tenure of teachers in high-poverty schools. The researchers found that African American teachers in high-poverty schools are more likely to remain in a school as the number of African American students' increases; White teachers are likely to leave. Additionally, Scafidia and colleagues found that the challenge of teaching in a school with a concentration of high-poverty students is not the primary reason the White teachers leave, rather the teachers left a "particular type of poor school—one with a large proportion of minorities" (p. 145). Similar results were found in a Georgia study (Jonsson, 2003). White teachers left schools with large proportions of minorities whether the students were middle-class or low-income African Americans.

Villegas and Irvine's (2010) analyses of the research explain these variations in the attrition rates of Black and White teachers. Their work reveals that teachers of color and White teachers differ in their motivation for entering the profession. Teachers of color report a desire to work with students of color and to improve these students' educational outcomes and personal lives (Belcher, 2001; Kauchak & Burback, 2003; Horng, 2005; Rios & Montecinos, 1999; Su, 1997; Wilder, 1999). Irvine (2002) reported that African American teachers in her study tended to see teaching as a calling, reminiscent of the historic "lifting as we climb" philosophy. Dixson and Dingus (2008) and others (Lynn, 2006; Su, 1997) found that African American teachers in their investigations purposefully entered teaching to give back to the community by returning to teach in their community of origin. Their reasons for entering the teaching profession could help explain the attraction of teachers of color to schools in urban high-need communities and account for the higher retention rates of teachers of color in those settings. For example, using data from North Carolina and Michigan, Murnane, Singer, Willett, Kemple, and Olsen (1991) found that teachers of color in those states stayed in teaching longer than White teachers, even after controlling for district-level fixed effects like school size and poverty level.

In summary, the evidence suggests that, compared to White teachers, educators of color appear to be more committed to teaching students of color in difficult-to-staff schools and more apt to persist in those settings. Villegas and Irvine's (2010) work suggests that an increase in the numbers of African American teachers could alleviate the severe shortage of teachers for the students and schools with the greatest needs.

THE POTENTIAL OF TEACHERS OF COLOR
TO IMPROVE THE ACADEMIC OUTCOMES
AND SCHOOL EXPERIENCES OF STUDENTS OF COLOR

A second major justification for increasing the diversity of the teaching force, suggested by Villegas and Irvine (2010) underscores the academic benefits that students of color could derive from teachers who are knowledgeable about their cultural backgrounds. The argument suggests that teachers of color are particularly suited to teaching students of color because they bring to their work a deep understanding of the cultural experiences of these learners.

Villegas and Irvine's (2010) review concluded that, although the literature on the influence of African American teachers on the school achievement of their African American students is only beginning to emerge, several studies suggest some positive effects. In an impressive quantitative study, researchers Meier, Stewart, and England (1989) investigated the relationship between the presence of African American teachers and African American students' access to equal education. Specifically, they investigated the following question: Does having African American educators impact African American students' school success? The researchers' findings highlighted the importance of having African American teachers in desegregated schools. In school districts with large proportions of African American teachers, the researchers found the following:

- Fewer African Americans were placed in special education classes
- Fewer African Americans were suspended or expelled
- More African Americans were placed in gifted and talented programs
- More African Americans graduated from high school

The authors emphatically concluded that "African American teachers are without a doubt the key" to students' academic success (p. 6).

In her study of teachers' perceptions of African American male students, Couch-Maddox (1999) found that African American teachers were more likely than their White peers to describe African American male students as "intellectually capable." The African American teachers also reported that these male students engaged in positive school behaviors, such as completing homework, attending school regularly, and serving in leadership roles (Fenwick, 2001).

Dee (2004) reanalyzed data from Tennessee's Project STAR and concluded that racial pairing of teachers and students significantly increased the reading and math achievement scores of both African American and White students by approximately three to four percentage points. Interestingly, Dee reported that the race effects were especially strong among poor

African American children who attended segregated schools. The average African American child attends schools where 67% of students are African American and 75% are poor. This fact underscores the importance of research on race effects (Center for Educational Policy, 2006).

Clewell, Puma, and McKay (2005), using the Prospects database, investigated the question: Does exposure to a same-race teacher increase the reading and mathematics achievement scores of African American and Hispanic students in elementary schools? The researchers found that Hispanic elementary students with a Hispanic teacher produced higher test score gains in math. In reading, the same effect was noted, but only in the fourth grade. Fourth-grade African American students had significantly higher scores in mathematics when taught by an African American teacher.

Klopfenstein (2005) reported that the enrollment of African American students in Algebra II increased significantly as the percentage of African American mathematics teachers increased. Other researchers have found that African American teachers, when compared to their White counterparts, are more successful in increasing student scores in vocabulary and reading comprehension (Hanushek, 1992), as well as economic literacy (Evans, 1992). Ehrenberg and Brewer (1995), using an econometric model that accounted for the nonrandom nature of teacher assignment to schools, found that an increase in the percentage of African American teachers yielded gains in standardized test scores for African American high school students.

Also of note are findings that African American teachers influenced African American students' school attendance (Farkas, Grobe, Sheehan, & Shuan, 1990) and that these teachers had higher expectations for their African American students than their White counterparts (Irvine, 1990). Other empirical works, such as a study by Hess and Leal (1997), suggested a correlation between the number of teachers of color in a district and college matriculation rates among students of color.

The chapters in this section look at the added advantages to increasing the number of Black teachers. They pay particular attention to the significant role of teacher education and coaching programs in recruiting and retaining Black and Black ethnic teachers. These chapters examine what teacher preparation and coaching programs must consider as they seek to attract teachers to and cultivate them for the profession. For example, too often the refrain, when talking about the need for Black teachers, is "It's hard to find them." Given that the Black teaching force in the United States has dropped significantly, the question becomes, what is the nation's commitment to developing the Black teachers we know we don't have but say we need? David A. Byrd and Shailen M. Singh, in their chapter *Mending the Pipeline: Recruitment and Retention of African American Preservice Teachers in a Predominantly White Institution,* address the critical shortage of African

American teachers in the United States. They focus on the efforts at Texas A&M University's College of Education and Human Development which has invested resources—both human and capital—to recruit and retain preservice teachers of color.

In their chapter, *Human Capital Investment: Supporting the Development of Visionary Change Agents in Teacher Preparation Programs for Urban Schools and Communities,* Robinson, Allen, and Lewis draw on Human Capital Investment theory to construct an innovative plan for revolutionizing teacher education programs.

Turning attention to coaching Black ethnic teachers in London, England, Victoria Showmuni examines the effectiveness of a programme intended to improve the recruitment and retention of Black minority ethnic secondary school teachers. Showmuni puts Black minorities front and center in her chapter by providing details of an evaluation of a coaching programme for teacher candidates who commonly experience feelings of disconnect in their teacher education programmes. All three of these chapters bring hope to the possibilities for effectively preparing teachers to teach Black children.

Moving from the topic of recruiting and retaining Black teachers to specifically looking at teacher experiences, in his chapter, *Bad Boys to Master Teachers: Hip Hop Culture and the Making of Black Male Teacher Identity,* Bridges draws from a qualitative study of ten Black male K–12 teachers from the Hip Hop generation who are closely connected to Hip Hop culture and are deeply invested in supporting the academic, social and personal development of Black male students.

In section's final chapter, *The legacy lives, "I leave you a thirst for education" Dr. Bethune's vision in action: A study of the impact of an HBCU on teachers and educational leaders,* Starker, Mariella-Walrond, Leggett-Watson and Scott examine the experiences of a group of K–16 educators who are graduates of the HBCU Bethune-Cookman University. Their work examines how their HBCU teacher preparation impacted their current practices as teachers. Their chapter presents the ways in which HBCU teacher education programs not only add nuance to the discussion on teacher preparation, but reaffirm the importance and the relevance of HBCUs in the preparation of teachers.

CONCLUSION

The chapters in this section attest that the recruitment, retention, and professional development of Black teachers have positive benefits for Black students and the high-need schools that many of them attend. Unfortunately, Black teachers often work in various contexts and conditions that mitigate and often neutralize their impact. These conditions make their work more difficult, constrain their efforts to teach, and impact their expectations and their students' achievement. Their presence alone cannot compensate or obliterate the effects of decades of neglect and ineffective policies and practices in schools where students of color attend. Additionally, recent data suggest that Black teacher turnover is increasing (Ingersoll & Connor, 2009). During the 2005–06 academic year, for example, Black teacher turnover was 20.7% compared to 19.4% for other teachers of color and 16.4% for White teachers. These new data suggest that the teaching profession may not be able to continue to attract effective Black teachers in high-need schools without significant resources aimed at recruiting and retaining them.

NOTE

The terms Black and African American are used interchangeable in this section introduction.

REFERENCES

Alliance for Excellent Education. (2004). *Tapping the potential: Retaining and developing high quality new teachers.* Retrieved from http://www.all4ed.org/publications/TappingThePotential/TappingThePotential.pdf

Barton, P. E., & Coley, R. J. (2009). *Passing the achievement gap II.* Princeton, NJ: The Educational Testing Service.

Belcher, R. N. (2001, March). *Predictive factors for the enrollment of African American students in special education preservice programs.* Paper presented at the meeting of Partnership for Rural Special Education, San Diego, CA.

Center for Educational Policy. (2006). *A public school primer.* Retrieved from http://www.ctredpol.org/publiceducationprimer

Choy, S. P. (1993). *America's teachers: Profile of a profession.* Darby, PA: Diane.

Clewell, B. C., Puma, M. J., & McKay, S. A. (2005, April). *Does it matter if my teacher looks like me? The impact of teacher race and ethnicity on student academic achievement.* Paper presented at the meeting of the American Educational Research Association, Montreal, Canada.

Clewell, B. C., & Villegas, A. M. (2001). *Absence unexcused: Ending teacher shortages in high-need areas.* Washington, DC: The Urban Institute.

Clotfelter, C. T., Ladd, H. F., & Vigdor, J. (2005). Who teaches whom? Race and the distribution of novice teachers. *Economics of Education Review, 24,* 377–392.

Clotfelter, C. T., Ladd, H. F., & Vigdor, J. (2007, November). *Are teacher absences worth worrying about in the U.S.?* (Working Paper No. W13848). Cambridge, MA: National Bureau of Economic Research.

Couch-Maddox, S. (1999). *Teachers' perceptions of African American male students in an urban school system.* Unpublished doctoral dissertation, Clark Atlanta University.

Darling-Hammond, L. (2000). Teacher quality and student achievement: A review of state policy evidence. *Education Policy Analysis Archives, 8*(1). Retrieved from epaa.asu.edu/eppa/v8n1

Darling-Hammond, L., & Baratz-Snowden, J. (2005). *A good teacher in every classroom: Preparing the highly qualified teacher our children deserve.* San Francisco: Jossey-Bass.

Dee, T. (2004). Teachers, race, and student achievement in a randomized experiment. *The Review of Economics and Statistics, 86,* 195–210.

de Vise, D., & Chandler, M. A. (2009, April 27). Poor neighborhoods, untested teachers. *The Washington Post,* p. A1, A15.

Dilworth, M. E. (Ed.). (1992). *Diversity in teacher education: New expectations.* San Francisco, CA: Jossey-Bass.

Dilworth, M., & Brown, A. L. (2007). *Teachers of color: Quality and effectiveness one way or another.* In M. Cochran-Smith, S. Feiman-Nemser, & J. McIntyre (Eds.), *Handbook of research on teacher education* (3rd ed., pp. 424–444). Mahwah, NJ: Erlbaum.

Dixson, A. D., & Dingus, J. E. (2008). In search of our mother's gardens: Black women teachers and professional socialization. *Teachers College Record, 110,* 805–837.

Ehrenberg, R. G., & Brewer, D. J. (1995). Did teacher's verbal ability and race matter in the 1960s? Coleman revisited. *Economics of Education Review, 14,* 1–21.

Evans, M. (1992). An estimate of race and gender role-model effects in teaching high school. *Journal of Economic Education, 23,* 209–217.

Farkas, G., Grobe, R. P., Sheehan, D., & Shuan, Y. (1990). Cultural resources and school success: Gender, ethnicity, and poverty groups within an urban school district. *American Sociological Review, 55,* 127–142.

Fenwick, L. T. (2001). *Patterns of excellence: Policy perspectives on diversity in teaching and school leadership.* Atlanta, GA: Southern Education Foundation.

Foster, M. (1997). *Black teachers on teaching.* New York: New Press.

Gay, G., Dingus, E., & Jackson, C. W. (2003). The presence and performance of teachers of color in the profession. Retrieved from http://www.communityteachers.org/reports/presPerfTeachersofColoringProfess.pdf

Gordon, J. A. (2000). *The color of teaching.* New York: Routledge-Falmer.

Hanushek, E. A. (1986). The economics of schooling: Production and efficiency in public schools. *Journal of Economic Literature, 24,* 1141–1177.

Hanushek, E. A. (1992). The trade-off between child quantity and quality. *Journal of Political Economy, 100,* 84–117.

Hess, F. M., & Leal, D. L. (1997). Minority teachers, minority students, and college matriculation. *Policy Studies Journal, 25,* 235–248.

Horng, E. L. (2005, April). *Teacher tradeoffs: Poor working conditions make urban schools hard-to-staff.* Paper presented at the annual meeting of the American Educational Research Association, Montreal, Canada.

Ingersoll, R. M. (2004, November). *Why do high-poverty schools have difficulty staffing their classrooms with qualified teachers?* Washington, DC: Center for American Progress.

Ingersoll, R. M., & Conner, R. (2009, April). *What the national data tell us about minority and Black teacher turnover.* Paper presented at the Annual Meeting of the American Education Research Association, San Diego, CA.

Irvine, J. J. (1990). *Black students and school failure.* Westport, CT: Praeger.

Irvine, J. J. (2002). *In search of wholeness: African American teachers and their culturally specific classroom practices.* New York: Palgrave.

Jonsson, P. (2003, January 21). White teachers flee Black schools: Some see exodus in South as a new form of segregation. *Christian Science Monitor.* Retrieved from www.csmonitor.com/2003/0121/p01s03-usgn.html

Kauchak, D., & Burback, M. D. (2003). Voices in the classroom: Case studies of minority teacher candidates. *Action in Teacher Education, 25,* 63–75.

King, S. H. (1993). The limited presence of African American teachers. *Review of Educational Research, 63,* 115–150.

Kirby, S. N., Berends, M., & Naftel, S. (1999). Supply and demand of minority teachers in Texas: Problems and prospects. *Education Evaluation and Policy Analysis, 21,* 47–66.

Klopfenstein, K. (2005). Beyond test scores: The impact of Black teacher role models on rigorous math taking. *Contemporary Economic Policy, 23,* 416–428.

Lynn, M. (2006). Education for the community: Exploring the culturally relevant practices of Black male teachers. *Teachers College Record, 108,* 2497–2522.

Meier, K. J., Stewart, J., & England, R. E. (1989). *Race, class, and education: The politics of second generation discrimination.* Madison, WI: University of Wisconsin Press.

Miller, R., Murnane, R., & Willett, J. (2007, August). *Do teacher absences impact student achievement? Longitudinal evidence from one urban school district* (Working paper No. W13356). Cambridge, MA: National Bureau of Economic Research.

Murnane, R. J., Singer, J. D., Willett, J. B., Kemple, J. J., & Olsen, R. J. (1991). *Who will teach? Policies that matter.* Cambridge, MA: Harvard University Press.

National Association of State Boards of Education. (2000). *Ensuring quality and quantity in the teaching workforce: Policies that can make it happen.* Alexandria, VA: Author.

National Center for Education Statistics. (2004). *Status and trends in the education of Blacks.* Washington, DC: U.S. Department of Education Institute Of Educational Sciences.

Orfield, G., & Lee. C. (2007). *Historic reversals, accelerating, resegregation, and the need for new integration strategies.* Los Angeles, CA: UCLA Civil Rights Project.

Rios, F., & Montecinos, C. (1999). Advocating social justice and cultural affirmation: Ethnically diverse preservice teachers' perspectives on multicultural education. *Equity & Excellence in Education, 32,* 66–76.

Rockoff, J. (2004). The impact of individual teachers on student achievement: Evidence from panel data. *American Economic Review, 94,* 247–252.

Scafidia, B., Sjoquistb, D. L., & Stinebrickner, T. R. (2007). Race, poverty, and teacher mobility. *Economics of Education Review, 26,* 145–159.

Schott Foundation, The. (2009). *Lost opportunity: A 50 state report on the opportunity to learn in America.* Cambridge, MA: Author.

Su, Z. (1997). Teaching as a profession and as a career: Minority candidates' perspectives. *Teaching and Teacher Education, 13,* 325–340.

Vandevoort, L. G., Amerein-Beardsley, A., & Berliner, D. C. (2004). National board certified teachers and their students' achievement. *Education Policy Analysis Archives, 12*(46). Retrieved from epaa.asu.edu/eppa/v12n46

Villegas, A. M. (2006). *Racial/ethnic diversity in the public school teaching force: A look at trends.* Washington, DC: National Education Association.

Villegas, A. M., & Geist, K. (2008, April). *Profile of new teachers of color in public schools: A look at issues of quantity and quality.* Paper presented at the annual meeting of the American Education Research Association, New York, NY.

Villegas, A. M., & Irvine, J. J. (2010). Diversifying the teaching force: An examination of major arguments. *Urban Review, 42,* 175– 192.

Wilder, M. (1999). Re-examining the African American teacher shortage: Building a new professional image of teaching for the 21st century. *Equity & Excellence in Education, 32,* 77–82.

CHAPTER 7

MENDING THE PIPELINE

Recruitment and Retention of African American Preservice Teachers in a Predominantly White Institution

David A. Byrd
University of Texas Health Science Center at San Antonio

Shailen M. Singh
Texas A&M University

To address the critical shortage of African American teachers in the United States, one college of education at a large predominantly White research university in the South has invested resources—both human and capital—to recruit and retain preservice teachers of color. This chapter provides a description of the activities that have been implemented to help *mend the pipeline* of preparing diverse teachers. These activities include outreach programs targeted at early identification and matriculation of prospective students and intrusive retention efforts focused on providing the academic support structure necessary to enhance learning and improve graduation rates. Also included in this chapter are recommendations for future research on the subject and guiding questions colleges of education can answer to develop their own recruitment and retention program.

Teacher Education and Black Communities, pages 143–160
Copyright © 2014 by Information Age Publishing
All rights of reproduction in any form reserved.

While extant literature has demonstrated a persistent gap between the percentage of the nation's teachers of color compared to the enrollment of K–12 students from under-represented racial and ethnic backgrounds (Tenore, Dunn, Laughter, & Milner, 2010), few teacher education programs—especially those at Predominantly White Institutions (PWIs)—have adequately addressed this demographic shift through focused recruitment and retention programs. One large predominantly White research university in the South has dedicated resources to attract high school and community college students into its teacher education program. These initiatives include a summer enrichment program which targets urban youth to visit campus so they might learn about the teaching profession and a summer workshop that targets prospective transfer students from minority-serving community colleges. This chapter will provide the details of programs that have helped to increase this college's African American enrollment from 153 in 2001 to 285 in 2011. Efforts such as the implementation of high-impact experiences that have improved the college's four-year graduation rate from 40.9% to 63.4% over that same time period will also be described.

If one thinks of the production of under-represented teachers as a pipeline, it could be argued that leaks exist which prevent prospects from becoming certified teachers. The pipeline begins with the identification of students in high schools and community colleges who either exhibit the qualities of great teachers—compassion, patience, commitment to social justice, etc.—or demonstrate an interest in the profession itself. After identification, these students must be counseled on the admissions, financial aid, and matriculation procedures for an educator preparation program. Barriers can prevent students from ever enrolling at this stage (e.g., lack of financial support, familial commitments, or other barriers common to first-generation students) and not all institutions invest the financial and/or human resources necessary to mitigate these obstacles. Even when recruitment issues are addressed, retention efforts must be narrowly tailored to meet the needs of under-represented students—financial aid must continue to be provided, timely academic support and intervention must be available, and high-impact learning experiences grounded in peer-reviewed research must be created to assist students in their progress to completion. In this chapter, we share our experiences developing recruitment and retention programs designed to mend the under-represented teacher preparation pipeline.

The pipeline which helps train professional educators has many leaks (See Figure 7.1). For competitive admission predominantly White institutions, students might be lost early in the process by not being admitted as first-time in college (FTIC) or transfer students. Once students matriculate, they may struggle with the transition to the university environment and either leave due to a failure to acclimate or choose to return to a more familiar environment. Finally, those who progress to the end of the program

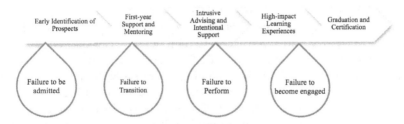

Figure 7.1 Graphical representation of teacher recruitment/retention pipeline with associated leaks at each stage.

could fail to gain their teaching credential because they do not pass their state certification exam.

PROFILES OF EDUCATION CANDIDATES

Although the enrollment in K–12 education of students of color has sharply increased in recent years, the production of teachers from under-represented racial and/or ethnic groups has not kept pace (Kirby, Berends, & Naftel, 1999; Broughman & Roollefson, 2000). According to the National Center for Education Statistics (NCES) (2007), one-third of America's student population in public schools in 2005 was a racial or ethnic minority. Hispanics accounted for 14% while 12% of students were African American. NCES predicts that by the year 2020, the minority population in schools will increase to 39% of the total population. Additionally, as Lewis, Bonner, Byrd, and James (2008) stated, "the research literature reports that African American males comprise approximately 2% of those enrolled in the 1,300 teacher preparation programs across the country (American Association for Colleges of Teacher Education [AACTE]), and 1% of the United States K–12 teaching force" (p. 225).

At competitive admission universities such as our Nation's flagship campuses, higher admission standards can serve as a deterrent for students interested in teaching as a career. Several studies have indicated that students interested in teaching as a career tend to have lower SAT scores, ACT scores, and scores on other college entrance exams (Gitomer, Latham, & Ziomek, 1999; Podgursky, Monroe, & Watson, 2004). These lower scores can directly impact individuals interested in recruiting students into colleges of education. As prospective candidates are identified, teacher preparation programs may not have the flexibility to admit underprepared students thereby decreasing the effectiveness of the recruitment efforts. Couple these data with the performance gap on standardized tests which exists between White high school students and their under-represented peers, and greater clarity is given to the need to help prepare African American and Hispanic prospective students and adopt alternative admission strategies so deserving students of color are afforded access to high-demand careers in education.

Guarino, Satibanez, and Daley (2006) provided a comprehensive literature review related to teacher recruitment and retention. Their analysis found that White females were more likely to pursue teaching as a career, but also found that minority teachers tended to be retained in the profession at higher rates. Particularly concerning in this study was the suggestion that teachers who serve in schools which predominantly serve low-income, underperforming students, and include higher proportions of racial or ethnic minorities are more likely to leave early in their profession—stressing the need to recruit teachers who share characteristics of the pupils they instruct.

A qualitative study of African American teachers by Gordon (2000) found that Black students generally viewed the teaching profession as unattractive. The reasons provided including that the profession was low-paying for the education that is required, that there is not enough educational support for students to succeed in their pursuit of teacher certification, and that there is a lack of encouragement and in some cases racist behavior by educator preparation programs that prevents African Americans from becoming teachers (Gordon, 2000). Recruitment efforts must encourage Black students and provide the financial support so student indebtedness is decreased, thereby making the selection of a service profession more attractive. Additionally, retention efforts must continually support and nurture under-represented learners so students feel the faculty and staff within the training program want them to succeed (Milam, 2010).

TEACHER RECRUITMENT EFFORTS

As indicated previously, effective recruitment efforts begin with the identification of prospects. In the particular college we identified, staff members visit urban high schools that serve a large number of under-represented populations and also visit community colleges in ethnically diverse regions as a means of identifying individuals who might become great teachers. Additionally, college representatives utilize future teacher organizations that are embedded within these schools (e.g., Texas Association of Future Educators, *Ready, Set, Teach!* classes, and Future Teacher Organizations at community colleges) by inviting these groups to visit campus to experience the campus community and engage in activities with faculty. These field trips are invaluable in both identifying prospects and providing the initial opportunity to extend a welcoming introduction to the opportunities on campus.

Identified prospects are entered into a recruitment database and contact is maintained throughout the admission and matriculation process so a welcoming message can be extended to these students and their parents. It is this database that is utilized to analyze recruitment effectiveness and serves as an invitation list for the programs delivered throughout the year. The following two examples of our recruitment activities demonstrate our options for exposing high school and community college students to the college's undergraduate programs.

Summer Enrichment Program

The Summer Enrichment Program (SEP) was created in the early 1990s as an opportunity for the college to expose prospective students to the opportunities available in the field of education. Specifically, the program is advertised as an educational experience for students interested in teaching in culturally diverse environments. It is the philosophy of the college that equally important to the increased production of certified teachers of color is the creation of in-service teachers—regardless of their racial or ethnic identity—who value and appreciate diversity and seek to expand educational opportunities for all students.

Effective recruitment strategies will inherently include tight linkages to retention practices that are based on empirical peer-reviewed evidence. The SEP is designed to engage prospective students with the support resources on which they can rely after matriculating to the university. These support resources include faculty—specifically faculty of color, the Student Success Center, the University Writing Center, and the Office of Multicultural Services, to name a few. As part of the admission application for the summer enrichment program, students are asked to write a response to the same essay prompts used in the university's admissions application. At one point during the student's time on campus, they are taken to the Writing Center and receive feedback on how their essays could be strengthened. Consequently, these teacher education prospects become more competitive for admission to the University and for available scholarships, but are also exposed to the usefulness of the Writing Center and the services it can provide once the student begins their post-secondary career on campus.

A high-impact learning experience highlighted by Kuh, Kinzie, Schuh, Whitt, and Associates (2005) as a strategy to increase student retention is the learning community. These opportunities to share learning experiences between students and faculty enhance learning and student engagement. The SEP involves undergraduate faculty so students can feel comfortable with the individuals with whom they will be sharing these experiences after they are admitted to the college. Faculty members are asked to present interactive experiential learning opportunities that engage students in the professor's research or instructional interests. Such presentations have included the use of technology to teach mathematic equations related to distance and time, social justice and multicultural issues in the classroom, and identifying and understanding learning disabilities in school environments. These presentations also serve the dual purpose of not just increasing faculty/student interaction, but also can introduce students to the need for teachers in high-demand fields such as mathematics, science, special, and bilingual education.

Summer Transfer Workshops

According to Cohen and Brawer (2008), students of color are increasingly enrolling in one of America's 1,173 public and private two-year colleges. The authors found that racially and/or ethnically under-represented students comprised 36.5% of community college enrollments—a 20% increase from the enrollment two decades earlier. As the cost of attending a university out-paces public funding of financial assistance (St. John, 2006), it is logical to expect the continued growth of community college enrollments in the future.

Any recruitment strategy that fails to address the unique needs of community college students will not adequately promote access for diverse populations. It is the responsibility of colleges and universities to disseminate specific information designed to assist in the transfer and matriculation of two-year students and to develop articulated transfer agreements when possible. Articulation agreements are tools designed to ensure the transferability of courses from one institution to another and can ease confusion and anxiety for prospective students (Cohen & Brawer, 2008).

The Summer Transfer Workshops in the college were created in 2005 as a mechanism to connect prospective community college transfers with the necessary information recourses to ensure students successfully matriculate to the four-year campus and to mitigate transfer shock that might arise from unfamiliarity with the campus, degree plans, and/or the faculty and staff at the University. At the workshop, students are introduced to admissions advisors who provide an overview of the application process and the minimum transfer requirements necessary to be admitted into the student's desired program. Financial aid representatives are also on hand to help facilitate the transfer of the Free Application for Federal Student Aid (FAFSA) information from one campus to the next. These individuals also spend time with students to discuss available scholarship, grant, and student loan opportunities that are available post-transfer.

Lewis and Middleton (2003) provided an overview of articles related to African American experiences in community colleges. By reviewing a decade of relevant articles, the authors found that although African Americans have often used community colleges as their conduit to higher education, several barriers have prevented their persistence to a bachelor's degree. The primary factors were centered on the themes of environmental factors—such as economic conditions and family constraints—and the need for a more diverse community college faculty. Although not all environmental concerns can be addressed by the CEHD, an effort is made to connect students with the support resources which may help overcome some of the barriers faced by under-represented transfers.

Following the presentations by University staff, College-level advisors and recruiters meet with the students to discuss the transferability of courses the students have taken and to provide an estimated time of graduation once students matriculate. All presentations are designed to give individualized attention because each student faces unique challenges depending upon the institution(s) students have attended and the types of courses they have taken in the past. It is the desire of the staff at the workshop to ensure that every student's concerns and or questions are addressed so as welcoming an environment as possible is created.

RETENTION EFFORTS

To effectively increase the production of teachers of color, colleges of education must be as equally concerned about the retention and graduation of their under-represented students as they are about recruiting these students initially. Braxton and McClendon (2001–2002) demonstrated that collegiate recruitment strategies should accurately and adequately provide prospective students with a clear view of what the student can and should expect in a collegiate setting. Accurately representing the institution to prospective students is vital to ensure students are familiar with the campus context to which they are applying. For PWIs it is important that recruitment publications and experiences do not misinform students. PWIs can sometimes appear to be a Historically Black College or University if publications are inaccurate. When students of color attend these institutions, they can feel misled and angry that they committed to study at an institution that is different from what they were expecting. This is a prime example of how recruitment strategies must keep retention in mind so students have a positive experience after matriculation.

The college identified for this chapter is committed to using its retention strategies as a showcase to both support and further its recruitment efforts. Several studies (Peltier, Laden, & Matranga, 1999; Hossler, 2005; Stage & Hossler, 2000) have focused solely on student attributes and behaviors that directly affect the likelihood of a student persisting through graduation, however the institution itself owes its students the commitment to do what it can to provide support, through intentional programming and services, to all recruited students (Tinto, 2010).

Many of the efforts the university has made illustrate the point that retention related efforts do not have to be costly in nature. Many of the programs illustrated herein can be easily replicated within the current economic context of tightened budges and restricted spending. The collegeis focusing on the shifting the culture of the college in an effort to weave retention related efforts into the fabric of daily operations. Below are a few examples of the efforts the college has made.

Undergraduate Student Success Center

The Undergraduate Student Success Center was established in 2008 to provide students with resources to support their academic and personal wellbeing. The center serves as a provider of resources, but more importantly it serves as a conduit for students to other on-campus resources. Terrion and Daoust (2011–2012) indicated that students are often unaware of the wide variety of services a campus can offer, and one of the intents of the center is to provide a *one-stop-shop* for students to not only find out about resources, but also to understand how to navigate the processes to access those academic support mechanisms. Essentially, the center serves as an academic "pharmacy" of sorts. For example, students struggling to engage with content related to their major will not only receive information related to effective reading strategies, but may also receive information related to free career testing and/or counseling services available on campus.

The center provides individual academic counseling where students have the opportunity to discuss the issues leading to any academic deficiencies. After one-on-one advising sessions regarding time management and study skills, the center then helps students to self-identify the root cause of their academic or personal challenges as well as the campus services that can assist them in improving their academic performance. By doing this, the center seeks not only to improve overall student performance, but to also assist students in understanding the ideal process of navigating the bureaucratic processes associated with being on a large PWI, to provide a more personalized approach to dealing with academic challenges.

The college has been intentional in developing strong links between recruitment and retention. Implied within the recruitment process is a college-wide promise to provide students with the tools and resources they need to be academically and personally successful. Braxton and McClendon (2001–2002) indicate that first year students, whether transfer or first time in college (FTIC), face a level of culture shock during their transition to the university setting resulting in high, and unexpected levels of stress.

The center, in partnership with college faculty and staff, seeks to minimize this transition period through a variety of services including free tutoring and evening workshops on a variety of success themes (e.g., time management, study skills, test taking, financial literacy, etc.). Students receive information regarding services through as many outlets as possible, including contact from advisors and faculty members, as well as through interactions with upperclassmen mentors. The services are all provided free of charge, and an intentional effort is made to schedule the availability of services around the typical student's academic routine. In other words, many of the services are available in the evening.

A key area of focus is to ensure that the center is not simply a *remediation* provider. Consequently, the center also provides workshops and resources related to high achieving students, specifically regarding career related workshops, and information regarding opportunities for students to engage in scholarly research. The center provides incentives for students to engage in undergraduate research, thereby incentivizing additional scholarly work and providing students with meaningful opportunities to engage with faculty members (Kuh, et al., 2010).

The college's leadership, in conjunction with the center, has made an effort to shift the focus of the academic probation and dismissal process to one that is more developmental rather than punitive. The process is shared with students as one that allows faculty and staff to provide students in need with additional one on one counseling. Students demonstrating high levels of academic need are provided individual academic plans, including strategies for time management and specific instructions on how to prioritize their study related tasks. The goal is to provide an experience that is more than just *additional hoops* through which the student must jump, and rather one that students recognize as being an example of the college's commitment to their success. Any student who has an anomalous semester—an uncharacteristically deficient semester in the middle of an otherwise good academic career—receives individualized contact from staff simply to check in to see whether the college can provide any additional support as they rebound from one poor semester.

High-Impact Practices

High-impact learning experiences have proven to be effective strategies to improve student learning, increase student engagement on campus, and empirical studies have demonstrated that these benefits have been particularly helpful in increasing the graduation rates of students of color (Kuh et al., 2010). California State University at Northridge, for example, identified that 73% of Latino students who participated in three or more high impact practices graduated in four years compared to the 69% rate of other non-Latino students who engaged in the same activities (Huber, 2010). Particularly beneficial are programs that "combine and concentrate other empirically validated pedagogical approaches into a single multidimensional activity" (Kuh, 2010, p. xi). The university has made an institutional commitment to increasing the number of available high-impact practices to students, and the college has integrated many of the practices in its operational culture. Below is an overview of the efforts the college has made:

Academic Advising

The college is making efforts to increase the intentionality behind its academic advising practices. Academic advisors play key roles in influencing both student achievement and overall student engagement (Kuh, 2010). Furthermore the state's higher education governing board encourages outcome-driven advising, prompting advisors to assess student learning (about curricular or other academic issues) as a result of academic advising. The board also encourages a high level of collaboration between academic advising offices and other college wide functions such as recruitment, admissions, and academic success related programs.

The college involves a wide group of faculty and staff in intrusive advising practices. First semester students are required to meet with their academic advisors during the preregistration period, during which time issues related study skills, time management, and class selection are discussed. Students are then referred to the Undergraduate Student Success Center should they need additional support.

First Year Learning Communities

The college has reframed foundational courses within individual majors to teach not only content, but also the processes associated with being both a successful student and a successful practitioner within the student's chosen profession. These clear indications and expectations have been proven to have a positive impact on overall student retention—in order to help student's succeed, it is incumbent on faculty to provide the metrics by which success will be measured (Tinto, 2010). Furthermore, research indicates that a student's level of commitment at the end of their first year can be a strong predictor of their intention to continue with their collegiate career and ultimately graduate (Tinto, 1993).

Specifically, the classes cover the skills associated with successful academic behavior. For example, instead of immediately discussing the syllabus on the first day of class, learning community faculty begin by talking about the purpose of the syllabus and how students should view the syllabus as a roadmap for the semester. Additionally, instead of simply providing assignment requirements, professors also discuss the ideal process by which students should complete assignments (i.e., meeting with the university writing center for assignments, ample study time for exams, etc.). The intent is to provide clear and consistent expectations regarding successful academic behaviors. These expectations can then be reiterated throughout the student's academic career.

The learning communities are also designed to provide increased engagement between faculty and students to provide a supportive environment and a more enriching experience that eases the student's transition into the university. Examples of experiences provided through learning communities include dinners at the homes of learning community faculty members, as well as outside of class social events (campus performance arts, sporting events, other off campus experiential learning opportunities, etc.). Each learning community is supported by an upper-class peer mentor. The college's peer mentor program assigns upper-division students to each learning community class to provide peer based academic support. The peer mentors are charged with coordinating group study sessions as well as serving as a resource to help FTIC students understand and navigate academic challenges. This additional support has proven to be a successful retention strategy both for low income, first generation students (Torres, 2004), as well as for students of color on predominantly white campuses (Hurtado & Carter, 1997). The college was able to enroll 100% of all first-time-in college (FTIC) undergraduates in a learning community for the fall of 2012.

Long Term Domestic/International Field Experiences

The college also provides students with the opportunity to participate in outside-of-class opportunities designed to provide students with a global perspective on their future profession. The college funds travel opportunities for students in courses which embed long-term field trips to both international and domestic locations. These faculty-led experiences provide students the opportunity to gain practical experience by applying in-class learning within the context of a different environment. In 2012, students in the college took trips to Gambia/Senegal, Mexico, Germany, Austria/Hungary, India, Costa Rica, and New York City, just to name a few.

Service Learning

Kuh (2010) indicated that service learning is characterized by giving students the opportunity to apply their classroom learning to local communities in an effort to better the quality of life of the community residents. Service learning also provides the occasion for students to engage in impromptu academic conversations with faculty members as they get to know them in a less formal and more personal environment.

The college was recently able to combine several high-impact practices through a service learning trip to the economically disadvantaged regions of their home state. The experience was offered to students in a learning community housed in the college's preservice teacher training program.

The students had been involved in a fall course which taught sociological issues in education and were taking a spring course about multicultural issues in education. The courses' content covered topics ranging from students examining their own cultural belief systems to information regarding the changing student demographics in the state. At the completion of the fall course students were provided the opportunity to travel to an impoverished area as a learning cohort. The trip was led by the faculty member who coordinated the students' learning community and also involved key members of the college staff, including the Assistant Dean for Undergraduate Academic Affairs, and the Director of Recruitment.

Students engaged with teachers in regional schools to gain a better understanding of the challenges their students face on a daily basis and to gain appreciation for the importance of family involvement in student success throughout K–12 preparation. Additionally, the learning community students were able to gain a wealth of practical information related to the impact of socioeconomic backgrounds and student persistence. Through a partnership with a local non-profit organization—a group charged with improving high school graduation and college attendance rates in the area—learning community students visited with families in the *colonias* near the schools they visited. *Colonias* are high-poverty communities that house many first-generation students. While visiting with families, students provided parents with information about building a college-going culture in their home and they distributed children's books that had been donated by a local second-hand book store.

In addition to the rich experiences, students were given the opportunity to engage with faculty and key staff on a personal level. The faculty and staff members who led the program became key providers of personal and academic support. Furthermore, providing the students with the opportunity to take an expense-free trip to further their education is a clear sign of the institution's commitment to the individual student's success. An additional benefit to the student was the ability to practically implement instructional theory they had been provided in the classroom by engaging in a service opportunity in the field. This provided the dual benefit of improved learning outcomes and increased engagement with college faculty and staff.

Integrating Successful Retention Strategies

Across the country, universities are being asked to recruit students from under-represented populations in an effort to create a diverse learning environment and to create a diverse population of graduates. However, many of these under-represented students come from academically deficient backgrounds, and to an extent are being put in a less than optimal position as it relates to skills necessary for academic success. The resulting relationship between the university and the student can be categorized as mutually beneficial: the student is put in a position to receive a quality educational experience, and the university receives a financial benefit as well as benefits related to diversity goals (Singh & Byrd, 2011). However the university must be cognizant of students' academic backgrounds and be proactive by providing retention related resources. Furthermore, the use of high-impact practice, including learning communities and service learning (among other) have been determined to have a positive impact on overall level of persistence and academic success for underserved populations (Swaner & Brownell, 2009).

IMPLICATIONS FOR PREDOMINANTLY WHITE INSTITUTIONS

A recent report produced by the Center for the Study of Race and Equity in Education at the University of Pennsylvania demonstrated the stark reality facing universities as they attempt to improve their graduation rates for African American students—specifically for Black males. The study found that Black males were often underprepared for college after leaving their K–12 institutions and accounted for fewer than 5% of the student enrollment in U.S. higher education. Additionally, Black males had the lowest college completion rates of all races/ethnicities and among both sexes with less than a third who entered graduating within six years (Harper, 2012). However, beyond these gloomy statistics, this report also provided a viable pathway through which PWIs can enhance the undergraduate experience for Black males.

Harper (2010; 2012) demonstrated that institutions must stop viewing student of color departure through a deficit lens. In other words, we must stop concentrating our research on the reasons under-represented students leave our campuses and begin identifying what systems were in place to support successful students and replicate those practices. Colleges of education are unable to replicate effective strategies if they have not been identified. Further research is needed to understand the characteristics of our successful students of color and the support mechanisms that have been most effective for increasing the graduation rates of under-represented populations.

Successful African American college graduates from predominantly White institutions were capable of navigating through colleges in which they were more likely to encounter microaggressions and instances of racism than they were to have interactions with students with similar identities. Racist encounters might range from racially charged jokes, to racial slurs written in common living areas (Harwood, Huntt, Mendehnall, & Lewis, 2012). Not only were the specific instances of microaggressive behavior troublesome, students also reported feeling marginalized with a lack of staff attentiveness to racially charged comments or behavior.

Harper, Davis, Jones, McGowan, Ingram, and Platt (2011) termed this as the burden of *onlyness* which was defined as "the psychoemotional burden of having to strategically navigate a racially politicized space occupied by few peers, role models, and guardians from one's same racial or ethnic group" (p. 190). This onlyness can also be evidenced by minority students being asked to represent the experiences of all students of color in classroom discussions (Watson, Terrell, Wright, & Associates, 2002). Research from Bonner (2010) discovered that gifted African American learners in higher education must establish viable relationships with faculty, must connect with peer groups to address their need for belonging, and must have adequate support from family units to succeed in college. Grier-Reed (2010) provided an example of a best practice called the African American Student Network (referred to as AFAM) in a large Midwestern PWI. Grier-Reed described AFAM as a networking group that provides focuses both on developing relationships with faculty, staff and students, and allowing students to make meaning of their own experience. Furthermore, Harper (2013) indicated that peer to peer interactions can provide students of color with valuable lessons on how to navigate through problematic campus environments by providing both roles models and sounding boards by which students can process through their experiences as a minority on a PWI. The pipeline that the college mentioned in this chapter has established has worked to accentuate these support structures for underrepresented students and serves as a model for other educator preparation programs seeking to increase the production of African American teachers.

Guiding Questions to Consider

Universities that are interested in developing a summer enrichment program designed to introduce students to specific curricular options such as teacher education should keep in mind a wide-range of issues that may not immediately come to mind. The following questions might help develop an experience that is rewarding for the students, fruitful for the college's enrollment management plans, and safe for all involved.

- What are the college and university policies and procedures for hosting a summer camp experience on campus (e.g., risk management paperwork, etc.)?
- What type of financial resources will be dedicated to the experience and is there the option to seek external funding?
- From which geographic regions will students be recruited to attend and how will they be contacted? Are there pre-existing relationships with individuals in schools who can assist with making these contacts?

- Are there legal implications for hosting minors on campus and what level of liability will the college take on by hosting these students?
- How will students be transported to and from the experience?
- In what ways can current and former students, faculty, and university offices be introduced into the students' on-campus experiences?

Colleges and universities interested in fostering a transfer-friendly environment should consider the following questions:

- From what colleges do the majority of transfers originate and how well does the four-year curriculum match up with the courses at these feeder institutions?
- What are the most common concerns expressed by transfer students in the undergraduate program and how can these issues be addressed before students matriculate to the university?
- How does the university convey a welcoming environment for all populations, specifically prospective transfers and under-represented populations?

Successful retention strategies should stem more from an organizational cultural shift. Retention related programming should be woven into the fabric of the college's operations. Daily operations (i.e., academic advising, academic probation, student advising, etc.) should have their intent reframed to be used as tools by which the institution can both reaffirm its commitment to retention, while also sharing clear expectations for student success related behaviors. Questions associated with this reframing process are below:

- What are the learning outcomes for academic processes such as advising or probation? What are we hoping that students know or understand about their role as a result of the processes?
- What do we expect out of our first year students? When are we sharing those expectations? Are we equipping them with the resources to meet those expectations?
- Who is engaged in our retention related efforts? Do we have a fair representation of both faculty and staff?
- Are our retention related efforts proactive or reactive? Are we waiting for students to make a mistake before intervening?
- What implicit messages are we sending to our students with every interaction?
- Who serves as mentors to our undergraduate students of color? Can these mentors adequately represent the diverse backgrounds from which our students originate?

CONCLUSION

To enhance the chances for the success of African American students in teacher education programs, we must improve the delivery of our recruitment and retention practices by utilizing observed data gathered from those who have graduated from PWIs in the past. Figure 7.2 describes an ideal pipeline for preparing preservice teachers of color. The pipeline provides seamless and supported transitions from intake (recruitment) through graduation. Furthermore, this ideal pipeline uses feedback loops which improve recruitment strategies. Retention strategies such as study abroad and learning communities can provide prospective students with an exciting view into what the university experience is like—and thus should serve as an excellent recruitment tool. Having former students who were successful as undergraduates return to campus to share their perspectives on the value of their university experience can also provide prospective students with additional rich information to assist them in decision making processes. Colleges and universities should intentionally design these experiences with post-event marketing in mind, and use them as a showcase to demonstrate the opportunities prospective students will be provided to supplement their in-class experiences.

Colleges of education must commit themselves to system change that improves K–12 education. To do so, these institutions must take ownership of the current context where the vast majority of teachers are from upper-middle class America and rarely look like the students they instruct. Through a dedicated recruitment program which focuses on the early identification of talented, diverse, preservice teaching candidates and a concerted retention effort that addresses the unique needs of our low-socioeconomic first generation students, it has been proven that colleges of education can transform the demographics of students choosing to pursue teaching as a career.

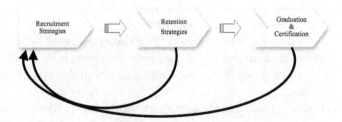

Figure 7.2 Recruitment/retention pipeline process with feedback loops.

REFERENCES

Bonner, II, F. A. (2010). *Academically gifted African American male college students.* Santa Barbara, CA: Praeger.

Braxton, J. M., & McClendon, S. A. (2001–2002). The fostering of social integration through institutional practice, *3*(1), 57–71.

Broughman, S., & Rollefson, M. (2000). Teacher supply in the United States: Sources of newly hired teachers in public and private schools: 1987–88 to 1993–94. *Education Statistics Quarterly, 2*(3), 28–32.

Cohen, A. M., & Brawer, F. B. (2008). *The American community college.* (5th ed.). San Francisco: Jossey-Bass.

Gitomer, D. H., Latham, A. S., & Ziomek, R. (1999). *The academic quality of prospective teachers: The impact of admissions and licensure testing.* Princeton, NJ: Educational Testing Service.

Gordon, J. A. (2000). *The color of teaching.* New York: RoutledgeFalmer.

Grier-Reed, T. L. (2010). The African American student network: Creating sanctuaries and counterspaces for coping with racial microaggressions in higher education settings. *Journal of Humanistic Counseling, Education and Development, 49,* 181–188.

Guarino, C. M., Santibanez, L., & Daley, G. A. (2006). Teacher recruitment and retention: A review of the recent empirical literature. *Review of Educational Research, 76*(2), 173–208.

Harper, S. R. (2010). An anti-deficit achievement framework for research on students of color in STEM. In S. R. Harper & C. B. Newman (Eds.), *Students of color in STEM: Engineering a new research agenda* (pp. 63–74). San Francisco: Jossey-Bass.

Harper, S. R., Davis, R. J., Jones, D. E., McGowan, B. L., Ingram, T. N., & Platt, C. S. (2011). Race and racism in the experiences of Black male resident assistants at predominantly white universities. *Journal of College Student Development, 52*(2), 180–200.

Harper, S. R. (2012). *Black male student success in higher education: A report from the national Black male college achievement study.* Philadelphia: University of Pennsylvania, Center for the Study of Race and Equity in Education.

Harper, S. R. (2013). Am I my brother's teacher? Black undergraduates, racial socialization, and peer pedagogies in predominantly white postsecondary contexts. *Review of Research in Education, 37,* 183–211.

Harwood, S. A., Huntt, M. B., Mendenhall, R., & Lewis, J. A. (2012). Racial microaggressions in the residence halls: Experiences of students of color at a predominantly white university. *Journal of Diversity in Higher Education, 5*(3), 159–173.

Hossler, D. (2005). Managing student retention: Is the glass half full or half empty, or simply empty? *College and University Journal, 81*(2), 11–14.

Huber, B. (2010). *Does participation in multiple high impact practices affect student learning at Cal State Northridge?* Unpublished manuscript.

Hurtado, S., & Carter, D. (1997). Effects of college transition and perception of the campus racial climate on Latino college students' sense of belonging. *Sociology of Education, 70,* 324–325.

Kirby, S., Berends, M., & Naftel, S. (1999). Supply and demand of minority teachers in Texas: Problems and prospects. *Educational Evaluation and Policy Analysis, 21*(1), 47–66.

Kuh, G. D., Kinzie, J., Schuh, J. H., Whitt, E. J., & Associates. (2005). *Student success in college: Creating conditions that matter.* San Francisco: Jossey-Bass.

Lewis, C., Bonner, F., Byrd, D., & James, M. (2008). Recruiting African American males into urban teacher preparation programs from university athletic departments. *The National Journal of Urban Education & Practice, 3,* 224–238.

Lewis, C. W., & Middleton, V. (2003). African Americans in community colleges: A review of research reported in the Community College Journal of Research and Practice. *Community College Journal of Research and Practice, 27*(9), 787–798.

Milam, J. (2010). (Re)envisioning teacher education. In V. Hill-Jackson & C. W. Lewis (Eds.), *Transforming teacher education: What went wrong with teacher training and how we can fix it* (pp. 3–36). Sterling, VA: Stylus.

National Center for Education Statistics (NCES). (2007). Table *220: Total number of degree-granting institutions and fall enrollment in these institutions, by type and control of institution and percentage of minority enrollment: 2005.* Washington, D.C.: Department of Education, 2007.

Peltier, G. L., Laden, R., & Mantranga, M. (1999). Student persistence in college: A review of research. *Journal of College Student Retention: Research, Theory, and Practice, 1,* 357–376.

Podgursky, M., Monroe, R., & Watson, D. (2004). The academic quality of public school teachers: An analysis of entry and exit behavior. *Economics of Education Review, 23*(5), 507–518.

Singh, S., & Byrd, D. (2011). Living in the shadows: Experiences of undocumented students. *Multicultural Learning & Teaching, 6*(2), 22–34.

St. John, E. P. (2006). *Education and the public interest: School reform, public finance, and access to higher education.* Dordrecht, The Netherlands: Springer.

Stage, F. K., & Hossler, D. (2000). Where is the student? Linking student behaviors, college choice, and college persistence. In J. M. Braxton (Ed.), *Reworking the student departure puzzle* (pp. 170–194). Nashville, TN: Vanderbilt University Press.

Swaner, L. E., & Brownell J. E. (2009). Outcomes of high-impact practices for underserved students: A review of the literature. Retrieved from http://www.aacu.org/inclusive_excellence/documents/ProjectUSALitReviewrevisedMar10.pdf

Tenore, F. B., Dunn, A. C., Laughter, J. C., & Milner, H. R. (2010). Teacher candidate selection, recruitment, and induction. In V. Hill-Jackson & C. W. Lewis (Eds.), *Transforming teacher education: What went wrong with teacher training, and how we can fix it* (pp. 93–118). Sterling, VA: Stylus.

Terrion, J. L., & Daoust, J. (2011–2012). Assessing the impact of supplemental instruction on the rention of undergraduate students after controlling for motivation. *Journal of College Student Retention: Research, Theory and Practice, 13*(3), 311–327.

Tinto, V. (2010). From theory to action: Exploring the institutional conditions for student retention. In J. C. Smart (Ed.), *Higher education: Handbook of theory and research, Vol. 25* (pp. 51–89). Manhattan: Springer Publishing.

Tinto, V. (1993). *Leaving college: Rethinking the causes and cures of student attrition.* Chicago: University of Chicago Press.

Torres, V. (2004). Familial influences on the identity development of Latino first year students. *Journal of College Student Development, 45,* 457–469.

Watson, L. W., Terrell, M. C., Wright, D. J., & Associates (2002). How minority students experience college: Implications for planning and policy. Sterling, VA: Stylus.

CHAPTER 8

HUMAN CAPITAL INVESTMENT

Supporting the Development of Visionary Change Agents in Teacher Preparation Programs for Urban Schools and Communities

Derrick Robinson, Ayana Allen, and Chance W. Lewis
University of Carolina

This chapter highlights a strategic plan for the development of Black teachers as visionary change agents in urban schools. The historical and present reality of Black teachers in urban schools sets the stage for strategic recommendations called Human Capital Investment. Human Capital Investment is a specialized and comprehensive set of recommendations designed for the development of change agents in the reformation of schools and communities. It is an aggressive plan consisting of specialized curriculum and pedagogy, teacher recruitment, and enriching field experiences which will create a pipeline for exemplary Black teachers to enter and impact urban schools.

Teacher Education and Black Communities, pages 161–188
Copyright © 2014 by Information Age Publishing
All rights of reproduction in any form reserved.

This chapter overviews Human Capital Investment as a detailed set of recommendations focused on revolutionizing university teacher preparatory programs. We will also provide recommendations for each stakeholder to ensure the successful implementation of Human Capital Investment.

> Until such time as institutionalized racism and structural poverty are eliminated as barriers to the educational achievement of Black students, an important component of their advancement will be teachers who perceive the structural barriers; who love the students for themselves; and who seek to guide students over the hurdles, to face the rising sun, as freed people. (Frederick & View, 2009, p. 604)

It has been substantially documented that highly qualified and culturally relevant teachers make a profound difference in the lives of students (Darling-Hammond, 2010; Gay, 2002; Ladson-Billings, 1995; NCTQ, 2004; NCTQ, 2013). Unfortunately, few teacher preparation programs in the United States are producing the caliber of a highly qualified teaching force that is dedicated and equipped to serve all students in spite of the social and institutional inequities that typically plague urban, low wealth communities and schools that predominately serve Black students (Darling-Hammond, 2010; NCTQ, 2013). This chapter begins with a historical overview of the African American educator experience from the emancipation of slaves post-Civil War up until the onslaught of desegregation. This historical context and subsequent conceptual review of current literature surrounding teacher preparation, frames our proposal of a transformative teacher preparation program entitled *The Human Capital Investment*. The Human Capital Investment is dedicated to the development of contemporary Black educators as visionary change agents who will be equipped to serve in urban schools. The Human Capital Investment calls for the strategic investment of money, resources, time, and effort into the systematic development of highly qualified, culturally relevant teachers which is a direct investment into the overall well-being of largely marginalized and often neglected communities (Wilson, 2012). This chapter highlights recommendations to develop teachers to enter urban schools and serve as change agents. In the preparation of Black teachers for urban schools, this chapter proposes that Historically Black Colleges and Universities (HBCUs) serve as fertile ground for their development because of its attraction of Black students and its historical allegiance to the Black Community.

HISTORICAL CONTEXT

African American Educators

African American educators[1] were visionary change agents in the Black community, for they were the anchors that held down and the pillars that held up the Black race. The postantebellum reality for African Americans posited education as the imperative and the great equalizer. Slavery's imposed illiteracy upon Black slaves, ignited their relentless pursuit of reading and writing. Moreover, literate Blacks were held in high esteem amongst the community (Anderson, 1988), which included Black teachers. Many of the Black educators and leaders during this time become literate under slavery, and those who did not become literate, understood the liberation that could ensue from literation (Anderson, 1988; Butchart, 2010). Teachers were the largest sector of professionals that provided leadership and a voice within and for the Black community (Franklin, 2009). They were revered, respected, and responsible for the success of future generations of Black leaders; which in turn secured the success of the entire race (Fairclough, 2007; Franklin, 2009; Gist, 2010; Kelly, 2009; Stanford, 1998). Black teachers exhibited a legacy of activism (Loder-Jackson, 2011) because they knew that education was the door to liberation (Anderson, 1988) and that they held the key that opened that door:

> Teachers shared a belief that education would liberate the black masses from ignorance, degradation, and poverty. They insisted that the colored race would sink or swim according to the education that they received. A people impoverished by slavery and benighted by enforced ignorance, urgently required lessons in freedom. Whether their classrooms were in redbrick, Gothic-towered universities or ramshackle schoolhouses of rough-sawn planks, teachers saw themselves as leaders of the race. (Fairclough, 2007, pp. 7–8)

According to Frederick and View (2009), such liberatory spaces were created through struggling against racist policy and an oppressive sociopolitical context to instill cultural consciousness, promote academic excellence, and provide the tools for racial uplift. Black teachers also empowered Black students through culturally responsive (Gay, 2002) and emancipatory teaching (Frederick & View, 2009) Furthermore, resistance, resilience, and agency were the nature of African American teachers (Siddle Walker, 2001), for their responsibilities extended beyond the scope of simply imparting academic knowledge and skills upon their students

Black teachers' pedagogical strength, which emerged during the late 1800s and early 1900s (Gist, 2010) was instrumental to the learning process of Black students, and often times made up for the disparities in facilities, resources, and opportunities (Fairclough, 2007; Gist, 2010; Kelly, 2009). Black teachers embodied a variety of culturally based rhetorical strategies to engage student learning (Brown, 2009). Such culturally relevant strategies included the incorporation of the cultural characteristics, historical epistemologies, experiences, and perspectives of Black students, and using them as conduits for transformative teaching and learning (Gay, 2002). Moreover, such teaching practices lacked deficit perspectives and did not blame students, nor their familial and home situations when students did not learn (Kelly, 2009). Kelly (2009) affirmed that Black teacher's creativity, ingenuity, and action provided their students with strategies of opportunity. Frederick and View's (2009) comprehensive look at Black educators in DC from the 1800s to 2008 revealed that (a) love (high expectation and care in the context of schooling), (b) guidance (making implicit rules of society explicit for students in order to navigate schools and the larger society), and (c) sociopolitical critique (building liberation and transformational skills) were the emerging themes that fostered liberatory spaces for Black children in urban schools in spite of shifting policies and administrations.

Black teachers made life-changing investments in their students as well as taught said students the ways by which to make investments of their own with the hopes of leading a better life. It was understood that collective capital and social networks created power (Frederick & View, 2009). Kelly (2009) discussed situational pedagogies:[2] "Black teachers' emphases were not simply on knowledge with an economic payoff; they often emphasized knowledge which could increase racial awareness and pride, as well as knowledge of White racism and discrimination" (Kelly, 2009, p. 332). He contended:

> Black teachers in all-black schools had the task of uplifting the race beyond the acquisition of cultural capital. Their primary emphasis was educational capital—the skills, knowledge, and credentials that could be transferred into economic capital—that most poor and working-class black parents simply could not give their children. Given the lack of alternatives, educational capital was the accepted mode to social mobility for blacks in a segregated society enduring state-sponsored racism. Educational capital gave black people hope that formal academic standards or qualifications would be the "great equalizer" despite its limitations in an oppressive society. (p. 333)

Black teacher's explicit incorporation of educational capital, cultural capital, and economic capital into learning environments, helped Black students navigate their situated experiences and also helped them to demand respect as individuals and as a race (Kelly, 2009).

The Preparation of Black Educators

Black teachers were in high demand and low supply at the turn of the twentieth century. Black educators were trained in private normal schools, secondary schools, and Black colleges and universities (Anderson, 1988; Fairclough, 2007), with the majority of Black teachers' preparation taking place at Historically Black Colleges and Universities (HBCUs) (Hunter-Boykin, 1992). According to Anderson (1988), some normal schools even accepted students who had not gone to high school but who passed an examination, and high schools and junior colleges were considered to be adequate teacher preparation. In the early twentieth century, states required prospective teachers to hold a high school diploma for admission to the normal schools while colleges and universities also upgraded their teacher training programs. At this time, the majority of graduates were going into teaching, more so than any other postgraduate career (Anderson, 1988). During this time, the existing black educational institutions with the ability to develop strong teacher education programs consisted of (a) 16 land-grant and seven state normal schools, (b) approximately 50 public high schools and five city normal schools, (c) approximately 60 private colleges, and (d) the more than 200 private institutions offering secondary and normal courses (Anderson, 1988). Teacher preparation was essential for the uplift of the Black race. Anderson (1988) contended: "If black children were to learn, they would be taught by black teachers" (p. 110).

DESEGREGATION: A RIPPING OF THE SEAM
AND THE EXODUS OF APTITUDE

A Ripping of the Seam

Black teachers' commitment and dedication during segregation compensated for "poor buildings, scanty equipment, and lack of books" (Fairclough, 2007, p. 5). Siddle Walker (2009) contended: "Segregated schools were characterized by self-efficacious, committed, and well-trained black teachers; extracurricular activities that encouraged students to utilize their multiple talents; strong leadership that engaged parents in the support of the children's education, and institutional and interpersonal forms of caring that encouraged students to believe in what they could achieve" (p. 272–273). It was believed that desegregation would offer equal educational opportunity and access for Black children, however, it became the ripping of the seam in the fabric of Black education, altered the Black teacher's position in the community, consequently unraveling the quilt of the Black community. The subsequent experiences of Black educators during the postsegregation era remains still in need of a seamstress, a stitch, a safety pin for repair: "Ever since Reconstruction, black teachers acted as community leaders, interracial diplomats, and builders of black institutions. Integration underminded those functions and diminished the relative status of black teachers. For some black teachers, integration brought demotion or dismissal" (Fairclough, 2007, p. 4). In fact, the most well educated Black teachers who knew the most about teaching Black students were the ones systematically dismissed after desegregation (Siddle Walker, 2001). Likewise, the victories in the civil rights movement that pushed forth the paradigmatic shift in the education of Blacks through integration sadly resulted in significant job losses for Black teachers, who began to seek out other career opportunities (Gist, 2010).

The Exodus of High Aptitude Teachers

Desegregation and the successes of Civil Rights legislation, while opening up a multitude of opportunities for minorities and women, created societal shifts that were catastrophic for the urban poor. Wilson (2012) cited joblessness, female-headed households, economic shifts, larger labor pools, growing youth population and increased social isolation of the urban poor as harmful realities uncovered in the post-segregation inner city. Teaching, largely considered a female-dominated profession, diminished in attraction as career paths opened for women and minorities over the decades since desegregation (Irvine, 1990; Corcoran, Evans, & Schwab, 2004; Lewis, 2006; Auguste, Kihn, & Miller, 2010; Madkins, 2011). The 1970s and 1980s saw dramatic declines in the percentage of minority students, particularly from historically black colleges and universities, who chose to major in education (Irvine, 1990). In addition to a teacher shortage, the exodus of high aptitude teachers created a drain on the profession. Hoxby and Leigh (2004) noted that high-aptitude women, seeking greater pay parity with high-aptitude men, were pulled away from the teaching profession to enter occupations that offered greater compensation. The teaching profession, often characterized by pay compression that lowered pay-for-aptitude, pushed high-aptitude teachers out and increased the percentage of low-aptitude teachers (Hoxby & Leigh, 2004). According to Corcoran, Evans and Schwab (2004), 48.8% of high aptitude female college graduates in 1964 entered the teacher profession; however, by 1992, only 11.8% of high aptitude female college graduates entered the teaching profession. From 1963 to 2000, the shift in both low and high aptitude female teachers fell from 48 and 20% to 16 and 4%, respectively (Hoxby & Leigh, 2004).

Teacher quality has also suffered, as recent school improvement strategies focus on improving present teachers while ignoring the need to "upgrade the caliber of young people entering the profession" (Auguste et al., 2010, p.9). This brain drain, although universal in its impact on education, has become more pronounced in urban, low wealth schools. Darling-Hammond (2010) also noted that schools with populations greater than 90% minority or 75% free and reduced lunch may have as high as 25% of its teaching staff classified as unqualified. Citing data from a 2009 School and Staff Survey, Moore and Lewis (2012) noted that urban schools have the highest percentage of novice teachers. This observation is further supported by the National Council on Teacher Quality (2013) which highlighted that the novice teachers are most likely to be placed with the neediest students. Auguste et al. (2010) also reported that, compared to leading nations, the United Sates "recruits from the bottom two-thirds of college classes, and, for many schools in poor neighborhoods, from the bottom third" (p. 10).

A COMPELLING CASE FOR CHANGE

Educational and economic access cannot be left to chance for students in urban poor communities. The percentage of Black and low income students who access higher education immediately after high school, has increased from 41.7% and 31.2% in 1975 to 62 % and 50.6% in 2010, respectively (U.S. Department of Education, 2012). Despite these relative increases, random, unstructured successes cannot be the method for future generations. For success in urban low wealth schools to become systemic, high quality teachers with a unique ability to connect with urban students and a strong sense of vision must enter schools and communities to affect change. The production and development of change agents, therefore, must become the mission of teacher preparation programs. Based upon the review of the extant literature in regards to teacher preparation, several gaps have emerged:

- Decline in teacher aptitude, which has lowered teacher quality (Hoxby & Leigh, 2004)
- Decline in the integrity of teacher preparation programs, which has devalued the impact of education programs (NCTQ, 2013; Romanik & Miami-Dade County Public Schools, 2010)
- Decline in the integrity of the teacher field experience, which has created an simplistic, ineffective model for field experiences (Perry & Power, 2004)
- Decline in cultural synchronization between the teacher and student, which has impacted teacher expectations and student achievement (Irvine, 1990)
- Decline in cultural synchronization between school and community, which has led to "hidden conflict, hostility, infrequent communication, . . . and negative teacher and student expectations" (Irvine, p. 42, 1990)

Based upon the abovementioned gaps that are presented in teacher preparation and quality, there exists a compelling case for a change in the strategy of teacher recruitment, development, and transition into the profession. What follows is a proposal for promise in teacher preparation. It is an investment in human capital that is designed to create visionary change agents who will increase access for urban students. This proposal for promise is called, the Human Capital Investment program.

THE HUMAN CAPITAL INVESTMENT: A PROPOSAL OF PROMISE

The Human Capital Investment is a set of recommendations for the development of visionary change agents for urban classrooms. Framed specifically for Historically Black Colleges and Universities, Human Capital Investment recommendations call for the rigorous development of Black teachers to enter urban schools and affect change. The development of visionary change agents for urban classrooms, as shown in Table 8.1, requires a curriculum that merges content, pedagogy, interdisciplinary studies, communication skills, and community-based field experiences. The recruitment of the best and the brightest candidates for the program ensures the personal drive to endure rigorous development.

The development phase of the Human Capital Investment recommends moving students into a specialized cohort either within the university's college of education or as the college of education itself. To support these future change agents, it is recommended that advisors, mentors and

TABLE 8.1   HCI Recommendations

Recommendation	Description
Curriculum-Restructuring	Strengthening preservice curriculum through increased content concentration
Dual Certification	Enriching the specialization areas of teachers to enable interdisciplinary lesson planning
Interdisciplinary Studies	Providing future teachers with the pedagogical skills to apply varying perspectives to instructional delivery and work within a team of teachers
Technology Integration	Ensuring a fully immersed, instructional technologically competent teacher in urban classrooms
Pedagogical Training	Ensuring a culturally relevant pedagogy is modeled as the learning experience of future teachers
Interpersonal Skills	Provide specialized coursework to ensure effective communication and discourse skills in future teachers
Field Experiences	Provide effective and ongoing school and community field experiences directly related to course content
Innovative Capstone Project	Strengthen long-term research and resiliency among future teachers with a four-year project
Multi-Tiered Support	Providing continuous support to grow future teachers through the program and into the profession

affiliations with significant community and professional organizations surround these candidates throughout their four-year matriculation at the university. By offering consistent support, professional and community mentorship, and a cohort model for these future change agents, a familial environment is built that is welcoming to Black teacher education students (Lewis, 2006).

Curriculum

The Human Capital Investment proposal recommends, as standard, a four-year, 48-course, 144 credit hour curricula that begins with a preteacher summer program prior to the student's first semester. Research indicates that the coursework in many teacher preparations programs lack the difficulty and content concentration to create effective teachers that can have an impact on student achievement (NCTQ, 2013; Romanik & Miami-Dade County Public Schools, 2010). In a review of 1,120 teacher preparation programs by the National Council on Teacher Quality (2013), it was concluded that 62.4% of entering high school teachers lack the adequate coursework and testing to ensure content knowledge in the subject for which they will teach. The National Council on Teacher Quality (2013) also stated that, in STEM preparation, "70 percent of undergraduate elementary programs do not require teacher candidates to take even a single science course" (p. 43). In addition to rigorous coursework, students within the program are recommended to participate in field experiences, summer teaching institutes and a culminating innovation project. The Human Capital Investment proposal recommends an intense curriculum and sequence of courses that encompass content competency, pedagogy, interpersonal skills, urban and traditional education studies, and interdisciplinary integration. As shown in Table 8.2, candidates who accept the challenge of this program must complete 24 courses, 72 credit hours, in their content area. Including interdisciplinary elective content, the candidate will complete 90 credit hours, 63% of their program, in relevant content. The goal is to create change agents who are competent enough to teach their craft. In comparison, a student that majors in chemistry at Massachusetts Institute of Technology must meet a requirement of 13 courses within their major (Massachusetts Institute of Technology, n.d). A student with a double major in secondary science education/chemistry at the University of Maryland must complete 12 courses in chemistry, three additional courses in other sciences and two math courses (University of Maryland, n.d). In terms of content requirements, the Human Capital Investment proposal recommends that students are competitive with education and noneducation content students in similar concentrations.

A key difference between the recommended curriculum proposal and the traditional teacher preparation program is the concentration on content.

TABLE 8.2 HCI Course Credit Overview

	Content Competency		Pedagogy		Interpersonal Skills		Education Knowledge		Dual Certification Electives		Total	
	Courses	Credits	Courses	Credits	Courses	Credits	Courses	Credits	Courses	Credits	Total Classes	Total Credits
Year 1	6	18	1	3	2	6	1	3	2	6	12	36
Year 2	6	18	1	3	2	6	1	3	2	6	12	36
Year 3	6	18	2	6	2	6	1	3	1	3	12	36
Year 4	6	18	2	6	2	6	1	3	1	3	12	36
	24	72	6	18	10	30	4	12	6	18	48	144

Note: Graduation requirements for students in the HCI program are expected to complete 48 courses, 14 hours of coursework.

Research on teacher preparation in high-performing countries like Singapore and Korea indicated that at least 50% of the course preparation is devoted directly to content mastery (Ingersoll, 2007). Furthermore, high-ranking U.S teacher preparation programs such as Furman University also have over 50% of its program focused on content specialization (Furman University, n.d.; NCTQ, 2013).

Human Capital Investment Recommends Dual Certification and Interdisciplinary Studies

The Human Capital Investment proposal recommends that future change agents are encouraged to obtain dual certification in their area of interests and its natural complement. As shown in Table 8.3, a student is heavily encouraged to complement their concentration in math education with a science education, for example.

The recommendation that future change agents are dually certified meets several criteria that distinguish them from traditionally certified teachers. First, dual certification adds to the amount of content preparation that the teacher is afforded. As shown in Table 8.2, coursework in dual certification adds 18 additional content hours of study to the student's program. Second, the recommendation of dual certification also creates a teacher that can better adapt to the instructional needs of a school and student. A science teacher that is also certified in math, for example, is more equipped to provide mathematics instruction and/or tutoring to students when the need is present. Additionally, dual certification enables the future change agents to easily transition to interdisciplinary instruction. Critics of interdisciplinary instruction note that much of the literature on interdisciplinary instruction is based on the pros and cons of the individual teacher experience and their ability to work with instructors of different disciplines over time (Applebee, Adler, & Flihan, 2007). The training

TABLE 8.3 Dual Concentration Pairing

Concentration	Natural Compliment
Math Education	Science Education, Business Education
Science Education	Math Education, Physical Education, Technology Education
Social Studies	Language Arts, Art
Language Arts	Social Studies, Art
Art Education	Social Studies, Language Arts
Business Education	Math Education, Technology Education
Physical Education	Science Education

Note: The dual concentration pairings above are suggested pairings. HCI students may elect their own pairings that fit into their areas of interests.

of future teachers in dual disciplines, complimented by research exposure into interdisciplinary instruction, can serve to build professionals more amenable to a complex, interdisciplinary environment.

The recommendation of interdisciplinary studies as a pedagogical tool provides future teachers with opportunities to exercise higher quality instructional approaches. Interdisciplinary teaching, when teachers are properly trained in it, has the ability to increase student engagement and relevance of content (Applebee et al., 2007; Nava-Whitehead, Augusto, & Gow, 2011). Nikitina (2006) suggests three strategies, described in Table 8.4, that guide instructional approaches for interdisciplinary teaching.

Applebee et al. (2007), as shown in Table 8.5, details a continuum of interdisciplinary approaches that range from situational exploration to a fully synthesized curriculum.

TABLE 8.4 Three Strategies for Interdisciplinary Teaching

Strategy	Description	Core Area/Discipline
Contextualizing	Embedding history, culture, literature, or philosophical questions to examine the context of knowledge	Humanities
Conceptualizing	Establishing quantifiable connections between two or more disciplines with common concepts	Sciences
Problem-Centering	Applying modes of thinking from several disciplines to analyze real-world issues	Applied Sciences

Note: The information for this table was retrieved from: Nava-Whitehead, S. M., Augusto, K. W., & Grow, J. (2011). Bewitching ideas influence learning: An evaluation of an interdisciplinary teaching experience. *Journal of College Science Teaching, 40*(6), 65–69.

TABLE 8.5 Interdisciplinary Continuum

Curriculum Type	Description
Predisciplinary	Thematic: Everyday knowledge; disciplinary concepts undifferentiated
Disciplinary Correlated	Subject-based: Discipline-based concepts related to common topics across disciplines
Shared	Integrated: Concepts overlapping across disciplines; mutually supported disciplines
Reconstructed	Synthesized curriculum: Concepts reconstructed across disciplines

Note: Information for table retrieved from: Applebee, A. N., Adler, M., & Flihan, S. (2007). Interdisciplinary curricula in middle school and high school classrooms: Case studies of approaches to curriculum and instruction. *American Educational Research Journal, 44*(4), 1002–1039.

As additionally noted by Applebee et al. (2007), a solid academic discipline base is assumed for interdisciplinary instruction to maximize success. As such, the training of teachers to ensure a solid academic base is heavily recommended. Human Capital Investment is, therefore, a recommendation that future change agents are dually certified and trained in applying interdisciplinary instructional pedagogy. The combination of interdisciplinary studies and culturally relevant pedagogy creates a teacher that can address content from various perspectives and create empirical connections that help students relate to abstract concepts.

Technology Integration

Regardless of concentration choices, technology integration in all aspects of teacher preparation will also serve to be a distinguishing element between a model program and presently existing programs. Traditionally, a majority of teacher preparation programs offer educational technology as a stand-alone course (Duran, Fossum, & Luera, 2007). However, Duran et al. (2007) suggested that technology-proficient educators are the product of three elements: (a) core coursework; (b) effective faculty modeling of instructional technology; and (c) technology-enriched field experiences. Research indicates that teachers that are exposed to technology integration during the preservice are less apprehensive in using technology to enhance the learning experience of their students as teachers (Lambert & Gong, 2010). Bell, Maeng, and Binns (2013) provide qualitative research to suggest that integrating technology instruction into teacher preparation programs facilitates future teachers' ability to better engage their students and improves their planning and instructional approaches. These findings are also supported by research recommendations that support sustainable partnerships [between teacher preparation programs and schools] that facilitate discussions of best practices and implement those into both teacher education classes and in-service teacher professional developments" (Ottenbreit-Leftwhich, Brush, Stycker, Gronseth, Roman, Abaci, vanLeusen, Shin, Easterling, & Plucker, 2012). The investment into future change agents for urban students requires that those change agents have an accelerated skill set designed for the integration of twenty-first century instruction and technology. Human Capital Investment recommends that technology integration, as suggested by Duran et al. (2007), become part of the learning experience in their development.

Pedagogical Training

Complimentary to a strong focus on content competency, students in the HCI teacher development phase are also given intense coursework and practice in pedagogy. Chief among the pedagogical practices for instructors of these urban change agents is the recommendation of an immersed culturally relevant pedagogy as an instructional philosophy. What distinguishes this recommendation from culturally relevant courses presently taught in teacher preparation programs is the immersion of culturally relevant practices throughout all applicable coursework. Through the immersion approach to culturally relevant pedagogy, future change agents will not view the practice as compartmental but rather as innate instructional practice. As teacher preparation instructors "utilize students culture as a vehicle for learning" (Ladson-Billings, 1995, p. 161). future change agents will acquire and develop a content and instructional approach that is instinctively culturally relevant. Combined with the candidate's own cultural reference and structured field experience, culturally relevant pedagogy training will arm future teachers with the tools to bridge home, school, and community (Brown-Jeffy & Cooper, 2011). To build upon culturally relevant experiences, the implementation of instructional and field opportunities will assist these urban change agents to learn how to create teachable connections to content through real-world experiences. As shown in Figure 8.1, the umbrella of culturally relevant pedagogy is recommended to guide research-based all instructional strategies and adds to the instructional repertoire of future teachers.

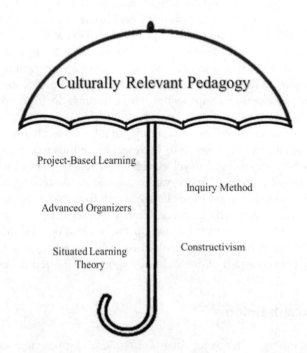

Figure 8.1 Umbrella of CRP.

Interpersonal Skills

A key component in teaching, particularly in urban schools, is the development of interpersonal skills to effectively deliver instruction. When addressing communities that have been historically marginalized, extra effort has to be made to bridge trust gaps. Historically, urban, low wealth communities have developed well-understood reasons to be distrustful of perceived outsiders which have contributed to social isolation (Payne, 2008). The employment of Black teachers, while a step in the right direction for cultural matching, does not guarantee a social connection between teacher and student. Urban change agents must be equipped with the ability to socially connect their content to student experiences. Therefore, the urban teacher must serve as "cultural translators" both teaching and modeling cognitive switching in order to enable trust with students and the community (Irvine, 1990, p. 126). Developing interpersonal skills, matched with content competency and culturally relevant pedagogy, creates a rigorous learning environment that empowers and supports children. The Human Capital Investment recommends courses that focus on developing key aspects of interpersonal skills. Along with coursework that explores culturally relevant pedagogy, social theory, and critical race theory, urban change agents should also leave a teacher preparation program skilled in public speaking, intercultural communication, and local/community studies. The goal of such coursework and skill development is to equip these future teachers with the ability to articulate content, make meaningful connections with students and the community, and understand the child in historical context to their environment. In Singapore, for example, teacher candidates are required to take courses in language enhancement and academic discourse to improve communication and professional interaction skills (Ingersoll, 2007). Field experiences that place the candidate in the community also serve the dual purpose of building interpersonal skills and building trust between school and community. Although primarily targeted for Black teachers, it is also observed that other marginalized minority groups also occupy urban schools. Therefore, it is recommended that programs consider extending culture matching practices to include other minority groups.

Field Experiences

Field experience presents an excellent opportunity for candidates to bridge theory and practice. Existing research on field experiences in teacher preparation programs has been mixed and inconclusive (Capraro, Capraro, & Helfeldt, 2010). Traditional field/clinical experience often designated as a 12–15 week, or upwards to a two semester, classroom experience commonly referred to as *student teaching* that culminates the preservice teacher's academic experience (Ronfeldt & Reininger, 2012). According to Ronfeldt & Reininger (2012), research indicates that quality of clinical experience, detailed as placement context, cooperating teachers, and university supervisors, has far more significance to effective teaching than length of experience. Based primarily on program support and cooperating teacher placement process, the National Council on Teacher Quality (2013) rated 70% of the 1,370 schools reviewed as having zero stars on the standard of student teaching. The observation of student teaching is extended by the National Council for Accreditation of Teacher Education (2008) in its assertion that universities must begin to, especially in urban settings, "serve the needs of the a particular set of students in a particular set of schools and communities" (NCATE, 2008, p. 15). Traditional field experience, in the form of student teaching, offers but one aspect of the student's life that the teacher must contend with. Perry and Power (2004) note that traditional teacher field experiences, characterized as a 1–2 semester classroom-only interaction, are often too simplistic and can only offer the teacher the chance to study observable behaviors. While the student-teacher may acquire surface understanding of student dynamics, focusing solely on observable behaviors does not offer the opportunity to frame behavior as contextual and relational. The Human Capital Investment program recommends that field experience be varied and offer the future change agent multiple entries into the world of the student and community that they are charged to change. Extending the university clinical experience to targeted schools and communities, as suggested by the NCATE (2008), builds a stronger connection to the students and families served.

Student Zones

Teacher field experiences in the Human Capital Investment program are centered on five zones that encompass the life of the student. As shown in Figure 8.2, the five zones of student interactions are: (a) Student, (b) School, (c) Community, (d) Interpersonal, and (e) Home.

Student Zone

Every student has his/her own unique outlook on life and his/her environment. While students in similar environments may encounter many common experiences, the individual student and his or her perspective must be the focal point. The individual student chooses the way in which (s)he views the world and responds. Students' response to their environment

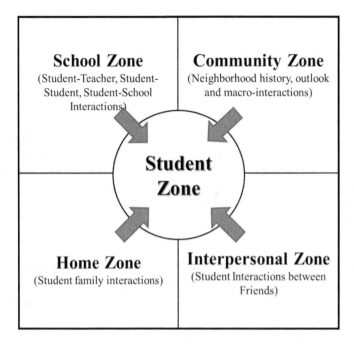

Figure 8.2 Student experience zones.

can be the unique combination of intrapersonal reconciliations with their other zones. As a result, the urban change agent must develop the ability to respect the power of the individual to analyze and critique his/herself, his/her environment, and adopt his/her own unique views.

School Zone

The school zone involves all of the unique interactions and relationships that occur in the school building. Future change agents will conduct inquiry in the dynamics of school climate and how those relationships impact student learning and success. Beyond the role of student-teacher, the change agent has the opportunity see the school from the multiple perspectives: (a) Student, (b) Teacher, and (c) Institution.

Community Zone

The community zone immerses the change agent in the macro-interactions of the neighborhoods from which the student emerges. Studying the history of the community, how the community interacts with business and civic institutions, and how members of the community interact within themselves, change agents will be able to gain useful insight into the ways in and by which community dynamics shape the collective outlook on life, values, and education. The Human Capital Investment program will partner with community leaders to create community mentors for future change agents as they perform field experiences in this zone.

Interpersonal Zone

The interpersonal zone takes the change agents on a journey into the life of the student as a human being. This field experience zone values all of the social interactions that shape the individual student's outlook and personal values. In this zone, change agents conduct inquiry into the activities and interactions that influence the child. From friendship bonds and recreational activities to social and mass media, the goal of the change agent is to develop both an appreciation and awareness of the trends, values, and uniqueness of youth culture.

Home Zone

The home zone allows the change agents to learn how family dynamics impact student perspectives. When possible, the change agent will spend time with families and attend family events to gain access to the interactions in this zone. Change agents will also work with family and social service departments to gain insight into the dynamics that students bring to a classroom. Work in this zone, when done with sensitivity and sincerity, will build trust between the change agent and families. The home zone is perhaps the most challenging of the field experience zones, yet has the potential to develop the future change agent's ability to teach and move beyond the observable behaviors noted by Perry and Power (2004).

Multiple, Varied Field Experiences

Human Capital Investment recommends that each course offered to future change agents permit the opportunity to participate in a field experience that is aligned to the specific coursework of the class. Functioning with the applicable aforementioned student zone, each field experience will contain a different perspective of the zone. Therefore, a *Methods of Teaching Mathematics* course will have totally different set of inquiry experiences than an *Education Psychology* course, although operating within the same zone. Further, the same *Methods of Teaching Mathematics* course can also have a variety of different experiences operating across multiple zones. The recommendation of varied, inquiry-based, field experiences over the duration of the future change agent's development will enable the continual production of high quality teachers with culturally relevant understanding of the dynamics that impact the classroom.

The Innovative Capstone Project

The urban change agents developed under the Human Capital Investment recommendations should be armed with the call of long-term vision to drive change in urban schools. To develop that sense of efficacy and long-term vision, Human Capital Investment recommends a four-year capstone project that will enrich the learning experience of change agents across the duration of the program. The capstone project should be based on the guiding principles of constructivism and action research.[3] The constructivist approach will create a learner-centered environment that is both inquiry- and problem-based for the future teacher (Smart, Witt, & Scott, 2012). The learning experience offered by the capstone project will also arm these change agents with a pedagogical approach to add to their teaching repertoire. The project requires the students in the program to decide a course of action that benefits the community, students and/or urban school. The project must be innovative and solution oriented. During the four years that the student is engaged in the Innovative Capstone Project, the student must meet annual milestones, detailed in Table 8.6, to ensure that the project remains on course for completion by graduation.

The experience of the Innovative Capstone Project immerses the future change agent in research related to their pathways and into the communities that they serve. The project will also prepare these change agents for graduate level work to encourage increased commitment to education. The use of action research as a guiding approach helps to bridge theory and practice and to enhance the personal and professional teaching philosophy of the future teacher (Honigsfeld, Connolly, & Kelly, 2013). To ensure that future change agents have the support and development of their projects, Human Capital Investment recommends enlisting an academic skills coach to provide specialized workshops to provide students with action research, writing, and statistical skills. Sela and Harel (2012) note that the use of action research should exist throughout the course of teacher preservice programs to impact the learning culture of the teacher. Along with community, school and program mentors, future change agents will be armed with an academic skills coach who provides resources and skills to support their

TABLE 8.6 Capstone Project Annual Milestones

Year	Annual Milestone
Year 1	Define the project and problem through established research
Year 2	Begin action research and gather qualitative data
Year 3	Pilot product and perform preliminary evaluation
Year 4	Present and defend project to panel

milestones. The culminating event for the four-year Innovative Capstone Project is a presentation defense before a panel of community, school, and university members.

Providing Support Services

While the Human Capital Investment recommends the recruitment of the best and brightest to enter this teaching program, it is paramount that continuous advising and ongoing support is provided to ensure the successful development of future change agents. Rogers-Poliakoff (2002) recommended a shared responsibility for the preparation of future teachers that expands across the entire university. Such a shared responsibility calls for a collaborative environment in which education and noneducation professors work to support future teachers (Rogers-Poliakoff, 2002). For example, university mathematics professors that teach preservice teachers might be encouraged to also expound on pedagogical processes of teaching math, provide more opportunities for student presentations, and require field experiences related to math instruction as class participation grades. This recommendation is different from other programs in that noneducation professors at universities are not systemically urged to teach pedagogical approaches to content or provide education-related field experiences of their students.

To further create a nurturing learning environment for future change agents, Human Capital Investment recommends a multitiered advising and mentoring structure. The successful implementation of this advising/mentoring structure creates two-fold success. First, this level of advising and mentoring raises the probability for successful completion of this rigorous program. Second, such support systems have the possibility of producing good habits of mind and improving the teaching culture of future change agents. Capitalizing on the experience that brought success to the teacher candidate, the future teacher should naturally extend the exercise of social capital to their future students.

The two-tiered advising structure provides the future teacher with two specialized advisors, a Master Teacher and an Academic Skills Coach. The Master Teacher, as detailed in Table 8.7, is a highly qualified, experienced urban teacher hired to apply classroom knowledge to practical usage. The Master Teacher should provide active teaching laboratories for the future change agents where they can model and assess teaching strategies. The teaching laboratory, much like the science laboratory connected to a science class, allows to student experiment with various teaching models such as inquiry, synectics, or advanced organizers.[4] The Master Teacher teams with preservice instructors to provide lab experiences that match the

TABLE 8.7   Human Capital Investment Support Tiers

Tier	Title	Description
Advisors	Master Teacher	• Highly qualified, experienced teacher of urban schools • Proven track record of success • Demonstrates effective teaching strategies and practices • Arranges and conducts workshops and seminars on teaching models for urban schools
	Academic Skills Coach	• Qualified academic skills coach • Arranges and conducts workshops and seminars on writing/research skills, presentation and communication skills, and other identified professional needs
Mentors	Community Mentors	• Community activists • Provides community history and current issues • Serves as liaisons for community-based field experiences
	School Mentor	• Qualified school teacher with stellar performance record • Articulates needs and visions of the schools • Serves a school-to-program liaison for school-based field experiences
	Peer/Team Mentors	• Provides peer support and constructive evaluation

pedagogical content learned in the student courses in the same manner that a chemistry lab class would match the content learned in a chemistry course. The Academic Skills Coach assists the student with the necessary skills to meet the challenge of the program, particularly the Innovative Capstone Project. This advisor provides assistance with writing, researching, presenting, and communicating as future change agents. The Academic Skills Coach works with professors to gain a better insight on the skills needed to provide a better focus for the student. Overall, the advising experience promotes the humanization of the collegiate learning experience (Museus & Ravello, 2010). Offering a personalized, skills-oriented advising experience will help the student to not feel alone in their collegiate challenges and provide a learning culture that they can carry over to their teaching practice. This experience also assists in providing a network of support to ensure that students are equipped to successfully navigate college life.

In addition to two-tiered advisors, Human Capital Investment also recommends a multitiered mentorship structure. As detailed in Table 8.7, a successful implementation of the program provides a future change agent with three tiers of structured mentorship: a) Community Mentors, b) School Mentors, and c) Peer/Team Mentors. The Community Mentor will serve a vital role in deepening the cultural experience of the future change agent. The Community Mentor, through facilitating community-based field experiences, helps increase the match between teaching styles and urban communities (Brown-Jeffy & Cooper, 2011). School Mentors are highly qualified teachers with a record of highly engaging interpersonal skills and ability to guide/mentor new teachers. The School Mentors, through informal seminars and constructive conversation, provides the future change agent with many of the intangible skills, such as relationship-building, maintain high expectations, and lesson adaptation, that make great teachers (Young, 2009). The difference between the school mentor and the master teacher is that the school mentor is a representative from the targeted schools/districts that the teacher program serves. Where the master teacher is housed entirely at the university and provides instructional laboratory experience, the school mentor is a highly qualified and effective teacher within the school district who can speak directly to the intangible needs and experiences present in specific urban school settings. It is recommended that the university and the school district work together to screen and select the candidates that assume the role of school mentor.

To affect an atmosphere of collegiality and camaraderie, the implementation of Peer/Team Mentors will add continual support for students. Future change agents, as shown in Figure 8.3, are to be assembled into two functional teams: a) Academic and b) Departmental. The academic team joins a set of future teachers in the various student primary certification areas. The purpose of this form of teaming will permit future teachers to share common experiences beyond their respective disciplines. Further, this teaming experience also mimics a common teaming practice within schools. Departmental teams assemble future teachers by their primary certification area. This level of teaming permits students to share common practices and challenges within their discipline.

The team mentoring component involves teams at different classification levels providing mentorships to the classes underneath them. For example,

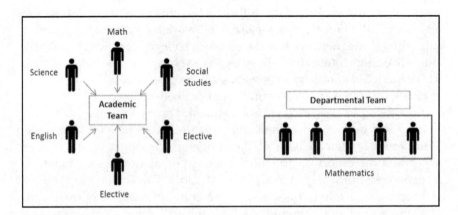

Figure 8.3 Peer teaming.

Teams in their junior year will become peer mentors of sophomores and so on. This level of mentorship provides opportunities for peers to share their fresh experience as students to newer students in the program. For the inaugural class of students in the program, peer mentorship will come primarily from students in the college of education or the professors themselves. Once the first cohort completes their first year, the Peer/Team Mentoring structure should become cyclical. Overall, the implementation of a multitiered mentoring program should offer future change agents an outlet to gain and share experiences as they move from college entrants into the teaching profession.

IMPLICATIONS

For it is obvious that if a man entering at the starting line in a race three hundred years after another man, the first man would have to perform some impossible feat in order to catch up with his fellow runner. (King, 1964, p. 134)

What does it mean to engage in Human Capital Investment? It means improving communities by investing the money, resources, time and effort into the one systemic, educational tool that guarantees school improvement and a better long-term quality of life: a highly qualified, culturally relevant teacher.

What is the potential impact of engaging in Human Capital Investment? The return on Human Capital Investment recommendations can be measured in both short and long term impact. According to the National Council on Teacher Quality (2013), new teachers that graduate from stronger programs are "contributing two more months of learning in a school year that graduates of weaker programs" (p. 10). Full engagement in Human Capital Investment can also be measured in the various value-added data collected by the university after the change agent enters into the community. The National Council on Teacher Quality (2013) also notes that 25% of teacher preparation programs ranked high in collecting data on its graduates for the purpose of guiding program improvement. The ultimate measure of Human Capital Investment is in the effect that its change agents have on the schools, students, and communities that they are charged to serve. In the long-term effectiveness, the impact of highly qualified teachers will make access to higher education a systemic certainty. Human Capital Investment, therefore, also has economic value.

What is the economic value of Human Capital Investment? Access to higher levels of education alone, according to the U.S Department of Health and Human Services (2012), can increase life expectancy by 9.3 and 8.6 years for men and women, respectively. Further, access to higher levels of education serves as a "consumption good" increases life satisfaction (Salinas-Jimenez, Artes, & Salinas-Jimenez, 2011, p. 423). Attainment of higher education levels also increases access to higher levels of income (United States Census Bureau, 2009). Therefore, a longer, more satisfying, and wealthier life is connected to the educational access, equity and acquisition that results from Human Capital Investment. For the urban, school-dependent, student, this access and equity is obtained through teachers that exercise a pedagogy that finds strengths and builds confidence (Jackson, 2011).

What is the educational value of a cadre of skilled, passionate, personable change agents trained to transform urban schools and communities? The annual development and production of high aptitude, culturally relevant, community entrenched teachers will create systemic pathways to equity and access for urban students. According to the National Council on Teacher Quality (2004), race, literacy level, subject area knowledge, and strong academic credentials have a positive impact on effective instruction for students. The development of change agents, Human Capital Investment, provides the tools to enable the urban student to "perform the impossible feat in order to catch up with his fellow runner" (King, 1964, p. 117).

What is the institutional value of Human Capital Investment to the university? The adoption of Human Capital Investment recommendations, in whole or in part, has direct implications in strengthening the design of the university's teacher preparation program. The optimal geographic location for the implementation of the Human Capital Investment program would be at a college or university that is situated within an urban school district. This positioning will permit a natural relationship between the program and the school district it intends to serve. Strengthening such a relationship attracts teacher candidates to the program because of the increased potential of placement upon graduation. Further, the optimal environment for program implementation would be the Historically Black College or University. The potential for added prestige offered by a strong nationally ranked teacher preparation program can reinvigorate the attraction and reaffirm the relevancy of Historically Black Colleges and Universities. Although implementation can work on any urban campus, such an environment offers an attraction to the communities that they serve and a return to the historical legacy that produced black teachers in the preintegration era.

NOTES

1. *African American* and *Black* as well as *educator* and *teacher* will be used interchangeably throughout the chapter.
2. Situational pedagogies: The responses and initiatives teachers gleaned upon to give their students the educational capital that in turn had the potential to impact their cultural capital towards human/economic capital (Kelly, 2009).

3. Constructivism is an approach to learning that emphasizes the learner as an active participant in the acquisition of their own knowledge (Smart et al., 2012).

Action Research is the "process of studying a real or classroom situation to understand and improve the quality of actions and instruction" (Johnson, 2008, p. 28).

4. Synectics is a teaching model that emphasizes problem-solving through the use of analogies and parallel connections (Joyce, Weil, & Calhoun, 2009).

Advanced organizers are presentation models designed strengthen a student's cognitive structure and enhance their retention of new information (Joyce, Weil, & Calhoun, 2009).

REFERENCES

Anderson, J. D. (1988). *The education of Blacks in the south, 1860–1935.* Chapel Hill, NC: University of North Carolina Press.

Applebee, A. N., Adler, M., & Flihan, S. (2007). Interdisciplinary curricula in middle school and high school classrooms: Case studies of approaches to curriculum and instruction. *American Educational Research Journal, 44*(4), 1002–1039.

Auguste, B., Kihn, P., & Miller, M. (2010). *Closing the talent gap: Attracting and retaining top-third graduates to careers in teaching.* A McKinsey Report: McKinsey & Company. Retrieved from https://mckinseyonsociety.com/downloads/reports/Education/Closing_the_talent_gap.pdf

Bell, R. L., Maeng, J., & Binns, I. C. (2013). Learning in context: Technology integration in a teacher preparation program informed by situated learning theory. *Journal of Research in Science Teaching. 50*(3), 348–379.

Brown, A. (2009). Brothers gonna work it out: Understanding the pedagogic performance of African American male teachers working with African American male students. *Urban Review, 41*, 416–435.

Brown-Jeffy, S., & Cooper, J. (2011). Toward a conceptual framework of culturally relevant pedagogy: An overview of the conceptual and theoretical literature. *Teacher Education Quarterly, 38*(1), 65–84.

Capraro, M. M., Capraro, R. M., & Helfeldt, J. (2010). Do differing types of field experiences make a difference in teacher candidates' perceived level of competence? *Teacher Education Quarterly, 37*(1), 131–154.

Corcoran, S. P., Evans, W. N., & Schwab, R. M. (2004). Women, the labor market, and the declining relative quality of teachers. *Journal of Policy Analysis and Management, 23*(3), 449–470.

Darling-Hammond, L. (2010). *The flat world and education: How America's commitment to equity will determine our future.* New York: Teacher's College Press.

Duran, M., Fossum, P. R., & Luera, G. R. (2007). Technology and pedagogical renewal: Conceptualizing technology integration into teacher preparation. *Computers in the Schools, 23*(3–4), 31–54.

Fairclough, A. (2007). *A class of their own: Black teachers in the segregated south.* Cambridge, MA: Harvard University Press.

Franklin, V. P. (2009). They rose or fell together: African American educators and community leadership, 1795–1954. In L. Tillman (Ed.), *The handbook of African American education*, Thousand Oaks, CA: Sage.

Frederick, R., & View, J. (2009). Facing the rising sun: A history of black educators in Washington, DC, 1800-2008. *Urban Education, 44*(5), 571–607.

Furman University (n.d.). *Secondary mathematics teacher education worksheet.* Greenville, SC: Furman University. Retrieved from http://www2.furman.edu/academics/Education/Programs/Documents/Worksheet%20Mathematics%20 2012-13%20FINAL.pdf

Gay, G. (2002). Preparing for culturally responsive teaching. *Journal of Teacher Education, 53,* 106–116.

Gist, C. (2010). Embracing the historical legacy of young, gifted, and black educators. *Black History Bulletin, 73*(1), 7–10.

Honigsfeld, A., Connolly, M., & Kelly, S. (2013). Demystifying teacher action research: lessons learned from a graduate education capstone experience. *Delta Kappa Gamma Bulletin. 79*(2), 15–21.

Hoxby, C. M., & Leigh, A. (2004). Pulled away or pushed out? Explaining the decline of teacher aptitude in the united states. *American Economic Review. 92*(2), 236–240.

Hunter-Boykin, H. S. (1992). Responses to African American teacher shortage: We grow our own through the teacher preparation program at Coolidge high school. *The Journal of Negro Education, 61*(4), 483–495.

Ingersoll, R. M. (2007). *A comparative study of teacher preparation and qualifications in six nations* (CPRE Policy Briefs RB-47).Consortium for Policy Research in Education.

Irvine, J. J. (1990). *Black students and school failure: Policies, practices, and prescriptions.* New York: Preager.

Jackson, Y. (2011). *The pedagogy of confidence: inspiring high intellectual performance in urban schools.* New York, NY: Teachers College Press.

Johnson, A. P. (2008). *A short guide to action research.* Boston, MA: Pearson.

Joyce, B., Weil, M., & Calhoun, E. (2009). *Models of teaching* (8th Ed.). Boston, MA: Pearson/Allyn & Bacon.

Kelly, H. (2009). What Jim Crow's teachers could do: Educational capital and teacher's work in under-resourced schools. *Urban Review, 42,* 329–350.

King, M. L. (1964). *Why we can't wait.* [Barnes and Noble Nook version]. Boston, MA: Beacon Press.

Ladson-Billings, G. (1995). But that's just good teaching! The case for culturally relevant pedagogy. *Theory into Practice, 34*(3), 159–165.

Lambert, J., & Gong, Y. (2010). 21st century paradigms for pre-service teacher technology preparation. *Computers in the Schools, 27*(1), 54–70.

Lewis, C. (2006). African American male teachers in public schools: An examination of three urban school districts. *Teachers College Record, 108*(2), 224–245.

Loder-Jackson, T. L. (2011). Bridging the legacy of activism across generations: Life stories of African American educators in post-civil rights Birmingham. *Urban Review, 43,* 151–174.

Madkins, T. C. (2011). The black teacher shortage: A literature review of historical and contemporary trends. *The Journal of Negro Education. (3), 417–427.*

Moore, J. L., & Lewis, C. W. (2012). *African American students in urban schools: Critical issues and solutions for achievement.* New York, NY: Peter Lang.

Museus, S. D., & Ravello, J. N. (2010). Characteristics of academic advising that contribute to racial and ethnic minority student success at predominantly White institutions. *NACADA Journal. 30*(1), 47–58.

National Council on Teacher Quality (2004). Increasing the odds: How good policies can yield better teachers. Washington, DC: National Council on Teacher Quality, Retrieved from http://www.nctq.org/p/publications/docs/nctq_io_20071129024229.pdf

National Council for Accreditation of Teacher Education. (2008). Urban teacher residency models and institutes of higher education: Implications for teacher preparation. Washington, DC: National Council for Accreditation of Teacher Education. Retrieved from http://www.ncate.org/LinkClick.aspx?fileticket=KqJqRodGoyM%3d&tabid=368

Nava-Whitehead, S. M., Augusto, K. W., & Gow, J. (2011). Bewitching ideas influence learning: An evaluation of an interdisciplinary teaching experience. *Journal of College Science Teaching, 40*(6), 65–69.

Nikitina, S. (2006). Three strategies for interdisciplinary teaching: Contextualizing, conceptualizing, and problem-centering. *Journal of Curriculum Studies, 38*(3), 251–271.

Ottenbreit-Leftwhich, A. T., Brush, T. A., Stycker, J., Gronseth, S., Roman, T., Abaci, S., VanLeusen, P., Shin, S., Easterling, W., & Plucker, J. (2012). Preparation versus practice: How do teacher education programs and practicing teachers align in their use of technology to support teaching and learning. *Computers & Education, 59*(2), 399–411.

Payne, C. M. (2008). So much reform, so little change: The persistence of failure in urban schools. Cambridge, MA: Harvard Education Press.

Perry, C. M., & Power, B. M. (2004). Finding the truths in teacher preparation field experiences. *Teacher Education Quarterly, 31*(2), 125–136.

Rogers-Poliakoff, A. (2002). Teacher preparation: Assessing teacher quality, administrative support, standards-based teacher preparation. *Basic Education, 46*(10), 1–26.

Romanik, D. & Miami-Dade County Public Schools (2010). *What the research tells us: Teacher quality and teacher preparation* (Information Capsule, Vol. 1002). Research Services, Miami-Dade County Public Schools. Retrieved from http://www.eric.ed.gov/PDFS/ED536511.pdf

Ronfeldt, M., & Reininger, M. (2012). More or better student teaching? *Teaching and Teacher Education, 28*(8), 1091–1106.

Salinas-Jimenez, M. M., Artes, J., & Salinas-Jimenez, J. (2011) Education as a positional good: A life satisfaction approach. Social Indicators Research, *103*(3), 409–426.

Sela, O., & Harel, M. (2012). The role of teacher education in introducing action research into the education system: A case study of an education college. *Current Issues in Education. 15*(2), 1–14.

Siddle Walker, V. (2009). Second-class integration: A historical perspective for a contemporary agenda. *Harvard Educational Review, 24*(2), 269–284.

Siddle Walker, V. (2001). African American teaching in the south: 1940–1960. *American Education Research Journal, 38*(4), 751–779.

Smart, K. L., Witt, C., & Scott, J. P. (2012). Toward learner-centered teaching: An inductive approach. *Business Communication Quarterly.* 75(4), 392–403.

Stanford, G. (1998). African American teachers' knowledge of teaching: Understanding the influence of their remembered teachers, 30(3), p. 229–243.

The Massachusetts Institute of Technology (n.d.). *Chemistry requirements for majors.* Retrieved from http://web.mit.edu/chemistry/www/academic/majors.html

The University of Maryland at College Park (n.d.). Curriculum requirements for the science education/chemistry double major program. Retrieved from http://www.education.umd.edu/EDCI/info/chemistry.htm

United States Census Bureau, (2009). Table *2b: Average monthly income by education, sex, age, and race and Hispanic origin, 2009.* Washington DC: United States Census Bureau, U.S. Department of Commerce. Retrieved from: http://www.census.gov/hhes/socdemo/education/data/sipp/2009/tables.html

U.S. Department of Health and Human Services, Centers for Disease Control and Prevention, National Center for Health Statistics (2012). *Health, united states, 2011: With special feature on socioeconomic status and health.* (DHHS Publication No. 2012–1232). Retrieved from http://www.cdc.gov/nchs/data/hus/hus11.pdf

Wilson, W. J. (2012). *The truly disadvantaged: The inner city, the underclass, and public policy* (2nd ed.). Chicago, Ill: The University of Chicago Press.

Young, E. (2009). What makes a teacher great? *Phi Delta Kappan.* 75(1), 39–40.

CHAPTER 9

AN EVALUATION OF AN IN-HOUSE COACHING PILOT STUDY WITHIN THE INSTITUTE OF EDUCATION, UNIVERSITY OF LONDON

20–20 Coaching TDA Project for the Recruitment and Retention of Black Minority Ethnic Student Teachers

Victoria Showunmi
Institute of Education

Students' success in Higher Education depends not only on their abilities but also on the support they receive. It has been known since the inception of access courses over a decade ago that nonstandard entry students and ethnic minority students are the two (not necessarily separate) groups that find Higher Education (HE) Institutions, for one reason or another, less welcoming than do White Anglophone students. This paper reports on a unique

Teacher Education and Black Communities, pages 189–207
Copyright © 2014 by Information Age Publishing
All rights of reproduction in any form reserved.

project known as "The 20–20 Coaching Programme" piloted at the Institute of Education, University of London.

The purpose of the programme was to provide an opportunity for Black Minority Ethnic (BME) student teachers to have access to coaching as a support for their particular needs. Experienced BME teachers were trained in coaching skills then matched up with BME student teachers from secondary schools across London. Evaluations of the project highlighted participants' positive responses to the programme in meeting these needs. This paper outlines the programme, its purpose and the process of selecting participants. It discusses participants' experiences of the programme, and concludes with ideas for improving and developing future programmes.

> My coachees was enthused by the process and each time we met it left her with a better understanding of the actions that she needed to take to enable her to achieve her long term goal." (BME Coachees on the programme)

INTRODUCTION

There is evidence (Showunmi 1996) at BME students find higher education more daunting than their White counterparts. If this is the case, these students could benefit from some additional support to set them on a path to success in higher education. Coaching is one such method of support that aims to improve confidence and performance. The provision of coaching to BME students in higher education could help them to tackle the particular difficulties they may experience and allow them to progress more successfully.

Coaching is a rapidly expanding discipline; however, its definition remains vague and is a frequent topic for debate amongst academics engaged in the field of mentoring and coaching (Griffiths & Campbell, 2009). Notionally, the perception of coaching is that it is about facilitating a change to behaviour and/or practice, enabling more effective performance. For that reason coaching is often associated with sport (Rodger, 2010).

Coaching can include various methods, such as Mezirow's (1998) Theory of Transformative Learning emphasises the importance of critical reflection. Here the coachee reflects on an experience or behaviour examining carefully what they would like to change in order to transform a situation in a more positive way. Transformation or change involves this process of exploring the old and looking towards the new (Scott, 1997). Mezirow (1998) argues that learning to think for oneself involves such critical reflection. From a coaching perspective, thinking for oneself is empowering and this is highly valued in the coaching process. It would seem in this highly competitive, contemporary society there is a surge in the demand for coaching. Being socially accepted and successful is becoming increasingly desirable and necessary

(Jamison, 2006). How people are perceived by others is paramount (Wrong, 1961). A reason for the increasing desire for coaching may be people's need to conform to and be successful in a particular social culture (Wrong, 1961).

Coaching, Mentoring, and Counseling

The terms "coaching," "mentoring," and "therapy/counselling" are often used interchangeably (Ives, 2008, Thomas & Smith, 2009). There is a perception that they are the same. Whilst they may come under the more generic umbrella of psychotherapy it should be made clear that coaching is not therapy or counselling which generally involves a one-to-one conversation, exploring a person's past experiences and behaviours, focussing mainly on emotions and feelings, in order to help them move forward in their lives (Vaughan Smith, 2007, Thomas & Smith, 2009). Contrary to this, the philosophy underpinning coaching is that it is solution focused, goal orientated and looks forward (Zeus & Skiffington, 2006; Ives, 2008, Griffiths & Campbell, 2009; Thomas & Smith, 2009). Coaching is presented as a tool to assist change and transformation, improving one's behaviour or skills to enable effectiveness in a chosen community (Connor & Pokora, 2007; Pask & Joy, 2007). Coachees generally use the coaching environment as a means to look at strategies to help them achieve their goals and move forward.

Coaching also differs from mentoring in that mentoring schemes in the United Kingdom and Western Europe have tended to emphasise mutuality of learning and the encouragement of mentees to do things for themselves and to offer a broader vision of both the role of mentor and the interactivity between mentor and clients. Watkins and Whalley (1993) define mentoring as "the process of helping another learn and enhance their professional role" and states that [a mentor] is not "a model for newcomers to imitate in any simple fashion" and does not involve "a management supervisor who is 'responsible' for the learner" (p. 130).

In contrast, coaching is a more recent trend that has progressed away from the idea of a subordinating apprenticeship or of sitting at the feet of a guru to receive wisdom on "expert" direction and become, at least in theory, a more learning centred and enabling process. Modern approaches to coaching emphasise learning rather than instruction and the importance of starting to facilitate learning from where the learner is.

In the education context, coaching and mentoring may be differentiated in the following way. Mentoring may be regarded as a person development centred approach, primarily embracing issues and personal development. However, on the other hand, coaching tends to be more performance centred. Mentoring may be a long-term relationship, which continues through job changes, while coaching may be relatively short term linked to a project or performance issue.

Although it has become particularly linked with performance on the workplace (Wrong, 1961), coaching also remains an essential part of successful education. Here at the Institute of Education, for example, a need was identified for a more formal support network for staff—particularly BME staff and students in higher education, who appeared to be experiencing particular difficulties. Therefore a confidential peer coaching service, given to student BME teachers by experienced BME teachers, was established as a way of developing deep personal learning, subsequently enabling more effective working practices (Carnell, Macdonald, & Askew, 2006).

At the end of the first year of this service, an evaluation was conducted, revealing positive benefits (Hargreaves, 2008). The results of this evaluation are presented in this paper. (The service is still in operation today and is growing exponentially.)

Coaching and Diversity in Education

Before going on to describe the IoE coaching programme for BME student teachers and assess its effectiveness, it is important to summarise some of the evidence that underpinned the establishment of this service.

It has been known since the inception of access courses over a decade ago that nonstandard entry students and ethnic minority students are the two (not necessarily separate) groups that find HE institutions, for one reason or another, less welcoming than do White Anglophone young people from grammar streams or public schools.

There have been growing concerns about the experiences and achievement of Black pupils (especially Black males) which underpins the call for more Black people to serve as teacher and lay mentor role models in schools. A recent article written by Maylor (2007) indicates the change in priorities for teacher recruitment in England (TTA 2003a, 2003b; see Carrington & Skelton, 2003 for an overview of teacher recruitment initiatives) to increase the recruitment of BME teachers against the continued debate for the need of representation of minority pupils in English schools.

Coaching, then finds its natural candidates among Black/ethnic minority students. When coaching or other support is effective, these students do well (Showunmi, 1995). Whilst much progress has been made in achieving racial diversity in lower and middle management, racial balance at the senior level remains elusive. David A. Thomas an American scholar, has examined the career progression of minorities in U.S. corporations (Thomas & Smith, 2009). His study reveals that "people of colour who advance the furthest all share one characteristic—a strong network of mentors and corporate sponsors who nurture their professional development."

In the light of evidence such as that given above, the idea of developing a coaching model at the IoE that would target BME students came about through various discussions with other coaches and working with student teachers. The purpose of these 20–20 coaching sessions was to enable BME PGCE, B Ed (hons) and Graduate Teacher Programme students to experience additional support from senior members of staff that were from BME backgrounds in London schools. When BME trainee teachers are recruited onto the various teaching programmes there is much evidence (Showunmi, 1995; Mirza, 2000; Maylor, 2008) to suggest that many schools experience difficulty attracting and retaining BME teachers. However, when we worked through the actual thought process it was important that the 20–20 coaching session should not be designed as a deficit model. As a team we were not primarily looking for people to come forward to be coached with problems but rather to move them on in their career direction. If, however, the student teacher did want to use the coaching session as an arena to unpack general issues that was still accommodated but not encouraged.

A really important element for the 20–20 Coaching session was that the coaches, as well as the coachees, came from a BME background. This was fundamental as it enabled the BME student teachers to talk through their experiences with people like themselves, who had probably faced similar challenges and fully understood their difficulties. There appears to be some evidence (Cornish, 2009) that black coaches can face a constant dilemma about whether to alter the way they behave in order to fit in, or accept that they will never fit in. One such dilemma is in the way they may communicate, as their style may be that of direct and full of passion.

It is very important to recognise in coaching that discrimination on the basis of race may happen (Cornish, 2009)—and even though Black British people who are either second or third generation may be virtually identical culturally to a White British person, they will have a very different experience in the workplace. This would be purely on the basis of racial differences alone. Therefore, it is vital that coaches for the coachees are able to have the capacity to respond to both actual and perceived racial discrimination.

Purpose of the 20–20 Coaching Programme

The purpose of the programme was to provide an opportunity for BME trainee teachers to access a coaching model that is supportive to their needs.

OBJECTIVES

The Key Objectives of The Programme Were

- To provide a platform for the coaches to talk through issues, challenges and aspirations with an experienced BME teacher as their coach
- To support trainee teachers in the development of their training whilst broadening them and allowing them to grow and reach their potential
- To develop a supportive and valuable approach for students to experience and ultimately use the strategies themselves
- To help Coachees learn about themselves as individuals and professionals, learning strategies during the process to resolve issues, make changes where necessary and move forward
- To encourage Individuals to talk through issues and how to take more control of the situation whilst on courses at the IOE and consider their own role as well as the impact on others through focused questioning and active listening

The Uniqueness of the 20–20 Coaching Programme

The "real "uniqueness for the 20–20 coaching was that the programme enabled both the coach and the coachee to enhance their professional development profiles, within a specific "space" for Black and Minority Ethnic teachers. Many of the coaches had attended various one day programmes, however had not found the opportunity to practice their acquired skill. In addition to this the coachee benefited from BME senior teachers that were willing to share 2–3 hours within their busy schedule to explore coaching from a cultural centred perspective. The coaching model was to empower the students with the understanding that they held the knowledge and coaching was just a mechanism to pull the information from within them.

METHODOLOGY

Participation on the Project

The 20–20 programme aimed to attract 20 trainee teachers and 20 coaches. However, we recruited 17 coaches who were willing to work with our trainee teaches. Subsequently, three of the coaches were unable to take up the coaching due to various circumstances. Therefore, in total the project had 14 coaches and 14 coachees.

The participants' backgrounds were African, African Caribbean and South Asian. Across both groups there were only five male participants. The age range for the coachees was between 25 and 48 and the age of the coaches was between 35 and 55.

Most of the coachees expressed an interest in the coaching programme as they thought it would be beneficial in their journey to becoming teachers. Some of the coachees had chosen teaching as their second career; however, for the majority it was their first choice after leaving college. The coaching programme attracted second and third year part time students studying on the B Ed programme. (The B Ed programme has been developed to train people working in school, either as unqualified teachers, overseas trained teachers or people undertaking others roles such as teaching assistants or learning mentors.) The programme of study for these students was part-time. In addition to this some students from the Teach First programme (equivalent to Teach America Programme) and the employment based route also came along.

The Coaches wanted to become part of the process as a way to give back to the wider community. The coaches were experienced senior teachers who included principals, deputy principals, heads of departments and local government education officers.

Recruitment Process

The coachees were recruited various ways that included a combination of posters, announcements on blackboard, tutors and general talking to students. However, the recruitment of coachees was left too late, as most of the Post Graduate Certificate in Education (PGCE) students had completed the year and were only coming back to finalise loose ends. If the programme were to be run again it would be important to start the recruitment of trainee teachers during the start of the spring term.

The coaches were recruited through the Institute of Education, University of London schools network, along with personal contacts and targeted emailing to a selection of London schools. .When the message started to go into schools, coaches contacted the team for further information. The coaches came from different schools across London. It was crucial that most coaches recruited were from Black and ethnic minority backgrounds

Our Approach as a Team

The team that organised the project, including the facilitators, consisted mainly of colleagues from a BME background. One facilitator however, was a White Scottish female who found the experience very different in the sense that "the shoe was on the other foot." This is her reflection.

> It was interesting for me to take part in this project as I realised very quickly that I was in a minority, something which I rarely experience. My colleagues talked about music, literature and cultures of which I had no knowledge and, at times, I felt rather left out and inadequate. I should point out that was not their intention—merely how I felt. I realised however, that my personality and expertise were what mattered to them and not my colour or background. I realised through the experience that the group needed to talk together about the particular issues many BME teachers feel and deal with. I learned much which can only lead to me having a better understanding of colleagues and their experiences which in turn may help improve my practice. The group were wonderful to work with and incredibly respectful of one another and all the facilitators. I had the feeling they were very sad when the project ended. (December 2010)

As a team we were able to work across each of our cultural experiences and use these experiences to develop our coaching model. The team consisted of two secondary teacher educators and a third had previous experience in school teaching although now taught Master's and doctoral programmes. The two teacher educators had worked closely together for many years and had set up a generic coaching programme for any trainee teacher studying at the IOE. One WAS Scottish (raised in Scotland) and the other Caribbean (raised and worked in London schools). The other member of the team was Black English, raised and worked in rural schools. Each of the team members brought a past insight from their teaching experience and an understanding of the importance of the need for an individual coach to enable people to negotiate the steps required to achieve their desired career pathway.

The team thought that training sessions for both the coaches and coachees needed to be interactive and functional. Therefore the sessions were organised with practise activities as the main focus. All the sessions began with a theoretical input on coaching and then lead into an interactive task. Some of the practice tasks were individually focused and others required the participants to work in small groups. The coaching team chose techniques that would permit the participants to reflect on the coaching experience. (The actual techniques will be discussed further on in this paper.) In addition to this, all of the participants were introduced to appropriate tools that could be used in coaching. Each of the tools was discussed and explored in detail.

How the Programme Was Constructed

The programme was designed to ensure that both coaches and coachees were able to have a practical coaching experience. All of the coaches attended two briefing/training sessions that informed them about the coaching model. The coaching model was based on Showunmi (1996) developed with trainee teachers in 1995. The model presented as an interconnecting circle that works in the following way: stage one: a team came together to develop the programme; stage two: trainee teachers signed up to the programme; stage three: senior teachers signed up to the programme; stage four: matching process; stage five: training for both coaches and coachees.

Initially, the student teachers worked together in randomly selected pairs, then each pair fed back their experiences to the group. Towards the end of this initial session, coachees were matched up with a coach and the process of them working together began.

The coachees (trainee teachers) and coaches (experienced teachers) were invited to a briefing session or briefed on an individual basis All of the participants were briefed on expectations from them as coaches and coachees. An opportunity to be reflective on coaching moments was built into the programme.

Overall, the coaching lasted for four months. Every two weeks, the trainee teachers (coachees) met with the team to report and reflect on their experiences. Notes of these sessions were taken by the team. Every month, both coaches and coachees came together with the team to reflect on the process. Again, notes were taken by the team. In addition, coaches and coachees were asked to write comments on post-it notes.

Programme Session Activities and Orientation

The 20–20 Coaching programme consisted of two briefing/training sessions for the coaches, followed by one briefing/training session for both the coaches and coachees together. After the coaching, there was a final session with both groups to capture feedback for future work.

The programme adopted a goal orientated focus to the coaching, and coaches were trained accordingly. Ives (2008) describes various approaches within the coaching paradigm which reflect a goal orientated approach. A humanistic approach looks at how the person's own desire to change in a positive way is the driving force in achieving full potential—something which all participants in the programme aspired to. A behaviour-based approach advocates working towards a change in behaviour in particular environments or contexts, which again comes from a desire to develop personally and become more effective. Finally, an adult learning approach sees coaching as a method of deep and everlasting learning. Adult learning explores theories such as reflection and experience to construct new learning. All these approaches support the previously mentioned philosophy of coaching as one that assists in change and transformation for the purpose of greater effectiveness within a community.

Both the coaches and coachees participated in a variety of activities. The following provides a breakdown of the various activities.

SETTING GROUND RULES

- Brain storming ideas for rules for the group including, of course, confidentiality, respecting each other's time by making and keeping appointments, switching off mobiles in sessions, etc.

LISTENING ACTIVITY

- In this activity, the group was asked in pairs to discuss their favourite book, film and piece of music. They were then asked to introduce their partner to the group. The idea was to become aware of the skill of listening.
- Participants were asked to note how their partner knew they were listening (i.e., body language, eye contact, affirmative nods, words etc.).
- They were asked what, if anything, interfered with listening (i.e., Outside noise, own busy life, too much information being given out and so on).
- They were made aware of the need, before a coaching session, to clear your head and prepare for the session ahead.

BUCKETS

- In this exercise, the coach asks the coachee to draw as many buckets as they felt they had in their life and draw a line as to how full they were. Examples can be: too many meetings, email overload, marking, home life, etc. They were then asked to select the bucket(s) they would most like to reduce or empty and to discuss, with assistance from the coach, how this might be done and how realistic it would be. Then they were asked to set goals.

TIME LINES

- In this exercise the coachees were asked to sit on a chair a distance away, for example, at the back of a room. They were asked to think about where they would like to be in six months (or can be years or any time they wish to make it realistic). They then discusses this with coach for 5–10 minutes. Then they move chairs forward to three months time, then move forward again one month. They discussed how they were going to achieve goals in the time set.

TWO CHAIR ACTIVITY

This activity can be used in different ways.

- Difficulty in making a decision (a dilemma). The coachee sits in one chair which denotes one decision choice. The coach talks through with the coachee how they feel in this position (positive aspects, negative aspects, what they might say or do). The coachee then sits in other chair which represents the other decision, and follows the same routine. They then shift between the chairs and see which decision "feels" best.
- This process can also be used to try out a prospective difficult conversation. The empty chair can be the person the coachee is going to have the difficult conversation with. Some issues to discuss could be practised.

DRAWING ACTIVITY/VISUALISATION

- The coachee is asked to put a dilemma onto paper in the form of a drawing or diagram—whatever they feel. The drawing/diagram should consist of the situation now and how the coachee would like it to be. The coach talks through the drawing/diagram with the coachee, exploring solutions and setting targets.

FORCE FIELD ANALYSIS

- This involves discussing the pros and cons of a new situation.

RESULTS AND DISCUSSION

Feedback from participants was analysed from the following sources:

- Notes of the fortnightly discussion/reflection meetings with the trainee teachers (coachees)
- Notes of the monthly discussion/reflection meetings with the coaches and the coachees
- Comments on post-it notes made by coaches and coachees
- Feedback forms filled in by coaches and coachees at the end of the four months of coaching

Much useful information about the effectiveness of coaching for BME trainee teachers by BME coaches was obtained from the meetings and post-it notes. These findings are summarised and discussed below.

Tackling Isolation

The coaching sessions revealed that a common experience of coachees was a feeling of isolation because of their race—and this was explored and tackled within the coaching sessions.

Many of the coachees spoke about feeling isolated in the school. They were in a position that held responsibility as a trainee class teacher, yet felt powerless as a BME member of the team. Some of the coachees faced an uphill battle to keep pushing themselves forward so that they were on the radar of others. The constant emotional push was both draining and isolating and made it hard for them to cope. Evidence suggests (Haberman, 2004) that when coping mechanisms fail, then stress increases and threatens the teachers' mental and physical wellbeing ultimately leading to teachers quitting or burning out. Haberman uses a behavioral definition of burnout and defines it as a condition in which teachers remain as paid employees but stop functioning as professionals.

During the sessions many of the coachees shared experiences of needing to prove that as a BME teacher they were the "good Blacks" and therefore the right choice for the school. Interestingly enough this is something that the coaches (experienced teachers) spoke about too. All of the coaches spoke about their journey to the top as an uphill struggle, and even now that they had reached their goal it was still a struggle.

Because the notion of isolation was real for both the trainees and the experienced teachers, the coaching sessions helped both to make some sense of what they were dealing with whilst navigating the education system. The coaching process, and being part of the interactive groups, empowered the coachees and in turn increased their confidence as teachers. As their confidence increased, their feeling of isolation and helplessness was eased.

The following quotes heighted the way in which coaching helped to tackle their feeling of isolation:

> Working with my BME coach helped me not to feel so isolated.

> I really appreciated the time and space with other trainee BME teachers.

Benefits of Group Interaction as Part of the Coaching Programme: Feeling Part of a Wider Community

Many felt that being BME was something that they had to battle if they were to get through the school placement experience. The 20–20 Coaching Programme made it possible for the Black trainee teachers to come together as a group and not have to justify why they were together. The coachees thought that it gave them a sense of belonging to a wider community of Black educators. Ogbu (1999) describes this as being part of a "collective identity." Based on a ethnographic study carried out in (1980) Ogbu uses the term "collective identity" as a way of connecting with the notion of belonging and pride that many Black people felt they had lost as an "other" in their professional lives.

The following comments by participants highlight the significance of group interaction with other Black trainee teachers as part of the coaching programme.

> Good to know that there are other Black people experiencing issues relating to their teaching experience

> Knowing that there were other Black teachers experiencing similar issues was reassuring for the coachees

> Having somebody who looks like you... knowing they too have had to navigate the system is very helpful

> The group experience was crucial as I never expected it would work... I thought that being in an all Black group would be negative... instead it was so uplifting

Providing the space for the interactive group experience contributed to the 20–20 coaching programme's uniqueness and success. Being able to share their collective experience in a designated space with other BME trainee teachers was invaluable. Knowing that they were among other BME trainee teachers on the 20–20 coaching programme eased the internalised questioning of their rights and needs as BME trainee teachers.

Tatum (1997) said that

> ... racial identity can escape conscious attention, especially if one is a member of the dominant racial group. It is essential that teachers understand these processes if they are to respond effectively to the reactions White students often have when confronted with issues of race and racism when they haven't yet examined their own racial identities.

Tatum (1997) argues that "it is a healthy part of psychological development to seek out racial identity groups" and that, "racial grouping is a developmental process in response to an environmental stressor, racism." Joining with one's peers for support in the face of stress is seen as a positive coping strategy. She goes on to say that forming and having access to one's own racial groups can lead to more productive and healthy intergroup interactions in educational settings.

Clearly, the opportunity for regular group interaction with the other BME trainees as part of the coaching process played a significant part in the success of the programme. It is recommended that BME coaching programmes should be designed to incorporate this group discussion and reflection.

The Importance of Having BME Coaches for BME Trainee Teachers

The findings also revealed that having BME coaches for BME trainees had a significant positive effect on the success of the coaching. The following quotes from participants highlight the importance of having access to BME coaches as part of the coaching process:

> The coach that I had was very experienced teacher and was able to relate to my experience... I really believe that having a Black coach to me was important.

> I had been part of the other coaching programme... for all trainee teachers and was not going to sign up for this one. I thought I would just come along just to see and was so surprised it was an interesting experience.

> The 20–20 coaching programme should be available for all minority teachers as our experience is so different.

> Some of the exercises really made you think about who you are and where you want to be.

> This was really helpful for me as a Black gay male. Believe me it is hard training to be a teacher as everything is being stacked against you.

All of the coachees who took part in the programme expressed the positive benefits in having access to an experienced Black teacher. Having somebody who actually understood what was going on in their teaching placement without the need of constant explanation was seen as crucial to their overall development.

The Feedback Forms: General Comments About the Coaching Programme

As part of the evaluation process we asked the coaches and coachees to place their thoughts against five questions on a feedback form. The comments on the feedback forms also revealed a positive response to the coaching from both coaches and coachees. However, none of these comments referred to racial background. This was a fault of the form's design—and in future studies, the feedback form should specifically refer to race. Nevertheless, the forms provided much useful information on the general effectiveness of the coaching programme.

The first question on the form asked: "What did you hope to get out of the service?" The following responses from participants will be valuable for the design of future coaching programmes—although most of the participants' aims were in fact addressed in the coaching sessions.

- Clarity, advice, guidance, help, a long term coach and coachee relationship
- Put my thoughts together and find the answers from guidance
- I had no preconceived ideas but have been able to reflect on my future
- To make me a better person! Self development
- Guidance—I wanted to gain confidence and find out within myself if teaching is really what I want to do and if I am competent enough
- For the coachee to reach their goals—or at least know where they wanted to be
- To develop my skills and in a new area
- Advice, help with better understanding of what concerns me and what I need to do in the future
- To understand my weak areas and how to overcome these, to focus

The second question asked: "What was most useful about the coaching session?" and responses are listed below.

- Questions that allowed internal focus/reflection
- Strategies that allowed long, medium, and short term goal making
- Made me realise what I can do in future. Also showed me the way to further my learning
- Talking to an outsider yet a professional in education about own ideas about teaching and learning
- I agree! I realised how much I can do!!!
- Helped me to think through problems
- To be a good listener—it was difficult
- To understand the difference between a mentor and coach
- Giving the coachee time to think and speak, being a good listener, giving guidance-helping them to make the choices

It was clear from the above comments that the coaching programme had been able to provide a wide range of guidance and support—including listening skills, confidence-building, planning, goal-setting, help with tackling problems, and time for reflection and discussion.

The third question asked: "What suggestions might you have for a future project?"

- Perhaps we can have more sessions
- To extend this in schools to help teachers on the job
- To have this opportunity through how my studies, possibly with the same person
- An extensive course for coachee
- Longer sessions with coaches

- To have a chance to get to know the coaches a little before we're paired up
- Maybe we could also coach 1st year students
- This is something that would benefit students at the start of their course of study
- Personally, I would have taken 3–14 questions and written them down, then have them answered by writing, then I could have more time to think and reflect

The main thrust of the participants' requests was to ask for more: longer sessions; more sessions; and extending the programme to qualified teachers and first year trainees. This attests to the value of offering such coaching programmes.

The fourth question asked: "What was least useful about the coaching session?"

- Yes, coaching sessions should begin earlier in the course
- Small talk
- Can't think of anything that was not useful
- I agree!
- So do I
- Me too
- Short time, I would prefer longer term "relationship"
- The coaching sessions would be more useful at the beginning of term and then follow up sessions to see if goals have been achieved or how far I have come to reach my goal
- Start coaching session earlier will prevent students—dropping out/ less stress etc.
- At the beginning would be ideal!
- I think coaching would be great while you are on your Newly Qualified Teacher year! If there is opportunity for this I would love to hear about it!

It was gratifying that most participants found all parts of the programme useful—with criticisms centring on the need for more, mirroring the response to the previous question. However, several of the second year trainees felt that the coaching would have been easier and more valuable earlier in the training course—and this should be borne in mind for future programmes

The fifth question asked: "What was the best thing about coaching?"

- Setting goals
- Reflecting on the goals

- Be able to name and clarify inside "you" what it is you want to do
- Seeing the actual aspirations
- Questions made me think and step back—think "deep" process about to get there
- Pulling internally out of yourself
- Kept focus on task
- Had to answer my "own" questions—motivates
- "friendship" informal

It would appear that the goal-orientated model was the correct one to use, as many responses referred to goals, aims and aspirations. The value of time for reflection and "friendship" were again mentioned—further supporting the recommendation to keep the regular scheduled group meetings as an integral part of the coaching programme.

Limitations in the Programme

Clearly, this BME coaching programme was not flawless. If we were doing it today there would be several things that we would have done differently. For example, we may explore the possibility of training the coaches for longer periods and with more intensity—perhaps even with some accreditation. We would also explore the timings of the training as many of the coaches found it difficult to attend at the end of the day due to work commitments or personal commitments. Some of the coaches we felt did not experience enough training.

It might also be best to run the course in the first, rather than the second year of the training course—to enable trainees to feel the benefits of coaching earlier, and to avoid the clash with preparing for final exams and assessments.

Something which is necessary is for coaches to have support and ongoing development themselves. It would be useful to build this in more regularly in the programme. The one session we did have however, was very positively evaluated by the coaches.

However, the main thing is that the programme took place, and we were able to attract participants, which demonstrated a need for such a programme. Something else for us to think about would be opening out the service to non BME students.

Recommendations

In order for both the coaches and coachees to benefit from the 20–20 coaching programme, a much longer time period for intensive training for the coaches is required. The use of "real" practical experiences is crucial for the development of coaches, and therefore it would be adventurous to develop further practical training resources for the coaches. There needs to be a much clearer theoretical underpinning, giving coaches a deeper awareness of the concepts, processes and benefits of coaching activities.

In addition to this, the coaches and coachees would need to come together as a whole group more frequently to share and explore once the coaching relationship commenced. The notion of the whole group experience would enhance the professional development of all the people involved in the process. The regular scheduled times for group reflection for both coaches and coachees should become a routine part of future coaching programmes.

This study also highlighted the value of having coaching programmes specifically targeted at BME trainees and given by BME coaches, in which the coachees and coaches would share similar life experiences and challenges.

The final recommendation would be to develop a network for BME teachers who express an interest in coaching.

REFERENCES

Carnell, E., Macdonald, J., & Askew, S. (2006). *Coaching and mentoring in higher education: A learning-centred approach*. London: Institute of Education.

Carringon, B., & Skelton, C. (2003). Re-thinking "role models:" Equal opportunities in teacher recruitment in England and Wales. *Journal of Education Policy*, 18(3) pp. 253–265.

Connor, M., & Pokora, J. (2007). *Coaching and mentoring at work: Developing effective practice*. Maidenhead: Open University Press.

Cornish, T (2009). Coaching Black British coachees. In J. Passmore, (Ed.), *Diversity in coaching, working with gender, culture, race and age*. London: Kogan Page:

Griffiths, K., & Campbell, M. (2009). Discovering, applying and integrating: The process of learning in coaching. *International Journal of Evidence Based Coaching and Mentoring*, 7(2), 16–30.

Hargreaves, E. (2008). *Using mentoring and coaching to support work based learning: An evaluation*. Centre for Excellence in Work-Based learning for Education Professionals, London: Institute of Education.

Ives, Y. (2008). What is "coaching"? An exploration of conflicting paradigms. *International Journal of Evidence Based Coaching and Mentoring*, 6(2), 100–113.

Jamison, C. (2006). *Finding sanctuary, monastic steps for everyday life*. London: Weidenfeld and Nicolson.

Maylor, U. (2007) "They do not relate to Black people like us"|: Black teachers as role models for Black pupils. *Journal of Education Policy*, 24(1), 2009, 1–21.

Mezirow, J. (1998). On critical reflection. *Adult Learning Quarterly*, (48), 185–198.

Ogbu, J (2004). Collective identity and the burden of "acting White" in history community, and education. *Urban review*, 36(1). March 2004.

Pask, R., & Joy, B. (2007). *Mentoring and coaching: A guide for education professionals.* Maidenhead: Open University Press.

Rodger, F. (2010). *How is coaching in different social contexts constructed through activity?* Research project submitted for Doctorate in Education degree: Unpublished.

Scott, S. M. (1997). The grieving soul in the transformation process. *New Direction for Adult and Continuing Education,* (74), 41–50.

Showunmi, V. (1996). The Black perspective of mentoring. *Mentoring and Tutoring Journal, 3*(3), 12.

Showunmi, V., & Constantine-Simms, C. (Eds.). (1995). *Teachers for the future.* Stoke-on-Trent: Trentham Books.

Tatum D. B. (1997). *Why are all the Black kids sitting together in the cafeteria?: And other conversations about race.* New York: Basic Books.

Thomas, W., & Smith, A. (2009). *Coaching solutions: Practical ways to improve performance in education.* London: Continuum International Publishing Group.

Vaughan Smith, J. (2007). *Therapist into coach.* Maidenhead: Open University Press and McGraw-Hill Education.

Watkins, C., & Whalley, C. (1993). Mentoring beginner teachers—Issues for schools to anticipate and manage. *School Organisation, 13*(2), 129–138.

Wrong, D. H. (1961). The oversocialized conception of man in modern sociology. *American Sociological Review, 26*(2), 183–193.

Zeus, P., & Skiffington, S. (2006). *The coaching at work toolkit: A complete guide to techniques and practices.* Australia: McGraw-Hill Australia Pty Ltd.

CHAPTER 10

BAD BOYS
TO MASTER TEACHERS

Hip Hop Culture and the Making
of Black Male Teacher Identity

Thurman Bridges
Morgan State University

INTRODUCTION

Given the issues facing urban youth in schools today, and the lack of Black male teachers who serve their psychological, social and educational needs, research on the epistemologies of Black male teachers is salient. While examinations of the tenuous plights of Black males in schools and the larger society are important, researchers bear the responsibility to investigate, more keenly, the educational and cultural contexts through which Black male teachers develop their pedagogical orientations. This chapter seeks to contextualize and humanize the troubled schooling experiences of Black male teachers and make sense of the ways that Hip Hop culture both inform their teaching practice and shape their pedagogical identities. Drawing from a larger qualitative study of ten (10) Black male K–12 teachers,

Teacher Education and Black Communities, pages 209–223
Copyright © 2014 by Information Age Publishing
All rights of reproduction in any form reserved.

the author examines the narrative of one particular participant, who, as a youth, was labeled "at risk" and, as such, marginalized within the public school system. Now, as a classroom teacher, he draws from his own schooling and Hip Hop cultural experiences to help develop students' social, cultural and gender identities and respond to their specific academic needs.

Much of the existing research that address Black males educational experience, embraces a deficit oriented approach, focusing too often on suspension, expulsion and dropout rates, as well as gaps in their academic performance, as compared to White students. In similar comparisons, Black male teachers, though often applauded for their effective management of Black boys, are generally classified as an "at-risk" segment of the teaching workforce, due to their low and declining representation in the teaching work force. Equally, Hip Hop Culture, particularly Rap music, is unfairly criminalized and framed as the media through which Black males develop and manifest disaffected and antisocial behaviors in school and in the larger society. These dehumanizing and deficit theoretical frames, have resulted in two dominant ideas about Hip Hop Culture and Black males in school: one, as dangerous and the other, as endangered. Consequently, these perspectives relegate both Black male teachers and students to the margins of public schools and research on teacher identity.

This chapter investigates those critical moments, from the participant's perspective, when teachers and school administrators were negligent in their responsibilities to provide high quality instruction and emotionally safe learning environments. More importantly, it sheds light on the significant role that Hip Hop culture played in (a) healing the social, emotional, and academic wounds cause by his schooling experience; (b) developing humanizing ideas about what it means to be a Black male in the U.S. society; and (c) providing an existential vision for himself as a teacher and a humanizing pedagogical framework for teaching his Black male students. This analysis not only emphasizes the ways that Black males have been systemically excluded from schools, but, more importantly, situates Hip Hop as a significant venue through which many Black males, both teachers and students, defend and define themselves within the context of school.

THE RELATED LITERATURE

Black Males and Hip Hop

Hip Hop is a term used to describe the collective experience, modes of thinking, and epistemologies of urban youth. DJ Kool Herk is credited for discovering Hip Hop in the Bronx, New York around 1972 and, by 1974, Africka Bambaataa established Hip Hop as a community rooted in principles of peace, love, unity, and having fun. These principles are generally, but not exclusively, expressed through following specific elements of Hip Hop: Breakin' (Breakdancing), Emceein' (Rap), Graffiti art (Aerosal Art), Deejayin, Beatboxin', Street Fashion, Street Language, Street Knowledge, Street Entrepreneurialism and Education (KRS-One, 2003).

Hip Hop represents a coalition of artists who rap, write, act, teach, dance and perform for a living and in the early 1970s, many of such artists, and the communities they reflected, suffered under crippling poverty and rejection from the mainstream society. Historically, Hip Hop crews grew out of former gangs who would, rather than fight, engage in rap, deejay and dance battles (Bynoe, 2004; KRS-One, 2003; Rose, 1994). Hip Hop battles, which included rapping, dancing, DJing, was not about dehumanizing or debasing others but about demonstrating one's creativity, intelligence and wit. Through these Hip Hop battles, rap and dance competitions, community performances and the like, Hip Hop provided both a source of income and a cultural venue to amplify a collective outcry against the social, racial and economic injustices inflicted on, in particular, marginalized people of color (KRS-One, 2003; Bynoe, 2004)

As reflected in the personal account discussed in this chapter, Hip Hop served as a cultural counternarrative to the dominant beliefs about the humanity of Black people in the United States and around the world. According to KRS-One, "Within our community, Hip Hoppas are judged by the content of their character and skill, not by the color of their skin, their choice of religion, or social status" (p. 181). Particularly among Black males, Hip Hop provided a space to envision and manifest a reality whereby they were validated, accepted and productive.

Hip Hop as a culture, emerged out of resistance to hegemonic ideas and practices and provides urban a platform elevate their voices (Morrell, 2002). It is through Hip Hop that countless Black youth engage in a critical analysis of the ecological conditions facing marginalized groups in the U.S. and throughout the world (Hanley, 2007). Speaking from the perspectives of Black and Latino youth and to the needs of their families and communities, Hip Hop artists like Chuck D, KRS-One, Tribe Called Quest, D-Nice, Public Enemy and Poor Righteous Teachers, to name only a few, used Rap to teach about social and political movements throughout history and disrupt dominate beliefs about Black peoples (Hanley, 2007; Hill-Collins, 2006; KRS-One, 2003). It was through Hip Hop that urban youth were taught to end "Self-Destruction," to put "Ladies First," to "Fight the Power" and to "Heal Oneself." These messages helped to shape their identities in ways that promoted high self-esteem, community activism, economic empowerment, and a commitment to social justice (Bynoe, 2004; KRS-One, 2003; Rose, 1994).

According to Morrell (2003), "the influence of rap as a voice of resistance for urban youth proliferates through artists who endeavor to bring an accurate yet critical depiction of the urban situation to a Hip Hop generation" (p. 73). Black men, in particular, who were born between 1965 and 1984 and who are proponents of the original philosophy of Hip Hop, represent this Hip Hop generation (Collin, 2006). This population of Black men, who KRS-One (2003) calls, "Hip Hoppas" are defined largely by the intersections of their early involvement with Hip Hop culture as a powerful social and political voice for Black people in the United States and their experiences with race, class, and sexism in school and the larger society (Brown, 1999; Lynn, 1999, 2002). This unique interaction of experiences—one which engendered a sense of voice and agency and the other which perpetuated ideas of Black inferiority, bolstered Hip Hop's popularity as a social, emotional, spiritual and artistic safe haven, particularly for Black males.

It is important to point out that, as with all cultures, Hip Hop is multidimensional and has produced some cultural expressions that are not positive. The popularized and commercialized images and discourses around Hip Hop are often hyper-sexualized, materialistic and sometimes violent. The present state of popularized forms of Hip Hop, as perpetuated by the media, forces us to seriously interrogate its purpose and function.

The more contemporary and popular representation of Hip Hop is often in contradiction to the goals, values and responsibilities of its origin. The goal here is not to create a false dichotomy between good and bad Hip Hop, as I assert that Hip Hop culture represents the truth of the human experience. Morrell and Andrade (2002) posit, "Whether the power in its message can be used for good or ill, few can dispute the impact of Hip Hop culture on the lives of working class urban youth" (p. 89). However, the cultural forms of Hip Hop emphasized in this chapter are those that remain true to the original philosophy of the community-peace, love, unity, and having fun.

Black Males in School

Through an examination of my own schooling experiences and the educational narratives of Black men and boys, I understand why countless Black males consider public school as an institution that they barely escaped. In 2005, the Education Trust Foundation reported that only 12% of Black fourth graders reached proficient or advanced levels in reading and math, and 61% had not achieved basic level training. By the eighth grade, the same proportion of students fell below the basic achievement level while only 7% reached proficient or above (EdTrust, 2005). To exacerbate these disparities, Black boys endured punishment more often and more harshly in school (Brown, 2007) and accrued high rates of incarceration, drug and weapons offenses, and school exclusion (Noguera, 1996, 2003a, 2003b). Similarly, in 2006 the Justice Policy Institute reported that, "While African American youth comprise 17% of the youth population, African American youth represent 27% of all drug violation arrests. African American youth represent 32% of all weapons arrests, and were arrested for weapons offenses at a rate twice that of Whites" (Justice Policy Institute, 2006).

More recently, in the Schott Foundation's 2012 Report, *The Urgency of Now: The Scott 50 State Report on Public Education and Black Males*, data on Black male graduation rates reveals that little progress has been made in understanding the Black male experience in relation to schooling nor in addressing Black male disengagement from school. In an analysis of national graduation data from 2009–2010, The Urgency of Now report asserts, "in 38 of the 50 states and the District of Columbia, Black males have the lowest graduation rates among Black, Latino and White, non-Latino male and female students" (Schott, 2012, p. 6). Nationally, only 52% of Black males graduate from high school in four years, whereas 78% of White, non-Latino males graduate in four years (Schott, 2012). These data paint a grim picture of the Black male experience in public schools and showcase, what seems to be, a set insurmountable educational challenges.

Similarly, Black men and boys have been characterized in popular media and by social scientists as a dangerous and endangered species. According to Ferguson (2001), "the image of the Black male criminal is more familiar because of its prevalence in print and electronic media as well as in scholarly work. The headline of newspaper articles and magazines dramatically echo these alarming messages, where the presence of Black males in public spaces has come to signify danger and a threat to personal safety" (p. 78).

Ferguson (2001) suggests that schools embrace and perpetuate these negative stereotypes from the media to categorize Black boys' expressions of masculinity as vicious, aggressive, and insubordinate and that their behavior needs to be controlled. She asserts, "What is required from them is a performance of absolute docility that goes against the grain of masculinity" (Ferguson, 2001, p. 78). Davis (2003) further illuminates this point commenting that, "the social construction of young men as troublesome bodies is tied to the idea that Black men are similarly constructed as violent, threatening and menacing" (p. 297). For instance, males play style and behaviors are often misunderstood by [White] female teachers and are seen as defiant, aggressive and intimidating (Davis, 2006). These conceptions and dehumanizing ideologies shape social policies, educational reforms as well as school culture and discipline practices that marginalize Black boys in schools (Dance, 2002; Davis, 2006; Ferguson 2001).

Analysis of existing research about Black males suggests that many experience troubles in school, be they academic, social or personal. It also suggests that efforts to address the educational needs of Black males, has left us ill-equipped at understanding how they experience and make meaning of these school troubled experiences. During our interview, the participant posed the following question, "As a Black boy in America, why would I trust any teacher? Why would I trust teachers in general if teachers put me out of school, put me out of class, get mad at me because they don't understand me?" Similarly, when asked to address the shortage of Black male teachers, he replied, "Why would I re-enter an institution that I barely escaped?"

This chapter examines the narrative of one particular Black male teacher, Mr. G, who "barely escaped" school, but is now a teacher who remains committed to the lives and education of underserved Black male youth. Informed by his own Hip Hop experiences, he recognizes its power at capturing the minds of urban youth and uses Hip Hop to teach, motivate and entertain his students (Hanley, 2007; KRS-One, 2003; Marvin Lynn, 2002; Stovall, 2006b). The reward of utilizing a Hip Hop cultural framework, superseded and helped heal the pain and humiliation of his K–12 experiences and, as such, represent powerful opportunities for school systems, teacher education programs and teacher preparation organizations, to attract Black men who, like many Black male youth, have rejected school as a safe social, emotional and intellectual space.

BLACK MALE TEACHER PROFILE

In this section, I am examining Mr. G's beliefs and perceptions about teaching and learning as connected to his educational history. More specifically, I explore his beliefs about the challenges facing Black male students and the strengths and potential of Black male youth and how these understandings are connected to his own troubled schooling experiences and practice as a teacher. Further, this narrative shows how Mr. G's experiences and perceptions relate to Hip Hop, which he has identified as an important influence, connecting him to teaching and his Black male students.

Mr. G

Mr. G is a Hip Hop MC (move the crowd) and digital artist whose connection to teaching is directly connected to Hip Hop. He began his career as a freelance digital artist and videographer. Through a fellow artist friend, he learned about an arts instructor position, and, though he never planned to be an educator, decided to explore teaching as a profession. After accepting the arts instructor position, he later realized that several of his friends within the Hip Hop community were recently hired at his school. He described the school as having, a "Hip Hop vibe," meaning much of the cultural activities, curricular frameworks and critical discourses between and among students and teachers, were expressed through many of the elements of Hip Hop culture-rap, poetry, and oratorical battles.

Mr. G was born in Hip Hop's birthplace, the Bronx, New York, in 1979. In New York, he lived with both parents and attended racially and culturally diverse public schools. He maintained an A average throughout elementary school and was at the top of his class academically throughout most of his early school years.

Mr. G described himself as an obedient child that worked hard to please his parents, particularly his father, who demanded high academic performance. Reflecting on his father's disposition towards school, Mr. G recounted, "He was the type to be like, 'okay your homework is not written neat enough. Write it over'!" He dedicated several hours a week to homework assignments, required reading, school projects and preparing for his father's weekly math, science and language arts quizzes. Since his friends, teachers, and family members considered him to be bright student, Mr. G found himself working to live up to their expectations. He recalled,

> I would just grab books that were large and think—oh that's 500 pages, lets start on that now, you know what I mean? I was in the 4th grade reading on a 12th grade level, and it was nothing for me.

Under those conditions, he was an honors student and flourished in the advanced academic tract at school.

Mr. G, however, recalled a time in his educational career when he began to experience school differently. The "shift," as he articulated, happened in 1989, when his parents divorced and his family moved from New York to a low-income neighborhood in Washington, DC. In New York, he lived with both parents—who were educated, employed, and owned their home, and was shielded from the social conditions facing, in particular, people of color in impoverished communities. In 1989, however, Washington, DC was categorized as the murder capital of the nation, exposing Mr. G to the negative impact that drug abuse, poverty, and gang violence had on countless Black communities, but specifically his own.

During that time in his life, Mr. G began to question the relevance of school as a way to address the challenges facing his family and community. He also felt suffocated by rigid demands to sit, follow, and obey, all of which exemplified desirable school behavior. Mr. G perceived school as a place that inhibited his creativity and disregarded the socioeconomic needs of his community. Rejecting the established protocol for student conduct, he questioned administrators' authority and broke, what he considered, unreasonable school and classroom rules. He became one of the school's problem students and, as such, was frequently put out of class, debased by teachers and suspended from school.

It was also during this time in his life that Mr. G was exposed to Hip Hop. His involvement emerged as Hip Hop became more popularized in mainstream media. What first captured Mr. G's attention was that the style and diction of Hip Hop artists like Kool Mo D and Run DMC mirrored the men in his family, church, and community. He stated, "They looked like the people in the hood. They looked like my uncle, they dressed like my uncles." Mr. G says, "They were political and street at the same time." Likewise, the power and authority with which Boogie Down Productions (BDP) rapped, especially in the song *You Must Learn,* ignited in Mr. G, a desire to validate, through research, the messages in the music, share the music with friends and challenge teachers with the information he learned.

His earliest memory of being deeply connected to Hip Hop was through the movie, *Do The Right Thing by Spike Lee,* and the song *Fight the Power* by Public Enemy, both of which elevated the voices and showcased the experiences of people of color in marginalized communities. In Hip Hop, he heard narratives that reflected his sociocultural experiences in Washington, DC, saw Black communities fighting against oppression and acquired the language and knowledge to use as a weapon of resistance.

Freire (2007) describes Mr. G's tenuous school experience as a "process of domestication," against which students eventually fight, in search of a more humanizing and validating educational experience. He (2007) asserts,

> sooner or later, these contradictions may lead formerly passive students to turn against their domestication and the attempt to domesticate reality. They may discover through existential experience that their present way of life is irreconcilable with their vocation to become more fully human ... sooner or later they may perceive the contradiction in which the banking education seeks to maintain them and then engage themselves in the struggle for liberation. (p. 75)

As the academic year progressed, Mr. G grew in his disconnection and carried the "troubled student" onto middle school. He noticed early in the year, that his six grade teachers were less accommodating, provided fewer chances to reconcile missed assignments and used harsh discipline measures to address bad behavior. He was failing most and barely passing a few of his classes, and by the end of the first grading period, counselors and administers assigned him to the schools' remedial academic tract and instituted a management plan to address his academic and social challenges. Therefore, he was grouped with students that required specialized academic and social support to be successful in school.

That decision was based on an evaluation of his most recent academic performance and behavior in school, rather than a longitudinal analysis of his past grades, behavior or the social context of his life at that time. Mr. G recounted,

> The year before my grades dropped, I was a straight A student for 4 years. Then, all of a sudden, I was sitting in remedial classes and I was not a remedial student. I saw how they taught us like we were slow. But we were only in the sixth grade and they already wrote us off and nobody was formally testing us.

He asserted that much of his time in remediation was spent completing worksheets and watching movies. He recalled feeling trapped as he was well aware of his academic abilities, but lacked the voice and resources to fight against oppressive school policies-particularly tracking.

For Mr. G, Hip Hop provided the space, outside of school, where he excelled and expressed himself without judgment and fear of failure. He recalled writing lyrics, making beats and practicing break dancing as often as he could find time. He stated,

> I was writing rhymes and dancing even then. I would beg my mother to go to the mall because after I saw the movie Beat Street, I thought that's where break-dancers would be and I wanted to battle people. Then I would go to the library and read all day so I could have information to use in my rhymes.

In the middle of our conversation, Mr. G began to recite the following lyrics to Hip Hop artist, MOS Def's song, *LOVE*.

> It was love for the thing that made me wanna stay out. It was love for the thing that made me stay in the house. Spending time, writing rhyms trying to find words that describe the vibe that's inside my space, when you close yo' eyes and screw yo face.

The "thing" that both Mr. G and MOS Def described was Hip Hop. Mr. G suggested that Hip Hop was his tutor, mentor and friend, during that time in his life when he felt most misunderstood and rejected. It provided a space where his authentic talents, beliefs, and ideals could be represented, and to his delight, challenged.

In an interesting twist of fate, Mr. G reflected on another pivotal movement at school when things began to shift for him, again. He explained that in January of that academic year, his teacher suffered a severe hip injury and went on medical leave indefinitely. Mrs. Pratt, his new teacher, articulated her pedagogical framework as one that valued and respected student voice and pushed students beyond their expectations. Therefore, she gave the class an open platform to voice their perspectives about what they were learning and how it was being taught. She also encouraged students to share their educational stories and to critically examine and make meaning of their schooling experiences. Reflecting on being Mrs. Pratt's student, Mr. G stated,

> After our teacher was injured, we got a substitute and this lady was like, "I'm not teaching y'all like you are remedial. I'm teaching you like I teach every other class." I was able to just exhale because she actually taught us. I just remembered being in there like, so if this didn't happen, even if I did good in the 6th grade and got straight A's in the remedial class, they would put me in the 7th grade special education class and I would just keep going on that track.

By the end of the academic year, Mr. G, his mother, and Mrs. Pratt urged school administrators to reevaluate his placement in remedial classes. However, instead of considering his previous years test scores, grades, and accounts from his mother and teacher about academic his abilities, the school administrators required that he attend summer school to catch up and continue remediation until them deemed him prepared to reenter general education classes. By the second semester of his seventh grade year, Mr. G was admitted to general education classes, but was and remains socially, emotionally, and academically traumatized by that experience.

Though Mrs. Pratt gave him a platform, at school, to share his perspectives and recover academically, Mr. G situated Hip Hop as his most significant teacher, as it helped him develop and nurture his critical thinking skills and orientations towards social activism, as well as gave him a platform to express his perspectives, uninhibited. For him, "the flood gates started to open" as artists like Slick Rick, Public Enemy and NAS emerged within the culture. He described NAS as one of the first Hip Hop artists to create rap lyrics that sounded like traditional poetry. NAS appealed to Mr. G because of his ability to graphically express the experiences of people who live in poverty in both authentic and poetic ways, while at the same time selling millions of records.

The opened flood gates represents his deepened connection to Hip Hop as a cultural space where he could address personal and community issues, sharpen his talents and make meaningful connections with artists from a larger creative community. He stated,

> Hip Hop is a culture that allowed me to resolve the conflicts within myself and then resolve the conflicts outside of myself. I had to resolve the issues that were going on in my world and then outside of that little circle. Then when I saw that congruence with people with different nationalities, from other countries and different places around the planet, knew I was on to something.

These Hip Hop experiences helped Mr. G develop positive thinking about what it means to be a Black male, an artist and a teacher. They exemplified characteristics of Black manhood that mirrored his father and grandfather, whom he described as strong, caring, giving, expressive, intelligent and community oriented. What he found in Hip Hop was a positive representation of himself, reflected in the artists he so deeply respected and a venue to heal from the wounds inflicted by insensitive and rigid teachers and school administrators.

Mr. G suffered social, emotional and academic trauma due to these early school experiences. Even more heartbreaking for him, however, was the realization that without his parents' intervention and the efforts of one caring teacher, he would have remained a remedial student and been forced to carry that label through high school. He reflected,

> I see how you can fall through the cracks in the school system. I was only in 6th grade and I realize that I could just really get lost in this system. I came from New York where I was a straight A student, but when I came to DC, I didn't do too good. I was a bright kid. I was just bored and angry.

He says that Hip Hop kept him out of trouble because he spent most of his free time working on art, interpreting lyrics, or stretching—all in preparation for his next free style battle or break dancing competition. While practicing, he visualized himself being the best at a particular way of rhyming or dancing. He stated, "I was being the best me that I could be." Therefore, these preparation processes kept him busy and reestablished the confidence he lost as a result of his experiences in school. In turn, his parents were pleased that he was at least home and safe from the violence in the streets of Washington, DC. He reflected,

> Hip Hop was my individuality and my little bit of space. At the same time I was like wow, my mom don't really get it but is alright with me stayin in the house because I'm practicing, I'm writing, im messing with beats, I'm sittin home downstairs on the living room floor working for hours at a time.

Mr. G articulated in our conversations that the passion with which he engaged in Hip Hop culture and digital arts is fueled by his tenuous middle school experiences. Hip Hop gave him a sense of peace in knowing that he in fact, could learn and perform at high levels in many areas of his life. Hip Hop also gave him a feeling of unity and belonging within a culture that validated his experience and gave helped him to heal. He stated,

> Even at a time when a lot of music talked about a lot of sad stuff and there were a lot of sad things going on in the neighborhood, we also had the power and opportunity to make things right and better and it may not be over night,

but now we can do the same things in our songs and how we teach and how we relate to one another.

Throughout our interviews, he talked about how lucky he was to have a teacher, Mrs. Pratt, who, saw past reputation as a deviant student, and taught using a pedagogical framework that centered students' knowledge and experiences and elevated student voice. He felt that if not for her, he would have been forced to follow the prescribed remedial academic tract, which, as he asserted, would have caused him to eventually drop out of school. This realization was particularly troubling as it speaks to the experiences of countless Black boys who are unnecessarily placed in low tracked classes or in special education. He asserted that these factors contributed to the endangerment of Black boys in U.S. schools and, as such, fuels his efforts to make deep connections with his Black male students and to critically engage with Hop Hip in ways that uplift students' voice and develops their analytical and critical thinking skills.

HIP HOP AS A HEALER

I often observed, while reflecting his educational history, signs of tension (wrinkled brows and deep in and exhales) in Mr. G's face and body language. He was particularly troubled by the school's failure to properly test students and their reliance on subjective tracking measures like, in-school behavior and grades, as a rational to suspend, reject, and deny them of the right to receive a high quality education. Though fortunate to a have advocates that represented his voice, Mr. G developed low self-esteem and feelings of purpose, because of school.

As a youth, Hip Hop helped to harness his talents, rebuild his self-confidence and re-establish his self-esteem. During that turbulent time in his life, Hip Hop music and cultural expressions reflected, in large part, expressed resistance against and critique of the sociopolitical issues facing Black people in the United States. These early experiences had significant implications for shaping his beliefs about and commitments to ensuring the social, academic, and personal well being of his Black male students.

He asserted,

> You are serving true Hip Hop, you are serving the community because you come from the community. You are exposing the things that are happening. You are exposing the things that are going on in your life, and you are conveying it to other people [students] to give them strength, to give them hope, to give them some things to wish to for, or a way to get out of it.

How he understood the foundational ideals and goals of Hip Hop culture in relation to his commitment to mold and nurture Black male youth, as congruent with and intimately connected to his intrinsic motivations to teach. His troubled schooling experiences and relationship with Hip Hop, serve as a framework through which he engaged with his own "troubled" students. He believes that engagement with Hip Hop provides deeper insight into students' lives, and likewise, strengthens the teacher-student relationship. Mr. G described his teaching style as a "whole new approach" that foregrounds personal relationships to gain students' trust, love and respect. He recognized that many Black male students have difficulty trusting teachers and school administrators, whom they perceive as inclined to use exclusionary discipline measures (detention, in-and out-of-school suspension, expulsion) to manage undesirable behavior. Giving his own educational narrative, Mr. G enjoys and fosters symbiotic relationships with, particularly, Black male student, who largely relate to his story. He stated,

> What I do as a teacher is that I try my best to relate to the students as a brother, a father, and a mentor. I am a caring adult that is 100% invested in my students and their futures. And I believe that when a student feels that you love them unconditionally, then they'll buy into anything that you introduce.

Mr. G also described his teaching style as "learning through fun." "I gotta keep my energy high," he said, "because nobody should be more energized than me, you know." He believed that if he failed to remain up beat and positive, then students would grow tired of his class and become distracted. He stated further, "you'll feel a lot of energy, you'll see a lot of joking and you'll also see a lot of work going on." In his digital arts courses, students are allowed to listen to music and to work collaboratively on class projects. They laugh, crack jokes, and even engage in spontaneous battles where students challenge one another's creative abilities. At the same, they are highly productive, producing professional digital art portfolios, which they need for college and careers in digital arts and media.

Mr. G identified poorly informed and uncaring teachers as mitigating factors that contributed to much of his school failure. His fifth and sixth grade teachers, in particular, failed to make meaningful connections with him, exhibited low self-efficacy in relation to meeting his specific academic and social needs, and lacked the cultural capital to help him successfully navigate school. He, in turn, relates to and teaches students within the context of their lived realities. Reflecting on how that he exhibited care by telling "the truth" to a particular Black male student who too struggled both academically and socially in school, Mr. G stated,

> You need to understand that they [teachers, school, and school systems] have set themselves up to insure your failure, either by ganging up on you or not

being qualified to work with you. So if you want to show off to get your teacher back, you can't do that with a C or D. Get an A in the class first and then get kicked out if you want.

In explaining his motivation to teach students how to survive and succeed in school and the ways that he understands and relates to both Hip Hop and his Black male students, he made personal connections with the original tenets of Hip Hop culture (peace, love, unity, and having fun). He articulated, what he considers, an inherent connection between the perceptions of Black males and Hip Hop culture. More specifically, he understood the negative representations in Hip Hop and Black male students' experiences in school, as reflecting the dire socioeconomic conditions facing underserved populations, rather than mere expressions of antisocial or bad behavior. These tenets ground his teaching orientations and serve as a framework for how he engages Hip Hop and promotes the academic and social well-being of Black male students.

Data from this study suggests that a vigorous analysis of the educational and cultural experiences of Black male teachers can shape our thinking about who can and should teach and heighten our awareness of the influences of prior schooling experiences on the motivations and pedagogical beliefs of this population of educators. Mr. G's experiences as a K–12 student and his relationship with Hip Hop culture, grounds his commitment to shield students from the educational, racial, social, and political injustices that have long been historically perpetuated against Black children in public schools (Kitwana, 2002; KRS-One, 2003).

Given Mr. G's narrative, it is not unreasonable to believe that Black males, particularly those who have experienced troubles in school and are deeply connected to Hip Hop, may be particularly committed and well suited to embody and put into practice the types of pedagogical orientations that foster success among Black male students. This presents wonderful opportunities for school systems, colleges of education, and alternative certification programs to reconnect with Black men who, like countless Black male students, have rejected school.

REFERENCES

Brown, J. (1999). Factors that influence African American male teachers' educational and career aspirations: Implications for school districts recruitment and retention efforts. *Journal of Negro Education, 68*(3), 280–292.

Brown, T. (2007). Lost and turned out. *Urban Education, 42*(5), 432–455.

Bynoe, Y. (2004). *Stand & deliver*. Brooklyn: Soft Skull Press.

Dance, L. J. (2002). *Tough fronts: The impact of street culture on schooling*. New York: RoutledgeFalmer.

Davis, J. E. (2006). Research at the margins: Dropping out of high school and mobility among African American males. *International Journal of Qualitative Studies in Education, 19*(3), 289–304.

Davis, J. E. (2003). Early schooling and the achievement of African American males. *Urban Education, 38*, 515–537.

Ferguson, A. (2001). *Bad boy: Public schools in the making of Black masculinity.* Ann Arbor: The University of Michigan Press

Freire, P. (2007). *Pedagogy of the oppressed.* New York, NY: The Continuumm International Publishing Group.

Hanley, M. S. (2007). Old school crossings: Hip hop in teacher education and beyond. *New Directions for Adult & Continuing Education, (115),* 35–44.

KRS-One. (2003). *Ruminations.* New York: Welcome Rain Publications.

Lynn, M. (1999). Raising the critical consciousness of African-American students in baldwin hills: A portrait of an exemplary African American male teacher. *Journal of negro education, 68*(1), 42–53.

Lynn, M. (2002). Critical race theory and the perspective of Black men teachers in the Los Angeles public schools. *Equity & Excellence in Education, 35*(2), 119–130.

Morrell, E. (2002). Towards a critical pedagogy of popular culture: Literacy development among urban youth. *Journal of Adolescence & Adults, 46*(1), 72–76.

Morrell, E., & Duncan-Andrade, J. (2002). Promoting academic literacy with urban youth through engaging hip-hop culture. *The English Journal, 90*(6), 88–92.

National Center for Education Statistics. (2005–2006). from http://nces.ed.gov/

Noguera, P. (1996). Responding to the crisis confronting California's Black male youth: Providing support without further marginalization. *Journal of Negro Education, 65*(2), 219–236.

Noguera, P. (2003a). *City schools and the American dream: Reclaiming the promise of public education.* New York, NY: Teachers College Press.

Noguera, P. (2003b). The trouble with Black boys: The role and influence of environmental and cultural factors on the academic performance of African American males. *Urban Education, 38*(4), 431–459.

Rose, T. (1994). *Rap music and black culture in contemporary America.* Middletown, CT: Wesleyan University Press.

CHAPTER 11

THE LEGACY LIVES, "I LEAVE YOU A THIRST FOR EDUCATION"— DR. BETHUNE'S VISION IN ACTION

A Study of the Impact of an HBCU on Teachers and Educational Leaders

Tehia Starker-Glass
University of North Carolina

Helena Mariella-Walrond
Bethune-Cookman University

Allyson Leggett Watson
Northeastern State University

Lakia M. Scott
University of North Carolina

Teacher Education and Black Communities, pages 225–243
Copyright © 2014 by Information Age Publishing
All rights of reproduction in any form reserved.

As both the necessity of Historically Black College and Universities (HBCUs) and the quality of Teacher Education programs nationwide continue to be questioned, we contend that a careful analysis of teacher education programs at HBCUs not only will add nuance to the discussion, but more importantly reaffirm the importance of teacher education programs and the relevance of HBCUs. This chapter examines the experiences of Bethune-Cookman University graduates who are K–16 educators and the impact their preparation has had on current career practices. Examination of the factors that contributed and continue to contribute to their success are included. We also highlight their voice through narrative description and provide a sense of both a historical and present relevance of the institution and responsibility to the preparation of twenty-first century teachers of color.

INTRODUCTION

In a time when the quality of teacher education programs and the very relevance of Historically Black Colleges and Universities (HBCUs) are questioned, a chapter focusing on the positive contributions of teacher education program at HBCUs is particularly timely because it, not only highlights the contributions of teacher education programs and HBCUs, but gives nuance to the discussion of preparing Black students to become Black teachers. In the article "Teachers and Teaching for the New Millennium: The Role of HBCUs" (Irvine & Fenwick, 2011), the authors point out that HBCUs can play a significant role in recruiting, retaining, and developing of teachers who serve in high-needs schools and that HBCUs are uniquely positioned, not only to diversify the nation's teaching force, but to develop teachers who dispel myths, serve as role models, and focus on the whole child.

Arne Duncan, Secretary of Education, states "HBCUs have produced roughly half of all African American professionals and public school teachers" (HBCUs and Higher Education: Beyond the Iron Triangle: Remarks of Arne Duncan to 2009 National Historically Black Colleges and Universities Conference, 2009). Secretary Duncan continues, "Every day, African-American Teachers are doing absolutely invaluable work in helping to close the insidious achievement gap" (2009). This achievement and opportunity "gap" has been enforced via some of the same mechanisms that attempted to prohibit Blacks from getting education in history: under resourced schools, structured inequities, deficit oriented thinking, and so on. Despite setbacks, Black teachers and students have met such obstacles with hard work and perseverance. Now is the time to focus on Black teachers by acknowledging the places where the development Black teachers continue to thrive and multiply—the HBCU—and specifically Bethune-Cookman University, which is the emphasis of this study. Using the Last Will and Testament written by Dr. Bethune (1955), we will share the history of HBCU's and Bethune-Cookman University, investigate teacher education, and examine how the university has impacted teacher education alumni. Dr. Bethune Last Will and Testament is an essay that includes her final wishes and responsibilities for the next generation. She left us with nine maxims that prompt us towards progress (Smith, 1996). The nine legacies Dr. Bethune left us with were: love, hope, the challenge of developing confidence in one another, a thirst for education, respect for the uses of power, faith, racial dignity, a desire to live harmoniously with fellow men, and a responsibility to young people. Dr. Bethune's nine charges to us are her legacy for all to continue. We will integrate each of the principles throughout this chapter to reinforce the connection of what she instilled in HBCU alum, teacher educators, and teachers.

This chapter is personal to us, as the first and third authors are alumni of Bethune-Cookman, the second author was our academic advisor at Bethune-Cookman, and the fourth author is an alum of an HBCU. We approach this article with direct experiences from Bethune-Cookman, and seek to understand how others experienced Bethune-Cookman and the impact it had on their academic trajectory of becoming successful teachers in a diverse society.

Literature Review

I leave you the challenge of developing confidence in one another...—The History of Educating Blacks and the establishment of HBCUs.

The historical aims of education for Blacks have been to reproduce a working class society that is comparable to second-class citizenry. Even though the Reconstruction Period (1865–1877) allowed for some civil liberties, ex-slaves still had to fight for the right of access to public schooling. Anderson (1988) provides a detailed account of this narrative through reviewing Blacks' pursuits to become literate through native schools and Sabbath schools in the South. He also counters the arguments surrounding Blacks' rising interest in education after the Civil War—he contends that even before slavery was abolished, Blacks had a strong desirability to read and write; they saw education as a key to liberation, freedom, and opportunity. Woodson (1919) also elaborates that when continental Africans arrived to the states as a result of the Transatlantic Slave Trade, they were coming from highly educated societies and valued learning.

The tradition of learning is also highly visible from the language that emerged furring the time of the Emancipation Proclamation. Anderson (1988) tells of how ex-slaves were the first to "crusade for state systems of common schools" for Black children after the Civil War. It was not until the 1900–1935 period that public elementary schools became available to Black children in the South; long after common schools were developed for other American school children in the 1830s through the 1860s (Anderson, 1988). He elaborates that demand for educational opportunity for Black children however was limited in that most public school funds (money collected through taxes) were diverted to schools for white children. The Freedmen's Bureau in particular, along with Northern philanthropists, helped to establish formal schooling and education for Black children in the area (Anderson, 1988; Jackson, 2001; Lovett, 2011; Morgan, 1995). However, there existed a dichotomy of perspectives between the Whites of the North and the South. Whereas Northern businessmen saw opportunities for Blacks to be upwardly mobile, yet remaining in their social class lanes, Southerners expressed discontent with aims to educate Blacks. They saw the movement for universal education as a ploy for the freed slaves to rise against menial labor-intensive jobs, which would in turn be left for the poor White class. Still, Northern philanthropy pursuits extended to the formation of schooling in higher education for Blacks. In retrospect, universal education benefitted the poor White class more than Blacks (Anderson, 1988; Lovett, 2011).

One of the most discussed educational models in higher education for Blacks in the South was that of the Hampton-Tuskegee model. In the Hampton model of industrial education, Samuel Armstrong's ideas were positioned as the basis for conditioning Blacks to accept their roles in society as second-class citizens—even with higher education credentials. According to Anderson (1988), "Armstrong developed a pedagogy and ideology designed to avoid such confrontations and to maintain within the South a social consensus that did not challenge traditional inequalities of wealth and power" (p. 33). In this model, Blacks were admitted into school only to still till the fields and learn trades that would advance sharecropping and domesticated roles in a planter regime. Only after strenuous hours of manual labor were students provided opportunities to develop their intellect. However, the curriculum was that of rudimentary or secondary education and begged to challenge the Black intellect (Spivey, 1978). Students would become graduates to teach and spread the teachings of their education to other community members in order to serve as exemplar models of social class reproduction (Anderson, 1988; LeMelle & LeMelle, 1969; Spivey, 1978).

"I leave you faith . . . "—the development of HBCUs

Also during this time, northern philanthropy and Black religious organizations helped to open more than twenty-four private Black colleges in addition to the small Black institutions that had been established for high school and college-level instruction in Pennsylvania (Jackson, 2001). Wiggan's *Education for the New Frontier* (2012) discusses the historical underpinnings of Black institutions; specifically, Atlanta University's emergence as becoming a vehicle for Black education in Georgia. Two organizations in particular were discussed in terms of beginning educational institutions for Blacks; the American Missionary Association (AMA) and the African Methodist Episcopal Church (AME). The Freedman's Aid Society was also established by the AMA and various religious institutions in the North. It aimed to set up and teach schools in the South for Blacks and helped to found more than 500 schools and colleges after the Civil War (LeMelle & LeMelle, 1969). This particular organization significantly contributed to opportunities of primary, secondary, and postsecondary schooling for Blacks. Wiggan (2012) also briefly discusses the emergence of land-grant entities such as Alabama and Florida A&M Universities that were developed as a result of the Second Morrill Act of 1890, which provided Black students training related to specific to agricultural and mechanical fields.

By 1880, Jackson (2001) notes that nationally, 30% of the Black population was literate, but more than 40 higher education institutions (both private and public) were spread across the nation for African Americans. These Historically Black College or University (HBCU) systems are categorized as: public two- and four-year colleges/universities, private four-year college/universities, and land-grant institutions. The ways in which these institutions are categorized directly applicable to their funding sources; that is, many private institutions began and continue through philanthropic efforts, whereas others are state funded by way of land grants or other resources. Between 1895 and 1915, leaders from various Black institutions such as Howard University, Hampton, Wilberforce, and Tuskegee among others, attempted to form an agenda for the sake of racial uplift and harmony between liberal arts and industrial institutions.

Following, the U.S. Supreme Court case, *Plessy v. Ferguson* (1896), mandates that states provide separate but equal educational accommodations for African Americans. At this time, HBCUs provided African Americans with primary and secondary education, even though there were considered institutes or universities. Most HBCUs evolved to teaching post-secondary courses and through the years, accreditation and varied career-based programs ensued. By 1900, approximately 2,600 African Americans had postsecondary credentials and 55% of the population was considered literature and by 1927, there were 77 Black colleges and universities and over 14,000 students were enrolled (Jackson, 2001; LeMelle & LeMelle, 1969).

Soon after, the Civil Rights Act of 1964 outlawed discrimination against race, color, religion, and gender, and additionally ended unequal voter registration requirements and racial segregation in schools and the workplace.

The main goals of historically Black institutions were to become a resource for building human, social, and economic capital in the Black community; as the two most popular professions of graduates were teachers and clergymen. In 1965, affirmative action policies and practices were established that allowed for equal access to opportunities, in particular, admission policies to admit minorities into selective collegiate institutions. By 1969, the National Association for Equal Opportunity in Higher Education (AFEO) is founded and serves as a policy advocate for the 118 established historically and predominately Black colleges and universities (Jackson, 2001).

I leave you a desire to live harmoniously with your fellow man . . .—the changing face of the HBCU.

By the 1970s, college integration becomes more preeminent and as a result, 34% of Black students in college attend HBCUs, but nearly a decade later in 1980, the number decreases to 25% (Jackson, 2001). Former President Jimmy Carter declares a federal initiative to help provide funding to HBCUs; however, a year later, under the Reagan Administration, cutbacks to federal funds awarded to education put HBCUs in a state of financial peril. And in 1994, the percentage of Black students enrolled at HBCUs drops to 15%. Today, there are total of 105 historically Black institutions across the nation since 1837 where Cheyney University located in Pennsylvania was recognized as being one of the first colleges to provide high-school and college-level instruction to African Americans and Lincoln University (also located in Pennsylvania) was known to be the first institution for African American students to receive college-level instruction in 1854 (Jackson, 2001; National Center for Education Statistics (NCES). NCES (2012) reported that there are over 330,000 students enrolled in HBCUs; however, only 78% account for the African American student population. Added, the total number of African Americans enrolled in U.S. accredited institutions is approximately 3 million, but only 9% of those students are enrolled in HBCUs. However, as successful as HBCUs have become in their attempts to provide such opportunities, landmark legislation which advocated for racial integration in all schools and universities, have had adverse effects on Black student enrollment at HBCUs.

Despite the decline, HBCUs serve as the largest producers of Black students with higher education and advanced degrees (NCES, 2012). According to the UNCF, although HBCUs are only 3% of higher education institutions nationwide, HBCUs graduate 20% of African Americans who earn undergraduate degrees and 14% of graduate degrees. HBCUs graduate over 50% of African American public school teachers, and 50% of African Americans who graduate from HBCUs go on to graduate or professional schools (UNCF, 2013). Still, it is important to recognize the cultural importance that a HBCU holds for its African American constituents.

HBCUs have mission statements that created the idea of developing Black students academically, socially, professionally, emotionally, and politically. HBCUs do more than just academically educate students. They prepare students for the world in which they will live, and help them effectively navigate that world in way that will assist in success (Harris, 2012). "The HBCU experience offered Black students the opportunity to realize their potential in ways that affirmed their identity and challenged them to use their education to demand justice for both themselves and their community" (Albritton, 2012, p. 314). This is what we want for all students within and around communities across the nations. Unfortunately, some Black students don't get to see their potential until they get out of their K–12 classroom, and into an HBCU.

Teacher Education: A Historical and Contemporary Perspective

"I leave you a thirst for education . . . "—the development of teacher education

In the nineteenth century, the rise of public schools forged a new direction for teacher education programs in the United States. The call for primary and secondary teachers became evermore important because schooling served as a mechanism in socializing youth into participation of a colonized society. Targeted to attract and provide education in denser populations, former agrarian families and their students would soon be a part of the transition to vocational jobs and the growing impacts of industrialization (Gutek, 1995; Spring, 1997). In an effort to create basic curriculum standards for classrooms and through the formation of normal schools, teacher education programs began as early as the 1830s and with such emergence, marginalization of schools, colleges, and departments of education quickly ensued (Fraser, 2007; Gutek, 1995). History also evidences that with such a demand in the profession, the field became feminized and eventually denigrated early on; women taught in the primary grade levels and men held administrative positions or taught at the secondary level (Gutek, 1995; Milam, 2010; Spring, 1997). And with the popularity of teacher education programs, there became an increased emphasis on standards, certifications, and accreditations; one may argue that this was another imposed stumbling block to restrict African American teachers from teaching their own. However, opponents would argue that since there had not been many formalized measures to adequately assess if high school and normal school graduates would do well in the classroom, such standardization was necessary.

Gutek (1995) shares that normal schools usually took two years to complete and provided students with a base knowledge of course content in reading, arithmetic, and science, as well as instructed students on ways to lecture and conduct classroom activities. However, Milam (2010) mentions that there were limitations to this model; mainly the time it took to meet such requirements often proved to be costly. As a result, teacher institutes quickly emerged and its program was much shorter in time to complete while still focusing on the same components deemed necessary in the teacher education and preparation model. Growing interests also forged the transition of normal schools into becoming teachers' colleges, which further marginalized the field in terms of who would be considered an educator. As one could assert, these new standards and forms of stratification in teacher education trickled down to schools and districts and further perpetuated biased perspectives on what students could and should learn in the classroom (Gutek, 1995).

These perspectives continue to pervade current day practices; curriculum and instruction techniques are prescribed on the basis of cultural assimilation and mainstream uniformity as opposed to the recognition of diversity and difference that aims at providing access and opportunity for all. Currently, Black teachers make up 8% of the nationwide teaching population (NCES, 2010), although K–12 students of color are on a steady increase across the country. Teachers of color bring a cultural perspective to the classroom that other teachers may not be able to provide from a first-hand experience (Brooks, West-Olatunji, Blackmon, Froelich, et al., 2012). Watson & Shealey (2011) asserted:

> Prior to the Brown v. Board of Education decision which significantly changed the schooling experiences of Black students in this country, Black teachers represented the epitome of knowledge and wisdom in Black communities (Foster, 1991). However, the contributions of Black teachers and segregated Black schools have remained largely ignored by mainstream research literature (Walker, 2005). The mission of Black schools, which were the center of the Black community, was to instruct and serve (Irvine, 1989). This sentiment is alive and well and continues to thrive at Historically Black colleges and universities where the student population is predominately Black and many of whom represent first-generation college students (Mccray, Sindelar, Kilgore, & Neal, 2002). This commitment to service was the foundation for the work of Black teachers prior to and after desegregation. Siddle Walker (2005) chronicled this work and the quest for equality by Black teacher associations. (p. 268)

Teacher Education programs within HBCUs are invaluable, as they are on the forefront of two endeavors, they are the top producer of Black teachers nationwide, and the experience of the Black student and Black teacher are the reality on and near HBCUs. Next, we focus on Bethune-Cookman and their teacher education program.

"I leave you love..."—the History of Bethune-Cookman

In 1904 Mary McLeod Bethune founded the Daytona Educational and Industrial Training School for Negro Girls with $1.50, faith in God, and five little girls. Dr. Bethune's unwavering determination and entrepreneurial spirit stretched every limit and crossed every boundary as she pursued her dream. The Florida State Department of Education approved a 4-year degree program in 1941 in liberal arts and education. Today, Dr. Bethune's dream is a vibrant university located on what was, at the founding of the school, the city's trash dump. Bethune-Cookman has an enrollment of over 3,400 students and is a private, historically Black, United Methodist Church-related university. The B-CU mission is to serve in the Christian tradition the diverse educational, social, and cultural needs of its students. Thus, Bethune-Cookman University rests on a long history of preparing quality educators.

The Teacher Education Program (TEP) at Bethune-Cookman is state approved and NCATE accredited and prepares teacher in Business Education, Elementary Education, English, Education, Exceptional Student Education, Music Education, Physical Education, and Social Science Education. The program continually receives praise by public schools for the way it prepares students to work with all students. In addition, teacher candidates are praised for their professionalism and their ability to successfully manage their classrooms. The TEP is committed to meeting the challenges of providing a diverse teaching force that better reflects the diversity in today's schools and its responsibility to prepare quality teachers who implement strategies and accountability methods that meet the needs of all students in the classroom. The legacy of faith, scholarship, and service continue to guide the work of faculty, staff, and students in the TEP.

The mission of the TEP at Bethune-Cookman University is designed to support and carry out the mission of the University to serve in the Christian tradition, the educational, social, and cultural needs of its students and to develop in the students the desire and capacity for continuous intellectual and professional growth, leadership, and service to others. The implementation of this mission has led to the TEP commitment to providing a student-centered environment where teacher candidates experience the freedom to grow, reflect and become effective professional educators. Reflected in this mission is the belief that effective educators will be competent, caring, and committed to provide quality instruction to all learners. In addition, the School of Education at Bethune-Cookman University visualizes the TEP becoming exceptional in the preparation of effective educators who understand the importance of possessing Essential Knowledge, using Reflective Practice and Assessment and position themselves as Professionals committed to meeting the challenges of serving all learners in a world of rapid change and increasing diversity.

Since 1943, Bethune-Cookman University has graduated more than 13,200 students. Alumni are employed in the fields of education, medicine, business, politics, government, science, religion, athletics, and environmental sciences and continue to live the university's motto "Enter to Learn... Depart to Serve." As with other HBCU's, students and graduates have been "prepared students to use the implicit and explicit roles of teachers of color to prepare the next generation of students to be successful citizens" (Brooks, West-Olatunji, Blackmon, Froelich, et al., 2012). Dr. Mary McLeod Bethune's Last Will and Testament speaks of the value of education and creating racial harmony—both continue to guide the School of Education in its preparation of teachers who are able to teach all students well.

"I leave you respect for the uses of power . . . "

This research seeks to define an in depth account of from alumni in teacher education. The authors assert that participants find preparation from BCU to be a key component of career success in teaching and administration and professional contributions. The data from this research is reported in two phases; however, the two overarching questions that guide the research are as follows:

Research Questions:

1. How did your academic experience at BCU impact your preparation for current teacher practice?
2. What is the historical and present relevance of BCU in the preparation of 21st century teachers of color?

METHODS

Study Criteria

The rationale and purpose of this study was driven by the esteem and regard the authors have of a HBCUs, and Bethune-Cookman University in particular. Two of the authors from this study are alumni of Bethune-Cookman's School of Education. The other author is an executive administrator at Bethune-Cookman, and the last author is alum of an HBCU. This study was specific to graduates from Bethune Cookman University (BCU) formerly

Bethune Cookman College Teacher Education program. The purpose of this study provided intentionality regarding the methods of selecting subjects. Invitations for participation in the research were sent through various methods. The authors utilized social media as the primary method of gaining interest from potential participants prior to beginning the study. Written invitations and research previews were highlighted using Twitter, Facebook, LinkedIn and Google Chat. Each of the authors selected alumni friends connected in their respective social media pool. The authors posted invitations to participate on Bethune Cookman Alumni organization pages. The authors purposefully have reached out to alumni from the most recent graduating class, December 2012 and as far back as 1976 graduates. Additionally, the authors convey personal reflections using qualitative research through narrative discussion. The authors' voice describes their own triumphs and challenges as BCU alumni currently working in higher education and BCU administration.

Participants

The authors concerted a targeted effort to reach the maximum number of graduates from the BCU alumni program. The initial sample for the survey research invitations yielded 40 responses with individuals interested in participating. The authors initially set up a spreadsheet to organize participant email, graduating class and specific education major. Additional information collected was the social media method used to gain the response. We send personal messages and one round of reminders before the survey closed. The actual sample for the survey data was small with only 11 respondents. The authors are using this initial low response to identify ways to gather more participants for phase 2 of the study. While we believe it is important to clearly identify the ways we acquired the initial sample in our reporting, for this study we will discuss the findings from the qualitative portion. The quantitative sample ($n = 11$) and data analysis will be reported in the second phase of this study. The authors sent over 55 invitations with the survey link. There was a 4.2% response rate to the survey data. A total ($n = 11$) of the quantitative sent survey links were returned complete.

The respondents needed to match two specific criteria for this study. First, each participant must have graduated from Bethune-Cookman College/University. Secondly, each participant must also have completed the teacher education program through the School/Division of Education. Finally, we used the "snowball" (Creswell, 2005) method to gain more participation in the study and asked that current participants pass along the survey link. While each of these criteria are specific and were outlined in the invitation, the participant data is self-reported and reflected from the individual perception and shared truth.

Survey Instrument

The authors wrote 61 survey questions to answer the research intent. The survey categories were organized into nine sections. The first eight sections consisting of 56 of the 61 survey questions were written using Likert-scale. These sections included questions with (1) indicating Strongly Disagree to (5) indicating Strongly Agree. The final section will assist the authors in qualitative data collection and included open-ended questions. We have asked each survey participant to provide his or her name and contact information to continue this study in a second phase. The Likert-scale survey sections included: 1–2, demographic information and alumni graduating class; 3, teaching experience and current career placement; 4, characteristics of BCU faculty; 5, preparation after graduation; 6, personal career experiences; 7, teaching experiences and impact; and finally, 8, impact and referral for future BCU prospective students. The final questions in section 9 allowed for open ended responses and highlighted participant perspectives on characteristics of being a successful teacher, perceptions about HBCU's and career preparation and relevance of HBCU's in the coming century.

Qualitative Inquiry

The authors identified 11 participants' reflections and their own personal voice to include in the narrative portion of the qualitative research. Six questions guided the participants to think openly about their experiences at BCU in the teacher education program and how BCU shaped their current success and career. Using narrative discussion and thematic analysis (Braun & Clarke, 2006) the authors were able to formulate themes based on passages reported by the participants. Thematic analysis follows a structure of how to analyze qualitative data, and that procedure was followed in this study. Thematic analysis was used because of its structured technique of analysis, which supports triangulation of all authors analyzing the qualitative data. This level of inquiry allows for summary and reporting from the initial data set, " a written passage in a qualitative study in which authors to summarize, in detail findings from their data analysis" (Creswell, 2005 p. 249). The participants spoke clearly about the meaning of their education from BCU, the historical relevance of BCU and the need for HBCU's in the twenty-first Century. It was important that during the research we validated the findings and related the emerging themes to the initial data analysis. Because we worked with institutional administrators to help send out the research invitation, we relied on "authenticity and trustworthiness" (Lincoln & Guba, 1985) in the qualitative reports. We also corroborated the qualitative data in comparison with the quantitative Likert scale questions. If a respondent answered "strongly agree" to the level of preparation they received at BCU, we looked for a similar and more intricate response to exist in the narrative description. Additionally, the authors included self-reported narrative analysis and those reflections are present in the themes and findings.

Data Collection

The intent of the research is to identify specific characteristics, qualities and professional perceptions of BCU teacher education alumni. To obtain this information with accuracy the authors worked within the institution to identify a list serve of alumni across the country. In addition to a prescreening survey invitation protocol, the authors engaged alumni representatives from some of the most active alumni regions. Employing the survey method to answer the questions relating to demographics, personal impact, effectiveness of educational preparation and likelihood for recommending the institution was the most rational to fit the purpose of the study and answer the research questions. The authors incorporated the cross-sectional survey approach to gather specific information with this population at a single point in time (Creswell, 2005). The survey was lengthy in written form but easy to navigate and complete. Additionally, the authors utilized the survey data to collect qualitative data. The qualitative results will be reported in this work and the quantitative data will be reported in phase 2 of the study. The authors indicated in the participant consent that completion would take no more than 20 minutes. The authors with the help of a doctoral candidate and graduate assistant developed the web-based survey through Google Docs. In generating the live survey through Google Docs, the authors could keep an updated spreadsheet of the most current data. The authors' sent each potential participant the live hyperlink with the informed consent portion displayed in the first window. Respondents were sent an electronic invitation to participate via email, Twitter, Facebook and LinkedIn. The survey remained open and live for three full weeks and reminders were sent out in open social media posts. The results were compiled and analyzed immediately after the survey census date.

FINDINGS

Participants

Table 11.1 examines the demographics of the participants for this study representing 10 years of alumni.

TABLE 11.1 Participant Demographics

Gender	Male 45%	Female 55%
Racial/Ethnic Identity	Black 91%	White 9%
First Generation College Student?	Yes 27%	No 73%
Highest Degree Earned to Date	Bachelors 9% Masters 45%	Specialist 36% Doctorate 9%
Years Teaching	8–20 years	Mean = 13.27 years
Teaching Awards?	5 teachers have won either teacher of the month, or teacher of the year	

Qualitative Themes

As we analyze the data, we again are focusing the qualitative data on the two research questions. Each question will be answered via thematic analysis.

How did your academic experience at BCU impact your preparation for current teacher practice?

"I leave you love . . . "—love from faculty

Participants collectively discussed how well they were prepared for the "real world." Participants regularly discussed how the content they were taught in their program is still currently relevant. Participants also felt they were prepared to teach in any environment. "I was given the opportunity to intern in a school that prepared me to deal with children with varying ethnicities and socio economic standings." Along with teaching in multiple environments, participants consistently discussed the high expectations that were expressed by Bethune-Cookman faculty. Faculty consistently told students they were capable of being successful, and every endeavor that students encountered, success was the standard. Whether it was coursework, field experiences, extra-curricular activities, or Bethune-Cookman events, "You KNEW the faculty expect nothing but the best and would to do anything to make sure you achieved it." Participants share that faculty did whatever it took to set the bar for high expectations, then assisted students in reaching that high bar.

Participants discussed the characteristics of BCU faculty that assisted them in their success. Some of the characteristics that surfaced thematically were hard working, persistent, dedicated, and resourceful. One participant shared, "family—we were treated like family. For someone who had no family in the entire state, that genuine love provided much comfort." Another participant reflected. "I felt like we were a family and there was a sense of pride that grew as we went through the program together." The faculty at BCU expected participants to work hard, but also worked hard themselves. They spent many hours in addition to their office hours working with students to cultivate the skill set needed to be successful teachers. Participants also elaborated on faculty's persistence of high expectations. Another participant shared, "they refused to let us quit or hand in subpar work."

What is the historical and present relevance of BCU in the preparation of 21st century teachers of color?

"*I leave you a thirst for education . . .* "—the legacy and school motto connection.

Participants discussed a myriad of topics in relation to the historical and present relevance of BCU. It was pleasing to read that participants saw the connection between the two. A theme that surfaced from the question of a historical and present relevant of BCU was the connection to the university's founder, Dr. Mary McLeod Bethune, and the motto of the school, "Enter to learn, depart to serve." As one participant shared, "Dr. Bethune is known as a champion of education and her legacy has allowed thousands to follow in her footsteps . . . I am truly proud to be a part of Dr. Bethune's legacy." Participants felt connected to the motto of the school, and faculty worked to keep the motto in the forefront of students' minds as they progressed through their program. One participant shared, "Teachers of HBCU teacher education programs have received a unique education that prepared them to deal with any school setting regardless of any circumstances. The locations of most HBCU's were established in low-income areas and preservice teachers completed their hours in low-income schools. The settings were not always ideal, but prepared preservice teachers for any and every kind of situation." The experiences in a multitude of classroom environments during the field experiences prepared students to serve in any situation. Historically, Dr. Bethune would have her students go into the community and teach the children that lived in the neighboring community. It appears that this tradition of serving the underserved has remained over the years.

When participants were asked about the relevance of HBCU's currently and in the future, all participants stated that HBCU's are and will remain relevant in the future. Thematically, their responses reflected cultural connections, and the competence of BCU's TEP. Participants overwhelmingly believed that HBCU's are a great place for young Black students. There was a resounding agreement that is reflected in this statement: "Yes, I think the black college experience is fundamental for any African American. I will always believe that there is nothing like it in the world. My experience prepared me for where I am today." Another perspective shared about the cultural connection of the HBCU was discussed by another participant, "Yes, where else can young

African Americans gain higher education with people who look like them and have similar struggles. We have the rest of our lives to work in diverse settings; it is just a great experience to look back on." Yet another participant shared, "There will always be a need for HBCU's because there will always be African American students who want to learn more about their heritage and feel as though they are in a community that perpetuates pride and academic excellence within their own culture." Participants believed that HBCU's are the safe haven for Black students to thrive and connect to their culture.

The competence of BCU's TEP is another reason why participants believe that HBCU's will remain relevant in the future. Participants concur: "BCU's teacher education program has always been relevant because it prepares students to be the best teachers by keeping up with current educational practices." Another participant shares, "BCU is relevant in 2013 because the quality of teaching evident by being able to relate with any culture and provide real world experiences for students to learn with fidelity." Reflections of the characteristics that participants discussed previously support the idea that HBCU's will remain relevant in the future as well.

Conversely, HBCU's will remain relevant because some participants share that some Blacks will continue to be marginalized, therefore denied access at one point or another to a predominately white institution (PWI). As one participant states, "Many are turned away from larger state schools." Another participant shares, "Yes, HBCU's will be relevant for the next century because we are demonstrating to PWI's that we are have been on the same playing fields. Some just choose not to recognize, but now we are sitting next to them . . . How could they not see us?!"

REFLECTION

"I leave you finally a responsibility to our young people . . . "—the study, and legacy continue.

The authors found overwhelmingly that the participants' report very high levels of continued engagement and awareness about BCU in general and the BCU teacher education program. Additionally, the participants feel very strongly about the importance of HBCU's in the twenty-first century. In the narrative discussion, respondents spoke specifically about BCU faculty and the level of encouragement they received throughout their matriculation. The respondents also continued to discuss the importance of spreading the word about BCU so that others will continue to be a part of the BCU legacy.

As the authors reflect on maintaining the high quality education and relevance at Bethune Cookman and every other HBCU, Chamberlin

(2012) concurs, "a return to the emphasis on teaching, nurturing, and mentoring students will allow HBCUs to regain a competitive edge and retain a distinctive flavor. Most importantly, a return to the original HBCU mission will better prepare all students for navigating the path to fulfillment of their dreams" (p. 29). HBCU's have consistently done a superb job of instilling the campus mission in students so they understand the magnitude of attending an HBCU. It is important to continue the task of students understanding the legacy they are contributing to as a student of an HBCU.

The implications indicate that faculty can make the difference for students, as well as being introduced and held accountable to the motto of the school. Faculty who prepared students for the real world, held high expectations for all students, as well as developing a community of family resonated with participants. Incoming students need to be inculcated with the university motto so they know what the overarching expectation is. Participants stated that the university motto was held in high regard, and students knew they were to carry the legacy introduced to them.

The second part of this study's data is currently being analyzed via quantitative data that examines specific criteria of teacher education faculty, career experiences impact on participants' profession, and impact and referral for future BCU students. The authors seek to triangulate the quantitative data with the qualitative data. We hope to publish all of the data to again show the impact of teacher education programs at HBCUs.

What we know as the alumni of Bethune-Cookman and HBCU alumni across the country can concur: "All of them believe their HBCU experiences provided an unmatched capacity to build their educational foundation for continued academic success beyond completion of their undergraduate degrees" (Bettez & Suggs, 2012, p. 304). There are many HBCU alumni who have acquired advanced degrees and continue to contribute to the academy of teacher education. As long as we are matriculating from Bethune-Cookman or any other HBCU, we can continue the legacy of Dr. Bethune by leaving a thirst for education for the next generation of teachers and students.

REFERENCES

Albritton, T. J. (2012). Educating our own: The historical legacy of HBCUs and their relevanc for educating a new generation of leaders. *Urban Review, 44,* 311–331.

Anderson, J. D. (1988). *The education of Blacks in the South, 1860–1935*. Chapel Hill, NC: The University of North Carolina Press.

Bethune, M. M. (1955). My last will and testament. *Ebony Magazine, 10,* 105–110.

Bettez, S. C., & Suggs, V. L. (2012). Centering the educational and social significance of HBCUs: A focus on the educational journeys and thoughts of African American scholars. *The Urban Review, 44*(3), 303–310.

Brooks, M., West-Olatunji, G., Blackmon, A. T., Froelich, K., De La Torre, W., Montano, T. Peregrino, S., Quintanar, R., & Smith, R. J. (2012). Minority serving institutions and their contribution to advancing multicultural teacher education pedagogy. *Education, 133*(2), 349–360.

Chamberlin, J. D. (2012). HBCUs at a crossroads. *Diverse: Issues in Higher Education, 29*(18), 29–29.

Creswell, J. W. (2005). *Educational research: Planning, conducting, and evaluating quantitative and qualitative research.* (2nd ed.). Ohio: Pearson Merrill Prentice Hall.

Duncan, A. (2009). HBCUs and Higher Education: Beyond the Iron Triangle—remarks by secretary Arne Duncan to 2009 National Historically Black Colleges and Universities Conference. Retrieved from https://www2.ed.gov/news/speeches/2009/09/09022009.html

Fraser, J. W. (2007). *Preparing America's teachers: A history.* New York: Teachers College Press.

Gutek, G. L. (1995). *A history of the western educational experience* (2nd ed.). Long Grove, IL Waveland Press, Inc.

Harris, O. D. (2012). From margin to center: Participating in village pedagogy at historically black colleges and universities. *Urban Review, 44,* 332–357.

History (2013). Retrieved May 5, 2013, from http://www.cookman.edu/about_BCU/history/index.html

Irvine, J. J. (1989). Beyond role models: An examination of cultural influences on the pedagogical perspectives of Black teachers. *Peabody Journal of Education, 66*(4), 51–63.

Irvine, J. J., & Fenwick, L. T. (2011). Teachers and teaching for the new millennium: The role of HBCUs. *The Journal of Negro Education, 80*(3), 197–208.

Jackson, C.L. (2001). *African American education: A reference handbook.* Santa Barbara, CA: ABC-CLIO, Inc.

Lincoln, Y. S., & Guba, E. G. (1985). *Naturalistic inquiry.* Newbury Park, CA: Sage.

LeMelle, T. J., & LeMelle, W. J. (1969). *The Black college: A strategy for achieving relevancy.* New York, NY: Frederick A. Praeger, Inc.

Lovett, B. L. (2011). *America's historically Black colleges & universities: A narrative history from the nineteenth century into the twenty-first century.* Macon, GA: Mercer University Press.

Mccray, A. D., Sindelar, P. T., Kilgore, K. K., & Neal, L. I. (2002). African-American women's decisions to become teachers: Sociocultural perspectives. *International Journal of Qualitative Studies in Education, 15*(3), 269–290.

Milam, J. (2010). (Re) Envisioning teacher education: A critical exploration of missed historical moments and promising possibilities. In V. Hill-Jackson & C. W. Lewis (Eds.), *Transforming teacher education: What went wrong with teacher training, and how we can fix it* (pp. 3–36). Sterling, VA: Stylus.

Morgan, H. (1995). *Historical perspectives on the education of Black children.* Westport, CT: Praeger.

National Center for Education Statistics (NCES). (2012). *The traditionally Black institutions of higher education 1860–1982.* Washington, DC: National Center for Education Statistics.

Smith, E. M. (1996). Mary McLeod Bethune's "last will and testament:" A legacy for race vindication. *Journal of Negro History,* 105–122.

Spivey, D. (1978). *Schooling for the new slavery: Black industrial education, 1968–1915.* Westport, CT: Greenwood Press.

Spring, J. (1997). *The politics of an American education.* New York: McGraw-Hill.

United Negro College Fund (2013) (n.d.) Our member colleges: About HBCU's. Retrieved from http://www.uncf.org/sections/MemberColleges/SS_AboutHBCUs/about.hbcu.asp

Walker, V. S. (2005). After methods, then what? A researcher's response to the report of the National Research Council. *The Teachers College Record, 107*(1), 30-37.

Watson, A. L., & Shealey, M. W. (2011). Black women speak: Examining the experiences of black women in teacher education. In S. Moore, R. Alexander, & A. Lemelle, (Eds.), *The dilemma of Black faculty at predominantly White institutions in America: Issues for consideration in a post-multicultural era* (pp. 267–282). United States: Edward Mellon Press.

Wiggan, G. (Ed.). (2012). *Education for the new frontier: Race, education and triumph in Jim Crow America (1867–1945).* New York: Nova Science Publishers, Inc.

Woodson, C. G. (1919). *The education of the Negro prior to 1861: A history of the education of the colored people from the United States from the beginning of slavery to the Civil War* Kessinger Publishing (Reprinted 2004).

Woodson, G. G. (1933). *The mis-education of the Negro.* Mineola, NY: Dover Publications, Inc. (Reprinted 2005).

PART III

IMPLICATIONS FOR ACCESS, EQUITY, AND ACHIEVEMENT

THE CONTEXTUAL FACTOR OF RACE IN EQUITY, ACCESS, AND ACHIEVEMENT

Marvin Lynn
Indiana University South Bend

I have been waiting a long time for this book. As a scholar who has studied the work and lives of Black male teachers while examining the utility of critical race theory as a tool for further illuminating the experiences of Black men, I have often bemoaned the disunity between theoretically laden and practice-driven research. Much of the theoretically driven research tends to de-emphasize issues of method or give scant attention to the lives of research subjects. On the other hand, practice-based research sometimes ignores the existence of theory altogether; thereby ignoring broader social, cultural, political and economic issues that may impact the outcomes of the data in some critical way. My research has been concerned with situating Black male teachers' practices within a broader critical analysis of race and racism in U.S. society. It is appropriate that I write an introduction to a section of a book that is committed to highlighting research on Black education that is ably informed by relevant theory.

In my research, I have drawn on critical race theory as a tool for analyzing and situating the work and lives of African American men. Critical race theory is a useful analytical tool for helping us to think through questions related to equity and access.

Teacher Education and Black Communities, pages 247–252
Copyright © 2014 by Information Age Publishing
All rights of reproduction in any form reserved.

The theory forces us to situate the United States inside a historical context. We must, for example, reckon with the fact that the United States began as a slave nation with expressed policies for the extermination of Native peoples. American laws and policies upheld these practices and even made it illegal for citizens—of any color—to disobey them. Critical Race Theory—which comes out of the law—then rightly suggests that the laws themselves are racist in their construction *and* their unjust application. A law designed to maintain the enslavement of African people while threatening the livelihood of those who challenge such laws could is a racist law designed to uphold a White supremacist society.

CRT is primarily concerned with two issues: race and racism. First, race is a highly structured, multidimensional system of practices, beliefs upon which all institutions in our society are built, maintained and run. You will often hear critical race theorists articulate the notion that "race is a social construct." That is true. But that doesn't make it any less real in the lives of those who are affected by it. Let me explain. Race has no real basis in biology or physiology. It is, as our great African American sociologist W.E.B. DuBois called it "A matter of skin and bone." In one sense, it is meant to merely describe our physical differences. The problem is that discrete characteristics are also associated with those physical characteristics. So people with dark skin are Black or of African American heritage. However, according to racial logic—they are also viewed as less intelligent, lacking in morality, lazy and so on. People with light skin and a certain hair texture are called White or Caucasian. Whiteness is also associated with industry, intelligence, and innovation. A number of theorists have documented the Eugenics movement which developed in the 1700s as a pseudo-scientific method for explaining the differences between the races. Studies—which have long been debunked and proven to be wholly inaccurate and politically self-serving for Whites—were developed as a way to illustrate not only the physical differences but differences in mental capacity between the races and therefore prove that white men were politically and economically dominant because they possessed natural intellectual endowments that made it so. It was an application of Darwin's Theory of Natural Selection and Survival of the Fittest to humankind. It justified slavery, colonialism and apartheid. So the establishment of "races" necessarily led to a "theory of race" which was designed to provide explanation for a whole range of differences. This theory of race operates as global belief system that significantly impacts our institutional practices but also the way we see ourselves and each other. None of us are free from its grip.

Race affects White people and people of color in different but equally disastrous ways. White people, throughout the globe, enjoy a superiority complex and have a sense of entitlement whereby they expect to be treated more favorably than others and expect to control all resources and dominate our institutions in order to serve and protect their narrow interests. They expect to get the best jobs, get into the best schools and enjoy dominance at every level in our society. People of color on the other hand, often accept a kind of secondary status in a political, economic and social sense and also engage in acts of self-hatred—skin lightening, Black on Black crime and other kinds of practices that further instantiate a theory of race that dehumanizes us. Because this theory of race is so pervasive throughout all our societies it has led us to develop laws, policies, institutions and practices that promote this particular way of viewing the world. All White people benefit from racism on some level and all people color are disenfranchised by it in a myriad of ways. Our theory of race substantiates, provides fertile grounding for and further advances racism or White supremacy throughout the globe.

Racism or White supremacy operationalizes or is the enactment of our theory of race. It is a system of practices based on the belief systems inherent in our theory of race. By practices—I mean institutional practices of systematic discrimination, disenfranchisement and maltreatment of peoples of color throughout the world based on their race. Racism/White supremacy has multiple dimensions and operates at multiple levels simultaneously. Eduardo Bonilla Silva, in one of his early works on the subject, brings theoretical specificity to the issue when he argues:

> First, racialized social systems are societies that allocate differential eco- nomic, political, social, and even psychological rewards to groups along racial lines; lines that are socially constructed.

Next he says:

> After a society becomes racialized, a set of social relations and practices based on racial distinctions develops at all societal levels. I designate the aggregate of those relations and practices as the racial structure of a society.

In other words, Blacks become a permanent "underclass" in society either acting as servants or considered menaces. This is part of the racial structure of society. Either way, they are to be regarded with suspicion and treated accordingly—as you have seen in the multiple examples I have provided. In a racialized social system, Oprah Winfrey (even with her many billions) is part of racial underclass. Because she is marked as Black and her celebrity is not always evident to the average racist onlooker, she, at times, suffers the same treatment as "average Black folk" thereby marking her as a menace who is to be refused service whenever convenient. But what Bonilla Silva says is that Black people's status in this highly racialized social context not only marks us as permanent members of an underclass, it also establishes a socially sanctioned set of "rules of engagement" in our society that are entirely based on perceptions of the racialized other. The "rules of engagement" make it acceptable to systematically disrespect, mistreat, abuse and people based on their race.

Bonilla Silva also says that

> ... on the basis of this structure, there develops a racial ideology (What I am referring to as a theory of race) ... This ideology is not simply a "superstructural" phenomenon (a mere reflection of the racialized system), but becomes the *organizational map* that guides actions of racial actors in society. It becomes as real as the racial relations it organizes.

Slave narratives, for example, that provide accounts of older enslaved African women who reared young White children who often sucked from their breast are often shocked to discover how cruel and inhumane these children can behave toward them once they are taught "appropriate" behavior toward slaves. As a child of two or three, he regards the slave woman as something of a mother. He is then socialized to understand his role not as a child of the slave woman but as her owner; one who has total dominion over her. He is provided an "organizational map" (to use Bonilla Silva's terminology) that helps him understand his relationship to the slave: it is one of dominion and unbridled power. As any good slave master would, he takes full advantage of this at every opportunity. Bonilla Silva provides another example that sheds further light on this matter, he states that:

> ... most struggles in a racialized social system contain a racial component, but sometimes they acquire and/or exhibit a distinct racial character. Racial contestation is the logical outcome of a society with a racial hierarchy. A social formation that includes some form of racialization will always exhibit some form of racial contestation.

Racialized people will always put forth a demand for better treatment. Depending on the reach and power of the demand, the racialized social system will reconfigure itself, as necessary, in order to lessen the threat to its dominance. We saw this at the end of the U.S. Civil Rights movement and we saw this as Apartheid system officially came to a close. On its face, the racial caste system appeared to be breaking down. In the United States, you could no longer legally ban Blacks from public venues. Segregation was outlawed. Since that time, more Blacks moved into the ranks of the middle class. Graduation rates for Blacks drastically improved. Conditions overall for Blacks have improved in some ways but significantly worsened in other ways. I provided example of this previously. I talked about incarceration rates. I have not talked about health disparities illustrated by the overall low access to quality healthcare African Americans experience. I have not talked in great detail about the growing gaps in income and wealth attainment between Blacks and Whites. I urge you to examine Oliver and Shapiro's important book "Black Wealth/White Wealth." The research illustrates how inequalities endure even when a society no longer sanctions legalized forms of discrimination.

The chapters in this section draw attention to how access, equity and achievement intersect in the lives of African American students and the teachers who serve them. Two of the chapters, those by Kenneth A. Anderson and Felicia Moore Mensah, address the ways in which innovative strategies can be adopted in teacher education programs to improve access to high-level and culturally relevant mathematics and science for African American students. Moore Mensah's chapter, "Using Observation Prompts in the Urban Elementary School Field Placement," for example, charts the successful use of "guided observation prompts" during preservice teachers' field experiences to broaden their knowledge about diversity. As a teacher educator, I too have found it important to immerse my students in literature on the history of Black and Brown schooling experiences while guiding them to "look for" illustrative examples of key concepts learned about while in the urban educational context.

In *Equity in Opportunities to Learn Mathematics: Policy and Practice Implications for High-Achieving Black Students,* Anderson examines data from the High School Longitudinal Study (HSLS) and finds that there is a lack of parity in areas of access and equity for high achieving mathematically inclined Black students as compared to their non-Black peers. The author discusses policy recommendations for creating more equitable conditions for gifted Black students who show promise in mathematics.

In the final chapter, Ivory A. Toldson and Mercedes E. Ebanks examines student responses to the National Crime Victimization Survey: School Crime Supplement of 2009 (NCVS-SCS). Their findings reveal which students perceive their teachers to be more concerned about their academic and social success, and how more care and respect for them during the school day. The authors review suspension and expulsion, and school environment literature and finds great disparities that negatively impact African American students. This chapter includes suggestions for developing effective teacher education programs.

In conclusion, the chapters in this section draw on a rich theoretical base to examine policy and practice in K–16 education. In their totality, the chapters make evident the strong linkages between elementary, middle and high school and higher education—especially for Black students and their teachers. The problems with Black achievement in one setting produce and reproduce those same problems in other settings. All of these problems and their solutions are produced, shaped and informed by broader contextual factors such as Anti-Black racism (Gordon, 1995) or what Jody Armour (1997) calls "Negrophobia," cultural misunderstanding, classism, homophobia and sexism. I urge the authors to more strongly consider the intersections between these axes of domination. In particular, we need increased understanding of the particular ways in which African American males are constructed in a White supremacist context and how this shapes and influences who teaches, what is taught and how it is taught. The chapters in this section begin this all-too-important project in earnest.

REFERENCES

Armour, J. D. (1997). Negrophobia and reasonable racism. New York: New York University Press.

Gordon, L. R. (1995). *Bad faith and antiblack racism.* Amherst, NY: Humanity Books.

CHAPTER 12

EQUITY IN OPPORTUNITIES TO LEARN MATHEMATICS

Policy and Practice Implications for High-Achieving Black Students

Kenneth Alonzo Anderson
Howard University

This chapter investigates equity in opportunities to learn (OTL) among high-achieving students. Data from the High School Longitudinal Study of 2009 (Ingles, 2011) were used to examine diversity in OTL between high-achieving Black students and all other high-achieving students. Specifically, equity in (a) opportunities to take advanced coursework; (b) profile of teacher credentials and experience; (c) teacher instructional methods and beliefs; and (d) student evaluations of teachers were examined. Opportunities to take advanced course demonstrate the strongest associations with standardized achievement. One key finding suggests that OTL for high-achieving Black students across the United States are considerably more inconsistent relative to OTL for all other high-achieving students. Additional

Teacher Education and Black Communities, pages 253–272
Copyright © 2014 by Information Age Publishing
All rights of reproduction in any form reserved.

similarities and differences are noted and subsequent recommendations are provided.

Equity in Black schooling experiences has been a topic of interest for decades. In 1935, W. E. B. Du Bois published an article entitled, "Does the negro need separate schools?" As shown in the following quote, Du Bois advocated for equity in high-quality schooling experiences, irrespective of whether or not schools were integrated.

Likewise, Du Bois described conditions for proper education.

> They *[separate schools]* are needed just so far as they are necessary for the proper education of the Negro race. The proper education of any people includes sympathetic touch between teacher and pupil; knowledge on the part of the teacher, not simply of the individual taught, but of his surroundings and background, and the history of his class and group; such contact between pupils, and between teacher and pupil, on the basis of perfect social equality, as will increase this sympathy and knowledge; facilities for education in equipment and housing, and the promotion of such extracurricular activities as will tend to induct the child into life. (Du Bois, 1935, p. 328)

It is reprehensible, despite assertions like those put forth by Du Bois nearly 80 years ago, that equity in schooling experiences of Black and other underrepresented groups continues to remain a critical issue. Accordingly, this chapter was written to trouble equity assumptions regarding high-achieving students. It is the anticipation that lessons can be learned from this treatise and subsequent action will be taken to improve equity in opportunities to learn (OTL) for high-achieving Black students and all students.

This chapter addresses equity in a unique way. Whereas inequity and poor-quality schooling is often examined relative to effects on student achievement differences, this chapter focuses on inequity experienced by Black students when achievement outcomes are similar to their peers. Specifically, high-achieving Black students will be compared to other high-achieving peers with the intent to examine opportunities to learn (OTL). Here, OTL are defined as favorable conditions that promote academic development. Likewise, high achieving is defined as ninth-grade students with standardized mathematics (algebra) scores that are in the 80th percentile or higher (i.e., 5th quintile). High-achieving students were selected for investigation in this study because high-achieving Black students are faced with unique challenges (Graham & Anderson, 2008) and strategies for maximizing potential among high-achieving Black students are necessary (Ford, Moore III, & Scott, 2011). As such, equity in OTL may be conducive to maximizing potential of high-achieving Black students.

The phrase "opportunities to learn" was derived from Boykin and Noguera's (2011) text, *Creating the Opportunity to Learn: Moving from Research to Practice.* In this text, the author's describe research-based factors that enhance achievement for African Americans and Latinos. These factors include (a) multiple forms of student engagement (behavioral, affective, and cognitive); (b) guiding functions—factors that "can steer shape, govern, and intensify fundamental engagement processes" (p. 51); and (c) asset-focused factors—"contextual conditions in which teaching, learning, engagement, and guiding functions are manifest" (p. 69). Accordingly, ideas presented in the Boykin and Noguera text along with those cited by Du Bois (1935) provided theoretical guidance for this study.

REVIEW OF LITERATURE

Opportunities to learn are essentially components of school climate and can be examined from multiple perspectives. School climate, albeit difficult to define and measure (Zullig, Koopman, Patton, & Ubbes, 2010), can be thought of as character and life quality within a school (Cohen, McCabe, Michelli, & Pickeral, 2009). School character and life quality can be enhanced or diminished by factors such as interpersonal relationships, organizational structures, inherent values, and customs (Cohen et al., 2009). Additionally, school climate factors such as classroom context, school engagement, teacher-student relationship quality, and teacher credentials have been linked to student achievement (Barile et al., 2012; Boykin & Noguera, 2011; Dotterer & Lowe, 2011; Hopson & Lee, 2011; Ross, McDonald, Alberg, & McSparrin-Gallagher, 2007).

School climate can be examined from multiple perspectives. Fan, Williams, and Corkin (2011) noted that institutional and student perspectives offer critical insight. Thus, OTL will be examined from institutional and student perspectives, with a primary interest in institutional perspectives. Institutional perspectives were given priority to demarcate teacher professional development opportunities for high-achieving Black students based on teacher and institutional data. Specific dimensions of OTL that were examined in this study include: (a) opportunities to take advanced coursework; (b) profile of teacher credentials and experience; (c) teacher instructional methods and beliefs; and (d) student evaluations of teachers. A brief literature review of these topics is summarized next.

Advanced Coursework

Taking advanced coursework has been linked to positive outcomes success. Some of the outcomes include increased test scores, high school graduation rates, college enrollment, and enrollment in four-year versus two-year colleges (Long, Conger, & Iatarola, 2012). Enrollment in advanced coursework has been shown to be especially beneficial for ethnic minorities and students in disadvantaged schools (Long et al., 2012), but advanced course enrollment is often unrealized by underrepresented groups (Shifrer, Callahan, & Muller, 2013). More than 30 years ago, Pedro, Wolleat, Fennema, and Becker (1981) found that attitudinal and attributional factors contribute to advanced coursework enrollment. Shifrer, Callahan, and Muller (2013) also note that school processes may contribute to advance coursework enrollment.

Teacher Credentials and Experience

Teacher credentials such as professional certification and experience have been linked to student achievement. Much of the research has centered on the relationship between teacher credentials and standardized achievement, leading to generally weak associations that are highly dependent upon the design of the evaluative model (Goldhaber, Goldschmidt, & Tseng, 2013). Despite mixed results regarding standardized outcomes, professional development for teachers, like any profession, is important. Increased professional development and experience can lead to greater feelings of teacher adequacy, improved curriculum alignment with instruction, enhanced content knowledge, and enhanced knowledge of larger sociocultural factors that influence schools (Anderson & Olsen, 2006; Brayko, 2013; Kee, 2012; Polikoff, 2013).

Instructional Methods and Teacher Beliefs

Teacher dispositions influence instructional practice (Britton & Anderson, 2010) and these practices can influence achievement (Boykin & Noguera, 2011). Teachers have reported feelings of discomfort when teaching ethnic minorities (Kumar & Hamer, 2013) and Black teachers have reported have more positive beliefs about Black students (Natesan & Kieftenbeld, 2013). In response to underrepresentation of Black students in gifted and talented (G&T) programs, frameworks for enhancing inclusiveness of G&T programs have been proposed (see Ford, Moore III, & Scott, 2011). In general, G&T training is often limited and teachers often lack appropriate instructional strategies to appropriately support and challenge G&T students (Berman, Schultz, & Weber, 2012). While this study does not exclusively focus on students who are specifically identified as gifted and talented, instructional strategies and beliefs regarding high-achieving students are likely parallel to the G&T literature and will be examined in this study.

Teacher–Student Relationship Quality

Teacher-student relationship quality (TSRQ) is a common topic of interest in education. Capturing this construct is often difficult and typically relegated to survey data. Despite difficulty in measuring this construct, studies have found strong relationships between TSRQ and student outcomes (Barile et al., 2012; Boykin & Noguera, 2011). Research has also shown that factors such as positive TSRQ may not be sufficient for improving academic outcomes (Dotterer & Lowe, 2011). Considering the contributions of TSRQ to academic achievement, significance of race in the United States, and large racial discontinuity between Black students and teachers, student perspectives of TSRQ was examined in this study.

Research Question

Concepts presented in the literature review were used to inform the following research question:

Which opportunities to learn, if any, contribute to increased mathematics achievement for high-achieving Black students?

As noted, this research question will examine four OTL components: (a) opportunities to take advanced coursework; (b) profile of teacher credentials and experience; (c) teacher instructional methods and beliefs; and (d) student evaluations of teachers. Results will be compared with the effects of OTL on all other high-achieving students (i.e., "non-Black") students. Findings can be used to maximize Black student potential and inform future research.

METHOD

Sample

Data from the *High School Longitudinal Study of 2009 (HSLS:09)* (Ingels et al., 2011) were used to conduct this study. HSLS:09 is a nationally representative longitudinal study of ninth-grade students in the United States and the District of Columbia. HSLS:09 has a strong emphasis on science, engineering, technology, and mathematics (STEM) and was designed to examine student transitions across several domains: high school, postsecondary education, workforce, and adulthood.

HSLS:09 employed a longitudinal design with several data collection periods. Base-year data, gathered in 2009–2010, were used in this study because student achievement indicators were publically available. HSLS:09 sampling techniques included a two-stage sampling process to generate a national sample. A total of 21,444 questionnaire-capable ninth-graders were drawn from 944 public, public charter, and private schools. Ninth-graders selected during the base year were given an algebraic reasoning assessment and survey items that were believed to influence educational choice. Teachers, parents, guidance counselors, and school administrators also completed survey items that were designed to assess factors that influence education choices (Ingels et al., 2011).

A subset of the HSLS:09 sample was the population of interest in this study. Specifically, high-achieving students or students whose algebra achievement scores were higher than 80% (i.e., top quintile) of ninth-graders in the United States as measured by a standardized algebra assessment given by the HSLS: 09 research team. The algebra assessment was scaled using a mean of 50 and standard deviation of 10.

Measures

Race

Black students in this study were defined as students who identified or were identified as Black or African American, but not Hispanic. It is important to note that students who identified or were identified as "More than one Race," but included Black/African American as one of the identified races, were included in the comparison frame. This analytic choice was due to the author's inability to reconcile additional complexity associated with the "More than One Race" category.

Opportunities to Take Advanced Coursework

Opportunities to take advance courses were measured by whether or not the student was enrolled in mathematics during the fall semester of the freshman year. Opportunities to take advanced coursework were also measured by whether or not students were enrolled in Pre-Algebra, Algebra I, Algebra II, Geometry, or Trigonometry in ninth grade.

Profile of Teacher Credentials

Teacher credentials is a complex concept consisting of related variables; thus, a number or teacher characteristics were examined. These variables included: (a) the number of years that the teacher taught 9th–12th grade mathematics; (b) highest earned degree; (c) highest earned degree from an education department; (d) whether or not the teacher entered the teaching profession through alternative certification; (e) number of mathematics courses taken; and (f) teacher certification (certified via regular, advanced, or certified completing probationary period or not certified).

Teacher Instructional Methods and Beliefs

Teacher instructional methods and beliefs were measured by a host of items: (a) teacher efficacy; (b) teacher beliefs about overall teacher expectations at the school; (c) whether or not the teacher taught using small groups; and (d) group assignment practices. Teacher instructional methods were also measured by assessing teacher-reported emphasis on several mathematics domains: problem solving, reasoning, connecting ideas, preparation for further mathematics study, logical structure, mathematics history and the nature of mathematics, effective explanations, business/industry applications, speedy/accurate computations, increasing student interest, mathematics concepts, algorithms, developing computational skills, and test preparation.

Student Evaluations of Teachers

Student-reported responses to survey items assessed the level of agreement with the following prompts about his or her mathematics teacher: (a) treats some students better than others; (b) treats males and females differently; (c) makes mathematics easy to understand; (d) treats student with respect; and (e) treats every student fairly.

Analytic Procedure

A three-step analytic procedure was used to conduct this study. First, descriptive statistics of variables, including frequencies and measures of central tendency were examined. Second, principal components analyses of the various weighted OTL items were conducted to combine items into common factors. Before combining the items, a common metric was created by standardizing items using a mean 0 and standard deviation of 1. Scree plots were examined and components with eigenvalues greater than one were retained. Using promax rotation, individual items with factor loadings of 0.3 or greater on a single factor were retained and items that loaded on multiple factors were removed. Third, a series of multiple regressions using OTL metrics to predict tests scores of high-achieving Black students and all other high-achieving students were conducted. To ensure sufficient degrees of freedom, each group of factors were analyzed separately.

Since HSLS:09 was conducted using a multistage sampling design, STATA 12 was used to conduct analyses in this study. Balanced repeated replication estimation techniques were employed in this study using analytic and replicate weights provided by the HSLS:09 research team (Ingels et al., 2011). Analytic weights and replicate weights were used to generate accurate variance and population estimates of ninth-grade students in the United States.

RESULTS

Factor analysis results will be presented first, followed by descriptive statistics of the sample that represents the high-achieving population of ninth-graders. Thereafter, results associated with the primary research question will be shared. The primary research is listed below:

> Which opportunities to learn, if any, contribute to increased mathematics achievement for high-achieving Black students?

Factor Analyses

Principal components analyses led to the creation of six teacher-reported factors and two student-reported factors. These factors were labeled cognitive engagement, pragmatics, grouping strategies, teacher beliefs, teacher content preparation, teacher formal education, student evaluation of teacher dispositions, and student evaluation of teacher treatment of other students, respectively. Appendices A–C summarize the various factors, associated factor loadings, and items used to create the factors.

Descriptive Statistics

Population Estimates and Course Enrollments

Descriptive statistics in Table 12.1 show that Black students represent about 6% of the ninth-grade students in the top quintile. Based on HSLS:09 estimates, Black students make up approximately 13.5% of the U.S. ninth-grade population. Figure 12.1 shows the breakdown of course placements for high-achieving students. Relative to all other high-achieving students, smaller percentages of high-achieving Black students were placed in Geometry, Algebra II, and Trigonometry, –4%, –8%, and –9%, respectively. Likewise, relative to all other high-achieving students, larger percentages of high-achieving Black students were placed in Algebra I (+4%).

TABLE 12.1   Frequencies of High-Achieving Students

Group	Observations	Population	Percentage of Population
Black Students	158	43,524	6.00%
All Other Students	3,489	681,384	94.00%
Total High-Achieving Students	3,647	724,908	100.00%

	Ninth Grade Course Enrollment	
Course	Black Students	All Other Students
Pre-Algebra	~0	3,355
Algebra I	13,544	180,949
Geometry	20,555	337,358
Algebra II	3,857	108,058
Trigonometry	252	8,439

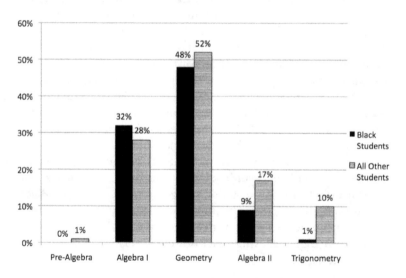

Figure 12.1   Breakdown of high-achieving student course placements. Due to the fact that all possible high school mathematics courses are not represented, the sum of the percentages for either category does not equal 100%. Only the most common mathematics courses were included.

Teacher- and Student-Reported Factors

Table 12.2 displays means and standard errors of teacher and student factors that were examined in this study. The means of the teacher-reported cognitive engagement, pragmatics, grouping strategies, beliefs, and formal

TABLE 12.2 Descriptive Statistics of Teacher and Student Factors

Factor	Black High-Achieving Students		All Other High-Achieving Students	
	Mean	SE	Mean	SE
Cognitive Engagement	1.55	0.89	1.10	0.21
Pragmatics	0.18	0.39	-0.26	0.14
Grouping Strategies	0.48	0.23	0.47	0.07
Teacher Beliefs	0.33	0.56	0.14	0.10
Teacher Content Preparation	-0.26	0.54	0.17	0.07
Teacher Formal Education	0.31	0.32	0.20	0.23
Student Evaluation of Teacher Dispositions	-0.20	0.68	-0.58	0.16
Student Evaluation of Teacher Treatment	0.04	0.19	0.19	0.04

education were higher for high-achieving Black students relative to high achieving "non-Black" students. The means of teacher content preparation were lower for high-achieving Black students relative to high-achieving "non-Black" students. Of the two student-reported factors, the mean student evaluations of teacher dispositions were higher for high-achieving Black students, but mean student evaluations of how teachers treat others was lower for high-achieving Black students, relative to high-achieving "non-Black" students. Standard errors of all factors were larger for high-achieving Black students, relative to high-achieving "non-Black" students. All standard errors for high-achieving Black students, save the teacher formal education factor, were at least twice the size of the standard errors for high-achieving "non-Black" students. The standard error for the teacher formal education factor was 0.39 times larger for high-achieving Black students, relative to high-achieving "non-Black" students. These larger standard deviations indicate a much wider range of experiences in opportunities to learn for high-achieving Black students, relative to high-achieving "non-Black" students.

Inferential Statistics

Advanced Coursework

Table 12.3 shows that for "non-Black" high-achieving students, enrollment in Pre-Algebra or Algebra I was negatively related to algebra achievement, but Algebra II enrollment was associated with an increase in algebra test scores that were equivalent to slightly more than 1/3 of a standard deviation. For "non-Black" students, geometry or trigonometry enrollment

TABLE 12.3 Multiple Regression of Course Enrollment Predicting Mathematics Scores of High-Achieving Students

Variable	B	SE B	t	95% CI
Black Students				
Constant	63.35**	0.52	122.58	[62.33, 64.37]
Algebra I	−1.66*	0.66	−2.53	[−2.95, −0.38]
R^2	0.06			
F	6.41*			
df1(1)				
df2 (199)				
All Other Students				
Constant	64.02**	0.48	133.18	[63.07, 64.97]
Pre-Algebra	−2.40*	1.09	−2.18	[−4.56, −0.23]
Algebra I	−2.07**	0.48	−4.28	[−3.02, −1.11]
Geometry	0.14	0.51	0.27	[−0.87, 1.15]
Algebra II	3.62**	0.55	6.56	[2.53, 4.70]
Trigonometry	2.97	1.53	1.93	[−0.06, 5.99]
R^2	0.19			
F	87.60**			
df1(5)				
df2 (195)				

* $p < .05$; ** $p < .01$

did not result in algebra achievement differences. Table 12.3 also shows that when high-achieving Black students were placed in Algebra I in ninth grade, their scores tended to decrease by .21 standard deviations. Due to the relatively low unweighted counts of high-achieving Black students in other courses, effects of enrollment in courses higher or lower than Algebra I could not be properly estimated.

Teacher Credentials and Beliefs

Teacher credentials (content preparation or formal education) were not strongly related to algebra test scores of Black or "non-Black" high-achieving students (see Table 12.4). Table 12.4 also shows that teacher beliefs were positively related to algebra test scores for high-achieving "non-Black" students, but effect sizes were minimal (+.03 standard deviations). Contrarily, teacher beliefs were not related to algebra test scores of high-achieving Black students, despite higher teacher-reported beliefs about high-achieving Black students, relative to all other high-achieving students.

TABLE 12.4 Multiple Regression of Teacher Beliefs and Credentials Predicting Mathematics Scores of High-Achieving Students

Variable	B	SE B	t	95% CI
Black Students				
Constant	62.83**	0.66	95.47	[61.52, 64.12]
Teacher Beliefs	0.08	0.28	0.28	[−0.47, 0.63]
Teacher Content Preparation	0.12	0.59	0.20	[−1.05, 1.29]
Teacher Formal Education	−0.38	0.32	−1.20	[−1.01, 0.24]
R^2	.11			
F	0.53			
df1(3)				
df2 (197)				
All Other Students				
Constant	64.25**	0.18	365.81	[63.90, 64.59]
Teacher Content Preparation	0.03	0.11	0.31	[−0.18, 0.25]
Teacher Formal Education	0.00	0.08	0.02	[−0.17, 0.17]
Teacher Beliefs	0.27*	0.12	2.32	[0.41, 0.50]
R^2	.01			
F	2.11			
df1(3)				
df2 (197)				

* $p < .05$; ** $p < .01$

Teacher Instructional Strategies

Of the three instructional-strategy factors assessed, cognitive engagement was positively related to algebra scores of high-achieving "non-Black" students (see Table 12.5). Although positively related, effect sizes were minimal (+.01 standard deviations). The mean for teacher-reported cognitive engagement of high-achieving Black students was higher (see Table 12.2), relative to "non-Black" high-achieving students; yet, no statistically significant relationship between algebra scores and cognitive engagement for high-achieving Black students was evident (see Table 12.5).

TABLE 12.5 Multiple Regression of Teacher Instructional Strategies Predicting Mathematics Scores of High-Achieving Students

Variable	B	SE B	t	95% CI	
Black Students					
Constant	62.44**	0.41	153.14	[61.63,	63.24]
Cognitive Engagement	0.18	0.12	1.58	[-0.05,	0.42]
Pragmatics	-0.10	0.24	-0.41	[-0.56,	0.37]
Grouping Strategies	0.07	0.43	-0.17	[-0.93,	0.78]
R^2	.11				
F	0.83				
df1(3)					
df2 (197)					
All Other Students					
Constant	64.13**	0.24	270.91	[63.66,	64.60]
Cognitive Engagement	0.07*	0.06	1.29	[-0.04,	0.19]
Pragmatics	-0.18	0.08	-2.01	[-0.35,	-0.00]
Grouping Strategies	0.14	0.14	1.06	[-0.12,	0.41]
R^2	.01				
F	2.45				
df1(3)					
df2 (197)					

* $p < .05$; ** $p < .01$

Student Evaluations of Teachers

For "non-Black" high-achieving students, evaluations of teacher dispositions were negatively related to algebra scores and student evaluations of teacher treatment of other students were positively related to algebra scores. Despite statistically significant relationships, effect sizes were minimal (-.01 and +.02, respectively). Contrarily, student evaluations of teachers were not significantly related to algebra scores for high-achieving Black students (see Table 12.6).

TABLE 12.6   Multiple Regression of Student Evaluations of Teachers Predicting Mathematics Scores of High-Achieving Students

Variable	B	SE B	t	95% CI	
Black Students					
Constant	62.97**	0.42	147.52	[62.12,	63.80]
Student Evaluations of Teacher Dispositions	0.07	0.06	0.86	[–0.06,	0.90]
Student Evaluation of Teacher Treatment of Other Students	0.27	0.32	0.86	[–0.35,	0.90]
R^2	.02				
F	0.65				
df1(2)					
df2 (198)					
All Other Students					
Constant	64.09**	0.14	456.54	[63.82,	64.37]
Student Evaluations of Teacher Dispositions	–0.05*	0.23	–2.29	[–0.10,	–0.01]
Student Evaluation of Teacher Treatment of Other Students	0.16*	0.07	2.18	[0.02,	0.31]
R^2	0.01				
F	9.02				
df1(2)					
df2 (198)					

* $p < .05$; ** $p < .01$

CONCLUSION

Equity in Opportunities to Learn

Descriptive statistics that were reported in this study may be more important than any inferential statistics reported in this study. Based on the very large standard errors of the means scores of the variables measured in this study for high-achieving Black students, relative to all other high-achieving students, it is clear that opportunities to learn for high-achieving Black students vary tremendously across the United States. These marked differences may provide evidence of why some high-achieving Black students are underachieving (see Ford, Moore III, & Scott, 2011). The next two sections address some ways to create an improved and more consistent experience for high-achieving Black students and high-achieving students in general.

Course Placement

Overall, findings show that for high-achieving students, course placement was the strongest indicator of algebra achievement is enrollment in Algebra II. Specifically, results show that placement of "non-Black" high-achieving students in Algebra II was particularly beneficial in increasing standardized algebra scores. However, the effects of enrollment in Algebra II and other advanced coursework could not be estimated for high-achieving Black students. Contrarily, enrollment of Black and "non-Black" high-achieving students in Algebra I was negatively related to algebra achievement scores. Moreover, data in the study show that relative to all other high-achieving students, a larger percentage of high-achieving Black students are placed in Algebra I (e.g., lower-level courses). Despite the negative relationship between Algebra I enrollment and standardized algebra test scores, these students still managed to earn scores that were in the 80th percentile or higher. Likewise, in terms of higher-level courses, smaller percentages of high-achieving Black students are placed in Geometry, Algebra II, and Trigonometry. These results may suggest that placement of high-achieving students in Algebra I could likely have been resulted in unchallenging environments for these students. Furthermore, enrollment percentages in Algebra I seem incredibly high for Black and "non-Black" high-achieving students since these students all earned algebra scores that were higher than 80% of all ninth-graders in the United States. Accordingly, findings indicate that placement practices for high-achieving students may require further scrutiny and modification to minimize underachievement. Enhancing placement practices could reduce regrettable placement rates of high-achieving students in lower-level subjects and provide learning opportunities that promote academic development.

The issue of placement is especially complex because the sole responsibility of placement cannot be attributed to high schools. For example, students in this study likely should have received Algebra I at some point before ninth grade, but if incorrect placement has occurred in earlier grades, then a cycle of mathematics displacement may continue through high school. As such, future research should examine placement processes in middle and high schools as well as coordination efforts between middle and high schools.

Implications for Teacher Education

Traditional factors that are thought to enhance achievement, such as cognitive engagement, pragmatics, grouping strategies, teacher beliefs, teacher content preparation, and teacher formal education led to nonexistent or weak associations with standardized algebra scores for "non-Black" high-achieving students, and were not reliably associated with standardized algebra scores for high-achieving Black students. The aforementioned practices are common components of teacher education programs and can be easily identified in the literature as key components of effective teaching. Findings in this study do not suggest that the factors examined are ineffective, but findings do indicate that the aforementioned factors failed to influence standardized algebra achievement. Considering the high stakes associated with standardized achievement and algebra mastery, this finding is substantial. Teacher educators must continue to examine effective approaches to improving standardized test scores as well as classroom-based indicators for high-achieving students.

One possible explanation may be that practices that are commonly used for students with average to below-average achievement may also be used widely with high-achieving students. Teacher educators must closely examine dosage and emphasis on high-achieving students as it relates to coursework, professional development, and practicum placements that allow preservice teachers to gain experience working with high-achieving students. Moreover, modification of program standards and key assessments that include indicators for high-achieving students are necessary. Results also indicate that high student ratings were negatively associated with achievement. Therefore, teachers should regularly monitor dispositions with the goal of promoting an appropriate balance between aspirations for positive regard and setting high standards.

Summary

In closing, this study set out to examine equity in opportunities to learn for high-achieving Black students, relative to all other high-achieving students. Based on findings, it is clear that enhancements to policies and practices related to advanced course placement procedures, student recruitment into advanced mathematics courses, and preparation of teachers to teach high-achieving students are necessary. It is the hope that this chapter provides a general overview of opportunities to learn for high-achieving Black students that will inform best practices and stimulate future research on this critical topic.

REFERENCES

Anderson, L., & Olsen, B. (2006). Investigating early career urban teachers' perspectives on and experiences in professional development. *Journal of Teacher Education, 57*(4), 359–377. doi:10.1177/0022487106291565

Barile, J., Donohue, D., Anthony, E., Baker, A., Weaver, S., & Henrich, C. (2012). Teacher-student relationship climate and school outcomes: Implications for educational policy initiatives. *Journal of Youth & Adolescence, 41*(3), 256–267. doi:10.1007/s10964-011-9652-8

Berman, K. M., Schultz, R. A., & Weber, C. L. (2012). A lack of awareness and emphasis in preservice teacher training: Preconceived beliefs about the gifted and talented. *Gifted Child Today, 35*(1), 18–26. doi:10.1177/1076217511428307

Boykin, A. W., & Noguera, P. (2011). *Creating the opportunity to learn: Moving from research to practice to close the achievement gap.* Alexandria, VA: ASCD.

Brayko, K. (2013). Community-based placements as contexts for disciplinary learning: A study of literacy teacher education outside of school. *Journal of Teacher Education, 64*(1), 47–59. doi:10.1177/0022487112458800

Britton, L. R., & Anderson, K. A. (2010, February). Peer coaching and pre-service teachers: Examining an underutilised concept. *Teaching and Teacher Education: An International Journal of Research and Studies, 26*(2), 306–314.

Cohen, J., McCabe, E., Michelli, N., & Pickeral, T. (2009). School climate: Research, policy, practice, and teacher education. *Teachers College Record, 111*(1), 180—213.

Dotterer, A., & Lowe, K. (2011). Classroom context, school engagement, and academic achievement in early adolescence. *Journal of Youth & Adolescence, 40*(12), 1649–1660. doi:10.1007/s10964-011-9647-5

Du Bois, W. E. B. (1935). Does the Negro need separate schools? The Courts and the Negro Separate School. *The Journal of Negro Education, 4*(3), 328–335.

Fan, W., Williams, C. M., & Corkin, D. M. (2011). A multilevel analysis of student perceptions of school climate: The effect of social and academic risk factors. *Psychology in the Schools, 48*(6), 632–647.

Ford, D. Y., Moore III, J. L., & Scott, M. T. (2011). Key theories and frameworks for improving the recruitment and retention of African American students in gifted education. Preparing teachers to teach Black students; Preparing Black students to become teachers. *The Journal of Negro Education, 80*(3), 239–253.

Goldhaber, D. D., Goldschmidt, P., & Tseng, F. (2013). Teacher value-added at the high-school level: Different models, different answers? *Educational Evaluation and Policy Analysis, 35*(2), 220–236. doi:10.3102/0162373712466938

Graham, A., & Anderson, K. (2008). "I have to be three steps ahead": Academically gifted African American male students in an urban high school on the tension between an ethnic and academic identity. *Urban Review, 40*(4), 472–499. doi:10.1007/s11256-008-0088-8

Hopson, L. M., & Lee, E. (2011). Mitigating the effect of family poverty on academic and behavioral outcomes: The role of school climate in middle and high school. *Children & Youth Services Review, 33*(11), 2221–2229. doi:10.1016/j.childyouth.2011.07.006

Ingels, S. J., Pratt, D. J., Herget, D. R., Burns, L. J., Dever, J. A., Ottem, R., Rogers, J. E., Jin, Y., & Leinwand, S. (2011). *High school longitudinal study of 2009 (HSLS:09). Base-year data file documentation (NCES 2011-328)*. U.S. Department of Education. Washington, DC: National Center for Education Statistics. Retrieved from http://nces.ed.gov/pubsearch

Kee, A. N. (2012). Feelings of preparedness among alternatively certified teachers: What is the role of program features? *Journal of Teacher Education, 63*(1), 23–38. doi:10.1177/0022487111421933

Kumar, R., & Hamer, L. (2013). Preservice teachers' attitudes and beliefs toward student diversity and proposed instructional practices: A sequential design study. *Journal of Teacher Education, 64*(2), 162–177. doi:10.1177/0022487112466899

Long, M. C., Conger, D., & Iatarola, P. (2012). Effects of high school course-taking on secondary and postsecondary success. *American Educational Research Journal, 49*(2), 285–322. doi:10.3102/0002831211431952

Natesan, P., & Kieftenbeld, V. (2013). Measuring urban teachers' beliefs about African American students: A psychometric analysis. *Journal of Psychoeducational Assessment, 31*(1), 3–15. doi:10.1177/0734282912448243

Pedro, J. D., Wolleat, P., Fennema, E., & Becker, A. D. (1981). Election of high school mathematics by females and males: Attributions and attitudes. *American Educational Research Journal, 18*(2), 207-218. doi:10.3102/00028312018002207

Polikoff, M. S. (2013). Teacher education, experience, and the practice of aligned instruction. *Journal of Teacher Education, 64*(3), 212–225. doi:10.1177/0022487112472908

Ross, S. M., McDonald, A. J., Alberg, M., & McSparrin-Gallagher, B. (2007). Achievement and climate outcomes for the knowledge is power program in an inner-city middle school. *Journal of Education for Students Placed at Risk (JESPAR), 12*(2), 137–165.

Shifrer, D., Callahan, R. M., & Muller, C. (2013). Equity or marginalization? The high school course-taking of students labeled with a learning disability. *American Educational Research Journal*, doi:10.3102/0002831213479439

Zullig, K. J., Koopman, T. M., Patton, J. M., & Ubbes, V. A. (2010). School climate: Historical review, instrument development, and school assessment. *Journal of Psychoeducational Assessment, 28*(2), 139–152.

APPENDIX A

Factor Loadings of Principal Components Analysis With Promax Rotation of Teacher Credentials and Beliefs

Scale	Teacher Beliefs	Teacher Content Preparation	Teacher Formal Education
Efficacy	0.65		
Expectations	0.68		
Years of 9–12 Experience			0.33
Number Math Courses Taken		0.61	
Certified in 9–12 Math		0.75	
Highest Degree From Education Department			0.57
Highest Degree			0.35
Did Not Enter Profession Through Alt. Certification			0.52
Certified			0.38

APPENDIX B

Factor Loadings of Principal Components Analysis With Promax Rotation of Instructional Strategies

Scale	Cognitive Engagement	Pragmatics	Grouping Strategies
Uses Small Groups			0.64
Group Assignment Practices			0.72
Problem Solving	0.37		
Reasoning	0.40		
Ideas	0.39		
Logic	0.35		
Explanations	0.33		
Computation Speed & Accuracy		0.58	
Interesting	0.31		
Computational Skills		0.58	
Test Preparation		0.47	

APPENDIX C
Factor Loadings of Principal Components With
Promax Rotation of Student Evaluations of Teachers

Scale	Student Evaluation of Teacher Dispositions	Student Evaluation of Teacher Treatment
Believes All Students Can Be Successful	0.36	
Mistakes Are Okay	0.36	
Treats Some Students Better Than Others		0.63
Makes Math Interesting	0.40	
Treats Males & Females Differently		0.73
Makes Mathematics Easy	0.39	
Treats Students With Respect	0.37	
Student Ideas Are Valued	0.40	
Treats Students Fairly	0.35	

CHAPTER 13

USING OBSERVATION PROMPTS IN THE URBAN ELEMENTARY SCHOOL FIELD PLACEMENT

Felicia Moore Mensah
Columbia University

INTRODUCTION

The composition of student populations in schools in the United States has become more and more diverse, with a projected minority student enrollment of 39% of the total school population by the year 2020 (KewalRamani, Gilbertson, Fox, & Provasnik, 2007), but the teacher workforce is predominantly White and female, despite modest gains in teacher diversity (National Center for Education Statistics, 2012). Hence, teachers have to recognize that schools and classrooms will be filled with students whose cultures, linguistic styles, ethnic, racial, and social class backgrounds will be different from their own. In addition, other diversities will also be present in classrooms, such as identity, sexual orientation, religious, and ability/disability. Unfortunately, many teachers find it difficult to be successful in teaching students who are different from them (Causey, Thomas, & Armento, 2000;

Teacher Education and Black Communities, pages 273–292
Copyright © 2014 by Information Age Publishing
All rights of reproduction in any form reserved.

Tatto, 1996), or to teach in urban schools that they perceive to be "urban, but not too urban" (Watson, 2011, p. 29), even though one of the major goals of teaching is "to foster the intellectual, social, and personal development of... [all] students to their highest potential" (Bennett, 1999, p. 2). Due to increasing diversity of students in public urban schools, and with emphasis on closing achievement and opportunity gaps for Black/African American and Latin(a) students, teacher educators have to prepare with greater success teachers to meet the needs of diverse students and schools (Lee, Eckrich, Lackey, & Showalter, 2010). In this chapter, I illustrate how the urban field placement is a prime place to learn about diversity and to prepare teachers for teaching. To facilitate preservice teachers' learning about student diversity, school culture, and science teaching in an urban field-based science methods course, the guided observation prompts serve as a tool for reflecting on and learning about diversity in two, predominantly Black/African American and Latin(a) public urban elementary schools in New York City.

DIVERSITY AND THE URBAN SCHOOL FIELD PLACEMENT

Foundational courses in teacher education and field placement experiences are viewed as primary places to prepare teachers for the practice of teaching (Ryan, 2006). Yet, there is an unspoken connection that needs to be made regarding urban field placement experiences—the connection to issues of student diversity and school culture when preparing teachers for teaching. For example, gaining practical experience f is confounded by preservice teachers' assumptions and biases about issues of diversity and teaching. In one study with elementary preservice teachers in a science methods course, Mensah (2009) found that the biases and assumptions preservice teachers held about diversity, teaching diverse learners, and teaching science came from their own cultural background and experiences, and many of the preservice teachers were unaware they held these views. Few of the preservice teachers had completed student teaching prior to enrollment in the science methods course, thus limiting their exposure of working within diverse school settings, working with students different from themselves, and not having the opportunity to teach science.

Furthermore, preservice teachers have their own ideas about what it means to teach and may hold strongly to these beliefs (Rodriguez, 1998; van Zee & Roberts, 2001). In fact, preservice teachers have had many years to build up notions of teaching from personal history (Lortie, 1975), and their ideas however may not represent the real work of what teaching and learning entails; consequently, they display negative images of science teaching (Mensah, 2011) or have deficit notions of the urban school context

(Roselle & Liner, 2012). In addition, preservice teachers may not have had opportunities to reflect on their views of what it means to teach students of diverse cultural and linguistic backgrounds (Johnson, 2002; Moore, 2008a; Picower, 2009).

Therefore, researchers offer several strategies and approaches in teacher education that reveal the beliefs preservice teachers have about teaching for diversity as attempts to mitigate factors that may hinder student learning. The literature actually speaks to early and frequent exposure in urban schools, community-based field experiences, and paired or coteaching models to promote preservice teachers' understanding of student diversity (Eick, Ware, & Williams, 2003; Gallego, 2001; Gardiner & Robinson, 2009). Others have redesigned teacher education courses and programs to support preservice teacher learning about teaching, diversity, and urban schools (Lee et al., 2010; Picower, 2009, Sleeter, 2001; Waddell, 2011). Still others have used writing or journaling within the field experience to promote learning about diversity.

JOURNALING IN THE URBAN FIELD PLACEMENT

Preservice teachers need opportunities to engage and reflect on student diversity and culture within classrooms (Mensah, 2009). One approach in preparing preservice teachers for diversity and to reflect on experiences while in the field placement is journaling or reflective writing. For example, Olmedo's (1997) research analyzed the journals and essays of White preservice teachers prior to and after fieldwork to determine if their views and beliefs would change after field assignments in urban school districts. Some initial beliefs that the preservice teachers had of students in urban schools were that urban students were unmotivated and deserved pity about their situations. Some preservice teachers felt it best to be colorblind, holding to the idea to treat all students the same. The views of the preservice teachers changed after their field experience. Those who initially felt that urban students were unmotivated found that students actually wanted to learn. The preservice teachers also learned that pitying students because of their social circumstances actually led to lowered expectations, and those who felt they had to be colorblind in order to be fair found that they were not differentiating instruction and not meeting the needs of their diverse students.

PURPOSE

There is an emergent body of research on the urban field placement and the preparation of teachers for these settings (Lee et al., 2010; Roselle & Liner,

2010; Sleeter, 2001). Still few studies pertaining to field experiences focus on student diversity, urban school culture, and science teaching. Therefore, considering previous research on the urban field placement, journaling, and the preparation of teachers for diverse settings, the purpose of this study is to describe how weekly guided observation prompts were used as an initial assignment in an elementary science methods course. The emphasis was on providing a rich, field-based experience, while focusing on issues of diversity in urban science teaching prior to formal student teaching internships through journaling. The research question for this study was: In what ways do guided observation prompts aid elementary preservice teachers in gaining a deeper understanding of student diversity, school culture, and science teaching in urban elementary schools?

METHOD

Setting and Participants

This study took place in a 16-week graduate level elementary science methods course at a large urban university in New York City (NYC). The science methods course, with a strong field-based component, was a required course for initial elementary teacher certification. There were nine female preservice teachers (PSTs) who participated in this study (Table 13.1; all names in the study are pseudonyms). These PSTs were diverse in terms of race/ethnicity and age; they were enrolled in the science methods course for one semester and had no prior student teaching experiences; they were seeking elementary school certification, and all nine wanted to teach in NYC public elementary schools. Information from initial surveys on demographic data and teaching experience was used to assign the PSTs to one of two local urban elementary school placements in East Harlem, NYC for the semester—Elementary School 1 (ES1) or Elementary School 2 (ES2).

From the Quality Review Report data from the Department of Education website, ES1 was a small K–5 school of approximately 150 students. Sixty percent of students were eligible for Title 1 funding; 57% of the student enrollment was Black/African American, 41% Latin(a), and 2% other races/ethnicities. Six percent of the student population was listed as English language learners and 26% was special education students. Overall, boys accounted for 55% of the student body and girls 45%. The school curriculum consisted of traditional subject areas of language arts, mathematics, and science, and additional "special" courses in art, swimming, and music. There was SMART Board technology in the science classroom that the school's science specialist, Ms. C, used occasionally for science instruction. The science specialist was the primary science teacher in the school for all grades.

TABLE 13.1 Preservice Teacher Profiles

Preservice Teacher	Race-Ethnicity,[a] Age (years)[a]	Previous Student Teaching (Y/N)	Previous Teaching/ Science Teaching Experiences	Plan to teach in NYC (Y/N)	School/Grade Placement
Ana	Caucasian, 23	N	Substitute teaching; assist teacher/ summer science camp teacher	Y	ES1, 1st
Lorraine	Caucasian, 21	N	None	Y	ES1, 1st
Tabitha	Jewish, 22	N	N	Y	ES1, 2nd
Kristi	Caucasian, 23	N	N	Y	ES1, 4th CTT[b]
Nora	White/Jewish, 22	N	Two summers teaching 5–6th graders in summer program	Y	ES1, 4th
Janine	African American-French, 21	N	N	Y	ES1, 5th
Rachel	Caucasian, 26	N	N	Y	ES2, 4th
Hope	Asian Indian, 27	N	Afterschool science program for elementary students; nutrition to 4–5th graders	Y	ES2, 4th CTT[b]
Valarie	Pakistani, 24	N	2 years in afterschool program for 4–6th graders	Y	ES2, 4th CTT[b]

[a] Self-identified from initial course survey; [b] CTT (Collaborative Team Teaching) classroom = Two teachers in the classroom with at least one of the teachers Special Education certified

Information from the Quality Review Report described ES2 as a PreK–6 school with a student population of 877 students. It was 94% eligible for Title 1 funding. ES2 was a racially and culturally diverse school, with 84% Latin(a), 15% Black/African American, 1% White, 1% Asian or Pacific Islander, and 0.25% American Indian. The student body included 44% English language learners and 4% special education students. Overall, boys accounted for 51% of the school population and girls 49%. The school curriculum consisted of traditional subjects, with an expanded two-period literacy curriculum, and extracurricular courses in physical education, food and nutrition, and chess. ES2 also has SMART Board technology in certain classrooms, which was acquired from one of the teachers who entered a competition and won this technology for the school. The science teacher, Ms. G, used the SMART Board in her classroom on rare occasions.

Procedure and Data Sources

Six PSTs were assigned to ES1 and three PSTs were assigned to ES2 for the semester. They spent at least two hours per week (approximately 28–32 hours for the semester) in their school placements. As a course requirement, the PSTs were given weekly guided observation prompts (Table 13.2) to introduce them to their school and students. The first five visits for the guided observation prompts focused on the school context and school culture, student diversity (i.e., selection of a case study student and whole class student diversity), science instruction, and science communication. The PSTs were encouraged to observe both the general classroom teacher and the science specialist. They could observe the general classroom teacher for the first hour and then accompany the class to science for the second hour, or start in the science classroom with the science specialist for the first hour and accompany the students back to the general classroom for the second hour. During their time in the school, which was not limited to simply observing, they were viewed as another teacher in the classroom. They interacted with the teachers and students on each visit, assisting in small and large group activities, and they also conducted brief interviews with students to plan a microteaching assignment (Gunning & Mensah, 2010). The microteaching assignment consisted of planning, teaching, and assessing a two-day science lesson in the science and/or general classroom taught later in the semester. The observation prompts served as contextual knowledge about the school and students in order to plan for microteaching. In addition, the PSTs interviewed the science specialist about her experiences and background in teaching science. For the final entry of the guided observation prompts (Week 6 Reflection), the PSTs were

TABLE 13.2 Weekly Observation Prompts

Observation Focus	Observation Prompts
Week 1: Context	What is the context of the school: student body make-up, grades, general classroom demographics, the school environment, classroom setting, school morale, physical environment, social environment of the school and classroom you are observing, etc.?
Week 2: Student Diversity	Who is a student least/most like me? Observe and work with this one student for the next month (case study student). How do I teach science for this student, and other students of linguistic, cultural, academic, and social diversity? Consider this student for your preassessment. What is the science curriculum in the classroom?
Week 3: Science Instruction	Is science being taught? How is science being taught? How are students learning and understanding science? How does my case study student learn science and understand science? What teaching strategies is the teacher using? Do students really understand science? What are students learning in other areas that can be used for making science more relevant and easier to understand?
Week 4: Student Diversities	How different are the students I am observing and will teach? Observe or work with a small group, along with your case study student. How can we assess what students know and understand in science? What kinds of assessment practices are being used in their science classroom?
Week 5: Science Communication	How well do students talk about science in the classroom? How well do students make connections between personal talk and language and the language of science? Record some specific examples of what students say in the science classroom where they are communicating their science understanding. How can you help your case study student talk about science in ways that build his/her understanding of science?
Week 6: Reflection	Re-read your journal entries. What did I learn about elementary science from observing and working with my case study student and other students in this classroom? What did I learn from the classroom teacher? What factors seem to be important in teaching and learning science? How will this field experience aid me in planning for my microteaching?

asked to reread their journal entries and provide summary paragraphs of what they learned from their observations in the school.

Collected at midsemester, the observation prompts served as the primary data source for this study. Additional sources from the course, such as written papers, lesson plans, informal conversations, and semistructured interviews (done at the termination of the semester), allowed for additional conceptual insight into the use of the guided observation prompts as a useful reflective tool in urban teacher education. As the instructor and researcher for this study, I also maintained a written journal where I recorded weekly notes from classroom discussions and observations, informal conversations with the PSTs, and teaching observations of the microteaching lessons done by the PSTs in their placements.

Data Analysis

For this study, the nine PSTs' six-week guided observation journals were collected and compiled into one case record document for analysis. The journals were coded using constructivist grounded theory (Charmaz, 2006). According to constructivist grounded theory, "both data and analyses are social constructions" (p. 31), such that "any analysis is contextually situated in time, place, culture, and situation" (p. 131). Hence, the data analysis was an "interpretive inquiry" in that "researchers make an interpretation of what they see, hear, and understand" from the data and the process of data analysis (Creswell, 2007, p. 39). By going systematically through the data and "actively naming data" (p. 47), defining what was significant in the data, and describing what was happening in the data, I went through a process of initial coding in order to understand the relevancy of the guided observation prompts on the PSTs' views of student diversity, urban schools, and science teaching. Initial coding was followed by focused coding, where I stayed close to the data (Charmaz, 2006) in order to produce codes and categories, consolidate the codes, and formulate theoretical interpretations of the data. I began this process by coding individual journal entries for each PST to capture individual learning. Throughout the process of analysis, I typed "memos" in the electronic files, using "gerunds" and other phrases to name and interpret the data (Charmaz, 2006). I moved from one journal entry to the next, identifying categories for comparative analysis across all journal entries from the nine PSTs (Charmaz, 2006; Strauss & Corbin, 1998). Within this process of grounded theory as a comparative method, "the researcher compares data with data, data with categories, and category with category," which I did for individual and group entries (Charmaz, 2005, p. 517). I also used the focus and content of the guided observation prompts to aid coding, such as "context," "school culture," "student diversity," "science instruction," and "science communication." Finally, I was able to collapse and finalize the major themes from the analysis process and gained insight into the usefulness of the guided observation prompts for urban teacher education.

Elements of rigor or trustworthiness of the themes as findings of the study were accomplished from using multiple levels of data interpretation as well as multiple data sources and theoretical lenses (Guba & Lincoln, 1989; Mensah, 2009). Adding to the trustworthiness of the study, the data analysis was systematic and grounded in the experiences of the PSTs' written journals, observations in the field, and conversations with the PSTs about their learning to become urban elementary teachers. I also used my knowledge of the school placements, which have been partnership schools for many years. Thus, I was very familiar with the teachers, students, and context at the two school sites.

FINDINGS

The six-week guided observation prompts were a valuable learning tool in introducing the nine PSTs to the urban school context and culture, student diversity, and science teaching. Three central themes from the study were *finding comfort in the urban school context, attending to academic and social needs of urban school students,* and *witnessing science as the marginal subject area in the urban school curriculum.* Each highlighted awareness and thoughts about urban schools as they worked with students of varying racial, ethnic, and linguistic backgrounds.

Finding Comfort in the Urban School Context

Being placed in an urban elementary school can be a frightening experience for PSTs who have not entered or spent time here in their past. The public images that circulate about urban schools in many cases cause trepidation for some PTSs new to urban settings (Mensah, 2009; Watson, 2011). The nine PSTs in this current study revealed some initial fears and biases about their images of the "inner city" school culture, students, and community. For example, Tabitha was imaging urban school children from notions of bad behavior or poor classroom management issues. She shared the following:

> I have lead a rather sheltered life myself and have heard all the horror stories about trying to teach in inner city schools, and so I am somewhat ashamed to admit that when I observed these "inner city kids" playing with parachutes during a science lesson just like any other kid I've met, I felt a sense of relief. These children aren't inherently different or worse behaved than any other children just because they are from the city. (Tabitha, Week #1; ES1, 2nd grade)

Similarly, some PSTs wrote about their initial preconceptions about urban schools in their journals and also discussed these ideas throughout the semester. They observed that their school placements were welcoming and nurturing, and many of them described their urban school as "comfortable" places not only for the students but also for them. Rachel liked the "positive, upbeat feel" of ES2, and she also noted how the security guard at the entrance of the school seemed to know each individual child. She commented about the student work displayed in the halls as a sign of care for student learning.

On Janine's first visit to her school placement, she talked about the sense of "community" and "family" she felt at ES1. She stated the classroom teacher she observed addressed the students as "scholars, please direct your attention up front" and "no matter what subject she discussed she would be sure to add 'scholars' to the end, like 'math scholars' and 'reading scholars.'" Janine also added:

> My overall feeling for the school is that it is a small well-known community inside. All the teachers know all the students, because at some point the students were their previous students. The kids stick up for each other and they all respect each other. They play in a friendly way, almost like family. They know each person's dislikes and each is willing to speak for each other when given the chance. I think I will have no problem getting to know the kids; they seem very accepting. (Janine, Week #1, ES1, 5th grade)

Making connections to community and family and reflecting on their time in the field, the PSTs revealed how their thinking about urban communities and urban students changed over the six weeks and the semester. For Tabitha, it was not believing what she had "heard" about urban schools, but grounding views and perspectives from personal observations and experiences at ES1. The PSTs commented that their urban school placement, for example ES1, was a "comfortable" space, while others mentioned the "almost like family" feeling and being accepted as a teacher in the school by the students, the cooperating teachers, and the staff. The school culture and student diversity played an important role in what and how the PSTs viewed their time in their school placements and shaped a better image of the urban school context, which was inclusive of caring schools, playful students, and family-like communities where you are respected and known. Their initial introduction to the urban school community through the guided observations helped to dispel negative preconceptions and deficit notions about "inner-city kids" and urban schools.

Attending to Academic and Social Needs of Urban School Students

Though all of the guided observation prompts had a focus on students in the urban elementary classroom, observation prompts for Week 2 and Week

5 were particularly focused on student diversity. Hope stated, "there were vast differences between students that cannot be overlooked" (Hope, Week #5, ES2, 4th grade). The PSTs selected a case study student to interview him/her about science and to use this information to plan for microteaching. They were asked to work with the case study student (individual diversity) and a small group of students (group diversity). For selecting a case study student, the PSTs had to select someone "least or most like" them. Even though most of the PSTs commented that the students they were observing were not like them in terms of ethnicity or race, being that the two schools were predominantly Black/African American and Latin(a), they still were able to connect with one student in the selection of a case study student. For example, Nora wrote that "in terms of racial and cultural diversity, pretty much none of the students are like me." Therefore, she gave more consideration to "students' personalities" and was able connect with one student:

> I watched a girl named A. She seemed to be very excited about school and paid fairly close attention to the teachers, despite the fact that most of the students were talking when they were supposed to be listening or working quietly. Even though A appeared to be slightly more outgoing and participatory in class than I was at her age, I still felt the strongest connection to her out of all the students. (Nora, Week #2, ES1, 4th grade)

Recall that the school placements were diverse in a number of ways, especially in terms of socioeconomic status, learning needs, cultural, and linguistic diversity. Both were classified as Title 1 schools, and both schools over recent years had increasing enrollments of Spanish-speaking students, where Spanish was the first language. The PSTs reflected on the bilingual students and their particular needs in science and in the general classroom. Ana spoke with Ms. C the science teacher at ES1 about the student demographics:

> Ms. C told me that almost half of her kindergarten science class speaks only Spanish, and that overall many of the students are bilingual. In fact, she wanted to know if I spoke Spanish. (Ana, Week #1, ES1, 1st grade)

The first grade class that Ana was assigned to had many students who spoke Spanish as their primary language. Ana described her interactions with an English language learner (ELL) student named O, who was also her case study student. When O got excited about learning, she would speak in Spanish rather than English. Ana reminded the student, "I don't speak Spanish." Ana commented:

> As a preservice teacher who plans to teach in the NYC public school system, I wonder if I should be taking Spanish language classes. While it's not a require-

ment that I speak Spanish, I think it would better prepare me for communicating with students. (Ana, Week #2, ES1, 1st grade)

D was a fourth grade student at ES1 who caught Kristi's attention in the classroom because "he was so excited to share in the class during group share time" (Kristi, Week #2, ES1, 4th grade). Kristi noted that D had difficulty with reading and spelling and later realized that English was D's second language. From interacting with D and the other students in the classroom, Kristi believed that it was "absolutely necessary that they [the students] be exposed to scientific language as much as possible and yet most of this happens through the worksheets, which many of them pay very little attention to" (Kristi, Week #6, ES1, 4th grade). Kristi thought that in the science classroom more time should be devoted to whole group discussions where bilingual students can develop "the language of science" (Kristi, Week #6, ES1, 4th grade). She also commented about her urban school classroom being "understaffed" in supporting students like D:

> With two teachers and 25 kids, it is impossible for each child to get the direct attention they need. Many of the students are bright and inquisitive, but with many of them being English language learners or Special Education students, they require a lot of support. Unfortunately, between these special needs and the behavioral problems within the classroom, the teachers are not only understaffed for the responsibilities they have, but they often spend a good part of the day disciplining and attempting to control the students. (Kristi, Week #1, ES1, 4th grade)

All of the PSTs reflected on student diversity in their urban school placements and gave attention to the selection of a case study student—someone they could connect with and build a relationship with over the semester. Both schools were experiencing increasing numbers of English language learners, and the PSTs noted the importance of having academic and social support in the classroom especially for students of linguistic diversity and even for their teachers. The PSTs mentioned science teaching and learning with students of diverse backgrounds and discussed how science was positioned in their field placements.

Witnessing Science as the Marginal Subject Area in the Urban School Curriculum

A third theme was highlighted from the PSTs' journals. They witnessed science as a marginal subject in the overall urban elementary school curriculum (see Mensah, 2010; Spillane, Diamond, Walker, Halverson, & Jita, 2001; Tate, 2001). Within the course, we discussed the low status of science not only in ethnically/racially diverse urban schools but more widely in elementary schools; therefore, their observations confirmed this. For instance, Ana talked about the lack of science for the first graders at ES1:

> Science is given much less time than English, math, and social studies. It is often greeted with enthusiasm as a break in routine. However, the little amount of time allotted to science becomes problematic when students are unable to make connections between lessons from weeks before. I believe if the class had science more often, it could lead to better retention and understanding. (Ana, Week #6, ES1, 1st grade)

Rachel shared similar sentiments about the limited amount of time students spent in science at ES2:

> The students are supposed to have three or four science periods a week; at least one in Ms. G's class, possibly two. However, the science class is often cancelled if school is closed, or there are other school activities such as assemblies and school pictures booked for the same time. (Rachel, Week #1, ES2, 4th grade)

Rachel also expressed how science was "eliminated" from the school schedule, which also made it difficult for students to retain what they were learning in science class, a similar comment made by Ana at ES1. Ms. G, the science teacher at ES2, mentioned that "retaining information is one of the most challenging problems" she has with her students and attributed this retention problem as a consequence of "teaching science only once a week, if that. When another event is scheduled, science can be one of the first subjects to be eliminated from the schedule" (Rachel, Week #1, ES2, 4th grade). Rachel added that "Ms. G feels science is extremely important for a student's education. She thinks it is disheartening that science is being limited and removed from schools" (Rachel, Week #1, ES2, 4th grade).

The same way that science held a marginal status in urban elementary schools, students with particular needs were marginalized from learning science as well. Science learning was not a priority for them because "many of the special education students rarely attend science class and instead go to what they call "'therapy'—missing out almost entirely on their science education" (Kristi, Week #4, ES1, 4th grade). Kristi, who was placed in a Collaborative Team Teaching (CTT) classroom at ES1, also shared the following in her summary reflections about the marginalization of science as a "disposable subject" compared to other subject areas:

> The students at ES1 are clearly being shown by example that Science is a distant second to Math and Reading in their education.... The kids simply do not have the time to get a quality science education in their current curriculum. Sometimes students have music lessons in place of their science class. It

is treated as a disposable subject, alongside art and music, to be addressed if there is the time. (Kristi, Week #6, ES1, 4th grade)

The PSTs witnessed science as a low priority, "distant second" subject and reflected on the implications of no science in urban elementary classrooms. For example, Kristi shared: "Teachers must be aware of the importance of science education for all students and treat it as equal to the subjects of Reading and Math" (Kristi, Week #6, ES1, 4th grade). The elementary schools that the PTSs observed did not have science as a major part of the urban school curriculum. They commented that not all students were receiving science instruction, noting bilingual and special education students as most marginalized in learning science.

From the observation prompts, the nine PSTs reflected on many aspects of urban schools, such as the school context and culture. They were able to think more deeply about student diversity, such as their case study student's academic, linguistic, and social needs. They discussed the marginalization of science in their school placements, and were "given excellent insight into elementary science teaching" from their time in schools (Ana, Week #6). Overall, the guided observation prompts allowed the PSTs to gain valuable, experiential knowledge about urban school culture, student diversity, and science teaching.

DISCUSSION AND IMPLICATIONS

A key goal in teacher education is to provide meaningful opportunities for PSTs to gain professional knowledge and teaching experience prior to becoming full-time classroom teachers. Where, when, and how PSTs are provided with these experiences and what they get during these experiences imply challenges in teacher education regarding field placements. There are also challenges in finding opportunities for preservice teachers to work within diverse, urban schools with populations of students they most likely will teach. Being aware of the realities of urban schools—their context, culture, students, and curriculum—means acknowledging the range of diversity issues found there and providing learning experiences that enliven a broader knowledge of urban schools and the many roles teachers play in these settings. Findings from this current study speak to teacher education in three important ways and connect to previous work on urban field placements and the preparation of PSTs for diverse learners.

First, the six-week guided observation prompts generate both practical and theoretical insights into PSTs' learning about urban schools. The guided observation prompts serve as a reflective tool that elicits initial ideas about urban schools, communities, students, and teaching.

Similar to findings in other studies, early exposure and journaling for PSTs help alleviate fears, address misconceptions and stereotypes of urban schools, and provide a context for on-going discussions in the preparation of teachers for diverse students (Garmon, 2001; Hiemstra, 2001; Lowe, Prout, & Murcia, 2013). The PSTs in this study change their initial views and generate their own perspectives and relationships with the predominantly Black/African American and Latin(a) students in their school placements. They invalidate negative images and stereotypes about "inner-city" kids and schools, which are based upon second-hand reports of what others "heard" and not on their first-hand experiences from what they see. Revealing assumptions, biases, and stereotypes are necessary goals for teacher education practices; otherwise, PSTs may perpetuate practices and maintain misconceptions that marginalize students, while also hindering their professional growth and learning as teachers (Mensah, 2009).

The PSTs' observations also disclose some of the realities, constraints, and possibilities of teaching in urban schools and working with Black/African American and Latin(a) children of varying educational needs. The ability to view urban schools, which are increasingly being populated with Black/African American and Latin(a) students, as rich environments for teaching and learning, become places to advocate for social justice (Moore, 2008b), and sites for holding high academic standards of excellence for all students (Brown, Benkovitz, Muttillo, & Urban, 2011). Both advocacy and excellence should be discussed in teacher education programs as topics in urban school teaching.

Second, the findings of this study also build upon and extend the work of Eisenhardt, Besnoy, and Steele (2011–2012) in their framework of assignments requiring their PSTs to collect data about two diverse elementary students during a twelve-week placement. The PSTs experience cognitive dissonance as some of their preconceived notions about students and teaching conflicted with their field study experiences. What this current study connects and extends to that work and of other researchers is the opportunity for PSTs to critically reflect on their personal experiences within urban field placements that give explicit attention to understanding context, culture, and content through purposefully crafted observation prompts. The prompts allow the PSTs to enter urban schools with focused intent on learning about their placements. For example, being present to make observations and connections directly, the PSTs build relationships with Black/African American and Latin(a) students, learn about pedagogical, social, and institutional issues in urban schools, and interact closely with classroom teachers in learning about their roles as urban teachers. But, to have this access to urban schools, schools of education and even content methods course instructors have to foster relationships with urban schools through school-university partnerships that foster mutually beneficial relationships for preservice and inservice teacher development (see Mensah, 2010).

Finally, as a science teacher educator, I am not only concerned with where, when, how and what kinds of experiences PSTs get in their preparation as urban school teachers but I am also concerned with preparing urban science teachers who have the skills and knowledge and desire to work within ethnically, racially, and linguistically diverse schools, many of which are populated with Black/African American and Latin(a) students. Researchers stress the importance of science education for all students, particularly students most marginalized from participating in science (Lynch, 2001; Mensah, 2010; Rivera Maulucci, 2010). In the science methods course many issues regarding teacher preparation and student learning serve as major discussion points in the development of culturally responsive science teachers. The reflective comments from the guided observation prompts offer an approach for the preparation of culturally responsive science teachers, who have an "affirming attitude toward students from culturally diverse backgrounds" (Villegas & Lucas, 2002, p. 24) and are able to see the marginalization of science instruction for diverse students (Tate, 2001). However, in order to reach this level of awareness, PSTs must first reveal and confront their biases and assumptions about teaching for diversity, as well as question their assumptions about who can do science (Mensah, 2009; Moore, 2008a).

Researchers offer many approaches in teacher education to prepare teachers for urban school placements, hoping to develop teachers who are equipped to work with students from diverse cultural backgrounds and experiences (Picower, 2009, Sleeter, 2001). The guided observation prompts bring out issues pertinent to teaching Black/African American and Latin(a) children. These are children from diverse cultural, linguistic, and social backgrounds, with many having language and learning concerns. These issues need to be discussed early and throughout teacher education and continue through professional development. This can occur by offering PSTs multiple and varied occasions to visit urban schools, work with diverse student populations here, and to teach within these settings. This study suggests that this occur prior to full-time student teaching internships where PSTs are introduced to urban school issues earlier in their preparation as teachers and also within content methods courses. Rushton (2003) notes that PSTs have to overcome "culture shock" as student teachers during their internships in inner city schools. Journal entries from the current study allude to the idea that culture shock may be diminished if PSTs are given opportunities early in their preparation to observe, write, reflect, and discuss issues relevant to urban school teaching, particularly in cases with high numbers of Black/African American and Latin(a) students in urban school placements. PSTs need real time in urban schools; in fact, these are settings they have not previously had opportunity to observe and teach but are places they most likely will be as teachers.

CONCLUSION

The PSTs in this study—who are ethnically and racially diverse as well—develop personal relationships within their urban school placements, enabling them to dispel preconceived notions of urban schools and students; they give particular attention to the academic and social needs of urban school students; and regarding the teaching of science, they witness science as a subject area not given much priority in the urban elementary school curriculum. The current study addresses the preparation of PSTs for urban school teaching, with a focus on learning about student diversity and science teaching, prior to student teaching. The experiences provided for the PSTs occur within a field-based content methods course and relate the importance of having early experiences to think about urban school teaching in a purposeful, guided way. Overall, the guided observation prompts provide the content for conversations about teacher education and the preparation of PSTs for urban school teaching. The guided observation prompts offer focused attention on the urban school context, culture, and content prior to formal student teaching internships.

Researchers note that in typical field placements and internship experiences, PSTs focus on routine tasks, procedural concerns of time management, lesson planning, and classroom management (Moore, 2003; Zeichner & Tabachnick, 1981). This leaves PSTs little time to focus on fundamental issues of student and school diversity during their field placements. Therefore, the guided observation prompts serve as a useful tool in the preparation of culturally responsive teachers (Villegas & Lucas, 2002). If we want to act responsibly to the growing diversity of our schools, we must address how teachers view Black/African American and Latin(a) students and develop approaches in teacher education that allow them to view urban schools, students, and communities in affirming ways. We need methods that support PSTs' development as urban school teachers; they are entering urban school, which are increasingly becoming more diverse. Within these settings, we want teachers who view urban schools as comfortable and welcoming communities for teaching and learning. Further, these schools need dedicated teachers to advocate for academic excellence for all students and in all content areas of the urban school curriculum.

REFERENCES

Bennett, C. I. (1999). *Comprehensive multicultural education: Theory and practice.* Needham Heights, MA: Allyn & Bacon.

Brown, K. M., Benkovitz, J., Muttillo, A. J., & Urban, T. (2011). Leading schools of excellence and equity: Documenting effective strategies in closing achievement gaps. *Teachers College Record, 113*(1), 57–96.

Causey, V. E., Thomas, C. D., & J Armento, B. (2000). Cultural diversity is basically a foreign term to me: The challenges of diversity for preservice teacher education. *Teaching and Teacher Education, 16*(1), 33–45.

Charmaz, K. (2005). Grounded theory in the 21st century: Applications for advancing social justice studies. In N. K. Denzin & Y. S. Lincoln (Ed.), *The sage handbook of qualitative research* (3rd ed., pp. 507–533). Thousand Oaks, CA: Sage Publications.

Charmaz, K. (2006). *Constructing grounded theory: A practical guide through qualitative analysis.* London: Sage Publications Ltd.

Creswell, J. W. (2007). *Qualitative inquiry and research design: Choosing among five approaches* (2nd ed.). Thousand Oaks: Sage Publications, Inc.

Eick, C. J., Ware, F. N., & Williams, P. G. (2003). Coteaching in a science methods course: A situated learning model of becoming a teacher. *Journal of Teacher Education, 54*(1), 74–85.

Eisenhardt, S., Besnoy, K., & Steele, E. (2011–2012). Creating dissonance in preservice teachers' field experiences. *SRATE Journal, 21*(1), 1–10.

Gallego, M. A. (2001). Is experience the best teacher? The potential of coupling classroom and community-based field experiences. *Journal of Teacher Education, 52*(4), 312–325.

Gardiner, W., & Robinson, K. S. (2009). Paired field placements: A means for collaboration. *The New Educator, 5*(1), 81–94.

Garmon, M. A. (2001). The benefits of dialogue journals: What prospective teachers say. *Teacher Education Quarterly, 28*(4), 37–50.

Guba, E. G., & Lincoln, Y. S. (1989). *Fourth generation evaluation.* Newbury Park, CA: Sage.

Gunning, A. M., & Mensah, F. M. (2010). One pre-service elementary teacher's development of self-efficacy and confidence to teach science: A case study. *Journal of Science Teacher Education, 22*(2), 171–185.

Hiemstra, R. (2001). Uses and benefits of journal writing. *New Directions for Adult and Continuing Education, 90,* 19–26.

Johnson, L. (2002). "My eyes have been opened." White teachers and racial awareness. *Journal of Teacher Education, 53*(2), 153–167.

KewalRamani, A., Gilbertson, L., Fox, M. A., & Provasnik, S. (2007). Status and trends in the education of racial and ethnic minorities. Retrieved from Education Statistics Services Institute–American Institutes for Research, National Center for Education Statistics http://nces.ed.gov/pubs2007/minority-trends/index.asp

Lee, R. E., Eckrich, L. L., Lackey, C., & Showalter, B. D. (2010). Pre-service teacher pathways to urban teaching: A partnership model for nurturing community-based urban teacher preparation. *Teacher Education Quarterly, 37*(3), 101–122.

Lortie, D. C. (1975). *Schoolteacher: A sociological study.* Chicago, IL: University of Chicago Press.

Lowe, G. M., Prout, P., & Murcia, K. (2013). I see, I think I wonder: An evaluation of journaling as a critical reflective practice tool for aiding teachers in challenging or confronting contexts. *Australian Journal of Teacher Education, 38*(6), 1–16.

Lynch, S. (2001). "Science for all" is not equal to "one size fits all": Linguistic and cultural diversity and science education reform. *Journal of Research in Science Teaching, 38*(5), 622–627.

Mensah, F. M. (2011). The DESTIN: Preservice teachers' drawings of the ideal elementary science teacher. *School Science and Mathematics, 111*(8), 379–388.

Mensah, F. M. (2010). Toward the mark of empowering policies in elementary school science programs and teacher professional development. *Cultural Studies of Science Education, 5*(4), 977–983.

Mensah, F. M. (2009). Confronting assumptions, biases, and stereotypes in preservice teachers' conceptualizations of science teaching and diversity through the use of book club. *Journal of Research in Science Teaching, 46*(9), 1041–1066.

Moore, F. M. (2008a). Preparing preservice teachers for urban elementary science classrooms: Challenging cultural biases toward diverse students. *Journal of Science Teacher Education, 19*(1), 85–109.

Moore, F. M. (2008b). Agency, identity, and social justice: Preservice teachers' thoughts on becoming agents of change in urban elementary science classrooms. *Research in Science Education, 38*(5), 589–610.

Moore, R. (2003). Reexamining the field experiences of preservice teachers. *Journal of Teacher Education, 54*(1), 31–42.

National Center for Education Statistics. (2012). *Digest of Education Statistics, 2011* (NCES 2012–001), Introduction and Chapter 2; U.S. Department of Education, National Center for Education Statistics, Schools and Staffing Survey, Teacher Data Files, 2007–2008.

Olmedo, I. M. (1997. Challenging old assumptions: Preparing teachers for inner city schools. *Teaching and Teacher Education, 13*(3), 245–258.

Picower, B. (2009). The unexamined whiteness of teaching: How White teachers maintain and enact dominant racial ideologies. *Race Ethnicity and Education,12*(2), 197–215.

Rivera Maulucci, M. S. (2010). Resisting the marginalization of science in an urban school: Coactivating social, cultural, material, and strategic resources. *Journal of Research in Science Teaching, 47*(7), 840–860.

Rodriguez, A. J. (1998). Strategies for counter resistance: Toward a sociotransformative constructivism and learning to teach science for diversity and for understanding. *Journal of Research in Science Teaching, 35*(5), 589–622.

Roselle, R., & Liner, K. (2012). Pre-service teacher vision and urban schools. *Journal of Urban Learning, Teaching, and Research, 8*, 45–52.

Rushton, S. P. (2003). Two preservice teachers' growth in self-efficacy while teaching in an inner-city school. *The Urban Review, 35*(3), 167–189.

Ryan, A. M. (2006). The role of social foundations in preparing teachers for culturally relevant practice. *Multicultural Education, 13*(3), 10–13.

Sleeter, C. E. (2001). Preparing teachers for culturally diverse schools research and the overwhelming presence of whiteness. *Journal of teacher education, 52*(2), 94–106.

Spillane, J. P., Diamond, J. B., Walker, L. J., Halverson, R., & Jita, L. (2001). Urban school leadership for elementary science instruction: Identifying and activating resources in an undervalued school subject. *Journal of Research in Science Teaching, 38*(8), 918–940.

Tate, W. (2001). Science education as a civil right: Urban schools and opportunity-to-learn considerations. *Journal of Research in Science Teaching, 38*(9), 1015–1028.

Tatto, M. T. (1996). Examining values and beliefs about teaching diverse students: Understanding the challenges for teacher education. *Educational Evaluation and Policy Analysis, 18*(2), 155–180.

van Zee, E. H., & Roberts, D. (2001). Using pedagogical inquiries as a basis for learning to teach: Prospective teachers' reflections upon positive science learning experiences. *Science Education, 85*(6), 733–757.

Villegas, A. M., & Lucas, T. (2002). Preparing culturally responsive teachers: Re-thinking the curriculum. *Journal of Teacher Education, 53*(1), 20–32.

Waddell, J. (2011). Crossing borders without leaving town: The impact of cultural immersion. *Issues in Teacher Education, 20*(2), 23–36.

Watson, D. (2011). "Urban, but not too urban": Unpacking teachers' desires to teach urban students. *Journal of Teacher Education, 62*(1) 23–34.

Zeichner, K., & Tabachnick, B. R. (1981). Are the effects of university teacher education washed out by school experiences? *Journal of Teacher Education, 32*(3), 7–11.

CHAPTER 14

COLLATERAL DAMAGE IN THE CLASSROOM

How Race and School Environment Influence Teachers' Attitudes and Behaviors Toward Their Students

Ivory A. Toldson
Mercedes E. Ebanks
Howard University

This study examined how school safety and fairness directly influences teachers' classroom attitudes and behaviors and indirectly shapes student outcomes. Researchers used critical race theory and humanism as heuristic frameworks to conceptualize the process by which children of diverse backgrounds learn and develop in the classroom and how teachers experience the school environment. The study participants included all Black, Latino, and White students who completed the National Crime Victimization Survey: School Crime Supplement of 2009 (NCVS-SCS). Students of all races, who perceived their teachers as more caring, respectful, and empathetic, and less punitive, generally reported higher grades. Black

Teacher Education and Black Communities, pages 293–315
Copyright © 2014 by Information Age Publishing

students were less likely than White students to perceive empathy and respect from their teachers, even when they were making good grades. Similarly, Black students perceived their teachers to be significantly more punitive. Implications included suggestions for developing effective teacher education programs.

Racial disparities in discipline, grade retention, placement in special education, and assignment to honors classes suggest that Black students' in the United States have a very tenuous presence within the school system. According to an independent analysis of the National Center for Education Statistics High School Longitudinal Study of 2009 (Ingels et al., 2011), 17.9% of Black males and 13.7% of Black females have repeated a grade, compared to 8.1% for White males and 5.6% for White females. Twenty-five percent of Black males and 14.5% of Black females have been suspended or expelled from a school, when the national average is 9.8%. Twenty-nine percent of the parents of Black students reported receiving a call from the school regarding problem behavior with their son or daughter, compared to 14% of the parents of White students.

The extent to which racial biases in schools and classrooms contribute to racial disparities in academic success is a subject of debate. Today, of the more than 6 million teachers in the United States, nearly 80% are White, 9.6% are Black, 7.4% are Hispanic, 2.3% are Asian, and 1.2% is another race (Toldson, 2011b). Eighty percent of all teachers are female. Relative to the composition of P–12 students in the United States, the current teaching force lacks racial and gender diversity. Black men represent less than 2% of the teaching force, of a student body that is 7% Black male. By comparison, White female teachers comprise 63% of the teaching force, of a student body that is 27% White female (Toldson, 2011b). Some school advocates suspect that teachers who lack cultural proficiency may relate to Black and Hispanic students in a manner that undermines their potential. This study specifically examines how race and school environment influence teachers' attitudes and behaviors toward their students.

LITERATURE REVIEW

Race, School Environment and Student Discipline

Elevated public awareness and perceptions of violence have increased schools' reliance on suspensions, zero tolerance and other exclusionary disciplinary policies (Christle, Nelson, & Jolivette, 2004; Skiba & Peterson, 1999). One study found that Black students with a history of disciplinary referrals were more likely to receive negative perceptions and less deference from teachers (Gregory & Thompson, 2010). There are also general concerns about the reliability and subjectivity in disciplinary referrals (Vavrus & Cole, 2002; Wright & Dusek, 1998). Through ethnographic research, Vavrus and Cole (2002) found that many suspensions resulted from a buildup of nonviolent events, where one student often carries the brunt of many students' misbehaviors. However, some studies suggest that school culture and administrative leaders can mitigate high suspension rates (Mukuria, 2002). For example, regular monitoring and analysis of narrative disciplinary referrals have been recommended to improve precision and application of disciplinary measures that are consistent with the students' infractions (Morrison, Peterson, O'Farrell, & Redding, 2004; Sugai, Sprague, Horner, & Walker, 2000).

With respect to disproportionate suspension rates among Black students, many studies have noted the influence of ecological variables beyond the school (Day-Vines & Day-Hairston, 2005). Eitle and Eitle (2004) found that Black students were more likely to be suspended in majority Black grade schools. Cultural expressions of certain behaviors, such as movement and speech, may be misinterpreted as threatening to teachers who lack cultural awareness (Day-Vines & Day-Hairston, 2005). Another study revealed that natural adaptations to life in some impoverished areas indirectly influence the students' chances of being suspended from school (Kirk, 2009). Few studies have examined suspensions and disciplinary referrals among Hispanic students. One study noted Hispanic students' rates of suspensions and number of referrals were generally greater than Whites, but less than Blacks (Kaushal & Nepomnyaschy, 2009).

Improving teacher efficacy and teacher–student dialogue and aligning their mutual understanding of school rules also demonstrated effectiveness (Pas, Bradshaw, Hershfeldt, & Leaf, 2010; Thompson & Webber, 2010). "Whole-school" and schoolwide interventions that focus on schoolwide improvements in instructional methods, positive reinforcement, such as teacher "praise notes" (Nelson, Young, Young, & Cox, 2010), behavioral modeling, and data-based evaluation, have also demonstrated effectiveness (Bohanon et al., 2006; Lassen, Steele, & Sailor, 2006; Luiselli, Putnam, Handler, & Feinberg, 2005). Resilience and skill building among students also reduced behavioral problems and subsequent disciplinary referrals among students (Wyman et al., 2010). Attention to students' mental health may also reduce suspensions and disciplinary referrals among Black male students (Caldwell, Sewell, Parks, & Toldson, 2009).

Race, School Environment, and Empathy, and Respect

Research evidence suggests that persons of a privileged social group need to make conscious adjustments to develop authentic relationships with less privileged groups (Ullucci, 2011). Standard rubrics of evaluating teachers, such as knowledge, pedagogy and organization, are insufficient because they do not account for the vast diversity in the classroom or the sociocultural context of education (Nieto, 2006). Therefore, the teaching force, which is approximately 80% White, needs to develop mechanisms for teachers to cultivate empathy and respect for students of a different race. Empathy, moral and spiritual values, and self-interest are three factors that motivate people from privileged social groups to promote equity in the classroom (Goodman, 2000).

Exposing teacher educators to different cultures is one strategy to increase their cultural awareness and empathy toward racially different students (Houser, 2008; Marx & Pray, 2011). Multicultural training workshops have also been identified as a strategy to help teachers develop an awareness of their personal biases that may threaten their capacity to empathize with other races (Pickett, 1995). Some pedagogical methods have been evaluated that have demonstrated effectiveness in helping teachers develop and convey empathy toward their students. For example, one approach instructs teachers to allow students to self-reflect and connect classroom lessons to their community environment (Rios, Trent, & Castaneda, 2003). A sense of social justice, insight, and the ability to challenge conventional wisdom help teachers to cultivate an empathetic understanding of their students (Nieto, 2006).

A relationship between respect and academic success for Black males was found through analyzing three national surveys (Toldson, 2008). High-achieving Black male students reported that their teachers were interested in them "as a person," treated them fairly, encouraged them to express their views and gave extra help when needed. Teachers who were effective also routinely let their students know when they did a good job. Overall, Black male students who were successful perceived their teachers to be respectful people who treated them like they matter and nurturing people who builds up their strengths, instead of making them "feel bad" about their weaknesses.

Toldson (2011a) found that schools with more gang activity had lower overall levels of academic achievement among students. Students in schools with gang activity were also more likely to report being distracted from doing schoolwork because of other students misbehaving. These findings collectively suggest that, teachers and administrators in schools with more gang activity are perceived by students to spend more time confronting problematic students, which may compromise the academic priorities of the school.

Students in schools with less gang activity are more likely to report that teachers care about students, treat students with respect, spend less time punishing students, and are less likely to report that teachers do or say things that make students feel bad about themselves (Toldson, 2011a). Black students are significantly more likely to experience disillusionment with their teachers (Lewis, James, Hancock, & Hill-Jackson, 2008). Many teachers, particularly in urban school districts, may become disenchanted because they feel they have little control over the conditions and circumstances that weaken student achievement (Toldson, 2011a).

THEORETICAL FRAMEWORK

Researchers used critical race theory and humanism as heuristic frameworks to conceptualize the process by which children of diverse backgrounds learn and develop in the classroom and how teachers experience the school environment. Critical race theory (CRT) examines White privilege and institutional racism. When viewing a racially diverse classroom with the tenants of CRT, a White teacher who takes a "colorblind" approach to teaching Black and Latino students, and ignores social inequalities, inadvertently promotes a racially prejudiced hegemony (Kohli, 2012). In previous studies, critical race theory has been used to demonstrate instructional techniques to develop agency and activism with students (Knaus, 2009), as well as the dynamic that leads to harsher punitive measures at majority minority schools (Zirkel et al., 2011).

This study also used humanistic perspectives to explore interpersonal dynamics between teachers and students that are conducive to a healthy learning environment. Humanistic psychology is based on the principles that in order for a person to grow and mature, they require a nurturing environment that provides them with genuineness, unconditional positive regard, and empathy (Rogers, 1992). Genuineness is defined as an openness and self-disclosure, unconditional positive regard is the feeling of acceptance, and empathy is expressed in the ability to listen to and understand. Humanistic theorists believe that both educators' feelings toward their students and knowledge of culture are important to the learning process (Barr, 2011). Humanistic teachers do not separate the cognitive and affective domains; rather they insist that schools need to provide students with a nonthreatening environment so they will feel secure to learn. Once students feel secure, learning becomes easier and more meaningful (Boyer, 2010).

RESEARCH QUESTIONS

Studies have found that teachers who lack cultural proficiency may not be able to relate to minority children and therefore may undermine their academic potential. Teachers' level of empathy, feelings of safety, and racial views can influence students' performance, grades, and disciplinary actions (Day-Vines & Day-Hairston, 2005). Toldson's (2011a) findings suggest that schools with more gang activity distract administrators and teachers from academic instruction and refocus priorities to problematic student behaviors. A noticeable void in the literature was research that examined the intersection of race and school environment on teachers' attitudes and behaviors toward their students. Four research questions are proposed for further investigation:

1. Do teachers' attitudes and behaviors toward students influence their academic success?
2. Does students' race influence teachers' attitudes and behavior toward their students?
3. Does the school environment influence teachers' attitudes and behaviors toward students?
4. Does the influence of the school environment depend on the race of the student?

METHOD

Participants

The study participants included all Black, Latino, and White students who completed the National Crime Victimization Survey: School Crime Supplement of 2009 (NCVS-SCS). The database was selected for this study because it had a clear indicator of academic success; had adequate Black and Latino adolescent representation; was a national survey that included multiple states and geographic areas; and had adequate measures of contributing factors, such as school environment and school safety measures. The database is indexed for public analysis at the *Interuniversity Consortium for Political and Social Research* (United States Department of Justice Bureau of Justice Statistics, 2010).

Procedure

Using data from the Bureau of the Census, the Bureau of Justice gathered data for the SCS as a supplement to the NCVS. The NCVS-SCS used a stratified, multi-stage cluster sample design. The Bureau of Justice described their selection of respondents as a "rotating panel design," in which households were randomly selected and all age-eligible individuals became members of a panel. Those selected in the panel were interviewed every six months for a total of seven interviews over a three-year period. The Bureau of Justice designated the first interview as the incoming rotation and the second through the seventh interview were in the continuing rotations. After the seventh interview, the household leaves the panel and a new household is rotated into the sample.

The NCVS-SCS surveyed 12- to 18-year-old adolescents who attended school in 2009. The survey population responded to questions regarding crime prevention measures employed by their schools, their participation in after-school activities, their perception of school rules, the presence of weapons, drugs, alcohol and gangs in their schools, and their fear of victimization at school. The NCVS-SCS used paper and pencil interviewing and computer-assisted telephone interviewing. Initial interviews were conducted in respondents' households and subsequent computer-assisted interviews were conducted by an interviewer calling from a centralized telephone facility using an automated version of the paper instrument to administer the questions.

The Census Bureau's Disclosure Review Board (DRB) vetted data collected for the NCVS-SCS. For confidentiality and anonymity, recoding procedures and a control number scrambling routine were performed before the file was released for public use. Responses to the NCVS-SCS are confidential by law under BJS Title 42, United States Code, Sections 3735 and 3789g and by the Census Bureau under Title 13, United States Code, Section 9.

Measures

School Environment and Classroom Dynamics

Fourteen continuous items were used that allowed students to rate various aspects of their school environment and dynamics within their classrooms. With the exception of the first two items, students rated these questions on a four-point scale with 1 indicating "strongly agree" and 4 indicating "strongly disagree." For the first two questions, the response options ranged from 1 indicating "never," to 4 indicating "most of the time." Where appropriate, items were reverse coded for analysis.

The first group of questions measured the level of distractions the students experienced from other students' misbehavior and teachers' disciplinary practices. The two questions asked, "How often do teachers punish students during your classes?" and "In your classes, how often are you distracted from doing your schoolwork because other students are misbehaving, for example, talking or fighting?"

The second group of questions measured students' knowledge, understanding and perception of school rules. The survey items included, (a) If a school rule is broken, students know what kind of punishment will follow;

(b) The school rules are strictly enforced; (c) The punishment for breaking school rules is the same no matter who you are; (d) "Everyone knows what the school rules are; and (e) The school rules are fair.

The third group of questions asked students whether they believed their teachers were caring, respectful, and nice. Specifically, the survey asked whether students agreed with the following statements: (a) Teachers do or say things that make students feel bad about themselves; (b) Teachers treat students with respect; and (c) Teachers care about students.

The final group of questions measured whether students had adults at school that cared about them. The survey asked if students agreed to the following: (a) At school, there is an adult who helps me with practical problems, who gives good suggestions and advice about my problems; and (b) At school, there is an adult I can talk to, who cares about my feelings and what happens to me.

Grades

NCVS-SCS recorded academic achievement with the item, "During this school year, across all subjects have you gotten mostly..." Students who participated in this survey responded by indicating the letter grade, A through F, that they were most likely to achieve during the school year. Codes for the categories were modify so that students who reported mostly A's received scores closer to 4.0, and those reported mostly F's received scores closer to zero.

School Safety

School safety was recorded with an index that included students' responses to questions that inquired about gang activity at the school and behaviors in response to threats at the school. Twelve dichotomous, yes or no questions were used to determine if students altered behaviors in response to violent threats at the school. Examples include staying away from hallways or stairs, cafeteria, school restrooms, activities, or avoiding school all together.

Gang activity was measured with two questions. The first question was a dichotomous yes or no question asking, "Are there any gangs at your school?" The second was a continuous variable that asked, "During this school year, how often have gangs been involved in fights, attacks, or other violence at your school?" The response choices were: (a) Never; (b) Once or twice this school year; (c) Once or twice a month; (d) Once or twice a week; or (e) Almost every day. To normalize distribution of responses, these two questions were reconfigured to create the following categories for this study: (a) No gangs—those responding "no" to question one; (b) No gang activity—those responding no to question one, and "never" for question two; (c) Some gang activity—those responding "once or twice this school year" or "once or twice a month" to question two; and (b) A lot of gang activity—those responding "once or twice a week" or "almost every day" to question two.

The resulting index ranged from 1 to 16. A score of 1 indicated the students' school has no gangs and the student does not feel he or she needs to avoid any areas of the school to remain safe. A score of 16 indicated the student attends a school with a lot of gang activity, has to avoid most areas of the school to remain safe, and may have avoided school altogether because of safety concerns.

Analysis Plan

The principle analytic technique used in this study was a 3 x 4 factorial analysis of variance ANOVA, whereby three levels of race (Black, White, and Latino) and four levels of academic achievement were tested for their independent main effects, as well as interactions between the two factors. General linear modeling approaches were used to reveal differences in the relationship between academic achievement and associated variables along race lines. The hypothesized relationships between academic achievement and external measures were tested and accepted or rejected based on the p-value (tested at .01). Means plots are displayed for select variables to display the linear relationship between various indicators of academic achievement and hypothesized covariates, across races. The plots include a dashed reference line on the Y-axis that marks the estimated mean of the variable of interest. The reference line is useful for determining the distribution of scores around the mean for various levels of academic achievement.

Structural Equation Modeling (SEM) was used to test the relationship between hypothesized causal factors and the equivalence between models that were constructed for Black, White and Latino male students. Using information gathered from multivariate analysis, the researcher selected variables for a path model to confirm their relationship in a trajectory model that evaluated the relationship between the school environment, classroom dynamics and student outcomes. AMOS 17 was used to test model fitness and calculate regression estimates of direct and indirect effects. Invariance between races was estimated for the overall model and the path estimates by imposing a series of model constraints through nested model comparisons.

RESULTS

Descriptive Information

Participants of this study included 8,986 Black, Latino, and White male and female students who completed the NCVS-SCS of 2009. The racial and gender composition of the participants were consistent with the demographics of the middle and high school Black, Latino, and White students in the United States. Fourteen percent was Black, 21% was Latino, and 65% was White. Eighteen percent of the participants attended school in the Northeast region of the United States, 25% in the Midwest, 34% in the South, and 23% in the West. The mean age of the participants was 15 years old. Ninety-two participants attended public schools and 88% attended the regular school that most students in their neighborhood attended. The most common mode of transportation two and from school was a private vehicle (51%), followed by a school bus (37%). Most students (61%) lived within 15 miles of their school.

The Relationship Between Race, School Environment, and Academic Success

A factorial ANOVA was used as a preliminary test for three research questions: "Do teachers' attitudes and behaviors toward students influence their academic success; Does the school environment influence academic success; and Does students' race influence teachers' attitudes and behavior toward their students? Table 14.1 displays the means, standard deviations, and F-ratios of aspects of the school environment that have a hypothesized relationship with academic achievement among Black, Latino, and White male students. The table marks variables that are significant by race and academic achievement. All six of the variables analyzed had a significant relationship with academic achievement. Mean scores with a negative relationship with academic achievement, such as "Unsafe School," get smaller when reading from left to right as academic performance increases. The opposite is true for variables, such as "Teachers Care for and Respect Students," with a positive relationship with academic achievement. Two of the six variables, "Unsafe School" and "Teachers Punish Students," were significant for race prior to performing any post hoc analyses.

Although initial tests found no significance for race and "Teachers Care for and Respect Students," post hoc analysis revealed that Black students perceived care and respect from their teachers significantly less (p < .001) than White and Hispanic students. Figure 14.1a reveals that the difference in perception is most pronounced among higher achieving students, where Black students reporting mostly A's perceive less care and respect than the average of all students. Similar racial differences were found in students' reports of punishment from teachers. Black students were significantly more likely to report that teachers punish students, which was most pronounced as academic success diminished (See Figure 14.1b).

TABLE 14.1 Means, Standard Deviations, and F-Ratios of School-Related Factors That Are Related to Academic Success Among Black, White, and Latino Students

	Race	D's & F's M (SD)	C's M (SD)	B's M (SD)	A's M (SD)	Total M (SD)	F-Ratio Race	F-Ratio Achievement
Teachers Care for and Respect Students 3 strongly disagree–12 strongly agree	Black	8.94 (2.29)	9.01 (1.87)	9.18 (1.67)	9.47 (1.75)	9.20 (1.77)	2.12	18.82**
	White	8.84 (1.45)	9.18 (1.57)	9.55 (1.38)	10.04 (1.44)	9.71 (1.47)		
	Latino	8.87 (1.61)	9.23 (1.67)	9.56 (1.46)	9.77 (1.44)	9.52 (1.52)		
	Total	8.87 (1.64)	9.16 (1.66)	9.50 (1.45)	9.96 (1.48)	9.61 (1.53)		
Unsafe School 1 very safe–16 very unsafe	Black	3.25 (2.08)	2.46 (1.83)	1.95 (1.64)	1.95 (1.65)	2.12 (1.73)	47.43**	24.47**
	White	2.02 (1.61)	1.65 (1.28)	1.47 (1.00)	1.33 (0.88)	1.44 (1.01)		
	Latino	2.94 (1.95)	2.21 (1.54)	2.03 (1.41)	1.79 (1.29)	2.04 (1.45)		
	Total	2.51 (1.86)	1.95 (1.50)	1.66 (1.23)	1.44 (1.04)	1.64 (1.25)		
Fair School 5 strongly disagree–20 strongly agree	Black	15.88 (2.45)	15.58 (2.76)	15.90 (2.44)	15.95 (2.65)	15.84 (2.56)	2.69	7.45**
	White	14.67 (2.22)	15.16 (2.14)	15.81 (2.25)	16.23 (2.29)	15.89 (2.29)		
	Latino	15.32 (2.30)	15.67 (2.27)	16.02 (2.24)	15.97 (2.25)	15.90 (2.26)		
	Total	15.07 (2.30)	15.38 (2.31)	15.87 (2.27)	16.17 (2.32)	15.89 (2.32)		
Teachers Punish Students 1 never–4 most of the time	Black	3.13 (0.81)	2.90 (0.90)	2.59 (0.88)	2.55 (0.86)	2.67 (0.89)	4.68**	15.02**
	White	2.78 (0.88)	2.64 (0.83)	2.54 (0.82)	2.44 (0.79)	2.51 (0.81)		
	Latino	3.03 (0.84)	2.76 (0.93)	2.58 (0.83)	2.51 (0.87)	2.62 (0.87)		
	Total	2.92 (0.86)	2.72 (0.88)	2.55 (0.83)	2.46 (0.81)	2.55 (0.84)		

(continued)

TABLE 14.1 Means, Standard Deviations, and F-Ratios of School-Related Factors That Are Related to Academic Success Among Black, White, and Latino Students (continued)

	Race	D's & F's M (SD)	C's M (SD)	B's M (SD)	A's M (SD)	Total M (SD)	F-Ratio Race	F-Ratio Achievement
Classroom Distractions	Black	2.94 (1.12)	2.56 (0.99)	2.43 (0.89)	2.25 (1.01)	2.44 (0.96)	1.51	12.53**
1 never–4 most of the time	White	2.84 (0.88)	2.58 (0.91)	2.42 (0.88)	2.29 (0.84)	2.39 (0.87)		
	Latino	2.55 (1.03)	2.51 (0.92)	2.38 (0.87)	2.31 (0.84)	2.40 (0.88)		
	Total	2.77 (0.97)	2.56 (0.93)	2.41 (0.88)	2.29 (0.85)	2.40 (0.88)		
Student Feels Supported	Black	3.25 (0.86)	3.27 (0.64)	3.37 (0.56)	3.35 (0.62)	3.34 (0.60)	1.57	4.19**
1 strongly disagree–4 strongly agree	White	3.41 (0.54)	3.30 (0.57)	3.34 (0.57)	3.44 (0.56)	3.38 (0.57)		
	Latino	3.29 (0.64)	3.25 (0.58)	3.32 (0.60)	3.41 (0.58)	3.33 (0.59)		
	Total	3.35 (0.63)	3.28 (0.59)	3.34 (0.57)	3.43 (0.57)	3.37 (0.58)		

Note: M = Mean; *SD* = Standard Deviation; $^*p < .01$; $^{**}p < .001$

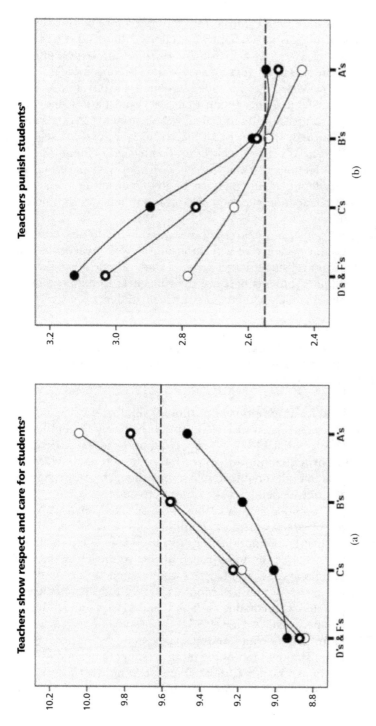

Figure 14.1a & 1b Means plots of race (separate plots) and grades (X Axis) on teacher attitudes and behaviors (Y Axes) as reported by Black, Hispanic, and White students. Note: ● = Black students; ◑ = Hispanic students; and ○ = White students. The dashed reference line on the Y-axis marks the estimated mean of the dependent variable. **Main effects for grades and race.

Black students who reported "mostly C's" reported more punitive behavior among teachers than White students who reported "mostly D's and F's."

The analyses of academic achievement revealed the largest effect size for feeling unsafe at school (eta-squared = .03). Feeling unsafe at school also had the largest effect size for race (eta-squared = .02). Post hoc analysis of feeling unsafe at school found that Black and Latino students felt significantly more unsafe at school than White students. As indicated in Figure 14.2a, although students of all races who feel unsafe at school are also less likely to have higher levels of academic achievement, Black and Latino students' feelings of being unsafe at school was above the mean, regardless of academic standing. Figure 14.2b demonstrates a relationship between academic achievement and classroom misbehavior, but no differences between races.

Although causality cannot be established, overall the results of the factorial ANOVA found evidence of a relationship between teacher attitudes, teacher behaviors and students' academic success. The analysis also found evidence that Black students perceive their teachers to be more punitive and less respectful and empathetic towards their students.

The Structural Path of School Environment, Classroom Dynamics, and Student Outcomes Across Black, Latino, and White students

SEM was used for three primary purposes. The first was to find causal links between the correlated variable in the three research questions that were tested with factorial ANOVA. The second purpose was to determine, if the school environment influences teachers' attitudes and behaviors toward students. Finally, the analysis tested if the influence of the school environment on teachers depends on the race of the student.

Exogenous and endogenous variables were selected for a path model to test their direct effects on teacher attitudes and behaviors and indirect effects on students' grades and feelings of support. In the model, events hypothesized to occur earlier were placed further to the left of the model. In this model, school safety and fairness were treated as correlated exogenous variables, classroom misbehavior, teacher attitudes and teacher behaviors were treated as mediating variables, and grades and student support were outcome variables. Figures 14.3, 14.4, and 14.5 display the path models tested for Black, White and Hispanic students, respectively. The initial maximum likelihood test of the model resulted in a good overall fit, $\chi^2(18) = 29.20$, $p = .05$, $\chi^2/df = 1.62$, comparative fit index (CFI) = .99, root mean square error of approximation (RMSEA) = .02, and normed fit index (NFI) = .98.

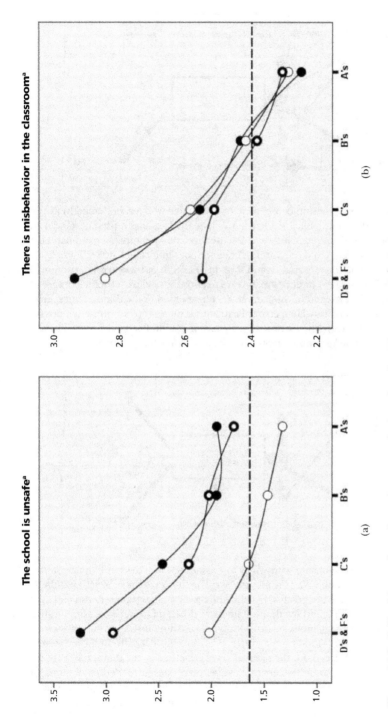

Figure 14.2a & 2b Means plots of race (separate plots) and grades (X Axis) on school and classroom dynamics (Y Axes) as reported by Black, Hispanic, and White students. Note: ● = Black students; ◉ = Hispanic students; and O = White students. The dashed reference line on the Y-axis marks the estimated mean of the dependent variable. *Main effect for grades. **Main effects for grades and race.

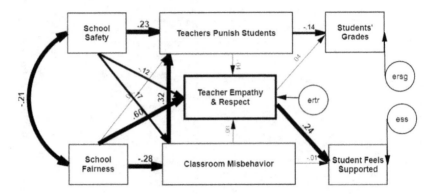

Figure 14.3 The relationship between factors associated with teacher empathy and subsequent grades among Black students. *Note:* The thickest lines represent standardized path estimates that are greater than .20, the medium lines represent estimates that are between .10 and .19, and the thinnest lines are not significant. Curved lines with two-way arrows represent covariance and straight lines with one-way arrow represent paths. The minus sign (–) indicates an inverse relationship. All path coefficients are significant (p < .01), except for the parameters represented by the thinnest lines. Ertr, ersq, and ess represent associated error of exogenous values (error representations for teachers punish students and classroom misbehavior are hidden from figure). Data from National Crime Victimization Survey —School Crime Supplement (2009).

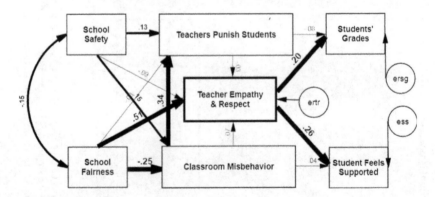

Figure 14.4 The relationship between factors associated with teacher empathy and subsequent grades among White students. *Note:* The thickest lines represent standardized path estimates that are greater than .20, the medium lines represent estimates that are between .10 and .19, and the thinnest lines are not significant. Curved lines with two-way arrows represent covariance and straight lines with one-way arrow represent paths. The minus sign (–) indicates an inverse relationship. All path coefficients are significant (p < .01), except for the parameters represented by the thinnest lines. Ertr, ersq, and ess represent associated error of exogenous values (error representations for teachers punish students and classroom misbehavior are hidden from figure). Data from National Crime Victimization Survey —School Crime Supplement (2009).

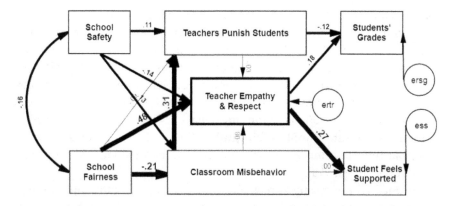

Figure 14.5 The relationship between factors associated with teacher empathy and subsequent grades among Latino students. *Note:* The thickest lines represent standardized path estimates that are greater than .20, the medium lines represent estimates that are between .10 and .19, and the thinnest lines are not significant. Curved lines with two-way arrows represent covariance and straight lines with one-way arrow represent paths. The minus sign (–) indicates an inverse relationship. All path coefficients are significant (p < .01), except for the parameters represented by the thinnest lines. Ertr, ersq, and ess represent associated error of exogenous values (error representations for teachers punish students and classroom misbehavior are hidden from figure). Data from National Crime Victimization Survey —School Crime Supplement (2009).

Invariance Between Races

Race differences between the path models and coefficients were further examined through SEM. The invariance of the path models across races was tested in three steps. First, the goodness of fit was calculated separately for Black, White, and Latino males. These preliminary evaluations confirmed an adequate fit of the data for all groups: for Black males, $\chi^2(6) = 8.74$, $p = .19$, $\chi^2/df = 3.8$, CFI = .99, RMSEA = .04, and NFI = .97; for White males, $\chi^2(6) = 11.38$, $p = .08$, $\chi^2/df = 1.90$, CFI = .99, RMSEA = .03, and NFI = .99; and for Latino males, $\chi^2(6) = 9.05$, $p = .171$, $\chi^2/df = 1.5$, CFI = .99, RM-SEA = .03, and NFI = .97. All fit indices were similar across race groups.

Second, all regression weights in the initial models with all races combined were constrained to be equal across race. The constrained model differed significantly from the unrestricted model, $\Delta\chi^2(26) = 31.89$, p < .01, indicating that the regression weights were invariant across race. The third was to constrain the structural covariance, while allowing the regression weights the freedom to vary across races. Results of this analysis did not indicate a significant attrition in model fit, $\Delta\chi^2(2) = 6.80$, indicating that the covariance between school safety and school fairness was not significantly different between Black, White, and Latino males.

Direct and Indirect Effects on Disciplinary Referrals and Grades.

Nested group comparisons confirmed structural invariance between the regression weights of Black, Latino and White students. Figures 14.3, 14.4, and 14.5 illustrate the path coefficients for each race of students, whereby several distinct differences emerged. First, note the direct effects of school safety on classroom dynamics. There is no difference in the effect of school safety on classroom misbehavior between Black and White students, yet unsafe schools significantly influence Black students' perception that their teachers are more punitive and lack empathy and respect for students in general.

Second, a very strong direct effect of teacher empathy and respect emerged for White and Latino students; however, the relationship was not significant for Black students. This is likely associated with the findings that Black students at higher levels of academic achievement perceive their teachers as significantly less empathetic and respectful. Finally, teachers' punitive actions toward students had a significant the direct effect on Black and Latino students' grades, but not on White students' grades. This is related to the finding that Black students at higher levels of academic achievement are more likely to report teacher punishment than White students with similar academic standings.

Monte Carlo parametric bootstrapping was used to measure the indirect effects of school safety and fairness on student outcomes. School safety significantly ($p < .01$) indirectly effected grades among all students; however, it only indirectly effected feelings of support among Black and Latino students. School fairness had significant ($p < .01$) indirect effects of feelings of support for all students, but did not have significant indirect effects for grades only for Black students.

Overall, SEM found evidence that school safety and school fairness directly influenced teachers' perceived level of empathy and respect toward their students, and indirectly influence students' grades and feelings of being supported. Invariance between nested models for Black, Latino, and White students suggest that the path to good grades and feeling support was significantly different across races. Notably, the overall safety of the school was a much stronger determinant of teachers' punitive behaviors, lack of empathy and respect toward Black students than it was for White students. Teacher empathy and respect led to greater feelings of being supported among all students; however, no relationship emerged between empathy and respect and students grades for Black students. Compared to White students, perceived punishment among Black and Latino students had a significantly stronger impact on students' grades.

DISCUSSION

On a basic level, this study found that teachers' attitudes and behaviors toward students and the school environment had a relationship with academic success among Black, Latino, and White students. Students of all races, who perceived their teachers to be more caring, respectful, empathetic, and less punitive, generally reported higher grades. These students were also more likely than low achieving students to perceive their school environment to be safe, supportive, and fair.

Black and Latino students were more likely to feel unsafe in their school. Black students were also less likely than White students to perceive empathy and respect from their teachers, even when they were making good grades. Similarly, Black students perceived their teachers to be significantly more punitive. A Black student who reported C's was far more likely to perceive their teachers to be punitive than a White student who reported D's and F's.

The overall safety and fairness of the school influenced teachers' empathy and respect for Black students significantly more than for White students, as reported by the students. Black students at unsafe schools also reported more punitive teacher behaviors. Among students of all races, school safety significantly indirectly affected grades, however for Black and Latino students, safety indirectly affected feelings of support.

When revisiting the theoretical framework, the findings demonstrate that teacher empathy is associated with improved academic outcomes, which is consistent with a humanistic perspective. With respect to CRT, racial dynamics appeared to alter the school environment along racial lines. White students' response patterns demonstrated a structure whereby teacher empathy and respect was central to students' academic success, school safety had no measurable influence on teachers' compassion for their students, and teacher punishment had no measurable impact on students' grades. Contrarily, Black students' response patterns reflected a dynamic, whereby school safety significantly diminished the overall level of empathy and respect that students perceived from teachers and punishment from teachers significantly reduced students' grades.

The results of this study have implications for policymakers, curriculum writers, teacher preparation programs, and professional development and training sessions. Teacher preparation programs should expand multicultural class offerings and incorporate multicultural emersion experiences. Teacher trainees' educational process should allow students to examine their own beliefs, biases, and attitudes toward other races. Courses should include discussions and assignments that encourage students to understand their fears and vulnerabilities which will enable them to be conscious of their decision making process to be fair to all students regardless of race.

Readers should consider several limitations within the context of the findings. First, since data were collected about socially desirable attributes, some participants may have used impression management during self-report procedures. Although all surveys were confidential, it is likely that some respondents may have embellished grades and other desirable attributes, and denied suspensions and other negative attributes. In addition, the survey was lengthy and solicited information beyond this study's scope. The length may have created some fatigue and led to "Yea-Saying" or "Nay-Saying," whereby respondents tend to select only the positive or negative answers on the survey. Finally, this study measures students' perceptions and does not objectively record teachers' attitudes or behaviors.

A special issue of *The Journal of Negro Education* established guidelines for effective teacher education programs (Toldson, 2011b), which are relevant to the study findings. Overall, effective teacher education programs:

- Should prepare teachers of all races, genders, and socioeconomic backgrounds to educate diverse classrooms
- Should contribute to eliminating the achievement and discipline gaps that exist between Black students and students of other races
- Use modern approaches to helping teacher trainees understand diverse classrooms, such as the use of multimedia, documentary film, service learning, and volunteering
- Use effective recruitment strategies to diversify America's teaching force
- Understand the influence of federal- and state-level educational policies on building teacher education programs to accommodate Black students
- Respect the unique role of historically Black colleges and universities in preparing and recruiting Black teachers
- Actively work to combat institutional racism and culturally biased assessments to promote teacher diversity and when training teachers to serve diverse classrooms

Recommendations for Educational Intervention and Future Research

Research on the effects of teachers' attitudes and its effects on Black, Latino, and White students is a vital concern as to develop culturally appropriate strategies to reduce teacher attrition, prevent high school dropout, and mitigate the impact of high stakes testing. School leaders need to understand how the teachers' negative attitudes and behaviors towards students originate and what interventions improve the learning environment. Future research should focus on studying the benefits of teacher preparation programs. Multicultural awareness, teacher philosophy and theory, and classroom management courses should encourage open dialogue about self-awareness, identify their own biases, judgments, and behaviors towards other races.

Local and national measures and educational policies should address students' feeling of safety, fairness, and support by school personnel. A replicate study should address the limitations of the current study and design a more specific survey with fewer questions to prevent fatigue and possible false responses. Future studies should also investigate if there is a significant difference between Black, Latino and White teachers with respect to their attitudes and behaviors toward Latino and Black students and the effects that may have on students and their perception and academic performance.

CONCLUSIONS

There are several important findings from this study, which contributes to the current literature base on teachers' attitudes on race, environment, and behavior toward Black, Latino, and White students. The current research addresses a topic that is often ignored because of the discomfort with discussing biases and unfair treatment within the education system. Students' perception of their teachers' attitudes and behaviors affect their learning experiences. This has an accumulating and detrimental effect on the future of children and their education, which affect communities and society, and long-term effects on the lives of these children.

REFERENCES

Barr, J. J. (2011). The relationship between teachers' empathy and perceptions of school culture. *Educational Studies (03055698), 37*(3), 365–369.

Bohanon, H., Fenning, P., Carney, K. L., Minnis-Kim, M. J., Anderson-Harriss, S., Moroz, K. B., et al. (2006). Schoolwide application of positive behavior support in an urban high school. *Journal of Positive Behavior Interventions, 8*(3), 131–145.

Boyer, W. (2010). Empathy development in teacher candidates. *Early Childhood Education Journal, 38*(4), 313–321.

Caldwell, L. D., Sewell, A. A., Parks, N., & Toldson, I. A. (2009). Guest editorial: Before the bell rings: Implementing coordinated school health models to influence the academic achievement of African American Males. *Journal of Negro Education, 78*(3), 204–215.

Christle, C., Nelson, C. M., & Jolivette, K. (2004). School characteristics related to the use of suspension. *Education & Treatment of Children, 27*(4), 509–526.

Day-Vines, N. L., & Day-Hairston, B. O. (2005). Culturally congruent strategies for addressing the behavioral needs of urban, African American male adolescents. *Professional School Counseling, 8*(3), 236–243.

Eitle, T. M. N., & Eitle, D. J. (2004). Inequality, segregation, and the overrepresentation of African Americans in school suspensions. *Sociological Perspectives, 47,* 269–287.

Goodman, D. J. (2000). Motivating people from privileged groups to support social justice. *Teachers College Record, 102*(6), 1061.

Gregory, A., & Thompson, A. R. (2010). African American high school students and variability in behavior across classrooms. *Journal of Community Psychology, 38*(3), 386–402.

Houser, N. O. (2008). Cultural plunge: A critical approach for multicultural development in teacher education. *Race, Ethnicity and Education, 11*(4), 465–482.

Ingels, S. J., Pratt, D. J., Herget, D. R., Burns, L. J., Dever, J. A., Ottem, R., et al. (2011). High school longitudinal study of 2009 (HSLS:09). Base-year data file documentation (NCES 2011–328). Washington, DC: U.S. Department of Education, National Center for Education Statistics.

Kaushal, N., & Nepomnyaschy, L. (2009). Wealth, race/ethnicity, and children's educational outcomes. *Children & Youth Services Review, 31*(9), 963–971.

Kirk, D. S. (2009). Unraveling the contextual effects on student suspension and juvenile arrest: The independent and interdependent influences of school, neighborhood, and family social controls. *Criminology, 47*(2), 479–520.

Knaus, C. B. (2009). Shut up and listen: Applied critical race theory in the classroom. *Race, Ethnicity & Education, 12*(2), 133–154.

Kohli, R. (2012). Racial pedagogy of the oppressed: Critical interracial dialogue for teachers of color. *Equity & Excellence in Education, 45*(1), 181–196.

Lassen, S. R., Steele, M. M., & Sailor, W. (2006). The relationship of school-wide Positive Behavior Support to academic achievement in an urban middle school. *Psychology in the Schools, 43*(6), 701–712.

Lewis, C. W., James, M., Hancock, S., & Hill-Jackson, V. (2008). Framing African American students' success and failure in urban settings. *Urban Education, 43*(2), 127–153.

Luiselli, J. K., Putnam, R. F., Handler, M. W., & Feinberg, A. B. (2005). Whole-school positive behaviour support: Effects on student discipline problems and academic performance. *Educational Psychology, 25*(2/3), 183–198.

Marx, S., & Pray, L. (2011). Living and learning in Mexico: Developing empathy for English language learners through study abroad. *Race, Ethnicity and Education, 14*(4), 507–535.

Morrison, G. M., Peterson, R., O'Farrell, S., & Redding, M. (2004). Using office referral records in school violence research: Possibilities and limitations. *Journal of School Violence, 3*(2/3), 39–61.

Mukuria, G. (2002). Disciplinary challenges: How do principals address this dilemma? *Urban Education, 37*(3), 432.

Nelson, J. A. P., Young, B. J., Young, E. L., & Cox, G. (2010). Using teacher-written praise notes to promote a positive environment in a middle school. *Preventing School Failure, 54*(2), 119–125.

Nieto, S. (2006). Solidarity, courage and heart: What teacher educators can learn from a new generation of teachers. *Intercultural Education, 17*(5), 457–473.

Pas, E. T., Bradshaw, C. P., Hershfeldt, P. A., & Leaf, P. J. (2010). A multilevel exploration of the influence of teacher efficacy and burnout on response to student problem behavior and school-based service use. *School Psychology Quarterly, 25*(1), 13–27.

Pickett, L. (1995). Multicultural training workshops for teachers. *Transactional Analysis Journal, 25*(3), 250–258.

Rios, F., Trent, A., & Castaneda, L. V. (2003). Social perspective taking: Advancing Empathy and advocating justice. *Equity & Excellence in Education, 36*(1), 5–14.

Rogers, C. R. (1992). The necessary and sufficient conditions of therapeutic personality change. *Journal of Consulting & Clinical Psychology, 60*(6), 827.

Skiba, R., & Peterson, R. (1999). The Dark Side of Zero Tolerance. *Phi Delta Kappan, 80*(5), 372.

Sugai, G., Sprague, J. R., Horner, R. H., & Walker, H. M. (2000). Preventing school violence: The use of office discipline referrals to assess and monitor schoolwide discipline interventions. *Journal of Emotional & Behavioral Disorders, 8*(2), 94.

Thompson, A. M., & Webber, K. C. (2010). Realigning student and teacher perceptions of school rules: A behavior management strategy for students with challenging behaviors. *Children & Schools, 32*(2), 71–79.

Toldson, I. A. (2008). Breaking barriers: Plotting the path to academic success for school-age African-American males. Washington, D.C.: Congressional Black Caucus Foundation, Inc.

Toldson, I. A. (2011a). Breaking barriers 2: Plotting the path away from juvenile detention and toward academic success for school-age African American males. Washington, DC: Congressional Black Caucus Foundation, Inc.

Toldson, I. A. (2011b). Diversifying the United States' teaching force: Where are we now? Where do we need to go? How do we get there? *The Journal of Negro Education, 80*(3), 183–186.

Ullucci, K. (2011). Learning to see: The development of race and class consciousness in White teachers. *Race, Ethnicity and Education, 14*(4), 561–577.

United States Department of Justice Bureau of Justice Statistics. (2010). National Crime Victimization Survey: School Crime Supplement, 2009. In Inter-university Consortium for Political and Social Research (Ed.). Ann Arbor, MI.

Vavrus, F., & Cole, K. (2002). "I didn't do nothin'": The discursive construction of school suspension. *Urban Review, 34*(2), 87.

Wright, J. A., & Dusek, J. B. (1998). Compiling school base-rates for disruptive behavior from student disciplinary referral data. *School Psychology Review, 27*(1), 138.

Wyman, P. A., Cross, W., Brown, C. H., Qin, Y., Xin, T., & Eberly, S. (2010). Intervention to strengthen emotional self-regulation in children with emerging mental health problems: proximal impact on school behavior. *Journal of Abnormal Child Psychology, 38*(5), 707–720.

Zirkel, S., Bailey, F., Bathey, S., Hawley, R., Lewis, U., Long, D., et al. (2011). 'Isn't that what 'those kids' need?' Urban schools and the master narrative of the 'tough, urban principal.' *Race, Ethnicity & Education, 14*(2), 137–158.

EPILOGUE

TEACHER EDUCATION AND BLACK COMMUNITIES

Implications for Equity, Access and Achievement

H. Richard Milner, IV
University of Pittsburgh

Several months ago, my wife and I visited preschools and daycare facilities to secure an appropriate "spot" for our twin daughters as we prepared to move to a new state. Our visits were pretty typical—each daycare tour guide talked about how wonderfully caring the adults were in her respective school. At the end of each tour, we were typically met by the school's director or associate and told about the philosophy of the school, some historical grounding, and a few insights about different teachers and their "styles" in the classroom. Rarely, were any substantive questions posed about our daughters. When questions were posed during our visit to these daycare facilities, the questions were surface-level at best: how old are the girls? When is their birthday?

What was especially annoying about our visits was the directors' consistent message that child's "play" would be the magic experience that would enable

Teacher Education and Black Communities, pages 317–321
Copyright © 2014 by Information Age Publishing
All rights of reproduction in any form reserved.

our girls to be not only "kindergarten ready" but also prepared for future academic and social success, especially within traditional schools. A bit aggravated by this claim, my wife and I often asked about other opportunities for our girls to explore, think, be creative, and develop. As African American[1] parents, at one facility, my wife and I were very concerned about the low numbers of African American students and adults at the school. We explained to the director that our daughters currently attended a facility where their co-teachers were White and African American. Also, in their classroom, there were three White American children, one Asian American child, and four African American children. We expressed how important it was for our children to be in a racially diverse environment and my wife shared how the girls' African American teacher was especially a great resource for our girls because she understood their hair on 'water-play' days, for instance. The African American teacher seemed to especially understand our girls' emotional needs. The director looked perplexed and pointed us to the one Black teacher we met during our tour. Or course, we would get "special" priority consideration because my becoming a new faculty member at the local university would be a "big deal." The director would do all she could to make sure our daughters were enrolled in that classroom if we requested.

However, although pleased with the performance of the one Black teacher in the school, the director warned us: her methods are very "nontraditional." She sometimes has her kids engaged in "mindless" drill and practice activities—approaches to child development that ran counter to naturalistic play that their daycare center advocated. The director joked that although her students tended to transition "fine" into kindergarten she practices too much "drill and kill" with her students.

Unfortunately, this storyline is not unique. The philosophy that young children learn and develop through play is a well-substantiated position in education research. However, children also learn and develop through additional methods as well. In general, although the directors saw my move to their city as a "big deal" at the university and in the city, they still believed they knew what was best for my children, two Black girls. Although we stressed how important it was for our children to have a teacher who addressed their socioemotional as well as their cognitive development, consistently across the sites we visited the directors were resolute: children learn through play. Period.

The problems identified above are emblematic of a central problem in teacher education: White teachers and White teacher educators tend to believe they understand what is best for all children without actually inquiring about and listening to the people and communities who know them best: Black students themselves, Black parents, Black family members and Black communities in general. The authors in this timely volume understand and take heed to the reality that Black people are best situated to answer and address the complex challenges Black students face. In a compelling fashion, the authors provide perspectives and insights drawn from their own experiences, the established literature, and empirical data to improve teacher education for and about Black communities. Indeed, as a field, teacher education suffers from many challenges that need serious attention. Related to the education of Black students, these challenges in teacher education include, but are not limited to the following:

- Increased external pressure to provide evidence of their effectiveness
- Structural incoherence between programs, where there is, perhaps, too much variation in terms of the level of curricula and instructional emphasis on equity and access
- Lack of consistency and commitment among teacher educators to address equity, access and social justice
- Increasing the numbers of teachers and teacher educators of color—especially Black and from diverse backgrounds (such as males) in the field
- Constructing and deconstructing curriculum and instructional experiences that meet the needs of all teachers, not just White teachers
- Addressing the uneven stress and burdens of teacher educators of color to be the diversity go-to person in teacher education programs

While the challenges outlined above provide a snapshot of some of the complex and essential issues teacher education must face, they are insipid in comparison to the task they face in preparing teachers to teach African American students in P–12 schools across the country.

In its simplest form, teacher education has done a meager job of preparing teachers to teach African American children although some progress is being made. The reasons for this lack of effectiveness is likely a consequence of many issues beyond the scope of this epilogue. This book is a resource to assist teacher education programs across the country in understanding Black students, their communities, and how to better meet their needs. Teacher educators may not focus much attention on preparing teachers to specifically consider what is essential to effectively teach African American students, and researchers have not necessarily studied this focus. Elsewhere (Milner, 2009), I reviewed the literature to identify scholarship and related practices that spoke directly to the preparation of teachers to teach African American students. What I found was similar to what was determined years prior. Ladson-Billings (2009) wrote: "almost nothing [literature] exists on teacher preparation specifically for African American students" (p. 8). Refreshingly, this volume fills this void and pushes for radical reform in teacher education, placing the education of African American children and Black communities at the very core.

The book covers many themes and perspectives that need attention in both the research community but especially in teacher education practice.

In many important ways, the text provides curriculum anchors to assist teacher education in knowing what to cover in teacher education programs committed to the preparation of teachers to effectively teach Black students. In particular, with equity and achievement for African American students as the aim, authors in the book stress the centrality of the following:

- Residential and nonresidential fathers in the Black community
- Recruitment and retention of African American teachers through pipeline and other mechanisms
- Voices of Black males in P–12 environments
- Access and equity in education for Black students
- Domain-specific teaching and learning for African American students
- Disciplinary and referral strategies to redress patterns for African American students

Finally, as this book suggests, there is a great need to prepare teachers with increased attention to African American students in P–12 classrooms because Black students consistently have been underserved. In essence, teachers often have low expectations for Black students, they "teach down" to them, and they often "water down" the curriculum.

The authors in this volume push teacher education to address many of the following important questions: (a) what are some cultural characteristics of African American students that must be addressed in order to effectively teach them? (b) What teaching practices appear to be the most promising for Black students and why? (c) What stakeholders are central to providing optimal learning opportunities for Black students (e.g., parents, policy makers, principals), and how can these stakeholders be used to draw upon to benefit Black students? (d) What policies enable and inhibit the success of Black students? Answers to these questions can help us rethink and radically shift the ways in which teacher education prepares teachers to teach all students effectively and especially the ways in which teacher education prepares teachers to teach African American students. Indeed, as the late Asa Hilliard (1992) explained, "any reform that benefits those students who are poorly served always works to the benefit of all" (p. 375). This is an important book for teacher education and Black communities that serves to benefit all.

NOTE

1. African American and Black will be used interchangeably throughout this epilogue. The term Black, as written here, also refers to individuals of the African Diaspora who identify as Black.

REFERENCES

Hilliard, A. G. (1992). Behavioral style, culture, and teaching and learning. *Journal of Negro Education, 61*(3), 370–377.

Ladson-Billings (2009). *The Dreamkeepers: Successful Teachers of African American Children* (2nd ed.). San Francisco: Jossey-Bass.

Milner, H. R. (2009). Preparing teachers of African American students in urban schools. In L. C. Tillman (Ed.), *The Handbook of African American Education* (pp. 123–140). Thousand Oaks, CA: Sage Publications.

ABOUT THE EDITORS

Dr. Yolanda Sealey-Ruiz is an Assistant Professor of English Education at Teachers College, Columbia University. At the core of her teaching and research agenda is an exploration of how diversity, particularly race, informs curriculum and pedagogy in literacy education in secondary and higher education settings. Concerned with Equity Pedagogy, her work specifically examines the racial literacy knowledge of teachers, the development and use of culturally responsive pedagogy in literacy classrooms, and the social and academic success of Black and Latino male secondary students. Dr. Sealey-Ruiz cofounded, with Erik Nolan, *UMOJA Readers and Writers*, a critical thinking and writing course for adolescent males of color at a New York City alternative high school.

Dr. Sealey-Ruiz provides professional development on culturally responsive education and racial literacy for teachers and administrators around the country. Prior to joining the faculty at Teachers College, she was a Research Associate with New York University's Metropolitan Center for Urban Education, where she led major research projects on the achievement of Black and Latino students in urban and suburban school districts in upstate New York and New Jersey.

Dr. Sealey-Ruiz's publications have appeared in *Teachers College Record, Urban Education, The Urban Review, Race, Ethnicity, and Education, Power and Education, Journal of Curriculum and Pedagogy, Journal of Negro Education, Journal of Adolescent and Adult Literacy, English Quarterly,* and *Adult Education Quarterly,* to name a few. She is an American Association of University Women (AAUW), National Council of Teachers of English (NCTE)

Teacher Education and Black Communities, pages 323–326
Copyright © 2014 by Information Age Publishing
All rights of reproduction in any form reserved.

Cultivating New Voices of Scholars of Color (CNV), and a Ford Foundation Diversity Fellowship recipient. Her Ford Fellowship provided funding for her research with Black male students and their teachers in London. In this current international research project, students, teachers, administrators, parents and community activists engage with the *Beyond the Bricks* community engagement tour which asks them to create action plans that will increase the social and academic success of Black males who attend schools in their community.

Dr. Sealey-Ruiz has served as Secretary for the American Educational Research Association's (AERA) Division K: Teaching and Teacher Education, the largest division within AERA. For two years, Dr. Sealey-Ruiz served as lead consultant for the New York City Department of Education's *Empowering Boys Initiative*, a pilot program that infused nontraditional, culturally responsive professional development in four New York City schools charged with increasing the social and academic success of their Black and Latino male students. Dr. Sealey-Ruiz received her M.A. in English Education from Teachers College, and her PhD in English Education from New York University.

Dr. Chance W. Lewis is the Carol Grotnes Belk Distinguished Full Professor and Endowed Chair of Urban Education at the University of North Carolina at Charlotte. Additionally, Dr. Lewis is the Director of the University of North Carolina at Charlotte *Urban Education Collaborative* which is publishing a new generation of research on improving urban schools. Dr. Lewis received his BS and MEd in Business Education and Education Administration/Supervision from Southern University in Baton Rouge, Louisiana. Dr. Lewis completed his doctoral studies in Educational Leadership/Teacher Education from Colorado State University in Fort Collins, Colorado.

Dr. Lewis currently teaches graduate courses in the field of Urban Education at the University of North Carolina at Charlotte. His experiences span the range of K–12 and higher education. From 2006–2011, Dr. Lewis served as the Houston Endowed Chair and Associate Professor of Urban Education in the College of Education at Texas A&M University. Additionally, he was the codirector of the Center for Urban School Partnerships. In 2001–2006, he served as an assistant professor of teacher education at Colorado State University. From 1994 to 1998, Dr. Lewis served as a Business Education teacher in East Baton Rouge Parish Schools (Baton Rouge, LA), where he earned Teacher of the Year honors in 1997.

Dr. Lewis has over 100 publications including 60+ refereed journal articles in some of the leading academic journals in the field of urban education. Additionally, he has received over $4 million in external research funds. To date, Dr. Lewis has authored/coauthored/coedited 10 books: *White Teachers/Diverse Classrooms: A Guide for Building Inclusive Schools,*

Eliminating Racism and Promoting High Expectations (Stylus, 2006); *The Dilemmas of Being an African American Male in the New Millennium* (Infinity, 2008); *An Educator's Guide to Working with African American Students: Strategies for Promoting Academic Success* (Infinity, 2009); *Transforming Teacher Education: What Went Wrong with Teacher Training and How We Can Fix It* (Stylus, 2010); *White Teachers/Diverse classrooms: Creating Inclusive schools, Building on Students' Diversity and Providing True Educational Equity [2nd Ed.]* (Stylus, 2011); *Yes We Can!: Improving Urban Schools through Innovative Educational Reform* (Information Age, 2011); *African Americans in Urban Schools: Critical Issues and Solutions for Achievement* (Peter Lang, 2012); *Black Males in Postsecondary Education: Examining their Experiences in Diverse Institutional Contexts* (Information Age, 2012); *Improving Urban Schools: Equity and Access in K–16 STEM Education* (Information Age, in press); *Black Male Teachers: Diversifying the United States' Teacher Workforce* (Emerald Publishing, in press).

Dr. Lewis has provided consultative services (i.e., professional development and research services) to over 100 school districts and universities across the United States and Canada. Dr. Lewis can be reached by e-mail at chance.lewis@uncc.edu. You can visit him on the web at http://www.chancewlewis.com.

Dr. Ivory A. Toldson is an associate professor at Howard University, senior research analyst for the Congressional Black Caucus Foundation, and editor-in-chief of *The Journal of Negro Education*. Dr. Ivory A. Toldson was recently appointed by President Obama as the Deputy Director of the White House Initiative on Historically Black Colleges and Universities (HBCUs). Dr. Toldson has more than 60 publications and research presentations in 32 US states, Puerto Rico, Dominican Republic, Scotland, South Africa, Paris, and Barcelona. He has been featured on C-SPAN2 Books, NPR News, The Al Sharpton Show on XM Satellite Radio, and WKYS 93.9, and his research has been featured on The Root, Essence.com, BET.com, The Griot, and *Ebony* Magazine. He gave expert commentary in three documentaries on Black male achievement: *Beyond the Bricks, Hoodwinked,* and the *Promise Tracker.* Known as a "myth buster," Dr. Toldson has publish reports challenging the merits of popular research reports and news sources that present negative statistics about Black people, which have been widely discussed in academic and popular media. He is a contributing educational editor for The Root and Empower Magazine.

Dubbed a leader "who could conceivably navigate the path to a White House" by the Washington Post, "a modern day Harlem Renaissance writer," by the New African Journal, and "Young Researcher of the Year" by Southern University, Dr. Toldson, according to Howard University's *Quest* Magazine, is "a much sought-after lecturer and researcher on a number of serious sociological and psychological issues that have implications for

African Americans." According to *Capstone* Magazine, "Toldson has spent a lot of time traveling across the country talking with teachers about misleading media statistics that invariably either link Black males to crime or question their ability to learn."

In 2005, Dr. Toldson won EboNetwork's Changing Faces award for outstanding literary achievement for is novel, *Black Sheep: When the American Dream Becomes a Black Man's Nightmare.* Dr. Toldson is also the author of The *Breaking Barriers* Series, which analyzes academic success indicators from national surveys that together give voice to more than 10,000 Black male pupils from schools across the country. Through his consulting firm, CREATE, LLC, he routinely works with schools to increase their capacity to promote academic success among Black males.

After completing coursework for a PhD in Counseling Psychology at Temple University, Dr. Toldson became a correctional and forensic psychology resident at the United States Penitentiary. There, he completed his dissertation on Black Men in the Criminal Justice System. Upon completion, Dr. Toldson joined the faculty of Southern University and became the fourth recipient of the prestigious DuBois Fellowship from the U.S. Department of Justice. He also served as the clinical director of the Manhood Training Village. He has received formal training in applied statistics from the University of Michigan, and held visiting research and teacher appointments at Emory, Drexel, and Morehouse School of Medicine.

ABOUT THE CONTRIBUTORS

Ayana Allen is the Post-Doctoral Fellow for *The Urban Education Collaborative* at the University of North Carolina at Charlotte. Her research interests focus on postsecondary access and success for underrepresented and marginalized groups of students, charter schools, and narrative and autoethnographic research methods.

Keisha Allen is a doctoral candidate in the Curriculum and Teaching program at Teachers College, Columbia University. Her scholarship focuses on the intersection of Black male identities and culturally sustaining pedagogies.

Kenneth Alonzo Anderson is a former middle school teacher and Associate Professor and Chairperson of the Department of Curriculum and Instruction at Howard University. Anderson's research interests include praxis- and policy-related issues related to educational equity, Black male achievement, middle level education, and content-area literacy development.

Thurman Bridges is an Associate Professor of Teacher Education at Morgan State University. His research explores the social context of urban education, Black male teacher identity, and Hip Hop pedagogy.

Travis J. Bristol's PhD research interests focus on the intersection of gender and race in organizations. Specifically, he examines how the various policy levers used by local, state, national, and international actors influence

Teacher Education and Black Communities, pages 327–332
Copyright © 2014 by Information Age Publishing
All rights of reproduction in any form reserved.

teacher and student outcomes. In 2013, Travis was awarded a Minority Dissertation Fellowship from the American Educational Research Association, a Ford Dissertation Fellowship from the National Research Council of the National Academies, and the Spencer Dissertation Fellowship from the National Academy of Education.

David Byrd is the Associate Dean at the University of Texas Health Science Center. His research includes increasing access to higher education for under-represented populations and reducing transfer shock at predominantly White institutions.

Suzanne C. Carothers is a Professor in The Steinhardt School of Education, Department of Teaching and Learning at New York University. A graduate of Bennett College in Greensboro, North Carolina, she received her Masters' Degree from Bank Street College of Education and her PhD from New York University in 1987. Dr. Carothers has done extensive teacher training and staff development work in a variety of settings for more than 25 years. Most recently she was awarded an honorary doctorate from Bank Street College of Education for outstanding achievement as a teacher, leader in education, and mentor.

Mercedes E. Ebanks is a graduate of Georgetown University and Howard University with degrees in Counseling Psychology. Dr. Ebanks has extensive experience as a bilingual school psychologist and behavior therapist in public and alternative schools in addition to serving several years with private practices, social service agencies, and nonprofit organizations in Washington, DC. She is cofounder of The MECCA Group LLC, a psychological and related services agency that provides therapy, evaluations, consultation, and trainings.

Leslie T. Fenwick is Dean of Howard University School of Education in Washington, DC and has more than 25 years of experience in higher education, public policy, philanthropy, and urban PK–12 schools. Dr. Fenwick held successive appointments as a visiting scholar in education and visiting fellow at Harvard University. Dr. Fenwick also served as associate dean of the School of Education and chair of the Department of Educational Leadership during her thirteen-year tenure at Clark Atlanta University.

Darrell Cleveland Hucks is an Assistant Professor of Elementary Education at Keene State College. His research interests include the schooling experiences of Black and Latino males, collective achievement, culturally responsive pedagogy, teacher education, literacy, and technology integration.

Jacqueline Jordan-Irvine is the Charles Howard Candler Professor Emerita of Urban Education in the Division of Educational Studies at Emory University in Atlanta. Dr. Irvine has received numerous awards for her research and teaching including the Distinguished Career Award from the SIG on Black Education of the American Education Research Association and Emory University's Thomas Jefferson Award—the highest award given to an Emory University faculty member for service and research.

Gloria Ladson-Billings is the Kellner Family Chair in Urban Education in the Department of Curriculum Instruction and Faculty Associates in the Departments of Educational Policy Studies and Afro American Studies at the University of Wisconsin–Madison. Her research interests include culturally relevant pedagogy, hip hop and youth culture connections to teaching, and critical race theory.

Brianna P. Lemmons, MSW is a Frederick Douglass Doctoral Scholar and doctoral candidate at Howard University School of Social Work in Washington, DC.

Marvin Lynn is Dean and Professor in the School of Education at Indiana University South Bend. His recent book, The *Handbook of Critical Race Theory in Education* which features state-of-the-art research in the field was published in 2013 with Routledge Press.

Helena Mariella-Walrond is the Associate Vice President for Institutional Effectiveness and Assessment and Associate Professor of Education at Bethune-Cookman University. Her research interests include curriculum theory and design, assessment, and multicultural education.

Lance T. McCready is Associate Professor of Urban Education in the department of Curriculum, Teaching, and Learning at Ontario Institute for Studies in Education, University of Toronto (OISE/UT). His research program focuses on the education, health, and well-being of urban youth, in particular Black male youth and queer youth of color. He recently published *Making Space for Diverse Masculinities*, a critical ethnography of gay and gender nonconforming Black male students in an urban high school; his current research and writing aims to advance queer color analysis of the educational trajectories of Black male youth.

Felicia Moore Mensah is an Associate Professor of Science Education at Teachers College, Columbia University. Her research interests are in diversity and social justice education with an emphasis on improving science experiences for PreK–16 teachers and students in urban classrooms.

H. Richard Milner, IV is Helen Faison Endowed Chair of Urban Education, Professor of Education, and Director of the Center for Urban Education at the University of Pittsburgh. His research, teaching, and policy interest include urban (teacher) education, African American literature, and the sociology of education.

Cheryl Moore-Thomas received her PhD in counselor education from the University of Maryland. She is a tenured associate professor and the associate dean of the School of Education at Loyola University Maryland. Over her professional career, Dr. Moore-Thomas has published and presented in the areas of multicultural counseling competence, cultural identity development of children and adolescents, college access, and accountability in school counseling programs.

Micia Mosely is an educational equity consultant and national facilitator. She supports schools and community based organizations through her independent consulting work and collaborations with the National Equity Project, The Posse Foundation, and San Francisco Coalition of Essential Small Schools. Her research interests include the success of Black teachers in urban schools.

Erik Nolan is a native of Brooklyn, New York and the founder of UMOJA Network for Young Men, Incorporated. A true drum major for youth, UMOJA focuses on developing young men holistically. Erik is also the creator and producer of a talk show highlighting young people. He is an alumnus of Virginia State University and is currently pursuing his MSW. He resides in New York with his wife and two children.

Derrick Robinson is a Doctoral Fellow for *The Urban Education Collaborative* at the University of North Carolina at Charlotte. His research interests focus on postsecondary access for urban students, discipline policy reform, and teacher preparation.

Lakia M. Scott is an urban education doctoral student at The University of North Carolina at Charlotte. Her research interests include: African American student perspectives on Historically Black Colleges and Universities, education for emancipation, and best practices for increasing urban student outcomes in literacy.

Yolanda Sealey-Ruiz is an Assistant Professor of English Education at Teachers College, Columbia University. Her research interests include the educational narratives of Black reentry women, racial literacy in urban teacher education, and the social and academic success of Black and Latino high school males.

Victoria Showunmi is a lecturer in education based in the Institute of Education, University of London. Her research interests include identity and leadership, Black girls experience in education, and teacher education.

Robert W. Simmons, III is an Associate Professor of Urban Education at Loyola University Maryland and the director of the Center for Innovation in Urban Education. His research interests include urban education, African American males in K–12 schools, Catholic schools in urban communities, science education in urban schools, and understanding the role of race and culture in K–12 schools.

Shailen Singh is the Director of the Byrne Student Success Center at Texas A&M University, and teaches courses in the Human Resource Development program. His research interests include work/family balance for higher education practitioners, as well as diversity issues in Higher Education.

Tehia Starker-Glass is an Assistant Professor of Elementary Education and Educational Psychology at the University of North Carolina at Charlotte. Her research interests include the motivational factors (self efficacy and attribution theory) of culturally responsive teaching within teacher education, and examining teacher education qualities at Historically Black Colleges and Universities.

Ivory A. Toldson is Deputy Director for the White House Initiative on Historically Black Colleges and Universities (HBCUs), a senior research analyst at CBCF, an associate professor of counseling psychology at the Howard University School of Education, and the editor-in-chief of the *Journal of Negro Education*. Dr. Toldson is credited with more than 40 publications, and research presentations in more than 20 U.S. states, Paris, Puerto Rico, the Dominican Republic, Scotland, and South Africa.

Allyson Leggett Watson is the Assistant Dean of Education at Northeastern State University. Dr. Watson has focused her research on urban education, faculty of color in higher education, and urban school and university partnerships. Dr. Watson is a graduate faculty member and has a substantial amount of teaching experience in courses such as educational research, advanced educational measurements and statistics, public school relations, and instructional strategies. In 2010, Dr. Watson founded Teaching & Urban Reform Network (TURN), a program to prepare preservice teachers in urban education and encourage effective pedagogical practices.

Audra M. Watson is a doctoral student in Urban Education Policy at the CUNY Graduate Center. She is also a Program Officer for Teaching Fellowships and Director for the WW-RBF Aspiring Teachers of Color Fellowship program at the Woodrow Wilson National Fellowship Foundation in Princeton, NJ. She was previously the Executive Director of Teacher Development for the NYC Department of Education where she planned and executed strategy for preservice through early-career teacher support